Rolling Stone

MAGAZINE

The

Uncensored

History

Rolling Stone

MAGAZINE

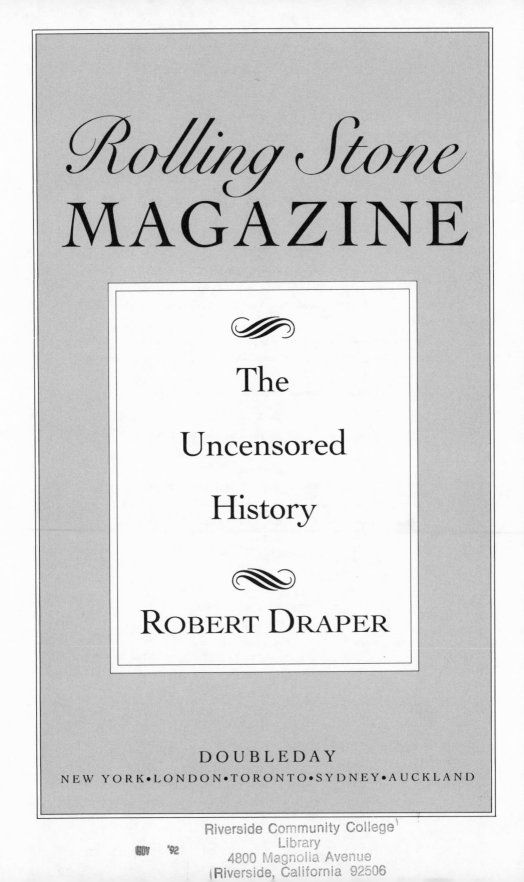

The

Uncensored

History

ROBERT DRAPER

DOUBLEDAY

NEW YORK•LONDON•TORONTO•SYDNEY•AUCKLAND

PUBLISHED BY DOUBLEDAY
a division of Bantam Doubleday Dell Publishing Group, Inc.
666 Fifth Avenue, New York, New York 10103

DOUBLEDAY and the portrayal of an anchor with a dolphin are
trademarks of Doubleday, a division of Bantam Doubleday Dell Publishing Group, Inc.

Library of Congress Cataloging-in-Publication Data

Draper, Robert.
Rolling Stone Magazine: the uncensored history / Robert
Draper.—1st ed.
p.   cm.
1. Rolling stone.   2. Wenner, Jann.   3. Rock music—Periodicals—
History.   4. Journalists—United States—Biography.   5. United
States—Popular culture—History—20th century.   I. Rolling stone.
II. Title.
PN4900.R6D7   1990
051—dc20   89-25627   CIP

ISBN 0-385-26060-1
Printed in the United States of America
May 1990
FIRST EDITION
RRH

To my parents, Claire and Bob Draper,
who endured three sons and three stereos

CONTENTS

PART 3
Malaise

PART 4
A Gathering of Moss

A U T H O R ' S   N O T E

*T*he history of *Rolling Stone* magazine is a story about music and journalism. At bottom, however, this is a story of people and their times, and the inextricable bonds between the two. Both the times and the people portrayed in this book have changed, for the most part, and the author asks that readers bear this in mind.

It is helpful to recall, for example, that while *Rolling Stone* staffers were experimenting with drugs, so were their peers—including their counterparts at other publications ... though in those newsrooms the drug of choice remained alcohol. One need not approve of such activity to recognize its cultural origins, or to draw distinctions between use and abuse.

Recalled Tim Cahill, one of *Rolling Stone*'s finest early writers, now a well-known author and occasional *Rolling Stone* contributor: "By the time I started working regularly for *Rolling Stone*, I'd been taking psychedelic drugs, until I began having these awful feelings. I'd think, Jeez, two hundred and fifty thousand people are reading what I'm writing, and maybe another two to five people are reading each copy; that's over a million readers that are gonna read what I wrote today. I think that's when I switched over to alcohol.

"But I have to say that people are always asking me what it was like in the early days. They're asking me about sex and drugs and rock & roll, and one of the things that people don't understand and can't appreciate is *how hard we worked*."

In the end, this book seeks to remember its subjects for what they produced, not how they lived. Virtually without exception, *Rolling Stone* has been produced every two weeks since October 1967.

Austin, Texas
November 1989

Rolling Stone
MAGAZINE

The

Uncensored

History

PROLOGUE

A memo from *Rolling Stone*'s National Affairs desk, scrawled across a World Wrestling Foundation press release which was transmitted via facsimile machine from the magazine's New York headquarters to the National Affairs desk of Hunter Thompson in Woody Creek, Colorado:

April 13, 1989

Jann

You crazy dilettante bastard—don't send me any more of this swill—get Robin Leach to handle the N.A. desk. They blamed me and Andy Young for Carter—but they will blame you for Bush. And yr. children will wallow in shame, while you ride free & giddy on yr. Hog. You better pray that Buddha (sp?) was wrong about Karma [or in] the Next Life you could end up scuttling around on some dung heap in Calcutta with only dim genetic memories of the life you once led on Fifth Avenue, when people whined like rodents at the sight of yr. beady red eyes. Selah. . . .

Anyway, let Ed Meese do yr. wrestling story. . . . For $5K a week I'll write you a tale of sex, treachery & madness that will make you scream in yr. sleep at night. Let me know.

Thanx,
HST

Dr. Hunter S. Thompson no longer writes for *Rolling Stone* magazine. The legendary author of *Fear and Loathing in Las Vegas* and *Fear and Loathing: On the Campaign Trail '72* is today a newspaper columnist, a reclusive observer of events rather than a roving participant whose "Gonzo journalism" once sought to erase all boundaries between subject and reporter.

Thompson erased them all too well. The *Rolling Stone* reporter became more famous than the people he was writing about. He stopped attending press conferences to avoid the ambush of autograph seekers. When he emerged to give lectures, drunken Gonzo disciples mobbed him and tried to tear the clothes off his body. Reporters hounded him night and day with interview requests. In the face of his astounding success, Hunter Thompson recoiled in fear and loathing.

Now he lumbers about in his Woody Creek shelter like a caged bear. His cabin is neat but cluttered with fan mail and old photographs of his eternal nemesis, Richard Nixon. He punches buttons on his satellite TV channel selector; he slaps a cassette of the Cowboy Junkies in the stereo and turns it up all the way; he takes leftovers from his refrigerator and tosses them outside for his peacocks to eat; he fills his body with chemicals, reads a few pages of the classics, kicks kitchen appliances across the room, hollers obscenities at his typewriter and grabs a nearby rifle and scrambles outside and pumps several shells into an empty beer keg.

Every so often, his claustrophobic world is violated by the sounds of beeping and humming. He glares venomously at his facsimile machine—his "mojo wire," as he calls it. Out rolls a communiqué from *Rolling Stone* editor, publisher and co-founder Jann (pronounced "Yon") Wenner. *How about an article on wrestling*, the editor suggests. *Or gunrunning. Or politics. How about just writing anything, anything at all, and returning to the magazine that you helped make and that helped make you, how about a renaissance, you rat bastard. . . .*

The inventor of Gonzo journalism reads these notes, defaces them with invectives and faxes them back.

Occasionally he counters with his own ideas. A possible epitaph for Abbie Hoffman, with implications for "who won the battle of the sixties," had Hunter Thompson mumbling to himself and scribbling notes for several days in 1989. A more lingering prospect was a novella entitled *The Princess of Camelback Road*. Fed up with reader complaints that Thompson never wrote about sex ("They said I was weird, or maybe even like Patrick Buchanan"), the journalist proposed in 1987 that Wenner excerpt his "tale of lust, treachery and frenzied, relentless sodomy," much as *Rolling Stone* had published Tom Wolfe's *Bonfire of the Vanities* chapter by chapter in 1984 and 1985.

Jann Wenner does not regard these counterproposals seriously. The editor of *Rolling Stone* last took a chance on his star writer in early 1984, when Hunter Thompson declared, "I'm going to the war zone," and boarded the next plane for Grenada. President Reagan's invasion of the island had all the earmarks of a Gonzo story: political folly, a flock of conventional journalists to serve as Thompson's Ed McMahons and a surreal, metaphorical backdrop.

A week or so later, Thompson arrived at the *Rolling Stone* office on 745 Fifth Avenue, bearing CIA propaganda posters and a notebook full of barely legible, stream-of-consciousness observations. Jann Wenner put up his star writer in a posh hotel and waited for the finished product.

He is still waiting.

The memos fly back and forth, like letters between old lovers long after the fall. The two men are bound by a wild, unaccountable history—nothing less and nothing else. Jann Wenner laments "what has become of Hunter," apparently referring to the Gonzo journalist's confessed abuse of drugs and alcohol. "Anything he wants to write, I'll publish," he says, in tones that betray not an ounce of hope.

Thompson, in turn, says that he no longer writes for *Rolling Stone* because "it's no fun anymore." He claims that the magazine he and others once regarded as the most dazzling publication in America began its slide into conservatism and mediocrity in 1977, when *Rolling Stone* abandoned its San Francisco roots for New York's pomp and glitter. He no longer reads *Rolling Stone*, and he has stopped sending Jann Wenner copies of his weekly column in the *San Francisco Examiner*. His 1988 best-seller, *Generation of Swine*, made no mention of his glorious association with Wenner's magazine. Those days, after all, were history.

HERE ARE A MILLION SUCCESS STORIES in the annals of the baby-boom generation, none greater or stranger than that of *Rolling Stone* magazine. In 1967, a twenty-one-year-old Berkeley dropout scraped together $7,500 from family and friends and started up a magazine. He did so because he was a rock & roll journalist whose work no one else would publish; also because he longed to meet his heroes: John Lennon, Mick Jagger and Bob Dylan.

By the end of 1969, Jann Wenner's two-year-old *Rolling Stone*—or simply *Stone*, as many affectionately called it in those days—was generally accepted as the most authoritative rock & roll magazine in the land. By 1971, *Rolling Stone* was what *Esquire* had been in the sixties and the *New York Herald Tribune* a decade before that: the breeding ground of explosive New Journalists like Hunter Thompson, David Felton, Grover Lewis and Joe Eszterhas. Two years later, the magazine began to make money. Three years after that, it helped elect a President. By 1989, *Rolling Stone*'s parent company, Straight Arrow Publishers, Inc., was worth perhaps $250 million —over thirty thousand times its value twenty-two years before.

None of this would have been possible without a few key individuals: acidheads, anarchists, commune dwellers, social lepers and parentless long-hairs who loved music and feared the morning sunlight. That having been said, *Rolling Stone* is a distinctly capitalist triumph. It prevailed because of entrepreneurship and a dedicated labor force; because debts were overcome and payrolls were met; and above all, because it satisfied a consumer demand.

The latter was no casual feat, since most segments of society had trouble figuring out just who or what the consumers were. Political activists pronounced them the New Left. Establishment journalists labeled them "hippies." Richard Nixon called them "bums." Jann Wenner, in the meantime, believed that the only common trait among this vast but amorphous constituency was an abiding love for music. And so Wenner's genius dictated a product that was as loosely defined and evolving as the generation it would serve. Its very nature was to avoid the set positions assumed by its psychedelic and left-wing counterparts in the underground press. *Rolling Stone* would keep on rolling, advancing through the years and gathering no moss.

It thus became a generation's voice—perhaps the only trustworthy voice; and for evidence, one need look no further than the pages of *Rolling Stone* itself. Conceived during San Francisco's Summer of Love, *Rolling Stone* championed a new pantheon of heroes—the Beatles, Dylan, the Rolling

Stones, the Jefferson Airplane, the Grateful Dead, Janis Joplin, Jimi Hendrix—until its loving gaze was distracted by the marching, charging feet of National Guardsmen on college campuses. Then the magazine deepened with hot blood. Came a crooked President and a crooked new decade, and *Rolling Stone* stopped talking about love and revolution. New Morality met head-on with New Reality. From 1970 until 1977, no magazine in America was as honest or as imaginative as what Jann Wenner called his "little rock & roll newspaper from San Francisco." Greater truths were its aim. That meant toppling false idols of every denomination—from Nixon, the FBI and the Nuclear Regulatory Commission to Woodstock, Charles Manson and the Symbionese Liberation Army.

Even in the blandest of times, *Rolling Stone* published good journalism —sometimes great journalism, and often on subjects no other American publication could or would touch. Its writers, after all, were at least as disaffected as its readers. Most of them were deemed unfit for the conventional newsroom, and the rest passed their days thrashing about like salmon in an aquarium. *Rolling Stone* plunged them into deeper, faster waters. Years later, few would remember the origins of Michael Lydon (*Newsweek*), David Felton (*Los Angeles Times*), Hunter Thompson (*Jersey Shore Herald*), Grover Lewis (*Houston Chronicle*), Joe Eszterhas (*Cleveland Plain Dealer*), Timothy Ferris (*New York Post*) and Howard Kohn (*Detroit Free Press*). It seemed as if they'd never been anything other than *Rolling Stone* writers.

They took up where Jann Wenner left off when the twenty-one-year-old editor wrote in his first column, "*Rolling Stone* is not just about music, but also about the things and attitudes that the music embraces." To a writer with a wild imagination, this was carte blanche. The music embraced irreverence, the fringes of American culture, lunacy in its most exalted forms, love, hope, fear, loathing. . . .

At bottom, however, *Rolling Stone* was about music. Often the magazine wandered from its central mission, but never for very long—sales figures always saw to that. Readers trusted *Rolling Stone*'s rock coverage, and so trusted even a writer like Grover Lewis, whose sign on his desk read: "I do not write no rock & roll." The magazine seemed to understand *exactly* how important pop music was. Teen magazines trivialized it; *Crawdaddy!*, the first American rock magazine, placed it on high with the utterances of Plato and Aristotle; and the straight press scorned or ignored it.

Instead of defining rock & roll, or deifying it, *Rolling Stone* covered it —a truly revolutionary idea. Its writers interviewed Bob Dylan, John Lennon, Mick Jagger, Janis Joplin, Pete Townshend and Eric Clapton with the sense of purpose a *Time* reporter would bring to an interview with Henry Kissinger. Musicians were *worthy* news figures, proclaimed *Rolling Stone*, and their music was worthy of analysis. Readers often disagreed, sometimes vehemently, with the magazine's seminal critics: Jon Landau, Greil Marcus, Langdon Winner, Jim Miller, Paul Nelson, John Morthland, Lester Bangs, Ed Ward and Dave Marsh. In the end, however, these disputes were always welcome, for they upheld Jann Wenner's larger argument: The music matters.

Wenner's mentor and *Rolling Stone*'s co-founder, Ralph Gleason, often said, "Don't analyze it. *Dig* it." But Gleason, a brilliant man of a thousand opinions, also subscribed to the corollary: *Something not worth arguing about was not worth digging.*

Perhaps *Rolling Stone* magazine grew out of an argument that was never settled.

It sprang, after all, from the restless impulses of Jann Wenner, America's most prominent editor/publisher of a magazine that does not feature nude women beneath its cover. Even those who despise Wenner rank him with the greatest editors of postwar American magazine journalism: Harold Ross of *The New Yorker*, Harold Hayes of *Esquire*, Clay Felker of *New York* and Warren Hinckle of *Ramparts*. If Wenner's agile mind does not approach theirs, his understanding of his audience and the tools at his disposal may have no equal.

"With the possible exception of Condé Nast," said Porter Bibb, who helped publish *Newsweek International* before becoming Wenner's first publisher at *Rolling Stone*, "he has attracted more talent than any other magazine publisher in this century. Furthermore, it doesn't matter what other editors you name: nobody had a better understanding of what was going on in this country in the sixties and seventies than Jann Wenner. And I don't think anybody's ever going to put together a journal that is as accurate a reflection of what's going on in the country as he did in *Rolling Stone*'s heyday."

Though he disapproved of his protégé's reckless business practices, Ralph Gleason nonetheless told a reporter in 1973, "He is a natural intuitive genius for this type of operation, whether you like him or not. If you gave me a million dollars to start a publication covering popular music and all aspects of popular American culture, I'd hire Jann. He's the best man for the job, period."

Gleason rightfully believed that Jann Wenner could not have pulled off *Rolling Stone* without his help. As with most great American success stories, luck had much to do with Wenner's ascendancy. *Rolling Stone*, in those critical early days that bury most new publishing efforts, enjoyed free office space and employees who were willing to work for peanuts. The record industry bankrolled *Rolling Stone*, advancing Wenner money after he'd drained the magazine's coffers on dubious expansion schemes. And musicians like Lennon and Jagger gave *Rolling Stone* their support long before it was obviously in their interest to do so.

But Wenner courted his good fortune. Like any of the great American entrepreneurs, from Henry Ford to Steve Jobs, the *Rolling Stone* editor had an indisputably brilliant idea. And he hustled to promote that idea, bearing the burden of his dream long after others would have laid it to rest.

His sales tools were peculiarly American. He was a vulnerable sort, pudgy and baby-faced, his inferiority complex plain for all to see, which made him a most unthreatening suitor. He charmed, he flattered, he eagerly played the fool. Like a child, he lacked any sense of history, and thus appealed to the child in everyone else with his starry vision of the future. These qualities did not translate well in crowds. But alone in an office room, one on one, Jann Wenner could spellbind with his boyish charisma.

Yet success is not always sweet beneath the candy coating. To implement his dream, Jann Wenner cut a multitude of ethical corners: stealing his initial subscriber list from another magazine, awarding himself shares of company stock so as to secure minority control, lying to advertisers about *Rolling Stone*'s readership and pocketing the magazine's subscriber dues while the rest of the staff worked for little or nothing. Those who have threatened Wenner in one way or another have lived to regret it. The man with the kitten's blue eyes will brawl in any ditch, personally soiling himself as no other publisher would, to protect his stunning achievement. Jann Wenner is a man of wealth and taste, but he is no gentleman.

From the very outset, Wenner proved his finest talent to be exploiting the talents of others. Absent any coherent method—his employee interviews often consisted of a single question, such as "What's your favorite Rolling Stones record?"—he hired individuals with virtually no experience and, as one of his former editors put it, "gave us enough space so that we could one day stand back and say, 'My God. I'm *good*.'"

On the warped and wonderful *Rolling Stone* career ladder, an occasional short story writer like Tim Cahill, with, as he put it, "no idea how to be a journalist," could be dragged out of his classroom and assigned stories ranging from Ravi Shankar to Bigfoot. A teenager like Cameron Crowe could earn the right to pen cover stories long before gaining the right to vote. Reporters from underground papers became associate editors; writers became bureau heads; pasteup artists became production directors; graduate students with a good album collection became record reviews editors; a former animal caretaker became copy chief; an "office chick" who made the coffee became the magazine's research editor; and night switchboard operators and fact checkers could and did ascend to the rank of managing editor.

"We fix broken careers," Wenner would tell a reporter with a smirk. But he did much more than fix the careers of Joe Eszterhas and Howard Kohn, who left their newspaper jobs under disreputable circumstances; he let the reporters reinvent themselves as writers. Eszterhas now wrote about narcotics agents, Kohn about Patty Hearst and Karen Silkwood—just as David Felton dissected the violent cults of Charles Manson and Mel Lyman, as Grover Lewis pioneered movie reporting, as Tom Wolfe wrote about astronauts and as Hunter Thompson covered the 1972 presidential campaign. These articles were among the finest stories published in the seventies, anywhere. It is fair to say that most of them would not have been written, or at least printed, without the encouragement of Jann Wenner.

Wenner incited his writers to take risks and avoid niceties. Though many codes of conduct he simply found too time-consuming to abide by, others he honestly believed were foolish and hypocritical. Chief among these was "journalistic objectivity." If the gloriously disengaged Walter Cronkite was the antidote to radio's Ed Murrow and print media's Henry Luce, Wenner's *Rolling Stone* marked a return to engagement. The editor knew his readers. They wanted it told to them straight. Wenner urged his writers to scrape away the bullshit. If the President lies, call him a liar; if Dylan is a poet, call him one.

Though younger than many of his employees, the editor's uncanny focus lent him additional authority. For *Rolling Stone* staffers—many of them cut off from their conservative families and uncertain of their place in the world—Jann Wenner became a father figure. They loved him, feared him and did all they could to win his favor. At least as often as not, they wished he would go away. They huddled together at bars or smoked pot on the office rooftop, cursing their boss for his tirades and his eleventh-hour issue changes. Like any self-respecting father, he made their lives miserable.

"We were always hassling to keep Jann out of the running of the paper," said Charlie Perry, *Rolling Stone*'s first copy chief. "But that's also when *Rolling Stone* was great. . . . It made for fireworks, both on the pages and behind the scenes."

"Jann was stamped by having a different mission than anyone else who worked there," said former music editor Abe Peck. "He was more of a businessman than any of his editors, and more of an editor than any of his business people. He was the unique fulcrum, the pivot point that made the magazine possible."

Wenner could be terribly generous, freely giving bonuses and paying hospital bills. Toward those who he believed crossed him, he could also be unspeakably vengeful. Those who left the fold without the father's permission were inevitable objects of his rage. He banished all traces of them; he spoke of them as expendables, belittling their contributions to *Rolling Stone* so as to diminish his own acute sense of betrayal and loss.

For *Rolling Stone* was a family—his, the only one he truly knew. The psychological scars of childhood were plain for any associate to see. An exceptionally talented child, Jann Wenner was also exceptionally lonely: ignored by his busy parents, misunderstood by his peers, desperate for acceptance and affection. His distinctiveness forever competed with his primal longings. From his adolescent days onward, Jann Wenner sought connections. His greatest goal in life was to be where the action was.

He was, as one of his former editors put it, "the original fan." It didn't matter all that much whether he was *seen* with stars. He simply wanted to *be* with them, to feel the glow of their charisma, to touch the sparks with his stubby fingers. Though he fantasized about becoming his generation's Henry Luce or William Randolph Hearst—the nickname Citizen Wenner was one he did not discourage—his own stature never preoccupied him as his surroundings did. Jann Wenner yearned to be in the company of greatness.

He reached for one constellation, then the next. As a Berkeley student he finagled his way into the debutante world. Then he discovered rock & roll. From Lennon, Dylan and Jagger he moved on to Tom Wolfe, Truman Capote and other vaunted literary figures. As politics captured his interests, he spoke now and again of running for office, some office or other. But that was never a serious prospect, even if one ignored Wenner's rather public history of drug consumption. No, Jann Wenner would settle for the company of greatness. Simply being there at those elegant Georgetown dinner parties was sufficient.

This behavior always flabbergasted Larry Durocher, *Rolling Stone*'s publisher in the early seventies and one of its true saviors. The sight of this brilliant young man fawning over celebrity politicians like a starstruck teenager sickened Durocher, but he was powerless to stop it.

"Jann suffers from an invisible talent," he would say. "There's no litmus test for a great editor. You can't throw a bucket of blue shit on him and see if he turns yellow. Now, I can't define his talent for you. But I know that he's gone through the last twenty years holding up a wet finger, and feeling the most subtle wind any human being on this earth can feel.

"*And he looks right through himself.* He doesn't see that talent. So when he looks at someone whose talent he *can* see—well, he's just always been starfucked for those people."

The ultimate groupie, they called him. But Jann Wenner's own yearnings helped him understand the yearnings of his readers. In his heart, and in theirs, *Rolling Stone* wasn't the mainspring of cultural enlightenment. It was what he often said it was, to the annoyance of his subordinates: "a little rock & roll newspaper from San Francisco."

"My theory is this," said Jon Carroll, one of Wenner's early associate editors. "The reason that *Rolling Stone* was successful is the same reason that *Playboy* and *New York* succeeded: each was the complete encapsulation of a single person's fantasy. Hugh Hefner wanted to be a playboy, and Clay Felker wanted to live on the Upper East Side of New York City. Jann wanted to be with rock stars. And it turns out that each fantasy was shared by enough people to create a successful circulation."

At the time of his employment, in 1970, Carroll misunderstood *Rolling Stone*'s mission. "I thought we were trying to save the world," he said. He and countless other staffers failed to appreciate one inescapable fact: *Rolling Stone* was Jann Wenner's magazine. It reflected his interests, not theirs.

And therein lies the unsettled argument.

"*Rolling Stone* magazine," said Larry Durocher, is "Jann in print." When Wenner founded the magazine, he brought both his brilliance and his insecurities to its pages. When the two forces found common ground, *Rolling Stone* sparkled. When they conflicted, the magazine fell ill. And so this marks *Rolling Stone*'s history: a curious tangle of inspiration and vulgarity, heroism and pettiness, joy and malaise.

———

They are all gone now, the magazine's famous critics and music reporters and New Journalists and political writers and photographers and art directors—gone from *Rolling Stone* and dispersed among the American media. They now occupy critical positions at *Newsweek, New York Times, Los Angeles Times, Vanity Fair, GQ, New York, Playboy, Vogue, Manhattan,inc., Esquire,* ABC, MTV, ESPN and a host of local newspapers and television stations. They are respected professors and wealthy publishing consultants, noted authors and editors and literary agents, playwrights and movie producers, record company publicists and band managers. Among the nation's liberal arts community, they have ascended to the positions of greatest influence. They have become the Establishment.

Perhaps the fact that they were all there at *Rolling Stone*, under one roof, for a few utterly remarkable years, is the story most worth telling. But it tells only one side of the greater story.

"They'll all tell you the same thing," said Robert Greenfield, *Rolling Stone*'s London correspondent in the early seventies. "All any of us wanted to do was write for the people who read *Rolling Stone*. That's why I worked for fifteen pounds a week in London: because people that I cared about read *Rolling Stone*. They'd read my stuff, and it was straight across—it was *communication*. That's why we wrote, and wrote at the top of our ability.

"And sooner or later, Jann just broke everybody's heart."

Greenfield was covering the infamous Rolling Stones tour of 1972 when word reached him that Jann Wenner had reassigned the story to celebrity journalist Truman Capote. Up until that moment, Greenfield assumed that *Rolling Stone* was more or less the *New Yorker* of his generation: a place where he would continue to write, side by side with other keepers of the faith, until he died.

Sometimes it was nothing personal. Staffers would be hired during the lucrative springtime, then dropped from the payroll when advertisers hibernated in the summer. Other staffers just didn't pan out, and others still (though remarkably few) viewed *Rolling Stone* as a step on the way to greener pastures and left of their own accord.

Far more often, however, the reasons for the departures were *entirely* personal. Somehow or other Wenner felt threatened by them, or hurt, or perhaps it all came down to restlessness again. These employer-employee melodramas: they were like torrid love affairs. Jann Wenner seduced them, made passionate love to them and then, with little warning, abandoned them. Often he followed this with flowers of a sort: a freelance assignment, a few extra weeks of severance pay, a party, a job offer to spearhead some new project. Sometimes the gesture worked, and they remained friends. Even those who came away with hard feelings had to admit that the whole experience was rather thrilling. Said Timothy White, *Rolling Stone*'s most prolific cover-story writer before quitting its pages in 1982, "Matching wits with Jann Wenner is some of the best fun you can have with your clothes on."

White's mistake was a common one: he gave in completely to the seduction—learning too late, in writer Lynn Hirschberg's words, that "once Jann owns you, you're dead." Though Timothy White would acknowledge a great debt to the *Rolling Stone* editor for letting his talents flourish, he never forgot the emotional price. "He didn't throw a monkey wrench in my career so much as on the *human* level," White said. "As time went on, he did unbelievably hurtful things that could only be attributed to cunning.

"Anytime anybody's shown him affection or warmth, he's turned around and screwed them. It's certainly true for me. They say you always push away that which you want to come closest. Well, Jann does a lot more than that. He aims a howitzer and fires."

One side of Wenner aimed for every soft spot, while the other seemed blissfully unaware of his own actions. "The thing was, it never really made sense," said Barbara Downey Landau, who began working for *Rolling Stone* as a proofreader in 1972 and eventually became the magazine's senior editor. "It would have been okay if he was giving you a hard time about something you had done or failed to do, but it was more like 'Hey, it's *your* turn to be publicly *humiliated!*' There is a certain kind of weakness that he would sense in people, and he used that to get to them. If they were down, he'd kick them. He was totally amoral in that way. But then he'd turn around and make you feel like he didn't really mean it, or that somehow or other things were okay.

"I really do not understand to this day why I care about this person," said Landau. "And I do, you know. He's a friend."

Perhaps because, in the words of former associate editor David Weir, "Jann doesn't have much conscience, but he has a lot of heart." To be sure, it was a strange game, this management technique of courting and bullying. But on certain levels, how could one dispute its effectiveness? An issue always went out, every two weeks. Novices and castaways did inspired work. *Rolling Stone* was still a family, with all the attendant friction and heartache. The family endured. What choice was there? Outside slouched a far drearier world. This was life in italics.

"In a sense, I regret ever having met the guy," said Grover Lewis, who successfully sued Wenner over a breach of contract. "The experience left me feeling soiled and angry. But on the other hand: we *were* putting out the best fucking magazine in America."

Lewis often pondered that dilemma. He felt truly proud to be associated with a magazine conceived by a man he truly despised. Was *Rolling Stone* a minor miracle? A major tragedy? Perhaps neither. Perhaps, as Larry Durocher suggested, it was merely a man in print, with Lewis and the others serving as unwitting biographers.

"In the end, Jann's a brilliant master at getting what he wants out of people," said David Weir, who co-wrote with Howard Kohn *Rolling Stone*'s stunning Patty Hearst stories. "What he lacks is loyalty and trust. He's too insecure to allow strong people to grow up around him and therefore catapult the magazine to what it *could* have been: easily the most important magazine of our time.

"That's what Jann missed. He let the talent dissipate, let it go all over the place instead of holding it in one place as the repository of the sixties. Then you could have said, 'Goodbye, *Atlantic Monthly*. Goodbye, *Harper's*. Goodbye, *New Yorker*.'

"He missed that. *He missed that.* That was his huge flaw."

ODAY *ROLLING STONE* MAGAZINE is a raging financial success. It is everything the *Rolling Stone* of the seventies was not: efficiently run, fat with revenues from fashion and automobile advertisers, professionally designed and editorially consistent. What admirers once called "the voice of the counterculture" (a responsibility Jann Wenner never accepted) now goes by other monikers. The magazine's associate publisher, Les Zeifman, calls it "the *Wall Street Journal* of rock & roll."

Zeifman joined *Rolling Stone* in 1977, when the magazine relocated to New York City. Though the move made perfect sense—virtually every American publishing house and national magazine is headquartered there—it was also perfectly symbolic. Jann Wenner's magazine changed almost overnight. Writers and editors left—gradually at first; then in droves. Often taking their place were famous New York writers, who wrote about famous New Yorkers.

The ties that bound the *Rolling Stone* family began to snap, one by one. Some staffers never adjusted to the new environment. Others, including Wenner, were thoroughly suckered in. They hung out with Manhattan's other newcomers, the *Saturday Night Live* cast, ghosting the city's nightclubs at all hours, dabbling in the urban drug of choice: cocaine.

In the swank new offices they still behaved as brilliant brats, but the rules were different now. For the first time ever, *Rolling Stone*'s editorial staff found itself battling daily with Jann Wenner's business lieutenants—battling over how the magazine should look, and what it should and should not say. The outcome of that war was preordained. For years and years, Jann Wenner swore that his magazine would one day boast a circulation of one million.

Back then, they laughed. *A million? Ridiculous. And wrong. Since when does* Rolling Stone *pander to the masses? It ain't our style.*

By the end of 1981, not a single writer or editor from San Francisco remained in the New York office.

————

Has *Rolling Stone* changed as drastically as America between 1967 and 1990? Probably not. In an age that christens Richard Nixon an elder statesman and finds Wall Street barracudas emerging from federal courts to wild applause, *Rolling Stone* evokes a warm familiarity. Its letters column still carries the quaint title "Correspondence, Love Letters & Advice." *Rolling Stone* music writers still approach their subject with suitable reverence and humor. Its political writers, especially William Greider, uphold liberal traditions even if many of the magazine's readers no longer do.

And it still publishes good journalism. In 1983, Jann Wenner paid freelancer David Black $26,000, plus expenses, to investigate AIDS, the sexual scourge of the eighties. The results, printed as a two-part series in the spring of 1985, were explosive. For his efforts, Black was assaulted by angry gays and given the National Magazine Award—the highest honor ever received by a *Rolling Stone* reporter.

The writer and his editors, Bob Wallace and Susan Murcko, returned from the award ceremonies and dashed into Jann Wenner's office, trophy in hand. Wenner looked up and smiled. "That's great," he said, somewhat distractedly.

David Black waited for the next words. Surely Wenner would suggest that they adjourn to the Plaza Hotel and pop a few corks.

Instead, the editor of *Rolling Stone* casually held out a bowl and waved it at Black. "Here," he said. "Have some popcorn."

The reporter went away befuddled. Perhaps Wenner's mind was elsewhere. Perhaps he was drunk on the vodka he kept in the refrigerator beside his desk. Likely as not the editor would be phoning David Black sometime soon, offering his award-winning reporter an exclusive contract, or at least assuring Black that Wenner was proud of him, that his work would always be welcome at *Rolling Stone.*

Jann Wenner never made this call. The AIDS investigation was a one-shot deal, suggestive of *Rolling Stone*'s lingering potential and nothing else. David Black was strung out to dry, a casualty of *Rolling Stone*'s war between its enduring conscience and its boundless commercial appetite.

This internal struggle, seen in virtually every issue of today's slick but self-conscious *Rolling Stone*, reflects a conflict greater than its own. It reflects two decades of stirred passions and best intentions, out of which emerged no clear moral consensus to replace the old. It reflects a generation's opaque triumph—1967's Human Be-In evolving into 1983's sheepish *Big Chill*. That triumph is *Rolling Stone*'s; the magazine is haunted by it.

Accordingly, contradictions haunt the magazine today. *Rolling Stone* no longer communicates "straight across" to its peers, for it deliberately abandoned them when MTV stimulated a new youth market in the early eighties. Now the magazine serves a different generation. Fittingly, it does so with a combination of earnestness and cynicism that is passed off as sophisticated marketing. But beneath the shrewdness lies real confusion.

Jann Wenner has often said, "There isn't a generation gap any longer." Yet his own editors do not agree with him. The gap in fact exists between *Rolling Stone*'s very soul and the young readers who have made Wenner a very rich man.

The pivotal readers in question constitute only 25 percent of the magazine's circulation. They are not *Rolling Stone*'s one million or so subscribers—the older, more sophisticated readers; the *Rolling Stone* faithful—for the simple reason that subscribers do not make magazines much money.

The real money comes from the newsstand. Every two weeks, anywhere from 190,000 to 220,000 consumers pay the full $2.50 for a copy of *Rolling Stone*. Many of them do so on sheer impulse. Most are "white teenage boys with zits," in the words of one former editor; of the politically charged era that gave rise to Jann Wenner's magazine, they have heard only rumors. Many cannot possibly be termed "the *Rolling Stone* faithful." Yet *Rolling Stone* does everything it can, every two weeks, to be faithful to them.

Most magazines, and indeed most individuals, cater to their greatest benefactors. Yet current and former *Rolling Stone* staffers liken Wenner's obsession with newsstand sales to a Wall Street fixation. The publisher ravenously devours all available data in pursuit of something his own editors do not believe exists: a reliable means of predicting what readers will buy. Since 1984, the cover of *Rolling Stone*—once so hallowed an icon that Dr. Hook sang about it in 1973—has been determined, in large measure, by focus group surveys and other research tools. A fabulous issue—that is to say, an issue with a fabulous cover—can push newsstand sales up to 300,000. On the other hand, the Reverend Charles M. Young's infamous Sex Pistols cover story in 1977 wallowed at 192,000. Said managing editor Jim Henke, "Once that happened, Jann's mind was pretty much made up about punk."

The lesson was learned all too well. Today, what *Rolling Stone* publishes and what it sells are often two entirely different things. As in the February 9, 1989, issue, serious articles on crack, *glasnost*, the war in Belfast and yuppie hucksterism are bundled up and shoved beneath a cover image of Jon Bon Jovi, the doe-eyed "lite metal" preteen idol. Editorial staffers insist that *Rolling Stone* is not "about Bon Jovi"—just as they insisted in the late eighties that the business staff's *Marketing Through Music* newsletter, which promoted corporate sponsorship of rock & roll, in no way reflected *Rolling Stone*'s opinions.

Similarly, when *Rolling Stone* first launched its sixties-bashing Perception/ Reality ad campaign in 1985, assurances were made all around that the magazine wasn't repudiating its roots. The campaign was simply pointing out to potential advertisers that its readers now used soap and were "card carrying capitalists." If the references to sixties "holdouts" were a little harsh . . . well, why couldn't a generation laugh at itself? If it could, surely it also could understand why *Rolling Stone* had to misrepresent itself occasionally, had to pander here and there. Compromise, as any reformed sixties "holdout" who voted for Ronald Reagan knew, was not the easiest pill to swallow. Sometimes, going down, the pill felt like a sword.

———

Certainly there was nothing smooth about the Axl Rose cover story of the August 10, 1989, issue. The enormously popular vocalist of Guns n' Roses demanded that the band's official biographer—a non-*Rolling Stone* writer with direct financial ties to Guns n' Roses—conduct the interview. In another era, when an Axl Rose would have needed *Rolling Stone* much more than the other way around, the editors would have laughed in his stupefied young face.

Instead, they granted his request, an unseemly concession to the shaky ground *Rolling Stone* today occupies. In point of fact, Axl Rose no longer needs *Rolling Stone* because its readers no longer rely on it as a music consumer guide. Nobody knows this better than Clive Davis, the former Columbia Records president whose financial sponsorship of *Rolling Stone* helped save the magazine from bankruptcy in 1970. In those days, Davis made Jann Wenner's publication "required reading" for his staff. Nowadays, the present head of the Arista label concedes that *Rolling Stone* "isn't essential reading."

Much of this is due to MTV's indisputable power over American youth. The rest, however, is due to Jann Wenner's complete ignorance of virtually every musical act that began recording after roughly 1975. The publisher of *Rolling Stone* shamelessly promotes his aging cronies: Art Garfunkel, Jackson Browne, Billy Joel, the J. Geils Band's Peter Wolf, Foreigner's Mick Jones and several others. (One music writer explained the magazine's rather timid record reviews by saying, "It is always a risk to rate too low anyone that Jann's had lunch with.") In all other cases, the index of newsstand sales is used to gauge a musician's worth. The generation gap—the one Wenner says does not exist—separates *Rolling Stone*'s first music critic from both his readers and his writers.

"To tell you the truth," said longtime contributor Mikal Gilmore, "I've given up trying to sell them music stories. They don't know how to pursue music with adventurousness anymore." Indeed, no writer wants to be the next Charles M. Young, selling to Jann Wenner a noble disaster like the Sex Pistols article. "Going to Jann is a crapshoot," says one editor. "You might hit him when he is really being smart and coherent and helpful and sweet. Then again, you might hit him when he's drunk and being a fucking asshole. So what do you do?"

What they do, according to music writer David Wild, is hedge their bets: "There's a certain amount of self-censorship that goes on by a bunch of us. We sometimes think, Oh, Jann won't go for that, and so we don't even ask. I think anyone who says that they don't get involved in that is being naïve."

Always Jann Wenner's employees spoke of him with pronounced ambivalence. But today there is no passion to the *Rolling Stone* staff's view of Wenner, one way or the other. He is simply an unpleasant fact of their existence—a figure to be endured, like a cranky and listless tenured professor. His presence is seldom seen and seldom missed, they say; his uniquely meaningful contributions seldom felt. As his employees, they still fear him, and the occasional backward glance to Wenner's accomplishments elicits occasional awe. But it has been some time since the staff of *Rolling Stone* expected magic from its leader.

"I don't think Jann has a vision for *Rolling Stone* anymore," said one of the magazine's top writers. "I think he *had* a vision, at one point, and he got it rolling, and now he's along for the ride."

BOB GUCCIONE, JR., THE EDITOR and publisher of *Spin*, views Jann Wenner as "the Dr. Faustus of the yuppie generation." It is Guccione's artful way of calling his competitor a sellout—artful, because the term "sellout" has lost virtually all meaning today except insofar as it dates the individual who utters it. After all, despite whatever it meant in the sixties, today selling out means one thing and one thing only: making money.

No one wrestled with the notion of selling out as *Rolling Stone*'s employees did in the sixties and seventies. Every single change in the magazine—its move from the old warehouse loft where *Rolling Stone* began, the abandonment of the magazine's quarterfold format, the use of four-color art, the restricted use of the word "fuck" in headlines, the acceptance of advertisements from liquor companies, then from tobacco companies, then from cosmetics companies, then from the military—was subjected to the kind of debate unimaginable to a young journalist of the nineties. Staffers agonized over these matters as if nothing less than society itself hung in the balance.

And it did, in a way. For these young men and women, both in the pages of *Rolling Stone* and behind its office doors, were harbingers of a swirling new culture. They were among America's first users of drugs, its first protesters and its first enthusiasts of "the San Francisco sound." When the Woodstock fantasy died horribly at the Altamont Speedway, they were among the first to face the music. Feminism was not born at *Rolling Stone*, but its women who struggled for equality triumphed in time to help promulgate the American feminist movement of the latter seventies. Quite correctly, the employees of *Rolling Stone* magazine saw themselves as leaders and tastemakers—the best minds of their generation. As preposterous as it may seem to a young magazine employee today, the *Rolling Stone* staffers wanted nothing so much as to set a good example for their peers.

When they did not, their readers cried "sellout"—a charge that perhaps no other magazine had ever yet faced. And in truth, *Rolling Stone* was always vulnerable. While generally free to lambaste musicians, the magazine's music writers refrained from criticizing record companies until the early eighties, when *Rolling Stone* no longer depended upon the industry's financial largesse. With relatively few exceptions, the magazine never saw much sport (or profit) in discovering unknown talent. In particular, its reluctance to cover black music is infamous. (Not coincidentally, *Rolling Stone* has never employed a single black writer. When black music critic Nelson George visited the magazine's office in the early eighties, he was startled by the sea of lily-white faces. "I thought I'd walked in on a California beach party," he said.)

While his staff has heatedly rebuffed all accusers, Jann Wenner's argument has consistently been that *Rolling Stone* never had a stance to sell out. In a wonderfully honest but generally misunderstood editorial, on the occasion of the magazine's fourth anniversary, the editor wrote:

> As attractive as it looks or may have looked, as lucrative and egoistic as the illusion is, we again disclaim for *Rolling Stone* the role as spokesman for anybody other than the people who write it and get it off the presses and onto the counters. We speak only for ourselves, hoping only that we do well in our own terms, as businessmen and journalists—that people will be interested in the same things we are, and at least respect our point of view.

The history of *Rolling Stone* is thus, for all its cultural resonance, intensely personal. Remarkable souls danced in and out of Jann Wenner's candy store. Some, like Tom Wolfe, Jacqueline Onassis, William Randolph Hearst III and Ralph J. Gleason, were eminences long before he met them. Others— most notably Hunter Thompson and *Rolling Stone*'s brilliant photographer Annie Leibovitz—became stars through their association with Wenner.

The rest never quite achieved fame. For most of them, this was fine. *Rolling Stone* was where they fell in and out of love, threw tantrums, lost sleep, did drugs—but above all else, where they worked like savages, seeking self-definition as they defined a culture in wild metamorphosis. "At *Rolling Stone*," said Timothy White, "each of us just wanted to see ourselves and those around us in our work, to remove those distances. In another time and place, we might not have gotten the chance to be so vulnerable and learn so much. And because of the catalyst of rock & roll, we not only wanted to discover the truth, but to dance with our secrets.

"*Rolling Stone*," said White, "was dancing with secrets."

———

Fame, of course, is another dance entirely.

Today forty-four-year-old Jann Wenner and fifty-one-year-old Hunter Thompson—two of the most colorful figures in postwar American print journalism—are wealthy and well known. Wenner has more money (his current worth exceeds $100 million), with an ostentatious lifestyle of private jets, country villas and choice social connections to match. Thompson, on the other hand, is the greater celebrity: he lopes along the lecture circuit, mumbles his way through guest appearances on *Late Night with David Letterman* and is protected by the citizens of Woody Creek like a sort of prehistoric pet.

The two have gone as far as any magazine could take them. In this uneasy success story, they occupy twin horns of the *Rolling Stone* dilemma: the price of commercial success and the limits of artistic freedom.

"Gonzo," Hunter Thompson mutters, and shakes his great bald head. "Sometimes I wish I'd never heard of the goddamned word."

A little self-pity massages the soul. Thompson is by no means a bitter man. He commands higher book advances than nearly any other American nonfiction writer, lives an unfettered life of sex and drugs and rock & roll and is left alone by the authorities. It puzzles him that he has achieved such notoriety. At bottom a shy and humble Southern gentleman, the Gonzo journalist graciously signs autographs and buys drinks for total strangers at the Woody Creek Tavern. He visits hospitalized neighbors. His eyes well up at the mention of fallen friends.

He is a deeply sentimental man, like his former employer. For all their differences, for all the lies and hysteria and dashed hopes, Hunter Thompson looks back on his *Rolling Stone* days with profound longing. It was quite a ride, that trip he took with Jann Wenner. God, they gave those bastards a scare.

Says Thompson, his long face a network of solemn wrinkles, "I've worked with Hinckle, Hayes—I've worked with all the best editors. Hey. When Jann was working, he *was* the best."

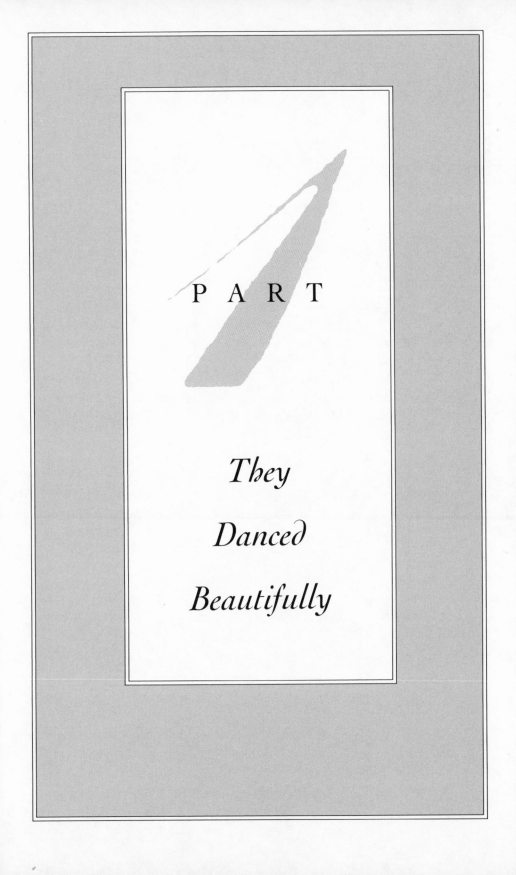

PART

1

They

Danced

Beautifully

Chapter One

"THE FREE-EST GENERATION THIS COUNTRY HAS SEEN"

"San Francisco is the next Liverpool," said the girl with the Benjamin Franklin glasses and the cheap antique dress.

"Oh, really," said Ralph Gleason, and he took down this information on his notepad. He was courteous enough not to laugh in her face. Would that he had a dime for every city that was calling itself the next Liverpool—he'd buy the Beatles, by God, and make them the permanent house band of 2835 Ashby in Berkeley. That would make Gleason's home the next Liverpool, and stifle these idiotic boasts once and for all.

San Francisco Chronicle columnist Ralph J. Gleason had dodged a lifetime's worth of bullshit in his thirty years as a music critic. He did not suffer fools, especially the archconservative variety, the sacred cows like Judy Garland and Bob Hope and anyone else who allowed himself to be photographed with venal tyrants like Lyndon Johnson and Richard Nixon.

"Don't follow leaders." It was one of Gleason's many favorite Bob Dylan lines. Gleason resented leaders for their actions; also, perhaps, because he was not among them—would never, in his view, receive the opportunity to lead. A person did not have to look hard to find the ethnic chip on his shoulder. "One part of him," said a friend, "was a classic New York Irishman of his generation, always braced for a rebuff, always on the lookout for any sign of condescension." Ralph Gleason, despite all the respect he would accrue as America's best-known music critic, harbored a sense of exclusion that put him squarely on the side of outsiders.

Among these, young people earned particular sympathy in Gleason's heart. God, what a mess they stood to inherit. Negroes treated like animals, artists behind bars for uttering a single word, boys shot down overseas in the kind of ridiculous war only the Best and the Brightest could dream up. . . . Give them a chance, he thought; how much worse can they do than my generation?

An annoyed reader once charged that the critic was an overgrown kid himself, a forty-eight-year-old schizophrenic who couldn't decide whether to split himself into three sixteen-year-olds or four twelve-year-olds. To which Ralph Gleason would reply, "Ah, well," and light his pipe. He knew a compliment when he heard one.

So Ralph Gleason listened patiently to the three kids seated in his living room: the failed commercial artist, the girl who claimed she'd lived in a tree in Mexico for a year and Luria Castel, the one with the funky glasses who did most of the talking. "San Francisco," she continued, "is the only city in the United States which can support a scene. New York is too large and confused, and Los Angeles is super-uptight plastic America."

She added, "San Francisco is Pleasure City."

Here Gleason could not hide his skepticism. Pleasure City? Not the San Francisco he knew. A few years back, maybe. You could spend long evenings, as Gleason did, roaming the North Beach beatnik enclave, catching hip music and live poetry gigs all along Columbus Avenue. But that was another time. Nightclubs like the Blackhawk weren't thriving anymore. These days, the only places that booked live bands were the topless bars on Broadway.

"Exactly," said Luria. "That's our point. That's why we're here. We don't want to have to go to a topless bar to hear the Byrds or the Lovin' Spoonful. It's offensive! We don't *like* bars. I mean, alcohol is our parents' trip."

Gleason didn't follow. What made San Francisco the next Liverpool if it wasn't music? San Francisco was a *banking center*, for Christ's sake. And it was beginning to look that way, too. All those fine fifty-year-old buildings demolished to make room for that awful skyline, those "prisons of plate glass," as he would say. All those buses clogging the Bay Bridge, those languid little ferryboats that just didn't fit someone's brilliant notion of progress now sitting in some grim shipyard somewhere out of plain view. Where was the Liverpool in this?

"Haight-Ashbury," Luria Castel said. "That's where it's all happening."

The three resided in the Haight district, a low-rent integrated community just south of Golden Gate Park. They lived in one of the many ramshackle Victorian homes, with a pot dealer and several dogs, and in fact they called themselves the Family Dog. Which, for the Haight, was not so unusual. People called themselves whatever they wanted to there, dressing as they liked, living communally and experimenting with marijuana and hallucinogens.

Changes were brewing in the Haight, the Family Dog spokesperson said. New artistic styles. An experimental mime troupe managed by a guy named Bill Graham. Weird stores like the Magic Theater for Madmen Only, where you could buy both antiques and drug paraphernalia.

And *music*. Gleason had undoubtedly heard of the Charlatans, a controversial group of long-haired acidheads in Edwardian clothes who'd spent the summer causing trouble as the house band in a Nevada saloon. The Haight was spawning other musicians as well, from Jerry Garcia's jug band the Warlocks to a fellow named Christopher Tree, who played the gong and the lute at the same time. The music fit with the neighborhood's taste for outrageousness; it belonged in the company of weird lights and incense and curious embroidery.

This was music you weren't supposed to sit and passively listen to, Luria said. In her view, sit-down venues like the Cow Palace were every bit as corrupting to music as the topless bars on Broadway.

So the Family Dog had taken matters into their own hands. They'd borrowed money from their parents, rented the Longshoreman's Hall at the edge of Fisherman's Wharf and were throwing a dance concert there.

"We want to invite the public to come and *feel good*," Luria said, giving Ralph Gleason a handbill. At the top it read:

THE FAMILY DOG PRESENTS
A TRIBUTE TO DR. STRANGE
SATURDAY, OCTOBER 16, 1965

Well. Interesting, definitely, Gleason thought as he bade goodbye to the Family Dog trio, closed the door and sat puffing on his pipe. Certainly worthy of a plug in his *Chronicle* column. But the new Liverpool?

He doubted it, and Ralph Gleason took justifiable pride in his foresight. Over the last three decades he'd done more to advance the careers of Miles Davis, Dizzy Gillespie, the Modern Jazz Quartet and Duke Ellington than any other writer. He was the first reporter to praise Lenny Bruce, then an obscure comic and social critic whose act Gleason caught in 1958 on Broadway, in a lesbian bar called Ann's 440. Other critics could churn out better copy, but none could match his vision. Every steering committee in town sought Gleason as an adviser. Every local musician hoped for kind words from the starmaker.

More often than not, Gleason would find something nice to say. At times, though, his pronouncements reduced performers to tears, and in one case led a musician to send Gleason a bag of sugar—not intended sweetly, as the critic was acutely diabetic.

For his perceived arrogance, Ralph Gleason had earned a sizable camp of enemies. Gleason looks like a dapper British spy, they'd say, and he sounds like a good-humored Eastern intellectual. But the man is egotistical, and self-serving, and downright diamond *cold*.

And he wasn't always right. No one knew this better than Gleason himself. Twice his judgment had failed him badly, and these mishaps haunted him. Back in the forties, young Gleason joined the fuddy-duddies in proclaiming swing jazz a commercial prostitution of Dixieland. His embrace of Charlie Parker's bebop came too late to save face.

The second gaffe was far worse. At the 1963 Monterey Folk Festival, Gleason and his wife, Jean, sat with friends and beheld the performance of a curly-headed folksinger who had become the darling of the East Coast record industry. This particular critic didn't see what all the hype was about. Turning to a friend, Gleason snorted, "Another New York Jew imitating Woody Guthrie."

In fact, Bob Dylan was from Hibbing, Minnesota, but that May, Gleason issued his dig in print. Dylan "tends to bore me," he said, "and sound oppressively mournful." The case was dismissed.

Six months later, Ralph Gleason reversed his stance. He personally apologized to Bob Dylan. In print he compared Dylan to Shakespeare. Dylan was the future, he declared, in the same breath relegating establishment jazz to the slag heap of the corrupt past. The musician and his girlfriend, Joan Baez, became Gleason's friends. One night as they drove around together in Gleason's red Volvo sedan, smoking pot, it occurred to him that if Dylan and Baez were indeed the future, then *good God, what if he suddenly lost control of his Volvo at this very moment?* On that night, he quit smoking marijuana once and for all.

So fervently did Gleason promote America's young protest singers, and then the Beatles and the Rolling Stones, that his fellow critics turned on him, saying he'd lost his mind. He hadn't; he knew just what he was doing. That was the way it was with Ralph J. Gleason. In the eyes of his peers, he was jumping the gun; in his own eyes, he was six months behind schedule, and furiously making up for lost time.

On this occasion, Gleason's timing was flawless.

———

The day of October 16, 1965, had begun with no dancing at all. Four thousand student demonstrators marched from the Berkeley civic center toward Oakland's Army base, singing the Beatles' song "Help!" while Beat poet Allen Ginsberg chanted and Ken Kesey's Merry Pranksters trundled along in their blood-red school bus. At the Oakland city line, a wall of four hundred Oakland city policemen in riot gear greeted them. The students halted. Eighteen Hell's Angels, the radicals' "violent brothers," materialized from behind the policemen.

"Cowards! Yellow motherfuckers!" the Angels sneered, and snatched away a protest sign. They advanced toward the students with raised fists. The policemen converged. By the end, a policeman suffered a broken arm, a massive Angel named Tiny got his head split open, several were arrested and the students never came close to the Army base.

It was a day of the times, angry and depressing. But history would also acknowledge the night, and its main event: the Tribute to Dr. Strange dance concert, the birth of the mad and wondrous and, some would say, calamitous San Francisco Psychedelic Era. On this evening American culture would explode like a stick of dynamite on a suburban lawn.

Ralph Gleason observed this from the balcony of the Longshoreman's Hall, his fists jammed into his Bogart trench-coat pockets, his pipe riveted between his teeth. From here he could see it all, and what he saw he could scarcely believe.

The dancers were robed in fantasy: Victorian lace and granny boots, straw hats with canes, derbies, sashes, elbow-length satin gloves, wine-dark velvet gowns. They snaked across Ralph Gleason's field of vision like a bizarre reordering of time itself: there went a go-go girl, a Robin Hood, a pirate, cowboys, pilgrims, hundreds and hundreds of strange children. The American Dream charged you with expressing yourself, and it never made sense to Gleason why people forsook this for the anonymity of gray flannel. There were hundreds at this event—an event *not* billed as a costume party—in brilliant agreement with Ralph J. Gleason.

They danced under pounding strobe lights, red, then white, then blue, to loud and murky music he had never heard before. There was an Oakland band that sounded British, and the infamous Charlatans dressed up like turn-of-the-century saloonkeepers. There were the soaring harmonies of the Jefferson Airplane, who had been recommended to Gleason a few weeks ago by a hysterical phone caller named Hunter Thompson. And there was the lead singer in the Great Society, a model named Grace Slick, in a purple mod dress and purple stockings, her hair long and tunnel dark, her voice high and stern like winter wind. Even in this cavern of glass and concrete, through the slapdash sound system, you could hear her words: *"Feed your head! Feed your head!"*

Apparently the dancers had been fed. They danced the Jerk, the Dog, the Hitchhike and the Hully Gully. But then hundreds of them, on no spoken cue, melded into a chain. They swished along in figure eights, and broke free, and danced dances that had no name. The bands played on, bathed in the weird protoplasm of the light show—playing *with* the dancers somehow, excited by the dance, like fish possessed by the voiceless yet insistent call to spawn.

Nearby the dancers stood a few Hell's Angels, several political types from Berkeley and a handful of older folk, all just as stupefied as Gleason. Gawking also was a man familiar to Gleason, dressed in a white Hindu suit: Allen Ginsberg. Only a week or so ago he had returned to San Francisco, the Berkeley demonstrations darkening his thoughts: "Here is the city," Ginsberg wrote, "here is the face of war."

War? Not here. Not tonight. Ginsberg had also spoken of a "revolution of the psyche," and that *was* here, in unbelievable numbers, all these young people in their psychic drag, dancing fearlessly. The poet shuffled through the proceedings, slack-jawed, while the purple goddess sang "Feed your head!" and Ralph Gleason gazed at the ornamental swirl of the dance, stricken: love at first sight.

Of this event he would write, in his column of October 18, 1965:

> Dixieland trumpet player Bob Scobey once said that dancing was "only an excuse to get next to a broad." Since the New Morality

supplies that need elsewhere, the dance floor is no longer the scene of the sexual expression it was. Now it is becoming a training ground for the free-est generation this country has seen . . .

Then the Gleason pronouncement:

. . . and they dance beautifully.

Before night's end, Gleason would come down from the balcony and join the dance.

————

That night a representative of the younger generation came up to shake Ralph Gleason's hand. He was a young man, or really only a boy: not yet twenty, baby-faced, with a mere babe's blue eyes peeking out from underneath a wavy thrash of brown hair. His lips were plump, almost feminine, and they moved at top speed, with words pouring out in an effusive rush, as if Gleason might turn his back and walk away at any moment.

Jann Wenner was his name. He'd been reading the critic's columns for some time now. The boy was himself a writer—trying, anyway—and a fan, both of Gleason and of the people he extolled in his column. The boy loved Dylan, loved the Beatles, loved the Stones, was as big a nut for rock & roll as there could possibly be, and as for this night . . . Well. What a night!

Ralph Gleason agreed with his new friend Jann Wenner. Yes, this night might very well make history.

Chapter Two

B O Y ' S   L I F E

One afternoon in the spring of 1964, Berkeley American studies undergraduate Greil Marcus sat in the apartment of fellow student Jann Wenner. The two had only just met, but Marcus was thoroughly taken with his new acquaintance.

Mose Allison was on the stereo as the quick-witted Wenner boy chatted about his experiences in Slate, the controversial organization that evaluated Berkeley teachers and caused a campus stir with its every utterance. Since last fall, Wenner had been a Slate rank-and-file insider, no casual feat for a freshman.

But then, he seemed to have the jump on everything. Wenner's off-campus apartment sat high on Waring, just south of Memorial Stadium, a truly enviable perch. He knew his campus politics and he knew his music. His words were aggressive, highly opinionated; ideas flew out of his mouth a dozen at a time.

"I thought he was really hip," Marcus would later recall. No doubt Jann Wenner would be in the thick of things when the collective student identity crisis detonated Berkeley—but purely by choice, as the crisis was not his. Wenner knew who he was and where he was headed, with or without anyone's help. While the Greil Marcuses of Berkeley were wondering aloud about their place in the world, Wenner had already staked his on a hillside, well above the confusion.

But just as Marcus was getting a fix on his host, his gaze fell upon an object pinned to a nearby wall. It was a page from the *San Francisco Chronicle*—the society page, upon closer inspection. There on the wall of this hip liberal's flat hung photographs of the haughty offspring of the San Francisco elite: luscious untouchable debutantes and their well-heeled escorts, all prim and oblivious, drinking up life by the silver goblet in these days of shattered glass. The great heirs, the great anachronisms. What were they doing on this wall?

So Jann Wenner's a hipster and a society boy, all rolled up into one soft package, Greil Marcus thought with some amusement. He did not dwell on it at the time. Marcus knew other fellows who cavorted with debs. Some people just went through that stage.

———

Six years later, Marcus wondered if the debutante ball would ever end.

This was 1970, a moment of fever, a year of lies and bullets. The Vietnam War had spread into Cambodia, and then into America itself. In this year, National Guard troops shot to death four students at Kent State. By this time Greil Marcus was one of *Rolling Stone*'s most respected music critics. From his desk he wrote about rock and revolution simultaneously, arguing, "No longer need one feel that he must give up his existing identity to become an activist."

Marcus was appealing to his readers; also, perhaps, to his friend and employer, Jann Wenner. If technologically skilled "system fuckers" could disrupt power lines, if former Green Berets could make plastic explosives, if Berkeley football players could "pledge to transform athletics into a meaningful counter-force to the Cambodian invasion," then imagine what the editor and publisher of a magazine as influential as *Rolling Stone* could do to aid the revolution.

To Marcus's dismay, Jann Wenner would not give the revolution his time. He wore pinstripes now, and around the warring world he breezed, getting stoned with his idols. Perhaps Jann had only been kidding when he told one of his first staffers that he'd created *Rolling Stone* so that he could meet John Lennon. In any event, by the tender age of twenty-four, Wenner had far outstripped that goal. He could brag that he and Lennon tooled around in limos together; that Bob Dylan paid him a visit one morning in a New York hotel room; that Mick Jagger had been his business partner; that Boz Scaggs was his friend whose record he co-produced; that his appointment book could pass for a social register of the music industry.

While America beat itself into a coma, Jann Wenner "was living out the debutante-world life that he had never completely lived out years before," said Marcus.

Yet the years would pass without any sign that the former Slate insider would ever forsake his stargazing ways—that the society page would ever come down from his wall. Plastered across his consciousness were the daughters of the San Francisco elite, then Lennon and Dylan and Jagger, then Tom Wolfe and Truman Capote, then Jimmy Carter and Jacqueline Onassis, then young and beautiful movie stars.

Always fresh faces, so the page itself would never yellow and wither on the wall. It would hang there forever.

———

The boy whose birth certificate read Jan Simon Wenner was born in New York City's Beth Israel Hospital on January 7, 1946. Conceived in the Jewish faith well after Hitler's suicide and only months before the *Enola Gay* dropped death upon Hiroshima, he sprang from the most fertile garden in the history of civilization.

A new dream was being born—right here, right now. The dream legislated a generation that would suffer neither tyranny nor poverty, would know only bottomless privilege. Integral to the dream was that generation's gratitude. One could only expect that these pampered legions would carry their parents' standard well beyond what Henry Luce called "the American Century." In their godliness, they might even conquer time.

The boy's parents had served their country—Ed Wenner in the Air Force, Ruth Simmons Wenner (known as Sim) in the Navy—and now searched, with the rest of America, for purpose. One night it literally cried out to them, at three in the morning. Ed Wenner reached for teary-eyed Jan, reached for the baby bottle and . . . it flashed. Could any routine today be more American than this? The father warmed to the idea as the son warmed to the milk: he who fed the baby-boomers would never want for food himself.

That same year the Wenners headed west, as did Ralph and Jean Gleason and the multitudes of other Americans scrambling to cash in on postwar promises. As many as one hundred and thirty thousand people a month in 1946 crossed the Arizona border into California, bypassing on their journey the moribund assembly-line towns and the industrial cities now chaotic with strikes. By 1947 the state bulged with three million inhabitants.

The migrating horde was like nothing American had ever seen. These seekers of milk and honey in no way resembled the raggedy supplicants of Steinbeck's *The Grapes of Wrath*. Nearly half of them ranged between fifteen and thirty-four years of age. They were younger than the average Californian, and better educated as well. The migrants formed a coveted new labor corps; and California, with eleven acres for every inhabitant, with the highest standard of living in the United States, absorbed them as no other state in the Union could.

The Wenners, like the Gleasons, chose the Bay Area over Los Angeles, already overcrowded and well on its way to becoming a city planner's miscarriage. San Francisco's twin sirens, Nature and Commerce, enticed Ed and Sim Wenner much as the gold miners were drawn a century before. For all its riches, the town also had grit. The 1906 earthquake along the infamous San Andreas fault had all but wiped out an area three hundred miles long and forty miles wide, yet San Francisco's rise from the rubble was a smooth success. Forty years later, skeptics predicted that war's end would do more lasting damage to San Francisco's economy. The imperial naval and military bases went, but the money stayed. For all its glimmer, San Francisco lived the craggy, resilient life of the Pacific's seal rocks. It feared no disaster.

Wenner's Baby Formulas, Inc., opened in 1947, in a vacant San Francisco butcher shop. The family lived across the Golden Gate Bridge, in the Marin County town of San Rafael. Known in later years as America's divorce capital, prosperous Marin was a quiet, communal answer to hectic San Francisco life. Here stood redwoods and unscarred hills, and smart houses with inviting front lawns. Creeks trickled down from the western hilltops; pedestrian boats chugged along San Pablo Bay to the east. Here all the promises of California collapsed into a lush and languid utopia.

Into this gilded era tottered forth Jan Wenner. By postwar estimation, the child had it made: precocious, energetic and obviously well fed, a beautiful blue-eyed boy imbued with the creativity of his mother and the entrepreneurial instincts of his father.

But the boy was lost in a house of dreamers. Ed Wenner's baby formula obsession meant that his mind was often away on business even when his body was planted in the Wenner living room. The man described by *Newsweek* as "a dark and stocky Walter Mitty who pursues his dreams" was not one to be whiling away his hours on the front lawn, tossing a baseball with his son. Why, Jan was a big boy now; he didn't need the bottle anymore. And soon Wenner's Baby Formulas, Inc., would be feeding 90 percent of all babies born within a 125-mile radius of San Francisco! Someday his son would appreciate this.

This made Sim far and away the dominant parent, a phenomenon hardly uncommon in the fifties. Yet, as she would herself confess, "I was a different kind of mother," a mother who had better things to do than lavish attention on her children, a mother who expected her son and his two younger sisters, Kate and Merlin, to cook their own food and do their own chores at a very early age. She was a businesswoman, a novelist, an artist—and as a hobby, a wearisome one at times, a mother.

Sim Wenner would not be tied down by umbilical cords or apron strings. She was well ahead of her time. Perhaps the whole Wenner family was. Both parents worked; housekeepers padded in and out. The children would know that they were lucky because the backyard swimming pool was always there to remind them. They would know that they were a family because every winter they skied together in Squaw Valley. This is how they would know each other, through monumental gestures and seasonal offerings. Ten years later, all five Wenners would live in separate cities.

———

In the fall of 1958, Ed and Sim Wenner packed up their eldest child and sent him some five hundred miles away from home. His new mailing address would be on the Palos Verdes Peninsula, south of Los Angeles, at the Chadwick School.

Margaret Lee Chadwick's boarding school stretched across fifty-five dreamy green acres crowning Academy Hill. From each edge of campus students could, if they so bothered, observe below the putterings of Los Angeles bedroom communities. More likely the communities looked up at them. It was a terrific privilege to survive the waiting list and attend Chadwick. Here one's child could mingle with the offspring of Judy Garland and Ronald Reagan and other prominent Hollywood performers. Here they could form lasting bonds with future Broadway stars, or even with future Russian spies.

Chadwick was known as an orphanage for rich kids. Beyond the school's progressive curriculum, discipline was taught here. Along the way, students would hopefully develop the sense of purpose their parents did not have time to instill in them. Along the way, a physically and socially awkward boy like Jan Wenner might come to view Chadwick as a glorious peak, rather than the world's most desolate island.

Not long after depositing him here, Jan's parents divorced. It was a divergence of two lifestyles, an impersonal thing really. Ed was a businessman, Sim was an artist. Things just didn't work out. Neither his father nor his mother took Jan back. No one called him and said, "Come home, we need to stick together."

Ed moved the $400,000 baby formula headquarters to the Los Angeles area, bought a house in Newport Beach and promptly remarried. Jan's sisters were sent off to other boarding schools. And Sim underwent a dramatic transformation: she grew her hair past her waist and began to affect the style and attitude of a hedonistic bohemian. She did not look, or behave, like Jan's or anyone else's mother.

Thus dissolved the Wenner family. The abandoned son would remember his anguish. Years later, he would tell his associates at *Rolling Stone* that in the divorce proceedings Ed and Sim Wenner fought over custody of their son; neither wanted custody. Sim Wenner would later dismiss this as "pure perception on his part," taking no account of the scar the perception left, deeper and more enduring than any flesh wound.

Not long after the divorce, Chadwick saw a new Jan—or Jann, as he was now spelling his name. He spread his talents all over the campus: acting in the Shakespearean Festival, writing articles for the Chadwick *Mainsheet* and a weekly column for the *Palo Verdes News*, editing the poetry anthology. Physically ungifted, he nonetheless involved himself in campus athletics as the varsity sports statistician. Zealously he pursued his own identity. In his sophomore class picture, only Jann Wenner wore a coat and tie.

"He operated on an energy level that was considerably higher than did most of us," one of his best friends said. "He was constantly coming up with ideas, and relaying those ideas in an excited, staccato-like voice."

His impatient bustle did not always wear well with his classmates. "He was pushy, he put people off," said another friend. "During Halloween, free doughnuts would be given out at school. And a certain kind of social convention, the kind your parents force on you, would tell the kids to bury their instincts, to be good, to just have one doughnut apiece. Jann would take five doughnuts. He didn't have that social convention. He took what he wanted."

Even Jann's English teacher, Mr. Holland, fondly called his pet student

Nox, short for "obnoxious." A rebel with flair, Jann smoked cigarettes behind the cafeteria after dinner, igniting them with the lighter he always carried while his girlfriend looked on in terror. Absolutely driven, they would say of him. Worthy of respect if not of fondness. A master of both put-downs and self-promotion. Next to his senior class photo in the 1963 Chadwick Dolphin yearbook, which he edited, are the words: "Greatness knows itself."

To some Chadwick students he was known simply as The Little Man.

As a senior, he dated Susan Weigel, a junior. Though well liked herself, she found that the more popular types "never could understand Jann, really. He was obnoxious and forceful, and not very nice, and weird." Susan recognized these unpleasant traits, but also found him articulate, freethinking and almost painfully vulnerable. She discovered early on his bitterness over his parents' divorce, and, despite all appearances, his fierce need for affection. "He desperately wanted to be liked," she said. "*Desperately*. He just had no idea how to go about it."

He took up with three classmates whose backgrounds were socially loftier than his own: Sheila Prell, whose family owned a prominent Las Vegas hotel; Andrew Harmon, son of a well-known movie producer; and Susan Weigel, a judge's daughter. Fascinated with his friends' heritage, Jann did not brag about his own. Being the son of a baby-food czar did not pack much social punch.

Jann learned this all too well during 1962's Christmas vacation, when he and Susan went skiing at the Sugar Bowl, a notorious magnet for the Bay Area elite. At the resort, Jann's girlfriend introduced him to her childhood friends. They were an impressive lot, these country-club heirs. Such poise they had, such elegant swagger. Many of them attended the venerable Thatcher School, compared to which Chadwick resembled a tawdry sweatshop.

They seemed friendly enough to Jann, who impressed them with his brashness and his fearless skiing. But their clannishness was overwhelming. To gain their unconditional acceptance, it appeared Jann Wenner would have to impale himself on his ski and spatter the snow with blue blood. One of the Thatcher boys nearly stole Susan away from him that week. She was torn, perhaps, between Jann's maverick charm and her own noble roots. She chose Jann, but too late to avoid anguish.

Yet he could understand, probably better than Susan Weigel, the appeal of this confederacy of beautiful young sophisticates. They inhabited a finer world, fraught with riches and spectacular tragedy. That this world balanced itself on one frail support—its own exclusivity—was not central in Jann

Wenner's mind. What mattered was that the world excluded *him*, for all time, with perfect indifference.

For every campus rebel, there is a campus All-American. Dennis Landis was his name, and Jann loathed him. Athletic, polished and brimming with self-confidence, the very image of Landis exaggerated Jann's own inadequacies. The two were born rivals. "They bantered," said Susan Weigel, "like little roosters."

During their senior year at Chadwick, a mutual friend named Bill Belding ran for student body president. Both Landis and Jann decided to campaign for vice president. Rather than engage in a popularity contest with Landis, Jann Wenner tried a back-door approach. He suggested that Belding and another classmate form a political slate with Jann—the Progressive Party —and run as a ticket. Jann warned Belding that if he didn't join the Progressives, Dennis Landis might form his own slate, and Bill Belding would be pulverized between the two great powers.

Belding signed onto Jann's ticket, discovering too late that his friend Landis had no slate of his own. "The Progressives," noted Dennis Landis later, "blew me and the other candidates out of the water. It was very skillful of Jann."

Jann's Progressives did not succeed in overthrowing the Chadwick administration, but they did make good on their promise to publish an alternative campus newspaper. *The Sardine*, a one-page leaflet, became Jann Wenner's soapbox. In its social column (called "Random Notes"), he plugged his own campus accomplishments while disparaging Dennis Landis's hook shot. Responding to student outcry, the controversial *Sardine* editor wrote, "We are not here to attack students, faculty, or the administration, but anyone who is afraid of critical appraisal or satire is implicitly recongnizing [sic] the truth in what we say. . . ." Jann then railed against the administration's ban on jean-cut pants. Subsequently, *The Sardine* was banned as well after just three issues.

No matter; Jann Wenner had made a good run of it, going out in a blaze of glory just two months before graduation. And now it was time to put away childish things. Like most of his friends, Jann applied for admission at Harvard. With his impressive résumé of extracurriculars and the honor of being one of only two Chadwick National Merit Scholar Finalists, he seemed a cinch for the Ivy League. Unfortunately, he had neither the alumni connections nor a grade-point average sufficient to gain entry. Harvard rejected him and accepted the other National Merit Scholar Finalist, Dennis Landis.

Humiliated, Jann Wenner made reluctant plans to attend the University of California at Berkeley for the fall of 1963.

———

On the evening of November 22, 1963, Berkeley freshman Barry Baron visited the apartment of his friend Jann Wenner. News of President Kennedy's assassination in a Dallas motorcade had swept the campus. With Kennedy as America's young, vigorous leader, the spirit pulsed with possibilities. Now that spirit lay cold on the table.

Baron let himself in, noticing that no lights were on, and looked around for Jann. He found him on the floor. "He was sitting with his legs crossed in front of a burning candle, in the dark," said Baron. "He was conducting a sort of vigil by himself in his apartment. I was as shocked as anyone else about Kennedy's death—but not moved to *that* extent.

"Jann always took himself very seriously—he was a very serious liberal Kennedy type. But I remember thinking at the time: Was he really that concerned, or was he just being dramatic? He *did* have a tremendous feel for theater."

At Berkeley, politics *was* theater—sometimes tragic, sometimes absurd—and Jann Wenner took to it like a country boy at Disneyland. Compared with Chadwick's puny graduating class of fifty-two, Berkeley seemed like a city-state, and in many ways it was: an enrollment of twenty-seven thousand, the liberal brain trust of the Bay Area and the crown jewel of the University of California system, the world's second-biggest university (after Calcutta), with an annual income of $580 million. More central to California society than Oxford to London or Harvard to Boston, the Berkeley campus in particular exerted a political grip on its city that, to some conservative malcontents, resembled a choke hold.

The founder of Chadwick's Progressive Party had entered the progressive motherland. Here at Berkeley, the stakes were higher than jean-cut pants. Students and faculty had shouted down loyalty oaths in the fifties and the House Un-American Activities Committee in the sixties. They protested the execution of convicted murderer Caryl Chessman; they reviled the growing military-industrial complex; they leafleted, picketed and sat in. The campus communicated through movements; to miss the movement was to dwell unknown, voiceless and disconnected.

The boy who sought connections showed up that first semester on the doorstep of Slate organizers Joan and Phil Roos, and after introducing himself said simply, "I want to work with you."

The Rooses were shorthanded and asked no questions. The "liberal Kennedy type" took his place among red-diaper babies and casual Democrats and went to work sorting the teacher evaluations. Before long, Jann became very close to the Roos couple. He spent many evenings in their living room, watching the news and telling them about his days at school. It was his first nuclear family. "When I become president of NBC," he vowed gratefully to the Rooses, "your daughter can be my secretary."

Jann Wenner, as a Slate insider, had burrowed into the heart of the Berkeley left wing. Such credentials would impress acquaintances like Greil Marcus, but Jann did not exploit his position to enrich his political awareness. Had he so chosen, he could have learned much from the Rooses and from Slate. Since its creation in 1958, Slate had assigned itself the task of fanning political embers, whether by coaxing the American Nazi Party to speak to Berkeley left-wingers or, in the fall of 1964, by calling upon Berkeley students to "begin an open, fierce and thoroughgoing rebellion on this campus." Politics, however, was not on Jann Wenner's mind.

Instead, he was more apt to chat about debutante balls. The socially libertarian Rooses were not startled by this preoccupation; a college boy, they believed, should experience it all. "The sixties were about self-development," said Joan Roos. "If that was the sort of thing that amused and challenged Jann, well, fine—so long as he wasn't directly stealing from the peasants in a traceable, linkable way."

When not at the Roos residence, Jann was consorting with Susan Weigel's fancy Thatcher friends who hadn't abandoned the Bay Area for the Ivy League. Sometimes they invited him to visit at their parents' houses. Jann returned the gesture, but with some apprehension. He'd come to view his own mother as an embarrassment. Sim wore long hair and flowing dresses, swore and used words like "groovy," smoked dope and entertained male guests. She was also, by this time, a published author, and while Jann harbored similar aspirations, Sim would be openly critical of his writing. The two seemed less like mother and son, more like older sister and kid brother.

"She was spectacular—quite the opposite of all our mothers," said a Thatcher friend. The visitors were enchanted by this free-spirited woman, just as they found Jann's flashy intellect so engaging. Yet their admiration was somehow lost on Jann. He still sought approbation, and on their terms, not his. Those who befriended Jann had trouble figuring out why this cocky rebel so desperately craved favor from the jet set.

"He was an exceedingly ambitious person, both professionally and socially," said one of his college pals. "Before the hippie era, there were lots of debutante parties—all very exclusive, of course. Jann had great ambitions to be a part of that scene, to be with the girls in the fancy parties in those fabulous estates.

"I myself was involved in that world. But I was a pretty conservative guy before '64—far more than he, of course: he wasn't at all. Here was this dope-smoking liberal on the one hand, and on the other hand there he'd be, with this glint in his eye—starstruck, I guess you'd say, begging for invitations to deb parties.

"Quite honestly, I thought it was hypocritical."

The friend had trouble explaining to Jann that a person just didn't beg his way into the elegant tented affairs. You were in, or you were out. Jann didn't listen. He bought his own dinner jacket. News of Jann's social obsessions filtered back to Susan Weigel, still at Chadwick and still being sent gifts by Jann. The thought of Jann crashing debutante parties disgusted her. She broke off their relationship.

Heedlessly Jann Wenner battered away at the ivory doors. By the fall of 1964, he was living in a glorious penthouse apartment on Carleton Street with three roommates, including Thatcher chum Ted Hayward. The penthouse had been Jann's idea. Ted Hayward thought it somewhat garish, much like the housewarming party Jann threw, which featured the kind of accouterments Hayward associated with frat houses.

Hayward had gone to the trouble, at Jann's behest, to invite his socialite friends, though it was not their habit to attend these nonexclusive affairs. At the party, one of the guests—presumably one of Jann's Slate friends—lit a marijuana cigarette, something the deb crowd found mildly fascinating. Otherwise, said Hayward, "my friends who came were appalled" by the popcorn and cheap jugs of wine, and left early.

For someone so ingratiating, Jann could be most ungracious. There was an aggressiveness to his insensitivity. At breakfast he gaily read aloud from the *San Francisco Chronicle*, which his roommates found no more entertaining than Jann's frequent attempts to play his guitar. The others also came to expect Jann to fudge on his share of the phone bill and, when his turn came, to cook hot dogs and beans and pocket the rest of the grocery money.

"Gradually," said Hayward, "I began to see the whole center of him, and what he wanted from me. I'd never met anybody who was motivated exclusively and purely by opportunism. In wonder—never really out of malice—I would sometimes find myself telling him, 'You are a *monster*! A complete and total *monster*!'"

One evening Hayward found Jann lying on his bed, sobbing uncontrollably. The sounds were deep and agonized. He had never seen his roommate so stricken with grief.

Hayward sat on the bed and put a gentle arm on Jann. "What's wrong?" he asked.

Still sobbing, Jann managed, "My psychiatrist died."

Hayward continued to comfort Jann, thinking, I didn't know he had a psychiatrist. What do I really know about this person?

Presently Jann Wenner stopped crying. He pulled away from his roommate, and staring at him with his red eyes, he bitterly told Ted Hayward: "I am *not* a monster."

By this time Jann was already dating a young woman he'd met at the Sugar Bowl ski resort, the daughter of a government official. She radiated class, and though she conveyed no interest in attending debutante balls, he found plenty of other moments to parade her in front of his friends.

Well after the fact, she would describe Jann as "one of the worst social climbers I've ever met. When we broke up, I felt a certain amount of resentment, because I thought maybe what had motivated our relationship was the idea that he thought he could benefit from my social connections."

Until then, the two were quite an item. The girl believed she loved Jann, though not because he had promised her that someday he would be "rich and famous." One evening, in Jann's penthouse, she let her boyfriend deflower her. A few nights later he had her over for dinner with the boys. For a tablecloth he used the very bedspread upon which the girl had lost her virginity. The bloodstain he situated directly underneath her plate.

The young woman did not know, but the roommates did. Jann chuckled throughout the meal, his joke lost on his girlfriend. Ted Hayward had trouble eating his food. *Monster,* he thought.

———

That fall the white tents came down. The Free Speech Movement had captivated the campus, and now even debutantes were marching.

The twenty-six-foot stretch of pavement along Telegraph Avenue girdling the Berkeley campus had never been of much consequence to Ted Hayward and his socialite friends. Perhaps this political vaudeville of leafleters, petitioners and soapbox debaters amused them. Perhaps, on bad days, the labyrinth of folding tables and scraggly leftists was yet another reminder of how overcrowded Berkeley had become.

On this matter, the social elite were no different than any other Berkeley student. They were all in the same dreary, rudderless boat. Classes were too large, curricula too rigid. The Board of Regents seemed more preoccupied with attracting research grants and Nobel laureates than preparing its undergraduates for the contentious world outside.

Discontent wafted like a storm cloud over Berkeley. The cloud broke on October 1, 1964, the day policemen arrested a young man named Jack Weinberg for distributing political material on Telegraph Avenue. From that moment onward, normal campus life descended into chaos. Students stopped going to class, rallied in the campus's Sproul Plaza and cheered the Free Speech Movement spokesman, Mario Savio, as their own Patton. Among the protesting masses were Jann Wenner's girlfriend, Jann Wenner's roommates and nearly every social prince Jann Wenner ever wanted to meet.

But not Jann Wenner himself. His professional ambitions, as with his social ones, would not lay fallow for any movement.

As a freshman, Jann wasted no time worming into the bowels of the news media. A friend of Sim Wenner's procured her son an entry-level job at NBC's radio affiliate. For twenty dollars a trip, he couriered NBC studio tapes to and from the airport. During the summer of 1964, while Republicans convened in San Francisco's Cow Palace, Jann fetched cigarettes for NBC's Chet Huntley. Soon he was reading NBC traffic reports over the radio.

Along the way, Jann obtained press badges. In any year they would have been treasured items. In 1964 they afforded a ringside seat to the student revolution.

At ringside he positioned himself, reporting the news rather than helping to create it. To his suddenly politicized friends, it seemed that only Jann Wenner, the hustling young opportunist, would not tumble into the drowning pool of the Free Speech Movement. With his press card, said one, "he could forever be the gadfly, never commit himself or take a stance on anything."

Instead, Jann gained his first professional experiences from the Movement. Accompanying one of the articles he wrote on the FSM was a photograph of Mario Savio behind a podium, addressing a massive, passionate rally . . . and to Savio's left, trench-coated, with microphone in hand, at the very edge of the action: Jann Wenner, cub reporter.

––––––

The bitter comments of his friends were not altogether fair. Jann's articles on the FSM were thoughtful and unquestionably sympathetic. Besides, if the whole purpose of the Movement was to encourage individual expression, one could not fault a young man for pursuing his own path.

Said Richard Black, a member of the Hearst family and a friend of Jann's from the debutante scene, "Jann Wenner had absolutely no political beliefs whatsoever. He was always a paparazzo in his heart. But Jann was motivated when none of us were. He had focus. Most of us were just hanging out at the Terrace."

The Terrace was an outdoor café across from Sproul Hall and a favorite campus gathering spot. Students sipped coffee and gossiped and theorized and soaked up the sun. During the fall of 1964, the singular Terrace topic was free speech. But the Cal administration eventually buckled, and in time so did the Movement. By the end of winter, Berkeley students had other things on their minds.

One crisp autumn afternoon in 1965, the talk on the Terrace drifted from revolution to drugs. Someone mentioned lysergic acid diethylamide, more commonly known as LSD, or just acid.

A conservatively dressed young man said to those gathered at the Terrace, "I'm gonna take some acid and do a psychology paper on it."

Among those within earshot was Denise Kaufman, a Berkeley student, FSM organizer and Ken Kesey compadre who had recently returned from a journey on the Merry Pranksters' bus. The short and pretty brunette eyed the young man with skepticism. Her first impression of Jann Wenner was that of an uptight, self-conscious preppie.

"Have you ever taken acid before?" she asked him.

"No," he replied stiffly.

"Do you have any idea what you're getting into?"

Jann fidgeted. He'd only heard the stories. In 1964 *One Flew Over the Cuckoo's Nest* author Kesey gathered a few wild souls and dubbed them the Merry Pranksters. Together they traveled in a multicolored school bus from coast to coast, dispersing their weird claptrap and, not incidentally, significant quantities of LSD.

The drug, first synthesized in a lab in 1938, was legal. A former Berkeley radar technician named Augustus Owsley Stanley III had spent the spring of 1965 manufacturing LSD capsules a million and a half at a time. Everyone knew someone who'd tried Owsley's acid. No one, as far as anyone knew, had ever died from it.

All the same, an acid trip was a roll of the psychic dice. Some people swore by the stuff, said it brought the beauty of routine life to the forefront of your consciousness, made magic out of ordinary sounds and shapes. The former Harvard professor Timothy Leary claimed you could take acid and sustain incredible orgasms, hundreds of them. But there were also those who just couldn't handle LSD. Dark and bloody nightmares reared up before them. The taking of acid was not a casual affair.

"You're going to do this alone?" she asked.

He said yes.

Denise Kaufman shook her head. "You're making a mistake," she said. "It's not a good idea to be alone for your first acid trip. You should have someone experienced with you."

Jann considered this. He looked up at her.

She said she would.

Denise Kaufman knew her LSD protocol. She borrowed some mellow records from one friend, a kitten from another. Back at Jann's apartment, she sat quietly while this unsettled young man fussed and paced, wondering why he had not yet come on to the acid. He bit at his nails. His clenched fist of a body moved back and forth across the room, then suddenly veered off and disappeared into a closet. He closed the door behind him.

He stayed inside the closet for hours. When he finally emerged, he was smiling and his blue eyes were soft and a little dizzy. The uptight, self-conscious opportunist had vanished. Jann sat next to Denise, and for hours they talked and listened to music and played with the kitten.

He fell in love with her, and with the forbidden fruit of the counterculture.

———

That fall he met Denise's friend Ralph Gleason at the Longshoreman's Hall dance party. Gleason was old enough to be Jann's father, but the two had something very much in common: an abiding love for rock & roll.

The music came to him, as it had to so many others, like a host of prodigal brethren, like seductive whisperers just outside the windowsill. They were an outcast's perfect heroes, for they were themselves outcasts. But Bob Dylan and the Beatles and the Rolling Stones made the fringe seem like the only place to be; it was where you broke rules, found true love and got the finest view of Middle America's rotting core. The music would find its way into the masses, but in 1965 it belonged to the fringe, and to the generation that occupied it. It belonged to Jann Wenner and other seekers of magic.

In 1965 the Beatles released "Eleanor Rigby," the Stones' nearly perfect "(I Can't Get No) Satisfaction" topped the charts and Dylan introduced his first rock & roll classic, "Like a Rolling Stone." The three songs, while musically different in every conceivable way, each chorused the campus themes of disenchantment and isolation. Their signature lines flew through the airways and out of the mouths of babes: *All the lonely people. How does it feel? I can't get no!*

Galvanized by their mutual infatuation, Jann Wenner and Ralph Gleason became fast friends. Together they attended folk festivals, taking in evenings at the Fillmore or the Avalon Ballroom and reveling in the growing power of the San Francisco scene. They cut a strange couple: this figure of studied elegance, graying and bespectacled, accompanied by a floppy-haired, acid-dropping happy puppy of a young man. Gleason himself was no stranger to self-promotion, but his was a subtle sales pitch. It amused him to watch young Wenner, an utterly guileless soul, pumping hands at the Matrix and shamelessly flattering every musician he could.

Jann became a frequent visitor at the Gleason household, then a fixture. The attention Ralph gave his new friend peeved the other hangers-on at 2835 Ashby. Many of these were Free Speech Movement leaders—virtual Gleason family members since Ralph befriended them in the fall of 1964, when no other Establishment reporter would offer a sympathetic ear. In the midnight hour they often sat and discussed strategy in his attic while his wife, Jean, served them coffee and cake. Gleason's daughters cut classes to iron Mario Savio's shirts.

Now in their place stood Jann, an FSM bystander. "I was a little irritated," said movement leader Michael Rossman, "because I couldn't see why, except out of the kindness of his heart, Ralph encouraged the kid so. I felt Ralph deserved followers who had a better moral dialect, more clarity in their words and deeds."

Yet the apprenticeship was not in vain. In February 1966 Jann persuaded the Berkeley campus paper, the *Daily Californian*, to let him write a music column much like Gleason's. The debut "Something's Happening" column, written under the pseudonym Mr. Jones—both title and pen name originating from Dylan's song "Ballad of a Thin Man"—set the tone early: controversial stands on local rock shows, a few jabs at hip entrepreneurs and at least one quotation per column of Ralph Gleason observations. Subsequent to the first entry, "Something's Happening" came adorned with a head shot of Jann with long hair, round sunglasses and a harmonica brace around his neck. This was Mr. Jones.

In these weekly columns, young Mr. Jones sang the psychedelic praises of acid ("One of these days Lyndon Johnson is going to try to find out why the 'leaders of tomorrow' are hung up on LSD instead of LBJ"); invented opportunities to quote Dylan and the Beatles; gushed over Mick Jagger's looks; bragged about reading all of F. Scott Fitzgerald's books; revealed where to buy good Popsicles and hobbit buttons; and reported on the doings of Ken Kesey, courtesy of information provided by Denise Kaufman.

In addition, Jann wrote about his own world. He couched these reports in nonsensical prose, cheaply imitative of Dylan's cryptic liner notes. But his friends understood the references. The boy named Jim who "had taken a trip on the Shotgun Express"—that was his society friend Jim Pike, a suicide victim. Those who knew about Jann's unconventional relationship with Sim understood the lines "Did Mrs. R. care that her son would soon be thin air? Did she wonder about his stare?" And people could not help but speculate that Blue Ned, the ephemeral protagonist in these quasi-fictional doodlings, was Jann's concept of his own alter ego and a reflection of his meek self-esteem: "Himself once wore a whispering mask named Blue Ned. The mask was immediately eyeless evidence of the many faces of Nowhere Man."

Readers not privy to the meaning behind the mush could still appreciate "Something's Happening" for its music news. Far more than Gleason or any other Bay Area reporter, Jann subjected the psychedelic scene to enthusiastic scrutiny. He reported on personnel changes at local radio stations; proclaimed the Jefferson Airplane "the best local rock and roll group" but predicted that the Grateful Dead "will make it the biggest"; derided cover bands awash in pseudopsychedelia; and suggested which concerts to go to and why. Mr. Jones was the Man on the Scene, the most reliable music information source around. He was doing his mentor Gleason proud.

———

By the summer of 1966, however, Jann Wenner began to weary of Berkeley. The manic pace of his first two years—Slate, the debutante scene, NBC, the Free Speech Movement, Denise and acid, Ralph and the Tribute to Dr. Strange—now assumed a drowsy limp. Life had become almost routine.

The downpour of adventure now only came in scattered showers. He'd spent a week in Mexico, where he held the hand of a female friend after she underwent a horribly primitive abortion. Denise had introduced Jann to Kesey's Pranksters, and Jann spent a day on the infamous bus with Beatnik legend Neal Cassady behind the wheel. That turned out to be a bummer, as Cassady persisted in giving Jann a hard time, calling him Jan and mocking his every comment.

He'd also formed a band, the Helping Hand-Outs, playing guitar and singing. "I'm as good as Eric Clapton," he was heard to brag. But the friends who heard his band jam could not agree, and the only clubs that would book the Helping Hand-Outs were the topless joints on Broadway.

So when Jann learned that his friend Richard Black and a Berkeley graduate student, Jonathon Cott, were going to spend the summer in England, he begged them to let him tag along. They were agreeable, but warned him that they were planning to attend film school there and how he spent his time was his responsibility. Jann assured them he would not be a bother.

Jann subsequently told his Berkeley friends he was going to spend the summer in a London film school, and thereupon packed his bags and dropped out of college.

The day Jann and his friends arrived, he made a beeline for the outrageous fashion kaleidoscope of Carnaby Street. There they strolled, the people he'd read about in magazines: mods, rockers, good-humored bobbies like windup dolls swinging their clubs, packs of pale and sharp-tongued cockney children. And then, the silver Rolls-Royce cruising past him, and a flash of blond hair in the window—it was Brian Jones, the Rolling Stones rhythm guitarist, it had to be. Already. God, this place could not be real.

He had arrived in the middle of a dream, and now sought to make his mark here. Hoping to drum up some freelancing work while in London, he'd persuaded Gleason to put him in touch with *Melody Maker*'s editor. He held out additional hopes of forming a band, a British version perhaps of his Helping Hand-Outs.

Yet above all, said Richard Black, "Jann was obsessed with meeting the Rolling Stones." By day he wore a porkpie hat and carried a camera and affected the pose of a photojournalist, hoping to confront the Stones. Jonathon Cott, a skilled interviewer, rehearsed Jann on appropriate questions to ask should opportunity strike.

In the meantime, Richard Black scored an invitation to an exclusive dinner party. Among the honored guests would be Paul McCartney. News of this threw Jann into a begging frenzy. Black was adamant, however; he simply would not smuggle Jann into the affair, no matter how high-ranking a Beatles fan Jann claimed to be. His refusal "put a sword through our friendship," according to Black.

Gradually the excitement abated, and Jann fell into despondency. *Melody Maker* would not publish Jann's analysis of the San Francisco scene. He hadn't gotten a band together. In the evenings Jann sat in his hotel room reading imported Marvel comic books, or cavorted with mods and Mersey-beaters and other Portobello Road scenemakers. He could not find the Rolling Stones.

Jann wrote Denise Kaufman, asking her to move to dreamy London and marry him. She accepted, then in a second letter hedged. Perhaps they could try living together in Berkeley first, she suggested.

Broke and depressed, Jann left London and flew to the U.S. East Coast. Old Chadwick and Berkeley friends now living in White Plains, New York and Cambridge took him in. He tried to write a novel. Several times he called Denise, demanding that she fly up to visit him. She refused. His pleas became more desperate. Jann Wenner was adrift, a Nowhere Man flailing about in the sixties.

Denise Kaufman visited Ralph Gleason and relayed Jann's despair. It disturbed Gleason to think of his gregarious companion in such emotional turmoil. He wrote Jann and delivered good news: a new weekly San Francisco paper was about to be published by some Gleason cronies. If Jann was interested, Ralph could put in a recommendation for a job.

Ralph Gleason's letter was heaven-sent. A month later, Jann Wenner was back in the saddle again.

———

The former Mr. Jones became the entertainment editor of *Sunday Ramparts*, an offspring of the borderline-subversive *Ramparts* magazine. His brashness around the office won him the same modicum of respect accorded the office mascot, a spider monkey named Henry Luce. For years Ralph Gleason, a member of the *Ramparts* editorial board, had quarreled frequently with staffers over the revolutionary importance of rock. Now here was this pudgy Gleason understudy similarly confusing politics and music. He also was suspected of smoking dope in the office—a definite no-no, as Big Brother likely had its eyes on *Ramparts* every hour of the day.

But, said art director Dugald Stermer, "he was willing to work hard and cover that beat which none of us cared about." *Somebody* had to listen to Joan Baez talk about her Gregorian chants, and reveal that "Grateful Dead" was a name from an Egyptian prayer that Jerry Garcia found while leafing through a dictionary, and remind readers that the Beatles were "*sine qua non* geniuses," and listen to white people sing the blues, and quote Ralph Gleason. Somebody had to be the low man on editor Warren Hinckle III's strangely ornamented totem pole.

From below, Jann gazed at Hinckle with a fan's fervor. He was in the presence of a legend. *Ramparts* may have begun in 1962 as a liberal Catholic news journal, but by the time Hinckle, a failed publicist and *San Francisco Chronicle* reporter, got his mitts on the magazine in 1964, it became a splashy outlet for Hinckle's muckraking whims. *Ramparts* attacked the Pope, the Warren Commission, Ronald Reagan and Barbie dolls with equal zeal, its prose hell-bent and its art slick and splashy. Advertisers shunned the magazine, but no matter: *Ramparts* made its money off subscribers, which grew in number from 20,000 in 1965 to 230,000 in 1967.

Ramparts also lived off the wealthy benefactors Hinckle seduced. It was almost eerie how the burly, eye-patched editor could round up moneyed liberals, woo them over lavish lunches—*never* on Hinckle's nickel—and walk away with a check good for the next extravaganza. The man blew money with style, they said: only first-class seats for Warren. Who could forget the time he confronted a domestic air strike in Chicago's airport, and instead of taking the train back to the West Coast, flew to London and from there returned to San Francisco?

Equally famous for his alcohol tolerance, Hinckle edited many an article from the barstool. For all his excesses, few questioned Warren Hinckle's editorial instincts. "I have no politics," he once told a reporter, and halfway meant it. The story was what counted. The story was the cause.

But Jann Wenner espoused the dubious cause of rock & roll. "Paul McCartney is the best white blues singer alive," he would tell fellow staffers, and they would have to admit it, the kid knew his turf. The question to them was: Did the turf mean anything? Jann smelled a rat when Hinckle, a born contrarian, assigned himself a *Ramparts* cover story on the psychedelic scene. "You've got only two writers on your staff who can do the story right," Jann said, meaning himself and Ralph Gleason. But Hinckle chose Hinckle, roasted the hippies, and Gleason resigned from the editorial board in protest.

Jann stayed on. Not just for the money did he endure his condescending treatment. The staff job meant instant access to musicians—indeed, Joan Baez came to *him*—and carte blanche at San Francisco rock clubs. When he wasn't sizing up the scene, Jann was sending out letters on impressive *Sunday Ramparts* stationery. His old friends noticed a change: Jann Wenner no longer flattered them or paid them any mind at all, except perhaps to tell them about the afternoon he spent with Timothy Leary or Eldridge Cleaver. Never again would he beg them for party invitations, shmooze at the Terrace or shiver beneath their imposing shadows. He had moved on.

And he had a new girlfriend. Her name was Jane Schindelheim, a dentist's daughter from New York. She and her sister Linda had been hired by *Ramparts* to open mail containing checks sent in for the Eldridge Cleaver Defense Fund. It was in the mail room that he first laid eyes on her.

She was beautiful, boyishly so, dark and fragile, with eyes that could appear both haughty and scared to death. Years later, Eve Babitz, in her short story "Bad Day at Palm Springs," was said to have modeled the story's elegant and mysterious character Nikki after her friend Jane: "Her skull, her cheekbones, the brutal cut to her mouth all were Egyptian and timeless. Her skin was the tone of the desert, no traces of rose, neutral." In this slag heap of mealymouthed politicos and mudslinging journalists, Jane Schindelheim radiated like delicate crystal.

Jann decided he would marry Jane Schindelheim. He told her this the first time they spoke at length.

———

Then the well ran dry.

Sunday Ramparts folded in May, and Warren Hinckle did not offer his entertainment editor a position on the regular *Ramparts* staff. Glumly, Jann considered his options. He was twenty-one but could not even consider returning to college, not after all he'd seen and done. Yet the local dailies already had columnists, and *Stereo Review* had turned down his two-thousand-word essay on the new Beatles album—too hyperbolic, they said, meaning they didn't see what was so special about the Beatles, meaning by extension that Jann Wenner and the straight press spoke separate languages, meaning his career path to big-time journalism terminated at a brick wall.

It did not seem fair. For four hysterical years he had scrambled, taking the scrambler's punishment, warding off the catcalls for *doing* while the world was *being*. Like his parents before him, Jann Wenner searched earnestly for his rightful chunk of the American Dream. He had played by all the tacit rules: learn what it takes, make the right friends, grab whatever opportunities come your way and wait for the rewards. The rewards never came. Only more wind in his face.

No satisfaction.

Jann Wenner took the civil service examination. Being a postman was a pretty hip job, and if nothing else, hip had high currency in the summer of 1967.

Chapter Three

"You're Probably Wondering What We Are Trying to Do"

The tribes gathered on January 14, 1967, a cloudless Pacific day. Across three-mile-long Golden Gate Park they walked, twenty thousand strong, negotiating their way to the park's Polo Fields—the spot decided upon after consultation with both an astrologer and a dope dealer wanted by the FBI. Some wore beads and loose Hindu robes, while others favored the ponchos and buckskin of the American Indian. Guitars dangled from their shoulders, bells from their necks, and in bundles of bandanna and brown paper they carried food to disperse among the winter flock.

It had all come to this, to the Human Be-In. At one o'clock, poet Gary Snyder stood atop the wooden stage and blew into a conch shell. Allen Ginsberg approached the microphone. "Ommmmmm," he said. Thousands and thousands chanted back: "Ommmmmmmmmm."

Jerry Rubin passed the hat for contributions to his latest legal defense. Timothy Leary, his hair and clothes

white and a flower behind each ear, intoned, "Turn on, tune in, drop out."
Music began. The city's greatest were all there: Grateful Dead, Jefferson
Airplane, Quicksilver Messenger Service, Big Brother and the Holding
Company, Country Joe McDonald and the Fish. The music was free. The
turkey sandwiches were free. Owsley's new White Lightning acid was free.
Every passing breeze washed the multicolored field with incense fumes and
marijuana smoke. Poets read, priests meditated and lost children were re-
turned to the stage by—could this really be happening?—Hell's Angels.
From the pale sky a lone man, a parachutist, fell to the earth. He got to
his feet and walked away and was never seen again.

By sundown the gathering picked up after itself and was gone.

The year 1967 was two weeks young. The wild, the gentle, the intellectual
and the curious—all stood on a city field, humming and listening, reconciled
and summoning. But summoning what? Who could account for this madness?
What in God's name did it foretell?

———

As Jann Wenner—now living in his mother's basement with his girlfriend
Jane—mulled over the relative merits of life as a mailman, San Francisco's
hippies celebrated the Summer of Love. Overnight, it seemed, the Haight-
Ashbury district had become a Calcutta of white middle-class children. The
Hashbury they called it now, a den of iniquity, a slum of cheerful migrants
looking only to hang out, drop acid and throw flowers at policemen.

Ever since the Human Be-In, city officials feared the worst. How many
would show up at the Haight's doorstep? A hundred thousand? Two hundred
thousand? There would be no food, no shelter. All these misbegotten runaways would deposit themselves in this shining city and sprawl across its
streets like an open sore.

Many blamed the Beatles. Last year's blasphemers ("We are more
popular than Jesus now," John Lennon had casually told a British journalist
in 1966) were this year's demon gurus. Gone were the teenybopper bangs;
now their heads sprouted hair in all directions. They dropped acid and said
they were the better for it. Paul McCartney visited the Haight in April and
gave the hippie experiment his stirring endorsement. Enormous supplies of
Owsley's liquid LSD were packed into airtight camera lenses and shipped
to the Beatles in London.

For some time now, Beatles songs like "Dr. Robert," "Norwegian
Wood" and "Yellow Submarine" suggested the group's fascination with

drugs. By June of 1967, all doubts vanished with the release of *Sgt. Pepper's Lonely Hearts Club Band*. The lyrical allusions ("Lucy in the Sky with Diamonds," "I get high with a little help from my friends") seemed more explicit than ever, but the music itself was the clincher. Backward tape loops, a reeling symphony and plainly amused vocals led even the most casual listener to conclude that the Beatles, the former cuddly crooners, were now permanent passengers on the Owsley Express.

But the *Sgt. Pepper* song that most eloquently referenced the San Francisco phenomenon was "She's Leaving Home." A sympathetic portrayal of a runaway, the song celebrated the girl's awaiting adventure while sternly reminding her parents, "Fun is the one thing that money can't buy."

And so they flocked to the Hashbury, Fun City. By early summer the sidewalks teemed with drug dealers, panhandlers and "self-expression" in forms Ralph Gleason could not have envisioned. The Diggers, the Haight's "worker-priests," administered free bean soup and set up racks of free secondhand clothes. The Hip Job Co-op put broke hippies to work hauling garbage or sitting babies. Mostly the new tenants avoided work, rent and similar hassles.

Outside the world hassled with itself. In Vietnam, the war escalated. In Detroit, Milwaukee and Washington, D.C., the streets raged with riots. And in Sacramento, a new California governor named Reagan pledged to break the back of the Berkeley rabble. Those who decried the Hashbury bazaar echoed the sentiments of San Francisco police chief Tom Cahill: "Hippies are not an asset to the community. These people do not have the courage to face the reality of life. They are trying to escape."

But was it as simple as that? As one hippie told a reporter, "When this many people decide a society is worthless, it's something to think about." Besides, this ragtag subculture had a vitality no one counted on. They shared food, floor space, clothes . . . everything they owned. The gathering was a peaceful one, glaringly different from the drunken brawls found every summer on the Fort Lauderdale beaches. By midsummer a second wave of visitors arrived at Hashbury: journalists and social scientists, and then, of course, politicians like Illinois senator Charles Percy and presidential candidate George Romney—early suitors to the Youth Vote.

Capitalism came, too. Weekend hippies and rubber-jawed tourists peopled Haight Street and wove through the legions of outstretched hands. The Gray Line Bus Tours offered a new "Hippie Hop," providing its customers with a "hippie glossary" and canned speeches:

We are now entering the largest hippie colony in the world and the very heart and fountainhead of the Hippie subculture. We are now passing through the "Beaded Curtain" and will journey down Haight Street, the very nerve center of a city within a city. . . . Marijuana, of course, is a household staple here, enjoyed by the natives to stimulate their senses. . . . Among the favorite pastimes of the hippies, besides taking drugs, are parading and demonstrating; seminars and group discussions about what's wrong with the status quo; malingering; plus the ever present preoccupation with the soul, reality, and self-expression such as strumming guitars, piping flutes and banging on bongos.

Author Richard Brautigan and others trotted alongside the buses, holding up mirrors to the tourists' faces and shouting, "Know thyself!"

The "Hippie Hop" was eventually suspended because of traffic snarls, but by then commercialism was an inescapable fact of Hashbury life. The Psychedelic Shop and other "head boutiques" upped the price of incense and sold "mod attire" no true hippie could afford. The Blushing Peony minted scores of buttons, the Drogstore charged fifty cents an hour for the privilege of sitting by the window and watching the parade, and Haight cooks wore beads and flipped Loveburgers.

The Establishment was not the only group making money in Hashbury, however. The counterculture, it appeared, could earn a living. Ralph Gleason's tireless advocacy of the scene in his five-times-weekly *Chronicle* column was paying dividends. The big San Francisco bands were landing fat recording contracts with major labels. The Jefferson Airplane's "Somebody to Love" was the number three song in the entire country. Packed houses and eventual prosperity came to the city's big rock ballrooms, the Avalon and the Fillmore. Local poster artists were now designing album covers; new clubs recruited light-show masters. Doing what they did best, some hippies were getting rich.

———

Others were getting stoned and sorting mail, but Jann Wenner was not fated to join their ranks. He loved both money and music, and as a local columnist had played some role in introducing the two. He belonged smack-dab in the middle. Often he took Jane to the ballrooms, leaving her to fidget by the bar while he circulated, glad-handing the musicians and concert promoters, staying in touch.

One day at the Gleason household, Jann pitched to Ralph the idea of co-authoring a rock & roll encyclopedia. Ralph liked the idea: Jann had the time, and Gleason had the file cabinets bulging with material. Soon Jann was digging away.

Before long, however, he was skulking about the Avalon Ballroom, visibly depressed. The encyclopedia project, he told Avalon manager Chet Helms, wasn't working out. Helms liked Jann, had always let him into shows free, and now sought to console the frustrated journalist.

"Well, look," said Helms. "I've got a project you might be interested in. A few of us are working on starting up this magazine."

Helms and his partners had in mind a counterculture-lifestyle magazine to be marketed in record stores. He'd already picked out a name: *Straight Arrow* magazine. Some twenty-six other counterculture rags (the best being the psychedelic *Oracle* and *Mojo-Navigator R&R News*, a purely music magazine) already littered the Haight, but *Straight Arrow* would have a bolder look and an editorial concept leaning toward the tribal aspect of hippie culture.

With Jann sitting in, the *Straight Arrow* organizers held several meetings to discuss strategy. A mailing list of potential readers was located at KFRC-AM, but beyond this progress was slow—or at least too slow for Jann Wenner, who stopped attending the meetings after a month or so. Chet Helms and the others thought nothing of it at the time.

———

A magazine of his own.

The idea seemed plausible enough. Ordinary hippies were publishing; he could blow their vain little scratch pads clear out of the water, and none would mourn their passing. The *Straight Arrow* self-appointed visionaries would fail as well. They had no sense of what people outside of their precious communes were interested in. Psychedelics were all well and good, but the shuffling ways of the counterculture tried Jann's patience.

Besides, Helms and his gang were interested in promoting "the tribal lifestyle." They were missing the point. The point was the music. That was the energy source, the Love Generation's big weapon. "Believe in the magic," sang John Sebastian of the Lovin' Spoonful, "it will set you free." He wasn't talking about the magic of tribal lifestyles.

Fuck the tribes, Jann thought. Kids communicated through music. As a bored Berkeley English major with a dimming interest in campus politics, Jann Wenner sat in a movie theater and in an ecstatic trance experienced the Beatles' *A Hard Day's Night.* No real plot, no real script, no real stance—*but it spoke to him.* Into his, and a generation's, bewildered face the Beatles shouted, "Life! Fun!" And now he believed, and would argue this point with great conviction, that if you spent an evening at the Avalon, you would walk away with more information about American youth, what they were thinking about and what really moved them, than could be gleaned from a year's worth of *Time* issues, a year's worth of political rallies and, for that matter, a year's worth of tribal life.

Paul Williams understood this. At the age of seventeen, the stringy-haired Swarthmore College freshman became terribly excited after reading an article in a British music magazine about the Rolling Stones' early days playing in London's Crawdaddy Club. A boy adrift became a fan anchored. Williams dropped out, found the nearest mimeograph machine and printed out issue number one of *Crawdaddy!* in February of 1966.

Crawdaddy!, billing itself as "a magazine of rock and roll criticism," had no precedent. Williams and his fellow writers weren't interested in competing against the industry trade papers or the teenybopper magazines. They wanted to put out a magazine that took rock seriously as a cultural phenomenon. In no time at all, *Crawdaddy!* became the talk of the music world.

Williams had visited *Sunday Ramparts*, and Jann, a *Crawdaddy!* reader, could not help but notice that Williams was even younger than he was. The two got along well; still, *Crawdaddy!* was not Jann's idea of entertaining journalism. Its writers fancied themselves essayists, sociologists and philosophers; they seemed unable to avoid using the word "I." Snobby all the way down to its ultra-spare, "This is for reading, not for looking at" graphics, *Crawdaddy!* was a magazine to be read but not emulated.

In castigating the *Crawdaddy!* approach, *Sunday Ramparts* writer Jann Wenner declared, "Don't believe anything you read about rock and roll, only what you see coming out of amplifiers." Even then, however, the young journalist did not really believe rock journalism had to be so forbidding. Now rustling in Jann's memory was the trip to England. Though distinctly British and at times terrifically boring, the music tabloid *Melody Maker* had made quite an impression on him. Here was a weekly that stayed on top of the scene—indeed, was supportive of and supported by (in the form of advertisements) the scene. San Francisco's *Mojo-Navigator* valiantly attempted this, offering interviews and rock gossip as well as record reviews; but the exciting little tabloid wasn't run as a business, and in August it folded.

The straight press was covering the Hashbury scene, and as only the straight press could. In their eyes the hippies were a riot waiting to be ignited; in their ears each San Francisco band sounded like the other. Seldom did they miss the chance to alarm readers with tales of acid-induced freak-outs and chromosome damage. The more pandering efforts, like *Esquire*'s "magazine for teen men only," *GQ Scene*, tried to reach the Love Generation with articles like "Staying Loose in a Necktie," "Looking Good While Holding Hands" and "Jimi Hendrix: Obscene and Vulgar? Or a Good Musician?"

These magazines lacked vision. More important, they lacked a visionary. Warren Hinckle may have offended Gleason and the hippies, but Jann could not help but be in awe of him. *Ramparts* was whatever the flashy, fearless editor said it was; *Ramparts* was, in the end, Warren Hinckle.

All the great publications were that way. Though it was co-founded by Briton Hadden, *Time* magazine's demeanor was vintage Harry Luce: cold, imposing and unabashedly conservative. Only a few months back Luce had died, a complicated genius, totally absorbed in his work, alone and largely unloved, but deeply respected. A brilliant mystery, like his journalistic counterpoint William Randolph Hearst, the sensationalist. These men threw ideas into the wind, threw money after the ideas and perhaps flung their souls in the bargain. But these men were *huge*—perfect fits in a huge and lonely mold.

From this mold of editor/publishers with household names came a new entry. If Jann Wenner needed a role model, the obvious choice was Hugh Marston Hefner, editor and publisher of the astoundingly successful *Playboy* magazine. Like Jann, Hefner arrived from the outside, a Chicago introvert with a nocturnal face, a born underdog. Spurned first by his peers, then by the New York publishing establishment, he set out in 1953 to become a legend. All it took was a $200 bank loan (using his 1950 Studebaker as collateral), with which he purchased the famous Marilyn Monroe nude photo from a calendar company; then another $10,000 from friends and hocked furniture. Issue No. 1 hit the stands on December of 1953 and made $26,000 without a single ad.

Hugh Hefner never looked back after that. In the Eisenhower fifties and thereafter, sex sold. Thus licensed, the pipe-sucking editor permitted himself a few indulgences. He penned, ad infinitum, a "*Playboy* Philosophy" which extolled the virtues of the swinging good life. *Playboy* featured fascinating interviews, occasionally outstanding fiction and the work of fine cartoonists. He entertained the rich and famous and dispatched his attorneys to defend noble causes. But nude women buttered Hefner's bread, and he did not forget this.

By 1967 the *Playboy* empire was worth over $70 million.

What was the magic in this? Only the belief, and the true believer.

Hefner, who put his first issue together in his kitchen, had even fewer connections than Jann. He was a square, a beatnik detractor who would promulgate "the UpBeat Generation." As *Playboy* editor and publisher, his hours were long but his contributions limited in magnitude. Even the name "Playboy" and the famous bunny logo were the ideas of art director Arthur Paul. Paul and several others could lay claim to the magazine's creative power. Yet only Hugh Hefner could claim that *he* was *Playboy*.

And now that call of ownership seduced Jann Wenner, twenty-one and restless in the Summer of Love. It was the call of his own identity. He, too, would *be* a magazine.

———

"Groovy, let's do it," exclaimed Ralph Gleason. Having departed the *Ramparts* editorial board, he now had a little time on his hands, and this idea of Wenner's seemed far more workable than the encyclopedia scheme. The timing for him, and for the scene, was perfect.

Jann's boisterous mannerisms notwithstanding, Ralph saw a lot of himself in the kid. As a college student in the 1930s, Gleason spent his evenings in the jazz clubs and his class hours catching up on his sleep or writing music reviews for the *Columbia Spectator*. Tossed out of Columbia for a college prank, Ralph immediately founded *Jazz Information*, an energetic four-page mimeo sheet. Seeing Jann Wenner goggle-eyed at the Fillmore, Ralph couldn't help but think of those Manhattan mornings when he'd stroll across 125th Street to Morningside and stare up at those enchanting marquees: Cab Calloway, Duke Ellington—legends, and *they were here* . . .

You had to say this about Jann Wenner as well: the kid was tougher than he looked. Ralph appreciated this. When the Gleasons moved to San Francisco in the late forties, Ralph took a job with an insurance company. He didn't like it, but Jean was pregnant and they needed money. Opportunity would come; in the meantime, stay alive and write your *Down Beat* columns after hours.

As long as Ralph had known him, Jann had been down on his luck. Magazines wouldn't publish his articles, girlfriends wouldn't marry him, Warren Hinckle treated him like a fat houseboy and his parents didn't seem to care what happened to him. Others might've crawled in a hole. Not this kid. He kept writing, kept his name circulating in the ballrooms and in the meantime did whatever it took to stay alive: living with his mother, pulling weeds in a concrete piling yard, doing mule work for NBC, taking the civil service exam, *whatever*. Jann Wenner was just a child. Maybe he didn't know much about editing magazines. But he damn sure knew how to survive, and that was lesson number one in the publishing business.

Ralph Gleason would take care of the rest. He'd worked with a number of fledgling publications, saw them come and go and had a sense of the pitfalls. Besides, if you wanted to start a music magazine in San Francisco, you could do worse than to have the famed *Chronicle* columnist as a consulting editor. Record companies would buy ads. Musicians would grant interviews. Radio stations would plug the magazine. Gleason would mean instant cachet for Jann's venture.

He also had an agenda of his own. Such a magazine could be his direct pipeline into the Love Generation—a generation prone, he would say, "to suffer the delusion that everything they are discovering is brand new." To Jann Wenner's endeavor he could bring a historical wealth, a perspective. In fact, Gleason decided he'd write a regular column for the magazine. He'd call it "Perspectives."

So yes, by all means. But there was another small matter, said Gleason. What would the magazine be called?

Jann Wenner was ready for that one. "*The Electric Newspaper*," he said. A psychedelic name for psychedelic times.

Gleason nixed it. He suggested the title of a Muddy Waters song, taken from an old proverb, and in turn borrowed for the name of a famous song and the name of a famous band.

Rolling Stone.

And the name of their publishing company? Jann had an answer for that one, too. It was a name he had heard somewhere before. "Straight Arrow," he said.

———

Joan Roos was surprised to see Jann Wenner show up on her doorstep again after all this time. But now the subject wasn't Slate.

It was money. Jann had a new project going, a magazine called *Rolling Stone*. He needed investors.

Phil Roos had just inherited a significant sum, and for tax purposes had given some of it to Joan. She passed $500 on to Jann, viewing it as a small but worthy cause—"like giving a woman money for an abortion," she said.

In exchange, Joan Roos said she'd like Jann to teach her how to dance to this new music he would be writing about. Jann never fulfilled the agreement, but shortly after receiving the check he returned with a piece of paper in his hand. It was a stock certificate, good for five hundred shares in Straight Arrow Publishers, Inc.

Joan Roos thought this was hilarious.

While the Diggers were serving up free bean soup and bread in Golden Gate Park, Jann Wenner was hustling money. Not everyone he approached was as amenable as Joan Roos. His society friend Richard Black turned him down cold. "The idea was great," said Black. "But I had no faith in Jann's ability to pull it off."

Another acquaintance didn't think much of the magazine's prospects. Instead, he invested his money in waterproof cement and lost a small fortune—a story Jann would delight in telling several years later.

Gleason agreed to pay for the dummy issue, then throw in an additional $1,500 for issue No. 1. Sim Wenner was good for $2,000, and Ed Wenner's wife, Dorothy, invested another $500. Jann himself sold $1,000 worth of Wenner's Baby Formulas, Inc., stock, a present from Ed Wenner for Jann's twenty-first birthday.

He then approached the Schindelheims. Jane's sister Linda contributed $1,000. Their parents matched that amount. That gave the *Rolling Stone* project $7,500 worth of venture capital—well shy of their $10,000 target, the amount Hugh Hefner had gathered to finance *Playboy*. Ralph Gleason tried a final potential investor, *San Francisco Examiner* music columnist Phil Elwood.

Sorry, Elwood said. It sounded interesting, but he was paying alimony and his new wife was pregnant.

It looked like $7,500 would have to do.

———

On June 18, at the Monterey Pop Festival, Jann and Ralph ran into Michael and Susan Lydon in the press section. Susan, a popular-arts journalist, had done some writing for Jann at *Sunday Ramparts*. Michael, a young *Newsweek* correspondent, had reported on the Human Be-In and various other hippie happenings. For a member of the straight press, his reportage was held in exceptionally high regard by the counterculture.

Somewhere in the conversation, Jann mentioned his new magazine. The Lydons were polite but inattentive. Tonight would be remembered for Jimi Hendrix's first American appearance, for the record-contract signings that followed the performances by Janis Joplin's Big Brother and the Holding

Company, the Grateful Dead, Quicksilver Messenger Service and the Steve Miller Band. Magazines came and went every day.

Two months later, Michael Lydon found himself sitting with Jann Wenner at Enrico's, a notorious writers' haunt just down the street from the *Ramparts* office in North Beach. Lydon's long-awaited story on the underground press had recently appeared in *Esquire*, and Jann was singing its praises.

In fact, Jann had made a decision. "I want you to be my managing editor," he told Lydon. "I'll pay you two hundred a week."

Lydon, Jann explained, would be perfect for *Rolling Stone*: young and hip, but a professional, embracing professional standards. The reporter was taken aback. Jann Wenner, virtually a stranger, was asking him to leave *Newsweek* for a job that paid less money and offered a substantial risk of failure.

But the virtual stranger seemed so sure of himself, so full of energy and absolutely certain of his and the magazine's destiny. Here he had Lydon at a disadvantage. It was as if Jann, in reading Lydon's articles, sensed where the writer's heart lay. Michael Lydon had been near the action all his life. In 1964 he went to Mississippi and took notes while watching Mario Savio teach black kids Spanish. A year later *Newsweek* sent him to London, where he interviewed Lennon and McCartney. The magazine transferred him to San Francisco at the beginning of 1967, and once again Lydon found himself in the center of the storm.

But always with pad in hand, tie around neck, while his peers banged on guitars or got dragged off to jail. It was starting to get to him, this detachment. "I was definitely feeling the call," Lydon said, "to join my contemporaries rather than working for the old system."

It was as if Jann Wenner was telling Michael Lydon about himself: "You *want* to drop out. You *want* to make less money. What I'm offering is *exactly* what you want."

"Okay," said Lydon. "Sure." But he refused to quit *Newsweek*. Somehow he would find time to handle both jobs.

At about the same time Jann made contact with Baron Wolman, a local photographer. The two met in March at a Mills College rock symposium featuring Gleason and other local music wags. Wolman was the event's official photographer, and Jann was writing it up for *Sunday Ramparts*.

Jann's obvious first choice as *Rolling Stone* chief photographer might have been Jim Marshall. Marshall had been on the scene for years; he was perhaps the best photographer of the counterculture, and certainly the most well known. But Marshall, a buddy of the Hell's Angels, had a nasty temper, and he liked to carry guns. He would also want lots of cash, and Jann did not have lots of cash.

Baron Wolman, though not as ubiquitous, was a meticulous, versatile photographer. Unlike the combative Marshall, Wolman was elfish and laid back, a professional voyeur who took great pride in his work. And Wolman, an astute businessman, was willing to work off-salary in exchange for stock. This was good, very good. He and Jann spoke the same language.

And incidentally, could Wolman spare a few hundred investment dollars?

Sorry, said Wolman.

Jann told his new chief photographer he wanted *Rolling Stone* to read professionally, like the trade papers *Billboard* and *Cashbox*, but to look elegant like *Sunday Ramparts*, with its Times Roman type, its classic headline faces and its Oxford rule borders. Indeed, Jann had already made a few inquiries at the *Ramparts* office. Dugald Stermer, the magazine's art director, was far too busy to help out with *Rolling Stone*. Production director John Williams, on the other hand, had been carrying out Stermer's instructions for years and needed a creative outlet of his own. *Rolling Stone* might be fun—and besides, he said, "this crazy kid was just so enthusiastic, so persuasive, he had this thing he really believed in. We all wanted to help him out." Williams volunteered to lay out *Rolling Stone* in his spare time.

Jann was thrilled. He then addressed Dugald Stermer. "By the way," he began. Mustering his full reservoir of audacity: "Can I use your design of *Sunday Ramparts* for my magazine?"

Stermer looked hard at the kid, then almost laughed. What did it matter? *Rolling Stone* stood no chance anyway. Besides, Stermer had borrowed much of the *Sunday Ramparts* design concept from *The Times* of London and the *New York Herald Tribune* Sunday magazine. Why not show a little goodwill?

"I don't care, go ahead," he said.

Jann still stood there. "And would you happen to have the *Sunday Ramparts* pasteup flats?"

The young publisher-to-be had acquired an art director, a design concept and free boards on which to compose his premiere issue. Few bandits made off this well.

Sunday Ramparts had been printed at Garrett Press, a small outfit located on Brannan Street in the San Francisco warehouse district. As Ralph Gleason pointed out to Jann, it made sense for *Rolling Stone*—identical in size and typeface to *Sunday Ramparts*—to use Garrett's compatible services. Besides, said Gleason, Garrett probably had untold reams of *Sunday Ramparts*-size paper sitting in a corner somewhere, waiting to be used. Maybe Jann could negotiate a good deal.

One more thing, said Gleason. "It's not uncommon for printers to donate a little of their warehouse space in exchange for the use of their services. If you approach it right," he told his protégé, "you might get office space in the bargain."

Jann met with Alan Seibert, the middle-aged head of Garrett Press. Armed with a by now well-rehearsed speech—"not a hippie rag," "fully capitalized," "Ralph Gleason," "*Newsweek*," "*Sunday Ramparts*-style graphics"— the young entrepreneur unleashed his roly-poly, blue-eyed charm. As it turned out, Seibert was a complete softie. He didn't think too much of the magazine's concept, but he liked the kid. With little deliberation, Seibert said that Garrett would be happy to do business with Jann. And as for workspace . . . well, the loft upstairs was really only being used for paper storage . . .

Alan Seibert gave Jann Wenner the entire loft, free of charge. A gold mine. Ralph would be tickled silly.

———

At the tail end of summer, *Rolling Stone* situated itself at 746 Brannan, an office that faced a tallow plant and the Acme Screw Works in the heart of the city's ill-reputed south-of-Market district. The old hands at Garrett, tough union men, eyed this shaggy aggregation of humanity with great amusement. Down the stairs came the old paper rolls and discarded type fonts; up the stairs trudged the longhairs, grunting under the weight of typewriters and mismatched furniture donated by the Gleasons and the Schindelheims.

"Look at 'em go," the Garrett employees said to each other, cackling. "Think they're gonna get rich and take over the world."

The loft was huge, with high ceilings supported by wooden stanchions, and a multitude of oversized windows. Against a wall on one end of the loft clanked the old Linotype machines, while on the other end the desk of Jann Wenner sat in the loft's single cubbyhole. As the printers downstairs heated and reheated the lead used for type, the burning odors wafted and filled the loft with an industrial reek.

Most of all, the lead furnaces produced heat. That late summer a hodgepodge of unpaid volunteers—radio station groupies, *Ramparts* handymen and the Schindelheim sisters—labored away at issue No. 1, sweating like miners. Susan Lydon sat behind one of the battered desks in a slip and underwear. Nearly four months pregnant, she feared the heat would cause a miscarriage.

After recruiting Michael Lydon, Jann had asked Susan, "What do you do around the house all day?" He thought she should chip in by typing address labels for the sample issue. It seemed like woman's work. Susan Lydon suggested that Jann go fuck himself. She was a writer; she would produce and edit copy. The task of label typing fell to her husband and Jann. She did, however, answer the phone, under Jann's orders, though in fact the telephone sat much closer to his desk than to hers.

"Susan," he said that first time, yelling over the hammering of the typesetting machine. "Get the phone."

"But, Jann," she protested. "You're right next to the phone. *You* get it."

The young editor/publisher demurred. "The phone should always be answered by a feminine voice," he said.

So Susan Lydon became receptionist as well. Virtually naked, high on speed, pregnant and sweating, she answered the phone, wrote a movie review and edited a long column analyzing the guitar styles of Jimi Hendrix and Cream's Eric Clapton. The writer, a Boston musician and student named Jon Landau, was a *Crawdaddy!* staffer. But Jann had lured him to the pages of *Rolling Stone* with a rather novel offer: he would pay Landau for his article, a benefit alien to the *Crawdaddy!* experience.

By day Michael Lydon did his work at *Newsweek*, using the bureau phones to make long-distance calls on Jann's behalf. Dispatched by *Newsweek* to Reno for a story, he caught Wild Bill Haley at the Cellar and returned to San Francisco with a Haley interview for *Rolling Stone*. At lunchtime and in the evenings, Lydon hunkered down at 746 Brannan, where he fine-tuned the premiere issue's lead article. The Monterey Pop Festival, he charged in this piece, was billed as a charity event but had instead lined the pockets of festival producer Lou Adler and his friends. Lydon had failed to get an interview with Adler, but he was otherwise proud of the piece. It was tough investigative journalism, a successful pursuit of a money trail—straight press reporting, but for the benefit of his peers.

Meanwhile, Jann Wenner bolted up and down the hillsides of San Francisco in the new Porsche his mother had helped him buy, a man with a million missions. Only recently he'd been contacted by Henry Rogers, the Beverly Hills publicist that represented the Doors, the Stones and others. Rogers's firm was looking for a young person well connected to the music scene, someone who could talk to musicians in their own language. Was Jann interested? Well, yes and no, he had this magazine and all. Jann left the door open. On October 3 the door was slammed shut: Rogers's people had hired a New Yorker. So that was that. *Rolling Stone* or bust. Call it the whisper of destiny. Jann Wenner was not fated to promote something that was not his. Onward.

For the sample issue—which would be sent to potential subscribers, advertisers and friends in high places—Jann needed a mailing list. He knew just where to go, and went there, to KFRC-AM. Saying he was with *Straight Arrow*, Jann Wenner asked for the mailing list that had been set aside for Chet Helms's magazine. It was the radio station's only copy; without it, *Straight Arrow* magazine would be doomed.

These matters took too much time to think through. Jann Wenner had no time, absolutely none. He snatched up the list, sold KFRC a full-page ad and resumed his breathless rounds. Days later, Chet Helms discovered the fate of *Straight Arrow*'s mailing list. Helms was stupefied. Things like this just didn't happen in the sixties. The magazine folded. (Jann today claims that *Straight Arrow* magazine folded before any of this happened.)

Jann Wenner sold more ads in the city, zigzagging through the Summer of Love, his sales pitch now as spare and efficient as a toothpick. Not wanting to be bested by KFRC, KMPX bought a full page. One poster shop bought a half; another, a full. *Great, great. Onward.* The Fillmore bought a quarter page—*thanks so much, cheap bastards, they were making a mint.* Two more quarter pages from a couple of Market Street businesses, small change in Berkeley and Mill Valley and Sausalito, an AM station in Los Angeles, *tomorrow the world!* And then Ralph's buddies at the record companies started sniffing around. A half from Chess Records. A full from Atlantic. Then, *banzai!*—a two-pager from Buddah Records, advertising the new Captain Beefheart record! *Yow! Give 'em center spread! Ring it up, a total of a thousand bucks' worth of advertising. Too groovy. But no time to gloat. Onward.*

For the *Rolling Stone* logo, Jann called the well-known psychedelic poster artist Rick Griffin. Griffin agreed, and hastily produced a draft of the words "Rolling Stone" in bold, almost regal script. The artist wasn't satisfied and wanted to refine the logo, but Jann did not give him that chance. Deadlines, deadlines. Onward.

More feature material was needed. During one of Jann's daily trips across the Bay Bridge to Berkeley, Ralph Gleason suggested contacting *Melody Maker* with an offer to trade copy. Thus came an up-to-date column on the London scene by the editor's son, Nick Jones, whom Jann promptly dubbed *Rolling Stone*'s "London correspondent." Further transatlantic inquiries yielded photos of the Beatles' wives in exotic Eastern garb and of

John Lennon in his first acting role. The movie, *How I Won the War*, was premiering at the San Francisco Film Festival at this very moment. Jann saw it, wrote it up, declared mysteriously in his review, "It's all pointless because that's the point of the film," and resumed his double-time pace—"like a monkey climbing a pole," an observer would later say.

The issue was filling out. Too much so, in fact. Ralph had convinced a Los Angeles writer named John Carpenter to hand over an exclusive interview with Donovan—a great acquisition, but far too long. They would have to two-part the interview. Jann clipped it thus:

Q. I understand you go to Amsterdam quite often.
A. Yeah, I drop over there, you know, to earn a few bob and
    things. That's money and ah, but . . .
    INCREDIBLE, BUT THERE'S EVEN MORE. In the
    next issue the Donovan interview continues. He talks about
    Gypsy Dave, the Maharishi, the Bob Dylan film, a fairy tale
    film he is making himself and ah, but . . .

Perfect. Tantalizing . . . like the John Lennon photo on the cover, like Baron Wolman's exclusive photos of the Grateful Dead just after they were busted, like the dozens of gossipy "Flashes" interspersed throughout the twenty-four pages, this issue was made to *move*. Lydon's Monterey Pop Festival story and Ralph Gleason's attack on TV racism would supply the controversy, while Jann's eight record reviews would add the necessary critical edge. ("Strange but quite nice," he wrote of one record. Another, he judged, was "quite well done.") In a half-page subscription ad for *Rolling Stone*, Jann's headline blared: "Can you dig it?" The question was rhetorical. *Of course* they could dig it . . . and would.

Eagerly Jann Wenner peered over the shoulder of John Williams at the *Ramparts* offices. It was the evening of October 17, fast becoming the morning of the eighteenth, and the premiere issue of *Rolling Stone* was being put to bed. While the editor/publisher fidgeted, the quiet art director meticulously pasted the typeset galleys and the photographic Veloxes onto the old *Sunday Ramparts* flats.

Jann Wenner breathed down the neck of John Williams, and the air from his anxious lips was altogether different from the incense-laden breeze that once blew through the streets of Haight-Ashbury. The Summer of Love was now over, both seasonally and by official proclamation. Eleven days prior, a casket was marched through Golden Gate Park and set aflame. "The Death of the Hippie, devoted son of mass media," they proclaimed the rite, and so torched the coffin—filled with beads and marijuana and the like—to purge the Hashbury of commercialism.

The smoke from the pyre still hung, it seemed, like new anxiety and resolution, like Jann Wenner's breath—like his words which on October 18, 1967, at about 5:30 P.M., fell down upon paper as the smell of burning lead hung over 746 Brannan:

> You're probably wondering what we are trying to do. It's hard to say: sort of a magazine and sort of a newspaper. The name of it is *Rolling Stone.* . . .
>
> *Rolling Stone* is not just about music, but also about the things and attitudes that the music embraces. . . . To describe it any further would be difficult without sounding like bullshit, and bullshit is like gathering moss.
>
> —*Jann Wenner*

That evening, a Garrett Press mail-room worker named Dan Parker came home to his wife in the Oakland suburb of Concord. He bent down to kiss her. She recoiled. The reek of lead fumes she was used to by now, but what she smelled this time was alcohol.

"Champagne," he muttered by way of apology, and fell into his chair. He said nothing more for a piece of time, his face a silent mask of bewilderment. Then he spoke, trying to assign words to what he had just seen:

These crazy hippies, a bunch of dumb kids, a couple of them attractive females though he'd heard one of them say "fuck". . . . Anyway, these kids were all standing around the presses downstairs, watching the machine spit out this . . . this awful, terrible, completely ridiculous *magazine*, he supposed you could call it. And one of them, the leader, a fat little kid, was getting all emotional, saying, "It'll never get better than this. . . ."

And then the next thing he knew, they were drinking *champagne*. Passing around the bottles, toasting to beat the band. And, well, sure, he had a couple of glasses. The kids were generous enough. But *shit* . . .

Dan Parker, future traffic manager of *Rolling Stone* magazine, ten years away from receiving a gold Rolex retirement watch from the choked-up fat little kid, shook his stupefied head. "It'll never make it," he said to his wife. "It doesn't stand a chance in the world."

Chapter Four

ROLLING THE STONE UPHILL

B astards!"

"Janno, calm down," Ralph Gleason said, exchanging glances with Michael Lydon while the young editor paced and swore. "You're not supposed to take it personally. They don't hate you. They're not laughing at you. This is just business."

Of the 40,000 copies printed of issue No. 1, some 34,000 had been returned—unsold. Hoping to save money, Jann and Ralph figured they could distribute *Rolling Stone* by themselves, picking and choosing retail outlets as best as they could. It now appeared that if they relied on their own ingenuity, *Rolling Stone* would go belly-up by the new year.

Thus began the roller-coaster ride, on a formidable incline. Much had to be done before Jann Wenner would convince anyone that he was the Henry Luce of the counterculture. Indeed, until he mastered the procedural esoterica of the publishing industry, Jann Wenner was just another Berkeley dropout with a magazine no one read.

The premiere issue of *Rolling Stone* had been on the newsstands only a few days when a letter arrived at 746 Brannan. The letter was from the American law firm representing the Rolling Stones, and its tone was solemn. "Use of the name Rolling Stone in connection with a newspaper concerned solely with activities in the pop music field," it stated, "is clearly an attempt on your part to confuse the public as to who is responsible or who is involved in same." It was a charge easily refuted (in fact, the legal threat was dropped shortly after the letter was sent), but an unsettling matter all the same. Jann had been heard to say that he'd founded *Rolling Stone* "so that I can meet John Lennon." He hadn't figured on pissing off Mick Jagger in the process.

Jann had promised to pay art director John Williams $200 per issue, but the coffers were empty. In true counterculture spirit, Michael Lydon had generously refused his $200-a-week salary; but that was before the assistant editor discovered the name of Herb Williamson, Jann's former editor at *Sunday Ramparts*, on the first issue's masthead, with the accompanying title "Managing Editor." As far as Lydon could tell, Williamson hadn't done anything to earn the superior designation. He felt double-crossed.

Susan Lydon wrangled with Jann as well. Her movie column for the second issue employed a style that did not sit well with Jann. In fact, he tore up the article, threw the pieces to the floor and jumped up and down on them.

"Never use first person!" he yelled. "That's not reporting!"

The piece was rewritten, and printed in the second issue without Susan Lydon's byline. At least Jann did not have to rely on her feminine telephone voice, as a new volunteer, a groupie named Henri, was now playing receptionist. One fortunate result of the first issue was that fresh bodies had arrived to help out. A KMPX disc jockey agreed to assist Jann in selling ads; a hippie with a van became "circulation manager." Both he and the deejay, and Henri, and seemingly every other frequenter of 746 Brannan who could follow a noun with a verb wrote articles as well.

Jann aspired to publish a magazine that would feature the clean, tasteful prose of *The New Yorker*. *Rolling Stone* was not quite there yet. The second issue's cover story on Ike and Tina Turner began with the very un-*New Yorker*-like sentence "Tina Turner is an incredible chick." The second installment of the Donovan interview concluded with the interviewer babbling to Donovan, "Thank you for spreading a little more magic." "London correspondent" Nick Jones had taken to ending his British column with a one-word sentence: "Love ..." Jann's London companion Jonathon Cott, now *Rolling Stone*'s "European correspondent," spent the first half of his James Brown concert review telling readers about the fine foreign films he'd been enjoying in Paris. Even Gleason, the staff's senior member, filled his column with banalities like "We are all one ... we are all victims."

Editorial would have to take care of itself. Jann Wenner, making his way through the minefield of the magazine business, had enough to deal with. Above all, *Rolling Stone* needed money to stay afloat. That meant accomplishing three objectives: getting copies sold on the newsstands, getting readers to subscribe and getting advertisers to open up their pockets.

Jann and Ralph approached Miller Freeman Publications, a small West Coast distributorship with twenty or so clients, including *Sea Magazine* and *Auto Week*. MFP's newsstand director, Ward Cleaveland, regarded Jann as a hippie who "didn't know what the hell he was doing." Cleaveland made an offer that would leave Jann with only 9 cents, or 36 percent, of the 25-cent cover price. *Ramparts* was getting 50 percent of every copy sold. Then again, *Ramparts* was hot property. Jann signed on the dotted line. At least he wouldn't have to wear out his Porsche hauling bundles of issues from one newsstand to the next.

Between sales of the next two issues, the nine pennies per copy added up to little. In fact, said Ward Cleaveland, "more copies were thrown out than were sold," but this was no great disturbance to Miller Freeman Publications. Cleaveland did not regard *Rolling Stone* as a prized account, and in fact "didn't give a damn if they stayed with us or not."

A month later, Stanley Binder of Acme News flew in from the East Coast to see Jann and Ralph. Acme, which handled *Crawdaddy!*, saw what MFP did not: that *Rolling Stone*, rough edges notwithstanding, could capture a large segment of the youth market. Flattered that a national distributor would think so highly of his magazine to make a special trip, Jann was prepared to sign with Acme right away. Ralph counseled patience. He suggested they show Binder's offer to attorneys.

Gleason's advice was in vain. That evening Jann and Stan Binder met for drinks in Binder's hotel room. Jann asked Binder if he'd like to invest $5,000 in Straight Arrow Publishers, Inc. Binder said no, thanks—just the account would be sufficient. A couple of glasses of wine later, Binder had the *Rolling Stone* publisher's signature.

The arrangement with Acme did not meet expectations. Despite Binder's encouragement, it seemed to Jann that Acme heaped attention on *Crawdaddy!*

at the expense of *Rolling Stone*. He began to talk about breaking the agreement only months after signing the contract. In the meantime, Jann hankered for cash.

The task of opening subscription mail fell to the Schindelheim sisters, who sat at a folding table and piled the money off to the side. Jann viewed this as his living allowance and dipped into the pile accordingly.

"Hey, you can't do that!" said one of Jann's assistants as she watched him snatch a wad of dollars from the table.

"I just did it," he said, and walked back to his desk.

One afternoon Jann sat with friends in a house on Potrero Hill, smoking dope. Jann was admiring the handsome wooden apparatus which held the joint.

"Where'd you get the roach clip?" he asked its owner, Robert Kingsbury, a man he had met only once before.

"Made it myself," said Kingsbury. "I make 'em out of hardwood knobs."

Jann took a toke and fingered the woodwork of the roach clip. Then he asked, "What do you think you could make these for?"

Kingsbury shrugged. "Maybe eighty cents apiece," he said.

"Could you make me some?" Jann asked. "I need a lot."

Sure, why not, said Kingsbury. "What do you need 'em for?"

"I want to give 'em away," said Jann, grinning devilishly. "As a subscription incentive."

And so page 23 of issue No. 5 featured a photograph of a 4¼-inch roach clip with the headline "This handy little device can be yours free!" With a subscription to *Rolling Stone*, the ad read, readers would receive this "essential accessory.... Act now before this offer is made illegal."

Gleason hit the ceiling. "Marijuana is *against the law*," he said, lecturing Jann in his acid Eastern voice. "You can cover it, you can joke about it— but you cannot sell dope paraphernalia through *Rolling Stone*. You just can't do that!"

Even by now, however, it was becoming clear to Gleason, the Lydons and others: as president of Straight Arrow Publishers, Inc. Jann Wenner could, and would, do with *Rolling Stone* whatever he wished. He'd received his mandate by acclamation, it seemed. Everyone, from the music industry to musicians to readers, could see that what Jann was up to was far worthier of serious attention than the Haight's underground dalliances.

Above all, this early approval was seen in the advertising contracts Jann procured from record companies. By the beginning of 1968, *Rolling Stone* had cracked almost every major account: Atlantic, Capitol, Columbia, Reprise, Elektra, A&M, Warner and RCA. Even when Paul Williams hired an outside ad agency, *Crawdaddy!* could not approach *Rolling Stone*'s early advertising success.

Some of these victories came courtesy of Gleason's reputation within the music industry. Most were not so easily won. Though Gleason would claim to a friend, "My introductory letter was his passport into all the record company offices," the passport usually got Jann no further than the receptionist. The impatient young publisher spent more time than he cared to outside office doors, lunging at the first opportunity to corner an executive and beg for a quarter-page ad.

Regardless, *Rolling Stone*'s potential was not lost on the industry. Atlantic executive Jerry Wexler became a subscriber by the second issue. Columbia president Clive Davis made *Rolling Stone* required reading for his staff. Though initially parsimonious with their ad dollars, by the summer of 1968 both companies signed long-term contracts with Jann. They saw the magazine, wrote Gleason, "not as a sales tool for their own product exclusively, but as a forum in which to discuss the music they sold in a publishing world which did not [previously] have such a forum."

"In a way that was barely appreciated at the time," said Michael Lydon, "it caught on very fast." By the second issue, publicity-hungry musicians like John Sebastian, the Righteous Brothers and Richie Havens were paying calls to 746 Brannan. Promotion, of course, worked both ways. The magazine's kind comments about Rolling Stones drummer Charlie Watts in a Jon Landau column were rewarded with a flattering letter from Watts, which Jann of course printed. When Beatles movie director Richard Lester held a press conference in San Francisco, a copy of issue No. 1 was pushed into his hand, whereupon Baron Wolman materialized with camera at the ready. The photograph of Lester clutching his copy of *Rolling Stone* appeared in issue No. 3.

To Gleason's chagrin, Jann Wenner discovered that as the music industry could use *Rolling Stone* for its purposes, so could Jann use the magazine for his. At times the young editor's motives seemed pure, even righteous, as when Jann himself penned a moving epitaph for "the Crown Prince of Soul," Otis Redding. Yet in that very same issue, Jann assigned Michael Lydon the task of ripping a Jimi Hendrix album on Capitol Records—as a favor to Hendrix's new label, Warner, Jann told Lydon. The assistant editor didn't think much of the Capitol album; nor, however, did he approve of Jann's ingratiating tactics. Still, Lydon wrote the slam, and in the following issue Warner became a *Rolling Stone* advertiser for the first time.

Seldom did Jann hesitate to drive a few nails into the coffins of competitors. He gleefully declared the death of *GQ Scene*, "a nowhere publication," and with equal zeal reported on the financial woes of the "dull, poorly-conceived and pointless" *Cheetah*. Fully a year before the folding of *Eye* magazine, the *Rolling Stone* editor was assuring readers of its doom.

Of particular amusement to Gleason was Jann's refusal to give favorable coverage to Simon and Garfunkel. The reason was simple, if not well known: Denise Kaufman, Jann's former girlfriend, had taken up with Paul Simon sometime after their breakup in 1966. By the middle of 1968, the duo's sound track for *The Graduate* had achieved such acclaim that the magazine's reticence was starting to look conspicuous. Finally, Jann himself wrote in a June 1968 issue, "Simon and Garfunkel have made a most amazing comeback . . ." Comeback from what? The news item did not specify. Gleason tittered like a schoolboy as he read the entry over the phone to Denise Kaufman.

Still, Ralph Gleason did not find much to laugh about on the subject of *Rolling Stone*. His association with the magazine, and specifically with Jann, now put his sterling reputation at risk. There was that damned roach-clip ad. In a similarly unclassy vein, Jann was exaggerating *Rolling Stone*'s circulation figures.

Worst of all, writers Ralph had brought into the magazine were now furious at Jann Wenner's arbitrary editorial practices. They wanted out. One East Coast writer fired off a missive to Jann and concluded, "I'm wondering if the *Rolling Stone* is supposed to be a newspaper or just your own personal ego trip."

Another letter, this one addressed to Gleason, was even more bothersome. "I realize that you have a million things to do that demand your time," the reporter wrote. "But, like it or not, *Rolling Stone* is more or less synonymous with Ralph Gleason. That being the case, I believe that you should keep a tighter supervision over the day-to-day affairs of the paper."

But Gleason could not do this. Jann Wenner was thoroughly unaccountable. He still called the Gleason household for advice—incessantly, in fact, so that Ralph was compelled to get a new, unlisted number. But unwanted counsel fell on deaf ears, or produced the opposite effect intended. It seemed to Ralph that Jann delighted in antagonizing his mentor. Ralph praised the new supergroup Cream; Jann methodically panned their latest album. Ralph lauded the debut of Creedence Clearwater Revival; Jann ran a negative review which took a jab at Ralph's favorable comments. Ralph demanded money for his columns; Jann did not pay Ralph, but did pay a guest columnist. On and on.

"He now feels he can get along without me very well," Gleason wrote a friend. "Okay, do it, baby."

Ralph told Jann he was quitting. Jann, now facing a mass exodus by disgruntled freelance writers, begged him to stay on. Gleason was unmoved. Jann, he said, had "a W. R. Hearst complex." On September 4, 1968, several weeks shy of the magazine's first anniversary, Ralph Gleason formally resigned as the vice president of Straight Arrow Publishers, Inc., and consulting editor of *Rolling Stone*.

———

Outside 746 Brannan, America did not attend to this new development. Amid the tumult of 1968, Gleason's departure amounted to barely a flicker, a firefly passing through a war zone. The year began with the Vietcong attacking the American embassy in Saigon, and grew uglier still with each passing month: the assassination of Martin Luther King, Jr., followed by a nightmare of riots near the Capitol; the assassination of Robert Kennedy, a harbinger of the violent Democratic convention in Chicago.

In this year of chaos Jann Wenner would seek order. On July 1 he married Jane Ellen Schindelheim in a small Jewish ceremony. As a wedding gift, Sim Wenner gave the couple her two thousand shares of Straight Arrow stock. Despite this and Jann's Porsche, the newlyweds were flat broke. Jane openly fretted about their inability to buy furniture for their new home, complaining that the only clothes they could afford were those at Goodwill. She and Jann often socialized with Baron and Juliana Wolman, whose tastefully appointed house in the Haight further reminded the Wenners of their shortcomings.

If life as the wife of *Rolling Stone*'s publisher had a glamorous side, Jane hadn't yet seen it. He worked incessantly, determined to master the business end of the magazine. When he wasn't hobnobbing at the Fillmore, he was reading books on business management. His hyperactive ways got on her nerves—Jann had turned her into an insomniac, she would tell a friend. Though she was an artist by trade before she came to *Ramparts*, Jann did not exploit her native talent at *Rolling Stone*, relegating her instead to the subscriptions table with her sister.

Still, Jann listened to his wife's suggestions. One was that he hire Robert Kingsbury, the roach-clip designer, as the magazine's art director. On its face the notion seemed preposterous. Kingsbury, a sculptor and art teacher, had never worked for a publication in his life. At forty-four, he was twice Jann's age. He despised rock & roll. Kingsbury's only viable connection to *Rolling Stone* at this point was that he was dating Jane's sister Linda.

But Kingsbury was brilliant and resourceful, a disciplined man with an income of his own and time on his hands. John Williams, still unpaid and overworked as he was by *Ramparts*, was more than happy to turn the pasteup boards over to someone else.

Jann agreed to pay Bob Kingsbury $300 a month, and the next day brought his new staffer to 746 Brannan. Standing at the entrance to the loft, Kingsbury gaped in dismay. No tables, no lamps—not so much as a ruler.

He turned to his new boss. "How the fuck am I supposed to do *anything* here?" Kingsbury demanded.

"Well," said Jann, grinning, "*you're* the art director...."

Resigned to his plight, Kingsbury began each morning with a circuitous route to work. Visiting various secondhand stores along the way, he slowly filled the loft with desks and chairs. He built his own drafting table, bought his own ruler. Jann did not pay Kingsbury that first month, and then confessed that he could only afford to pay staffers, including Jann himself, $200 a month. This rankled Kingsbury, even more so after discovering a provision written into the Straight Arrow bylaws entitling Jann to retroactive pay. But the challenges of designing *Rolling Stone* helped quell his hostility, at least for a while.

By this time, both Lydons had left to pursue freelance careers and most of the volunteers had vanished. The only ones left were Henri the groupie/receptionist, a woman who claimed to be a famous beatnik's daughter and a former animal caretaker who collected funky neckties.

The former animal caretaker, Charlie Perry, had been hired as a proofreader, though in a matter of weeks he would assume nearly all of *Rolling Stone*'s editorial duties. Perry, the archetypal *Rolling Stone* staffer, came to the magazine with no formal experience, yet with deep empathy for the counterculture and a willingness to show his loyalty by working around the clock for no money at all.

As a Near Eastern languages major at Berkeley, Charlie Perry—a hippie, albeit balding—shared a house with Owsley Stanley, the "LSD millionaire," and thus received a crash course in psychedelia. This led, it seemed, to a fascination with animal consciousness. Perry's postgraduate work as an animal caretaker ended, he said, "when one day I went into somebody's house and said hi and then looked at their dog and said, 'Oh, too bad, somebody's got his bone.' And I was right. I had recognized the body language of a dog when his bone had been stolen. I had to quit after that."

Perry was dealing marijuana when he learned that *Rolling Stone* needed a proofreader. He'd been reading the magazine since the first issue, was a fan and would work for free. That first day Perry wisely claimed for his exclusive use one of the magazine's few functional typewriters and one of the only chairs in the office that had a stable back support.

Jann liked the amiable pot dealer from the start. Perry had not been with *Rolling Stone* more than a few days when the editor asked him to take a look at an editorial Jann had been agonizing over for some time. It was Jann's denunciation of the Jerry Rubin-led "Yippies" who were urging young people and musicians to disrupt the Chicago Democratic National Convention. The article would be the magazine's most controversial yet.

Give it a good read, Jann told Perry, adding that he wanted the article to appeal to the psychedelic consciousness. Said the editor, "I want the *stoned* effect."

The Brannan groupies and hangers-on were faceless and interchangeable, matters of supreme indifference to Jann. But Charlie Perry was a natural copy editor, a semi-bald and semi-stoned encyclopedia of a man. The *Rolling Stone* editor was perturbed, then, when Perry told him one day, "Look, Jann, I've got a problem. My dope's run out, and I don't have enough money to fly down to L.A. and buy some more. I'm gonna have to get a job. There's this opening at the San Francisco Zoo, and—"

"Forty," said Jann. "I'll pay you forty an issue."

Perry saw his chance. "Forty a week," he countered.

Jann hesitated. "Uh, okay," he then said.

Charlie Perry and Bob Kingsbury became for Jann what Michael Lydon and John Williams had never been: loyal employees who worked in-house, accountable nearly every minute of the day to *Rolling Stone*. He added a third, his personal secretary, Gretchen Horton, a couple of weeks after hiring Perry. Horton's interview for the job was lackluster, but that same day she wrote Jann, stoned, and begged for the job:

> It's vital to me to be around some cool people . . . I dig, with heart, soul, & body, this music. It literally holds me together at times. I KNOW I'd really groove on the job . . . I'm a good secretary— and would really like to see you laugh! Peace—love—and please call me!

Dedication like that was hard to come by. Jann Wenner called Gretchen Horton and hired her as soon as he finished reading the letter.

———

In October of 1968, Ralph Gleason returned to the fold after a month's hiatus. But there was a catch: he wanted Jann to hire John Burks as managing editor.

Burks, like Warren Hinckle, had made a name for himself as the editor of the San Francisco State campus paper. Unlike Hinckle, who drove the publication $20,000 into debt, Burks was a model of efficiency. Later he started his own magazine, *The Observer*, then wrote copy for the *Oakland Tribune* before signing on with *Newsweek*.

At *Newsweek*, Burks and his co-worker Michael Lydon often discussed *Rolling Stone*. Burks viewed the publication as a potentially fine magazine disguising itself as incoherent fluff. In his opinion, many of *Rolling Stone*'s articles were little more than press releases, leading the cheers for every San Francisco band that stumbled its way into a record contract. Cover stories seemed poorly conceived; indeed, issue No. 11 had no cover story, only a photograph of Baron Wolman's wife, Juliana. Additionally, Jann Wenner's magazine frequently violated the First Commandment of magazine publishing: *Thou shalt always come out on time.*

Lydon passed John Burks's critiques on to Jann. One day Burks received a phone call. The voice on the other end said, "Hello, I'm Jann Wenner from *Rolling Stone*, and I understand you think our magazine sucks."

"Well," said Burks, "I think it's a long way from what it might be, yeah."

"Well, we're looking for a managing editor. Can we have lunch?"

Gleason pushed hard for Burks. The two had met three years earlier when Ralph agreed to write, free of charge, a column for Burks's new San Francisco weekly, *The Observer*. Their professional relationship soured after Burks, at the behest of his printer, censored a Gleason column that quoted Lenny Bruce using the word "fuck." The two argued heatedly over the matter and had not spoken since.

Nonetheless, Gleason was impressed with *The Observer*. It looked sharp and it always came out on schedule. Burks's experience and leadership qualities could be just what the magazine needed. And since *Rolling Stone* habitually printed the word "fuck" about once every column inch, Burks would not have to resort to self-censorship.

Jann threw on the charm and John Burks was in, for about half of what *Newsweek* had been paying him. The new managing editor hit the ground, said Charlie Perry, "at a hundred miles an hour." Burks abandoned the practice of using publicity photos for the magazine. He put an end to fawning interviews. By his decree, 746 Brannan became a newsroom, with Burks exhorting the *Rolling Stone* volunteers. Make the extra phone call. Hunt for offbeat angles. Find the story within the story. Think of yourselves as *reporters*.

Burks and Perry became a team, weaving and rewriting and, in a pinch, creating. A freelancer named Larry Sepulvado turned in a basically dull piece on Texas music, wherein brief mention was made of an albino blues guitarist. An albino blues guitarist—that's a howl, Burks thought, and then instructed Perry, "Call the writer. Ask him to tell me everything he knows about this albino guy." The final version of the Texas music article declared that the "hottest item outside of Janis Joplin" was twenty-three-year-old Johnny Winter. The plug eventually made Johnny Winter a very rich young man.

Neither Burks nor Perry could decipher the English of a Japanese fellow who wrote an article on the rock scene of his native land. Armed with a Japanese edition of *Billboard*, the two editors determined the hot Japanese acts, put paper in the typewriter and rewrote the piece from scratch. The pseudonym, Max E. Lash, was one of several employed by Burks and Perry to conceal a basic fact: *Rolling Stone* was largely the editorial product of two individuals.

"Smoke," Burks would say, looking up from the pasteup boards at four in the morning, addressing Perry by his favorite pen name, Smokestack El Ropo. "Smoke, I'm imagining a desert . . . desolate . . . a fierce wind blowing . . . There is a desolate, windy, gaping hole—do you see the hole here?"

"Why, yes," Perry would say, his eyes gleaming, "I believe I do," and with that would turn to his typewriter and conjure up a parody, a dope fable, and thereby fill the hole.

———

In early October of 1968, publicists for the Beatles announced that an album by John Lennon and his Japanese girlfriend, Yoko Ono, would be released as soon as distributors stopped wringing their hands over the album's cover, which featured frontal and rear shots of the two artists in their birthday suits.

Gleason, now back with *Rolling Stone*, urged Jann to seize the moment. Cable the Beatles office in London, he instructed the editor, and ask for the nude shots. Promise them you'll use the photos. It's a cinch we'll get incredible publicity out of it.

Jann hesitated, but Gleason was insistent. How do you know it won't work, he argued, if you don't try it? Jann wired Derek Taylor, the Apple Corp. Publicist. Taylor responded. The photos were on their way. In the meantime, Jonathon Cott scored *Rolling Stone*'s first-ever interview with Lennon.

Rolling Stone's anniversary issue would be its best yet. Ralph Gleason's column was back; John Burks had put together a remarkably comprehensive essay on creeping commercialism in rock & roll; Cott's exclusive with Lennon was accompanied by a photograph of the songwriter in all his uncircumcised splendor; and the cover revealed the backsides of Lennon and Ono, with the caption likening the couple to Adam and Eve: "And they were both naked, the man and his wife, and were not ashamed." Leaving no stone unturned, the cover headline promised "Forty Pages Full of Dope, Sex & Cheap Thrills."

Jann and Ralph got the publicity bonanza they had hoped for. In San Francisco, a newsstand dealer was arrested for peddling obscene material. In New Jersey, the postmaster would not permit copies to be mailed to East Coast subscribers. In Baltimore, a distributor feared reprisals by church groups and withheld the Lennon issue from the stands. Back at 746 Brannan, the phone did not stop ringing. America had discovered *Rolling Stone*.

"The point is this," Jann Wenner would gloat in print the following issue: "Print a famous foreskin and the world will beat a path to your door." The Lennon cover had been a public relations masterstroke. Eagerly Jann accepted the credit—diverting none of it, as far as anyone could tell, to Ralph Gleason.

His exuberance was understandable. *Rolling Stone* had stumbled its way to respectability for twelve months now—"about eleven months longer than many people thought we would last," Jann noted in the anniversary issue. With Gleason, Wolman, Kingsbury, Perry, Burks and Gretchen Horton, the magazine now rested on sturdy backs. Henceforth there would be no tentativeness, no all-consuming fear that two weeks would pass without there being money for an issue. *Rolling Stone* wasn't rich, but in a year that saw the fatality rate of new magazines climb to 95 percent, it had demolished the odds. Jann Wenner's publication would roll on into 1969, and Jane Wenner would buy furniture for their house.

The president of Straight Arrow Publishers, Inc., awarded his new staff Christmas bonuses in the form of company stock. It was a gesture of deep gratitude toward the people he would come to regard as his family. Tidings, it was, of comfort and joy.

The following month, Richard Milhous Nixon was inaugurated as the thirty-seventh President of the United States.

Chapter Five

SCRIBES OF A SOUND

> **REVIEWERS**
>
> **AND**
>
> **WRITERS**
>
> Rolling Stone is interested in receiving record reviews, movie reviews and book reviews from interested writers or those who would like to write. Any such reviews printed will be paid for. If you would like to give it a chance—and we are most interested in finding new reviewers—please send your manuscript with a self-addressed envelope to: Manuscripts Editor, Rolling Stone, 746 Brannan Street, San Francisco, California 94103.

"So what was Mick like in '64?" Jann Wenner anxiously asked his office guest.

It was a strange way to conduct a job interview, but twenty-two-year-old John Morthland maintained his habitual poker face. He was aware of the *Rolling Stone* editor's reputation for star worshipping, and besides, the question was often put to him. Here it was, after all, October of 1969, and Mick Jagger's band was strutting and leering and copulating its way through America for the first time in three years. Under these circumstances, only the woefully unhip would not demand information from the young man who had been the first known American ever to interview the Rolling Stones.

Morthland did smile to himself, however, as he greatly appreciated irony. The editor asked him other questions, primarily tests of Morthland's musical knowledge: "Who was Muddy Waters's piano player?" He correctly replied, "Otis Spann," but could have said "Dick Nixon" and the results would have been the same. Jann Wenner would hire him within a few months, and due in no small part to that isolated moment in 1964 just outside the Mojave Desert when the Rolling Stones answered a few clumsy questions and thus rescued a boy from the desert's anonymous doom.

Providence delivered John Morthland to an office desk at 746 Brannan. All around him—elbow to elbow, really, as space in the *Rolling Stone* loft was scarce by 1970—sat others with similar stories. And this was no accident. Their very presence in this room, in *Rolling Stone*'s pages, confirmed the genius of Jann Wenner's idea. Even the editor, however, did not anticipate this phenomenon: that his magazine, "a letter from home" as Gleason called it, would become a home for so many writers-in-waiting, so many Eisenhower orphans; and that as a direct result of this, *Rolling Stone* would by the end of the decade become a devastating critical force in the music industry.

The *Rolling Stone* ads represented more than an employment opportunity. The respondents did not want jobs so much as the chance to speak and be heard on a subject that meant something vital to them. This subject, this sound, bore no resemblance to the white noise of their adolescence. The fifties, those breezy postwar years, had been pure hell for them. The sixties promised excitement, maybe even change. . . . But a sense of purpose, for those who neither led nor followed, remained as elusive as any fantasy.

Among the new faces in the Garrett Press loft there were no Mario Savios, no rock stars, no rock magazine publishers. These were writers, maybe, eventually—and rock & roll disciples, indisputably: one minute the music was not there and then when it came into their lives it did not arrive in a neat bundle that could be picked up and put down like a baseball mitt. Miracles are not handled this way, and for them music *was* miraculous, like language and fire, proof of magic and thus maybe, eventually, of hope.

"Believe in the magic, it will set you free," however, was not the kind of effusive sentiment John Morthland employed, either in his record reviews or in everyday conversation. The Moth, as they called him around the office, preferred the style of understatement. His roaring passions he kept mostly to himself. The miracle that brought him here to 746 Brannan he would render as the punch line to the wry joke that was his destiny.

John Morthland was born in 1947, a total stranger to postwar prosperity. He spent the first years of his life in a Chicago tenement; then in the slums of Bergenfield, New Jersey; then on a farm in the heart of Pennsylvania's Amish country. His father was uneducated and worked odd jobs. Poor before the war and not much better off after it, Mr. Morthland was nonetheless a bullheaded patriot, proud to have served his country. "Say what you will of the Army," he often told his only son. "But it made a man out of me."

In the summer of 1957, Morthland's father announced at the dinner table that they would soon be moving to California. There were palm trees there, he told his wife and son and two daughters. "And when you cross the street," he added, his voice low and wondrous, "the cars stop and wait for you to pass."

Mr. Morthland tried without success to land a job in Disneyland. Eventually they moved to the site of the very first McDonald's hamburgers: San Bernardino, in southern California, at the edge of the Mojave Desert, where Air Force planes flew overhead, valiantly attempting to shatter the sound barrier, instead merely shattering the Morthland household's glassware.

John Morthland's father became a gravedigger at a cemetery which lay next to a miniature golf course. The son would remember that first summer in the Last Frontier as a formative one. He spent most of it sitting on a fence, watching the miniature golfers to his left, his father digging graves to his right.

Too small to engage in school sports, John reported from the sidelines for the high school paper and wrote the local daily's "Teen Scene" column. The teen beat meant church bake sales one Friday, Eric Burdon and the Animals the next.

As it happened, in 1964 a San Bernardino disc jockey had gotten his hands on an imported pressing of cover tunes recorded by a virtually unknown British band, the Rolling Stones. Quickly the Stones became a city favorite, and later it was decreed that the band would begin their first U.S. tour in San Bernardino. An interview would be granted to high school junior John Morthland, "Teen Scene" reporter.

Thankfully, it would not be remembered what young Morthland had asked the Stones—"Mick, what's your favorite color? Brian, if you had to do it all over again . . ."—but only that it was he, and none other, who had done the asking. The irony lodged itself. Thereafter John Morthland would attend Berkeley in 1965, and hear an LBJ aide speak on campus and utter such pallid lies about the American role in Vietnam that Morthland—the son of a Goldwater Republican—would be slapped awake from the deadest dream. He would grow his hair to his shoulders; no longer would he dine at his father's table. He would drop out, drop acid, register each semester to avoid being drafted. He lived each day on a single bowl of brown rice with an egg scrambled in it—proudly half starved, working at the campus bookstore rather than beg, short-haired, for his father's nickels.

These were the days that molded John Morthland. But in the very end, what meant the difference between a life of purpose and one of desolation —between his life as an acclaimed journalist and his father's as a forgotten itinerant—was knowing what Mick Jagger was like in 1964.

———

Jann Wenner met John Morthland because of Greil Marcus, who first met the editor that day in 1964 at Jann's apartment where the Mose Allison record played and the debutante photos hung on the wall. The two had not seen each other much after that. Regardless, Marcus observed the amazingly linear path of Jann Wenner's career, reading with approval the Mr. Jones column and then the weekly features in *Sunday Ramparts*.

"And in 1967," he said, "I happened to be walking down Bancroft right at Telegraph, and there outside a smoke shop was a stack of *Rolling Stone*, the first issue. And I bought one, and I hadn't read a paragraph of it before I realized: This is Jann's. I could tell by the design, the voice, and I flipped over to the masthead, and I was right. It made perfect sense."

And it made equally perfect sense for him to admire Jann's unwavering focus. Greil Marcus grew up with definite twin passions—liberal ideology and Elvis Presley—but without definite plans on how to make use of the two. At Berkeley he fashioned his own major, American studies, then became a political science graduate student, and perhaps after that would be a professor.

By 1964, however, Marcus was gripped in the rock & roll vise, his Presley side howling out, too far gone to be sedated by academia. Playing his favorite song—the Beatles' version of "Money"—for unmoved friends on one occasion, Marcus resorted to desperate measures. "See, here's what's going on," he said over the music. "Listen to what's going on in the in- strumental break here. What you hear is a metaphorical representation of the out-of-control technological forces of modern society grinding the individual down to nothing. Hear that scream? That's the gears of the machine, meshing, destroying the soul!"

"I was basically kidding," said Marcus, "but even in my sarcasm I was thinking, Well, why not? This makes sense." An unpublished critic was born.

Four years later, Greil Marcus bought *Magic Bus/The Who on Tour*, only to discover that the album represented not a live tour but rather the record label's desire to dump a collection of prereleased songs on the market until the band could complete its new material. Incensed, he penned a review of the album, lamenting over what the record should have been, and mailed the manuscript off to *Rolling Stone*. Marcus's review was published in *Rolling Stone*'s next issue, and Marcus received in the mail a check for ten dollars.

Boy, thought Marcus, this is really simple. He sent in more reviews and wrote for other publications as well, usually examining music as a social or political scientist might, seeking a record's broadest possible context—the kind of sweeping analysis for which Greil Marcus would one day be known worldwide.

In one such piece, Marcus attacked Ralph Gleason. Two weeks later, the young critic was at Gleason's house, hat in hand, asking for information on the Coasters only Gleason could supply. The *Chronicle* columnist let on that he'd seen Marcus's jab at him but hadn't lost any sleep over it. After that, the two became close friends.

One day at the Gleason household, Marcus told Ralph, "You know, the *Rolling Stone* record review section is just god-awful."

"Well," said Gleason, quite typically, "why don't you do something about it?" Marcus wasn't sure what that meant until a few days later, when Jann Wenner phoned him and issued the formal challenge:

"If you're so disgusted with the record review section, why don't *you* edit it?"

As Greil Marcus discovered the first day on the job, there had been no editor before him. Each issue's record review section comprised whatever had come in through the postal service in response to the help-wanted ads. It seemed to Marcus that most of the albums reviewed were either folk records or rock records reviewed as if they *were* folk. The writers picked apart the lyrics and then issued their bland verdicts—or ridiculously hysterical (yet still bland) verdicts, as when a reviewer summed up the Who rock opera *Tommy* by saying, "For the first time, a rock group has come up with a full-length cohesive work that could be compared to the classics."

Marcus would do his best to change all this. He put out calls to old friends: his old cruising buddy Barry Franklin from high school, Phil Marsh and Bruce Miroff from college. His good friend Langdon Winner he solicited as well; Winner brought along his roommate, John Morthland.

"Most of the people I was working with couldn't write," said Marcus. "So because I was a control fetishist I'd sit down and completely rewrite them. They didn't know enough to be pissed off." Don't pussyfoot around, Marcus exhorted his stable of reviewers. Say what you want to say. Cut 'em up, tear 'em to pieces.

———

One writer who needed no such encouragement was Lester Bangs. Three months before Greil Marcus's arrival, *Rolling Stone* received in the mail a sputtering, scathing condemnation of the debut record of the MC5, a "revolutionary band" recently lauded in a distinctly idiotic *Rolling Stone* cover story. Bangs bought the hype, bought the record and after listening, felt duped. Having seen *Rolling Stone*'s help-wanted ad, he took aim and fired.

Lester Bangs began to send as many as ten or fifteen reviews a week to *Rolling Stone*. Marcus printed two of these back to back in his first section. The first, assessing the much publicized debut of the Columbia Records artists It's a Beautiful Day, noted:

> The vocal harmonies sound a little bit like the Fariñas and a little bit like the Peanut Butter Conspiracy. In other words, kind of ethereal and kind of lame. Of course, I have a problem since I do not hear them but *smell* them, and what they smell like to me is rotted posies pressed between pages of Tennyson. . . . I hate this album. I hate it not only because I wasted my money on it, but for what it represents: an utterly phony, arty approach to music that we will not soon escape.

The bookend to this review declared Captain Beefheart "the only true dadaist in rock" and pronounced the avant-garde songwriter's latest album "a total success, a brilliant, stunning enlargement and clarification of his art."

It was Greil Marcus's way of presenting to *Rolling Stone* readers the critical vision of Lester Bangs. If, between these two reviews, a reader failed to understand where Bangs was coming from, it surely was not the fault of *Rolling Stone*.

The Bangs reviews kept coming in, dozens of them, accompanied by long, obnoxiously honest letters. Through the caterwauling prose Greil Marcus developed a composite of his star reviewer: a twenty-year-old women's shoe salesman living just outside of San Diego in a town called El Cajon; a sometime college student, hating every single minute of college life; a grounded Kerouac understudy, restless, hopeless, misunderstood, the music in his life ridiculed by everyone, all musicians ridiculous except the Velvet Underground; incredibly sensitive, probably unbearable . . . a real find.

Wanting to meet him, and figuring he was lonely, Marcus and some of the other reviewers persuaded John Burks to have Lester Bangs flown up to San Francisco. Bangs eagerly made the trip. Surprisingly, said Langdon Winner, this wild-man reviewer "had on nice corduroy pants with a cord sport coat, brown shoes—he looked like one of those straight people you avoided in high school. And filled with extravagant ideas, which I think had religious moral roots; very direct, with an aura of naïveté about him."

Indeed, Bangs naïvely assumed that he was delivered here to be offered a staff position, and was secretly crushed when no offer was made. But until 1973, when Jann Wenner banned him from the pages of *Rolling Stone* for showing disrespect toward musicians, Lester Bangs continued to bombard Greil Marcus and future editors with his ravings—some of them assigned, the vast majority unsolicited vitriol.

––––

From Yellow Springs, Ohio, came letters remarkably similar to those Marcus received from El Cajon. The Ohio correspondent, Ed Ward, was a New Yorker now stuck in a Midwestern beatnik refuge, Antioch College, whose curriculum he couldn't figure out. Ward, a fifth-year freshman, was bored and broke and waiting for a lifeline to fall out from heaven. He loved *Rolling Stone*, had been to San Francisco a few months before the Summer of Love and had reason to believe that it was the promised land. Marcus regarded Ed Ward's letters as cries for help.

Where Lester Bangs was all hilarity and righteous fulmination, Ward was a serious music student. Brought up on Gilbert and Sullivan, classically trained, Ed Ward by the age of eighteen had developed a keen ear for the way popular music was absorbing avant-garde techniques. Like Jann, he worshipped Dylan, but his interests extended to electronic music and the weird hybrids of the Deep South. Unlike some of Marcus's writers, Ward seemed deeply appreciative of the fact that rock & roll did not begin, or end, in Liverpool or the Haight-Ashbury. *Rolling Stone* published whatever Ward sent.

When Greil Marcus asked Ed Ward in early 1970 if he'd like to replace him as the reviews editor, Ward could have wept. He'd counted as the high point of his twenty-year-old life the months in 1967 he spent as a staffer for *Crawdaddy!* If Paul Williams hadn't treated his people so shabbily, he never would have left that angry letter of resignation pinned to the *Crawdaddy!* office wall by means of a butcher knife. He'd still be working there, unpaid and so what, sleeping on the office floor, living off doughnuts and pharmaceutical speed and pounding out first-and-final drafts of solemn interviews with the Rascals, the Youngbloods, other "serious artists." And now, a deliverance from Antioch, a chance to write about music *and be paid for it.* He might never have to eat brown rice again.

A few days later, another call came in:

"Hello, Ed? This is Gretchen Horton from *Rolling Stone.* I need to find out a few things. What is your birthday and what time were you born?"

Ward passed on the data. Then he asked what the hell was going on.

"Jann wants to make sure the staff is astrologically compatible," came Horton's answer. Her voice was wary. "So you're a Scorpio. Hmmm. We'll have to see how this balances out."

An astrological imbalance? Foiled by the stars? Ed Ward did not rest easy until the one-way plane ticket to San Francisco arrived.

———

The *Rolling Stone* critics, said Greil Marcus, wrote in happy oblivion, grateful simply for the outlet, "with absolutely no conception that the stuff we were writing would have any effect on anybody." Despite (or because of) this, the magazine's writers rearranged contemporary music's power structure in a way no periodical had before or would since.

Among critics, none approached the influence of Jon Landau. A former Brandeis University student, musician and record store clerk who used to engage in scholastic arguments with Paul Williams over the sociological importance of Beatles records, Landau cut his teeth at *Crawdaddy!* and *Eye* before coming to *Rolling Stone,* where his writing matured rapidly. Unlike Williams, Landau did not confuse the Doors with God; unlike Jann Wenner, he was not persuaded by the available evidence that the Jefferson Airplane —or any band from San Francisco—was America's answer to the Rolling Stones. He focused, almost cantankerously, as no other *Rolling Stone* critic did at the time, on black music.

Said Greil Marcus, "Jon wrote with enormous authority, and if he didn't know as much as he seemed to know, he still knew more than most did.

Once he wrote, 'I've been listening to blues for six months now . . .' And I remember reading it and thinking, Wow. *Six whole months*. He made it sound so impressive."

In *Rolling Stone*'s fifth issue, Landau panned the Rolling Stones' *Their Satanic Majesties Request*, going so far as to say that the failure seemed likely to "put the status of the Rolling Stones in jeopardy." A few weeks later, Stones drummer Charlie Watts thanked Landau for his comments and promised that the band would try harder next time around.

Three issues later, Landau addressed the much hyped Boston music scene, touted by MGM Records (who had just signed three local acts calling themselves Orpheus, Ultimate Spinach and Beacon Street Union) as "the Bosstown Sound." Industry wags awaited the verdict. Digging beneath the promotional layers, the New England-bred critic concluded scoldingly that the Bosstown Sound was a complete shill. MGM's brainchild died in its crib.

A month later, Landau broke a far mightier back. This time the subject was Cream, the British white-blues supertrio led by guitarist Eric Clapton. For two years, Clapton had been seeing his name scrawled across London concrete, followed by the words "is God." He and his band mates had known nothing but media adulation, commercial success and swarms of willing groupies. No less than Jann Wenner had tracked the Cream guitarist down in 1966 and informed Clapton, "Locally you are known as one of the world's top blues or rock guitarist [sic]."

So Clapton was quite unprepared for the Brandeis student's smirky judgment that "Clapton is a master of blues clichés . . . a virtuoso at performing other people's ideas." Damned by the faint praise, Clapton actually fainted while reading the Landau piece. Upon being revived, he decided then and there to dissolve Cream.

———

The consequences of other critical stances in *Rolling Stone* were often negligible. Negative reviews of Santana's debut and of *Led Zeppelin II* didn't stop either from topping the charts, for example. Other cases were more difficult to assess. CBS Records president Clive Davis was furious over Lester Bangs's *It's a Beautiful Day* review, but the group of the same name received little marketing support afterward. And it was well known that the magazine's frequent belittlings of Big Brother and the Holding Company upset the band's lead vocalist, Janis Joplin, who once said, "*Rolling Stone*? Those shits! They don't know what's happening, they're out in San Francisco feeling smug because they think they're where it's at!" Still, a somber Gleason column calling for Joplin to ditch her band was followed a few days later by her decision to do exactly that.

On the other hand, favorable play in *Rolling Stone* gave unknown or floundering acts a new lease on life. The magazine's Texas-music article brought into stunning relief the hitherto unknown albino guitarist Johnny Winter, who was consequently flooded with offers and eventually signed with Columbia for an unprecedented $600,000. Ronnie Hawkins, once the leader of a group of session musicians who later became the Band, found a sympathetic listener in *Rolling Stone* reporter Ritchie Yorke. Yorke's subsequent article resulted in a new contract for Hawkins, who sent Yorke a humble thank-you note and pledged to play a free concert of *Rolling Stone*'s choosing.

Those who doubted *Rolling Stone*'s credibility among its readers had little to say after the Masked Marauders incident. Grumbling aloud one day about the unseemly spate of "supergroups," "supersessions" and "super-concerts" afflicting the music scene, Greil Marcus said to friends, "I wonder what a *real* supersession would sound like—you know, Jagger and Dylan and Lennon. What would they play?"

Rather than wait for an answer, Marcus headed for the typewriter. Under the pen name T. M. Christian, he wrote:

> They began months ago, the rumours of an event that at first seemed hardly believable ... John Lennon, Mick Jagger, Paul McCartney and Bob Dylan, backed by George Harrison and a drummer as yet unnamed—the "Masked Marauders." Produced by Al Kooper, the album was recorded with impeccable secrecy in a small town near the site of the original Hudson Bay Colony in Canada.

The album, said Christian, featured McCartney singing "Mammy," Dylan imitating "early Donovan" and Jagger crooning something called "I Can't Get No Nookie."

Marcus took the Masked Marauders review to Jann Wenner, who could not stop laughing as he read it. He approved the review, and Bob Kingsbury designed a phony cover. To complete the ruse, the "Records" section of October 18, 1969, included not only the review of the Marauders' LP but also one of a legitimate "supersession" album by a band called Merryweather. In the latter review, critic John Morthland condemned all contrived "super" efforts—"with the sole exception of the Masked Marauders...."

As soon as the issue hit the newsstands, 746 Brannan was deluged with calls—and not all of them by consumers. Dylan manager Albert Grossman rang the office, saying he hadn't been in touch with Bob for a while and was this Masked Marauders shit really true? Stones/Beatles manager Allen Klein called to ask the same question.

In the meantime, a reporter confronted alleged Marauders producer Al Kooper. Was it true? Answered Kooper, for reasons of his own: "No comment."

Marcus could not let it die. He and Langdon Winner rounded up some Berkeley musician friends, sequestered themselves in a garage studio and recorded "I Can't Get No Nookie" and the rest. They took the tape to KMPX-FM, San Francisco's hippest station, and the session was aired. More hysteria. Motown Records offered to pay $100,000 for the tape. Instead, the Marauders cut a $15,000 distribution deal with Warner Brothers. Phony press releases were drummed up and faithfully printed in *Billboard, Record World* and *New York*.

By this time Jann decreed that enough was enough, and *Rolling Stone* exposed its own hoax. Gradually, very gradually, readers accepted the Masked Marauders as a product of their own wishful thinking.

Or most of them did. Years later, Greil Marcus's brother met some fellows who insisted on playing for him a truly rare bootleg recording. Steve Marcus laughed, and told them the tale of the Masked Marauders. The fellows shrugged, saying they didn't know anything about that but what Marcus was about to hear was a genuine Lennon/Jagger/Dylan supersession.

As the first notes sounded, Steve Marcus exclaimed, "This is it! I'm telling you, this is my brother's band!"

But his new friends refused to believe him. The Masked Marauders, darling of the critics, would live on.

Chapter Six

"It Was Like
Balling for
the First Time"

The caller told copy editor Charlie Perry he represented the American Society of Composers, Authors and Publishers, and he had a great story for *Rolling Stone*. ASCAP, he said, was going to start competing with BMI in licensing rock songwriters. In fact, an ASCAP convention was going to take place in the Bahamas, where this new strategy would likely be discussed.

"We'd be happy to pay your way," said the caller, "if you care to cover the convention."

"When's the convention going to be?" asked Perry.

Said the caller, "At your convenience."

Perry said thanks so much, and hung up.

On another occasion, a publicist contacted Greil Marcus and bluntly asked Marcus to have a particular record reviewed. Marcus said no.

The publicist growled, "I can have you fired."

Marcus said he doubted it and replaced the phone.

By 1969 all skepticism had been erased: *Rolling Stone* was here to stay, was well on its way to becoming an institution and was therefore worthy of corruption. Seemingly every sloe-eyed, thousand-toothed, well-tanned reptile in the music industry was breathing hot air into the phone lines of 746 Brannan, or slithering over for an in-person seduction. By all available evidence, they slithered back without so much as an ounce of flesh.

What Jann Wenner's magazine had achieved in two short years was astonishing. Its readership—once 6,000, now closing in fast on 100,000—trusted *Rolling Stone*, depended on it as one might a big brother. Readership surveys showed that very few of *Rolling Stone*'s faithful read *any* other magazine, on any subject. Perhaps no other periodical in America enjoyed so captive an audience.

Rolling Stone didn't talk down to its readers like a Walter Cronkite understudy. The writers talked in their own language, flaunting their blissful lack of objectivity. When a new ultracommercial band starring an unknown singer named Olivia Newton-John was announced by Monkees creator Don Kirshner, the magazine's news article described the press conference as "the greatest barrage of promotional bullshit in many years." In the April 19, 1969 edition, the magazine—in "Random Notes," *Rolling Stone*'s music gossip column—took an apparently unprovoked but vicious swipe at the drug methamphetamine and listed several means by which speed could be wiped off the planet. *Rolling Stone*, like the best of rock & roll, delivered its message with brutal honesty.

Readers expected *Rolling Stone* to take chances. It is possible that they counted on the magazine to do so. For cover stories, the magazine every so often shimmied out on the wobbliest possible limbs. Newsstand customers would be greeted by the unlikely images of Captain Beefheart, the "cosmic jazz orchestra" bandleader Sun Ra, a black street kid holding an underground newspaper or a middle-aged cowboy in his best rodeo threads. "The message," said John Burks, "was: 'We haven't lied to you yet, so believe us: this guy counts just as much as the John Lennon we had on our cover last issue and the Jimi Hendrix we'll have on our cover next issue.' "

Rolling Stone could be expected not only to see through industry hype but to point it out whenever it materialized. When radio jocks across the land issued the declaration that Paul McCartney had died in a 1966 car crash and had since been replaced by a double—that dozens of clues on Beatles records supported this theory—*Rolling Stone* cleared its throat and said: *Balls*. (Indeed, fully nine months before the Rumor saw print, a young man walked into 746 Brannan and brandished proof that Paul was dead. Burks sent him packing.)

It took a lot of nerve. Here was a magazine whose very existence depended on record company ads, whose record store distribution was handled by A&M Records (later by CBS), whose high editorial quality owed much to the industry's good graces . . . yet *Rolling Stone* seemed to bite every feeder's hand. It reviled the bands on which the record companies heaped the most money. It now attacked, with piranha-like glee, the Stones and the Beatles. (Dylan was spared until 1970.) *Rolling Stone* even went so far as to insult, in print, the advertisements Columbia Records placed *in the magazine*, declaring these "The Man Can't Bust Our Music" ads insincere, and ultimately causing Clive Davis to scuttle the whole campaign.

Anxious to extend their reach, *Rolling Stone* writers ventured forth into the world beyond the Bay. In the first year of operation, the magazine's San Francisco bias was as plain as any other ugly prejudice. Even its most experienced writers—Jann, Burks and Gleason—perpetrated the notion that good rock & roll music could not originate from any American city outside of San Francisco, except by the most absurd of coincidences. Fortunately, *Rolling Stone*'s newer writers dispelled the bias. Lester Bangs and Ed Ward championed distinctly East Coast acts like the Velvet Underground and Iggy Pop, while John Morthland and Langdon Winner wrote disapprovingly of releases by homegrown musicians Country Joe McDonald and Santana.

In so doing, *Rolling Stone* regularly infuriated its own readers. But the magazine's noisiest battles were not fought with either readers or the grayhairs of the record business. Those clashes usually involved Bill Graham.

The hollow-eyed, steel-jawed concert promoter was a Polish Jew orphaned by Nazis and raised in New York street fights. His face was a leather-bound book that read: "Don't fuck with me." After Luria Castel's Family Dog shows in 1965, Graham—then the director of the San Francisco Mime Troupe—sponsored a series of concerts featuring the Grateful Dead, the Jefferson Airplane and Janis Joplin. Before long, Graham had muscled his way into the forefront of Bay Area rock promotion. At the advice of Ralph Gleason, Graham reopened the old ballroom located on Fillmore and Geary in the heart of San Francisco's Negro district. By late 1966, the Fillmore, as it came to be known, was showcasing some of the most remarkable rock concerts the Bay Area would ever see.

Credit, when given to Bill Graham, was doled out grudgingly. He was an anti-hippie, brutally efficient, and he harbored no longing to go broke off rock & roll. One of Graham's earliest critics was Jann Wenner. In his first column for the *Daily Cal*, Mr. Jones cited the promoter's "extreme uptightness," and later wrote, "These weekend dances at the Fillmore Auditorium are being promoted by a little man named Bill Graham . . . [who] has turned these dances into money making schemes first and foremost. Whatever fun one has is strictly incidental to, almost in spite of, Bill Graham."

For all his tough talk, Graham's skin was paper thin. He tracked down young Mr. Jones and issued a furious rebuttal. Jann printed some of it, but then wrote, "I think he believes he owns the whole scene, and this is wrong."

In similar fashion, *Rolling Stone* gave Bill Graham his due while refusing to be intimidated by him. Early issues gave page-one coverage to his being fired as the Jefferson Airplane's manager, and referred to him as "the burgeoning Howard Hughes of the dance scene." Shortly thereafter, Graham canceled his advertising contract with *Rolling Stone*. Despite this, Charlie Perry wrote a sympathetic piece on Graham's troubles with his Fillmore East club in New York. But the article slightly misquoted the promoter at one point, triggering Graham's paranoia and the usual gale of obscenities.

In June of 1969, the Fillmore Corporation announced that it would co-sponsor free recording seminars. *Rolling Stone* dubbed the gesture "at once altruistic and self-centered." For this Graham threatened to sue. In a letter to the magazine, he accused Jann of letting his publication's "high ideals slowly crumble before the almighty dollar. . . . You have worked so hard at letting the public know where I've been at. I think it is time for the public to find out who you are and what the *Rolling Stone* stands for. . . . Stay tuned."

These threats, and their impotence, only testified to *Rolling Stone*'s growing power. The magazine was getting better and better, issue by issue. Jann's "John J. Rock" column was now "Random Notes" (the name directly lifted from his *Sardine* column in boarding school), and far spicier and savvier than before. Art director Bob Kingsbury and photographer Baron Wolman gave *Rolling Stone* a look unlike any psychedelic counterpart: clean, uncluttered, yet increasingly more ambitious and possessing the dimensionality of the sculptures in Kingsbury's home studio.

Nowhere was the magazine's improvement more striking than in its interviews with musicians. Titled "The *Rolling Stone* Interview" (with no apologies to *Playboy*), these question-and-answer profiles were typically, in *Rolling Stone*'s first year, reprints of *Melody Maker* interviews or transcripts of press conferences or simply pieces other magazines had passed on. By the fall of 1969, however, installments of "The *Rolling Stone* Interview" would provide striking glimpses into the personalities of John Lennon, Mick Jagger, Who guitarist/songwriter Pete Townshend and Doors vocalist Jim Morrison. The interview sessions were always lengthy, nothing like the morsels of time usually parceled out by record company publicists. If *Rolling Stone*'s interviewers were still learning how to ask the tough question, their subjects—eager, usually, for exposure in the magazine—met them more than halfway.

By the end of the decade, it no longer seemed fair to compare the writing in *Rolling Stone* to that in other "counterculture" publications. Jerry Hopkins, a former Los Angeles drug paraphernalia store manager who responded to the magazine's very first help-wanted ad, was consistently churning out brilliant features. While Hopkins roved the festival scene, Jann recruited a versatile in-house staff writer: Ben Fong-Torres, who had been writing for Pacific Bell's employee magazine and editing a bilingual Chinatown paper on the side. Meanwhile, Burks reeled in a talented and ambitious young Philadelphia journalist named John Lombardi while doing field research for a cover story on the underground press. By the beginning of 1970, *Rolling Stone* would also be receiving offbeat news reports from Chet Flippo, a Texan who had spent the early sixties as a naval intelligence officer in Morocco.

The magazine's great strides were due to a variety of factors. Clearly John Burks was one of them. They called the six-foot-seven, deep-voiced newsman a "jazz style" editor, and not just because of his taste in music or the way he absentmindedly drummed his pencils on his desktop. Burks improvised, pulling stories this way and that, throwing in some obscure nugget of reportage, sending out a second correspondent to complement the first. Often the results seemed wild and sloppy, zigzagging across the page like a Thelonious Monk score. Sometimes (though not always) that was the point.

Burks, after all, had done time in Fourth Estate prison camps. He saw *Rolling Stone* as an alternative to the stale and myopic musings of Establishment media. The stance had great appeal for writers like John Lombardi. "I had worked for a bunch of dailies in Philadelphia and South Jersey," Lombardi said, "and was extremely unhappy with what I had seen there. Their approach to the news didn't seem to have anything to do with the reality that I and my friends perceived.

"When I first got to San Francisco, my wife and I met up with John in North Beach and talked over Anchor Steam beer. John was talking an Us-and-Them philosophy, Them being the straight press, and I very much wanted to hear that. I mean, that's the sort of thing that brought me to *Rolling Stone*."

Above all, John Burks had the editorial staff's complete loyalty. Where Jann Wenner, younger and not overstocked with patience, might be more apt to focus on a journalist's shortcomings, the managing editor's style was more avuncular. He apprenticed them carefully, leading them to the heart of their stories and spinning them out again. Under his tutelage, creative individuals became writers—if not brilliant reporters, then honest ones at least.

Burks brought a newsroom sensibility to *Rolling Stone* while Ralph Gleason provided the magazine's broadly based musical perspective. "For having next to no physical presence in the office," said Ben Fong-Torres, "he was a *great* presence. He was the patriarch, though he didn't come across as that old, and we looked to him for guidance. If I were to smell a payola story, I could always send it past Ralph and he would just say, 'Look, this is garbage—here, these are some editorials from five years ago, copy 'em for your files, what you're talking about is part of a typical six-year cycle, and what you guys *really* ought to be doing is studying the jukebox industry, now *that's* where the scandal leads.'

"He could put you back in your place, or up on a higher level, whichever the situation called for. He was our encyclopedia."

———

But the man most deserving of credit for *Rolling Stone*'s success was twenty-three-year-old Jann Wenner.

Inordinate good luck was no longer an acceptable explanation. Alchemy seemed more like it. With only a few thousand in venture capital, he'd succeeded where *Crawdaddy!*, *Scene*, *Cheetah* and *Eye* failed. His hiring of Wolman and Kingsbury instantly resulted in a distinctly elegant look for *Rolling Stone*. By acquiring Burks, he acquired a newsroom. What he got when he signed up Marcus was not just a reviews editor but an entire bullpen of critics. Jann Wenner had the Touch.

First *The New York Times*, then *Newsweek* and a host of dailies dispatched reporters to San Francisco to probe this new phenomenon. Wenner, they concluded, was the real deal, a young man of taste and vision. The *Rolling Stone* editor/publisher began to give speeches at music conventions, call industry executives by their first names and field questions from other magazines about the future of rock. No longer was it necessary for him to introduce himself as "Jann Wenner—you know, the editor of *Rolling Stone*."

And if he attended to the applause, he did not yet believe, as some suggested, that the *Stone* could roll on its own momentum. Jann Wenner still worked long hours, still kept an eye on every major piece, still selected every cover, still badgered Bob Kingsbury incessantly about ways in which the design of *Rolling Stone* could be improved. To facilitate his brainstorming, Gretchen Horton bought her boss a dictating machine. She created a monster. Memos descended upon 746 Brannan like acorns from an oak in a windstorm.

His ideas could be excruciatingly bad, as when he declared to staffers that a new watermelon-flavored chewing gum out on the market had psychedelic overtones and thus warranted *Rolling Stone's* attention. At least as often, his instincts were dazzling. When Langdon Winner praised Paul McCartney's new solo album as a departure from overproduced Beatles records, Winner made no mention of the album's press sheet, on which McCartney took several digs at John Lennon, Yoko Ono and the Beatles.

Said Greil Marcus, "Jann told me, 'I don't want to run this review without taking this other stuff into account. Here's this sunny-sounding record—everything's coming up roses—that in fact has been made with a tremendous amount of bile. And I think the review should reflect that.'

"We must have argued two hours about this. Finally he convinced me. So I went and had a two-hour argument with Langdon."

Winner rewrote the review. He did not regard the incident as an example of wrongheaded meddling. "I took it as the sign of a strong and good editor," he said.

As with Warren Hinckle, Jann's editorial acumen was easily matched by a flair for promotion. The case of the groupies article made this abundantly clear.

Baron Wolman, always more fascinated with people than music, was intrigued by the legions of young women—some not so young, others a decade away from womanhood—who crowded the backstage area of rock concerts. Groupies, they were called: the girls with the band, erotic gypsies with, as Frank Zappa put it, "a taste for the bizarre."

Wolman thought they were a great untold story and said so. Burks, in typical fashion, assigned an ensemble of writers to the case, including himself. Groupies of all sorts were rounded up, photographed and questioned: "Why do you like living this way? Is there much competition? Which band is the kinkiest? Do musicians look after their illegitimate children?"

The result was a sensational article, one which Jann felt deserved sensational promotion. Enlisting the aid of a Columbia Records graphics staffer, he designed a promotional ad for the groupies issue and bought a full page in the *New York Times*. The cost—$7,000—all but emptied *Rolling Stone's* bank account. So untroubled by this was Jann that he spent additional money flying himself and Jane and Baron Wolman to New York to obtain first-run copies of the February 12, 1969, ad, which featured a Wolman photo of a particularly gaudy-looking woman accompanied by the headline: "When we tell you what a groupie is, will you really understand?"

The ad went on to explain what a groupie was, why this was an important thing to know and why only *Rolling Stone* was equipped to inform the reader on such matters. Plato was quoted: "When the mode of music changes, the walls of the city will shake."

At the bottom of the page was a subscription form. Few, as it turned out, responded—a total of three, it has been said, plus a fourth who sent a package containing dog feces. But Jann's audaciousness intrigued the New York press. Underground rags, it was noted, did not take out full-page ads in the *New York Times*.

————

Since May of 1968, Jann Wenner had been trying to score an interview with his idol, Bob Dylan.

The task would not be easy. Dylan, the J. D. Salinger of rock stars, did not make himself available to the press, and even less so since July 29, 1966. On that day, Dylan flew off his motorcycle and broke his neck. For nearly two years he recovered in complete seclusion, while rumors of his death haunted the Haight and other gossip mills.

In 1968 Bob Dylan emerged with *John Wesley Harding*, a collection of soft, almost grateful love songs and allegories. "He went off the bike and his life flashed before him and he is glad to be alive," Ralph Gleason noted. The singer/songwriter met the press, though nowhere near halfway. Despite the warmth of *John Wesley Harding*, his replies to reporters' questions were as evasive and mocking as ever.

There was so much about this gifted, perplexing man no one knew. Jann Wenner wanted answers. His first letters to Dylan brought no reply. Then, in late summer of 1968, Jann traveled to New York to meet writers and record executives, tape a few radio interviews and see the play *Hair* with his distributor, Stan Binder. After a night out on the town, he returned to his hotel. There was a message: "Mr. Dillon" had tried to reach him.

Another two months passed. Then the *Rolling Stone* editor returned to New York with his friend and neighbor Boz Scaggs, who was looking to cut a deal with Atlantic for a debut album featuring Jann as co-producer. The two checked into the Drake, and shortly thereafter received a call. It was Dylan. He would be by the next morning.

Dylan showed up an hour early, clad in sheepskin and leather. Jann, half asleep and buck naked, received his guest while Scaggs stayed in bed. The meeting was brief. Dylan was there to check Jann out, to hear the young editor explain why this interview was so important to him.

Fully eight months later, at the end of June in 1969, Jann Wenner's persistence paid off. The Dylan interview, printed in *Rolling Stone*'s second-anniversary issue, was fraught with the usual aggravations. Dylan would not talk about his accident and how it changed him. He refused to accept that his songs had even the slightest influence on youth culture. He ridiculed the significance of his lyrics, the significance of Jann's questions, the significance of social change. He was Bob Dylan, distant and elusive.

But because Jann Wenner was a serious Dylan fan, his questions were highly specific and informed. Dylan yielded little ground, but far more than usual. The result was a landmark for *Rolling Stone*. Other magazines quoted from the interview, and in the eyes of his peers Jann Wenner was a dragon slayer. Said Jon Landau, "As Ralph Gleason validated *Rolling Stone* in the early days, I think Jann's meeting with Dylan marked an even greater validation in the eyes of people like me."

———

Sitting in during the Dylan interview was a man named Charles Fracchia, a thirty-two-year-old investment banker from San Francisco. When Gleason resigned as vice president of Straight Arrow Publishers Inc., in the fall of 1968, Fracchia—an old friend of Baron Wolman's—replaced him on the board and invested $10,000 in the corporation.

Fracchia, who enjoyed high living and Mozart, fell down the rabbit's hole when he came to *Rolling Stone*. His first encounter with Jann Wenner was to be at Fracchia's private club, but the editor's long hair and jeans necessitated a change of venue. Fracchia had never tried drugs until he attended a Straight Arrow board meeting that took place at the Wenner household and featured scrambled marijuana and eggs for breakfast. Later came groupies, Bob Dylan, Bill Graham and the Rolling Stones. Charlie Fracchia was getting a crash course in the counterculture.

To his eventual chagrin, the well-appointed investor taught Jann Wenner a few things as well. During their first trip to New York together, Fracchia checked into the Plaza Hotel while Jann opted for the Chelsea, a nexus of hip sleaze that lost its appeal to Jann the moment he arrived.

"I can't stand the Chelsea," Jann told Fracchia the next day. "There's freaks all over the place. Can't you get me into the Plaza?"

Fracchia tried, but the Plaza was full. Instead, he called a friend who helped run the posh Sherry Netherland Hotel. "I got him a room," said Fracchia, adding wryly, "and before long he practically had a permanent suite there."

Fracchia's initial $10,000 was gone in an instant, so he and a few of his investment clients came up with another $30,000. But that wasn't enough either, especially when Fracchia got wind of the groupies ad. "I was horrified," he said. "Here we were, hand-to-mouth, and he tells me we've just spent seven thousand on an advertisement."

Still, Fracchia could not help but be impressed with his young business partner. Jann Wenner was getting a great deal of mileage out of relatively little money. In each other they discovered fellow expansionists. It was time to cut a few bold deals.

Mick Jagger called Jann in the spring of 1969. The Rolling Stones enfant terrible hadn't toured the States in three years, hadn't yet secured his role in the movie *Ned Kelly*; he was restless, looking for a creative outlet. Point-blank, Jagger offered to put up the money for a British version of *Rolling Stone* if Jann agreed to run the show. Jann flew to England in March, and together he and Jagger incorporated the Trans Oceanic Comic Company Limited. The first *British Rolling Stone* hit the stands in June.

In May of 1969, on a New York stopover between San Francisco and London, Jann purchased *New York Scenes*, an entertainment magazine for the East Coast's "nouveau hip." The magazine featured articles on rock, sex and how to get a cheap apartment in Manhattan. In exchange for ownership, Jann gave *Scenes* publisher Frank Enslow 10 percent of *Rolling Stone*'s stock. Charles Fracchia saw it as a sound investment, one that wouldn't affect Straight Arrow's cash flow unduly.

Both Gleason and Wolman thought Jann had lost his mind.

———

The summer of 1969 promised some forty music festivals across the United States—a season, so it was declared, of beautiful things, of abundant goodwill.

But the Family Dog's Tribute to Dr. Strange was nearly four years dead now, and since then much of that precarious innocence had been spoiled. A new thinking pervaded the festival atmosphere, one which promoted lies and hucksterism and preyed on the good-naturedness of musicians and their fans. The Luria Castels were replaced by former used-car dealers who made promises they had no intentions of fulfilling. Bands found their names on festival posters before they'd so much as seen a contract; top acts withdrew in a huff, while young hippies sat in the sod and smoked pot and tried to make the best of it. Money inevitably "ran out" before the final acts, who would then confront the hard choice of either refusing to play and thus alienating their loyal fans or playing for free and thus rewarding the promoter for his predatory ways. Usually they played for free.

Each and every festival caved in under the weight of greed, violence or rampaging incompetence. Jann Wenner, meanwhile, was embroiled in a festival fiasco of his own. In March of 1969, he, Gleason, Bill Graham, Chet Helms and several other unlikely allies laid plans for a free music extravaganza in Golden Gate Park. The Wild West Festival, it would be called: a nonprofit August weekend gathering of painters, puppeteers and the West Coast's finest bands. The organizers boasted that San Francisco, the cradle of the counterculture, would show other hapless cities how to put on a show.

By the end of July, however, the Wild West account was bone dry and its integrity under constant attack by left-wing fringe groups who charged that Jann and his fellow organizers were only trying to make a fast buck. One press conference followed another, a sound track of snarls and unanswered pleas . . . all of which degenerated, by early August, into the muffled death rattles of another festival not meant to be.

Painful experience advised, then, that the Woodstock Art and Music Fair would be yet another disappointment. The festival, originally planned for the artists' colony of Woodstock, New York, was chased out of town in May and relocated forty-five miles away in Wallkill. But the Wallkill residents wanted no part of it either; they applied for an injunction to keep the hippies out, forcing Woodstock Ventures to shuffle on down the road. Just a few weeks before the festival's August 15 opening, the organizers found a six-hundred-acre dairy farm fifteen miles northwest of Wallkill, in the postage-stamp town of Bethel. All this eleventh-hour deck shuffling did not bode well.

But the week of August 15 dawned, and no major act had yet canceled. The Bethel townsfolk regarded the probable onslaught with a passiveness not unlike that of the cattle chewing their way through the pasturelands of the Catskills. In Manhattan, in Boston, in Jersey, in San Francisco, word came down: Woodstock might turn out to be a trip, after all.

———

On Friday, August 15, at a disagreeably early hour, *Rolling Stone* staffers Jan Hodenfield, Greil Marcus and Baron Wolman climbed into a car and departed New York City, bound for Bethel. Hodenfield, the magazine's New

York bureau chief, had twelve days earlier suffered through a long weekend at the Atlantic City Pop Festival. This was his assignment; Wolman would be going to take photos for a book on rock festivals, and Marcus had been in New York anyway and figured he'd buy a ticket like the next curious hippie.

Eight miles from the festival, the *Rolling Stone* crew met a vicious traffic snag. Cars sprawled across the meadows, banging into each other, stalemated. Marcus, Wolman and Hodenfield agreed: this was an awful bummer. No other road to the festival existed, as far as they knew, and now everywhere around them, by unspoken acclamation, people were abandoning their cars, dragging out their blankets and bags of food—shucking technology, as it were—and walking.

After four hours of tedious maneuvering down a back road suggested to them by a friendly cop, the *Rolling Stone* staffers did the same. By early evening they arrived at the farm of Max Yasgur.

What they witnessed that first night was both wondrous and disturbing. A crowd of fifty thousand or so was expected, but this was at least twice that, and twice more were reportedly on the way. Instantly there was a food shortage and a water sanitation problem; instantly the portable toilets backed up, rebelling against the unprecedented numbers. That night it rained, not for the last time, and in short order the meadowland was reduced to a rank bog of shivering bodies.

The *Rolling Stone* crew left the mud village and checked into the Howard Johnson motel in nearby Liberty, where many of the musicians were staying. The atmosphere was raucous, with drugs in abundance. But reports of mounting chaos, of the festival being declared a disaster area, threw a shadow upon the gaiety, while outside the storm clouds threw stinging sheets upon Max Yasgur's children.

On Saturday Greil Marcus decided that chaos would overtake the Woodstock festival. He made plans to leave, but all flights were booked. Returning to Bethel the next morning, he discovered what Jan Hodenfield and Baron Wolman had themselves discovered the night before.

What was happening here defied historical precedent. Yasgur's farm had become the third-largest city in New York, a nation of a quarter of a million young people with long hair. A world without money, but also without starvation, as everyone shared what they had. People were on drugs here but not a soul died of overdose, and women took off their clothes but were not raped. Yes, it was a disaster, and a stunning victory over that disaster. The victory did not emanate from Luria Castel's Haight-styled vision, for there was no room to dance and it was too hot for costumes. And the leaders of the left could claim no credit for this—indeed, when Abbie Hoffman grabbed a stage microphone and began to issue his usual polemic, Who guitarist Pete Townshend swung his guitar and cut down Hoffman like foul ivy while the audience cheered. No, this was a triumph of the ordinary—a celebration of, by and for the masses.

Hodenfield had seen the reactionary *New York Times* editorial condemning the Woodstock wasteland as "an outrageous episode." How dead wrong they were, he thought, and he squeezed through the garbage and the exultation, scratching away at his notepad, determined to get every detail right, believing as he never had before that it would be up to *Rolling Stone* to set matters straight.

On Sunday afternoon it rained, again, and this time it seemed that perhaps the torrent would never stop. But it did, and helicopters punctured through the clouds and dropped flowers and dry clothes onto the field. The music continued all night long. At about four in the morning, Crosby, Stills and Nash played their first-ever concert-sized gig, admitted to the crowd that they were "scared shitless" and then performed brilliantly. Greil Marcus stood by the stage, stoned on fatigue, his mind jangled with images of children laughing in the rain, listening, his fine critic's faculties simply unequipped to sort out this bombardment.

Just a few hours later it was light. The rain had stopped; birds whistled overhead. Weekday was upon the world, and the Yasgur grounds looked like nothing so much as a muddy field of rags. Almost everyone had left the Woodstock festival now, and as Jan Hodenfield departed the proceedings, he could hear behind him Jimi Hendrix soaring through his psychedelic rendition of "The Star-Spangled Banner."

The guitar notes burst into the turquoise sky, one wild explosion after another. Hodenfield felt as if he were stepping into an entirely new world. The moment seemed declarative to him, the guitarist's electric anthem a clarion cry . . . for what, for *something*—what had happened here?

The *Rolling Stone* reporter made his way back to Manhattan, staggered to his office and slept there. When he had the strength to write, the words seemed to tremble on the page:

Nine days after the passing of the ABM bill by the United States Senate, an act bringing total destruction that much closer to being one man's temperamental reality, an army of peaceful guerrillas established a city larger than Rochester, N.Y., and showed itself imminently ready to turn back on the already ravaged cities and their inoperable "life-styles," imminently prepared to move onto the mist-covered fields and into the cool, still woods. "It was like balling for the first time," said one campaigner, her voice shredded, her mind a tapioca of drugs. "Once you've done it, you want to do it again and again, because it's so *great*."

And surely they *would* return to other Woodstocks, thought Greil Marcus as he drafted his article while vacationing with his wife in Colorado. "The limits have changed now," he wrote, "they've been pushed out, the priorities have been re-arranged, and new, 'impractical' ideas must be taken seriously. The mind boggles."

Joni Mitchell sang that on Woodstock weekend the world got itself "back to the Garden." Amid the bright and outrageous fruit, however, the crabgrass grew unseen.

Chapter Seven

THEY DIED
HORRIBLY

So enthralling was the Woodstock after-glow that when the Rolling Stones an-nounced they would be throwing a free concert as a "thank-you gift" to their American fans, no one laughed.

Graciousness, of course, was not the Stones' stock-in-trade. The band did not believe in encores, or in low ticket prices. "Thank you," from Mick Jagger's rubbery lips, oozed out in a vapor of sarcasm, suggesting at best a playful contempt, at worst something truly demonic.

The Rolling Stones, rock's ultimate narcissists, gaudy and uncouth practitioners of Western materialism, seemed to the Woodstock spirit what Hitler was to the 1936 Olympics. True, they proved they could be sentimental. On July 3, 1969, their former leader, Brian Jones, was found dead at the bottom of his swimming pool. Two days later, at a Hyde Park free concert attended by 250,000, Jagger read from Shelley—"Peace, peace, he is not dead, he doth not sleep, he hath but awakened from the dream of life"—and a thousand white butterflies were released from the stage and fluttered off into the heavens.

But by mid-October, three months after the butterflies and two months after the Woodstock miracle, the Stones were back in America and back to their old tricks. The best seats at their eighteen concerts would cost $12.50, an unheard-of figure, almost double what the Doors were charging. "It says," wrote Ralph Gleason of the ticket prices, "they despise their own audience." The American Federation of Musicians threatened to have the Rolling Stones deported.

Haughtily innocent, Jagger responded at a press conference, "I don't know how much people can afford. I've no idea. Is that a lot? You'll have to tell me."

On the evening of November 9, the Rolling Stones returned to the Bay Area for the first time since 1966, playing two shows at the Oakland Coliseum. The first set was a disaster: the band showed up late, the speaker system imploded and promoter Bill Graham wrestled with Stones tour manager Sam Cutler onstage underneath the piano. The second show went better, though again delayed for hours, and when Jagger flashed the V-for-victory sign and sang "I'm Free," the hard-bitten radicals who sought freedom for the Chicago 8 and the Oakland 7 booed him for his political insensitivity. Afterwards, the Stones defaced a backstage poster of Bill Graham's likeness, smearing it with cheese and liver pâté, and resolved to drop "I'm Free" from their set.

At the end of their touring road, Mick Jagger announced at a New York press conference that they would treat San Francisco to a free concert on December 6, the eve of Pearl Harbor Day. The hows and wheres were not detailed, but Jagger's personal secretary, Jo Bergman, soothed the skeptics. "Don't worry," she said. "We've always done everything at the end, at the last minute, and it works."

———

A few days later, Bergman flew west and showed up at 746 Brannan with a handful of associates. There Jagger's secretary confronted Jann Wenner's secretary, Gretchen Horton.

We need to make a bunch of phone calls in a quiet place, said Bergman. Can you spare an office?

Gretchen Horton did not see herself turning down a favor asked by the Rolling Stones. "Take Jann's office," she said. "He's out of town."

Returning to find Stones management planning the free concert in his office, Jann blew a fuse. Yet he confined his yelling to Gretchen Horton.

The *Rolling Stone* editor was still patching things up with Jagger over the *British Rolling Stone* mess.

The magazine venture had been pure folly from its inception. The editors Jo Bergman hired in London might have been right for the 1967 version of *Rolling Stone*, but not for the current and more professional rendition. The British staff's idea of good public relations was to throw a party for record executives and spike the punch with strychnine-laced LSD, which caused numerous hospitalizations.

Occasionally Jagger would stalk in and out of the London office, compelling the multitude of ultrafashionable hangers-on to sit up straight and put out their reefers. Otherwise, the singer only seemed to show interest in his magazine when opportunities arose to butt horns with Jann.

"Obviously," wrote an insider to Ralph Gleason, "it's a case of a couple of strong egos maneuvering for control of *Rolling Stone*." With Jagger's support, the British staff routinely threw out pages of what Jann wished them to print, and inserted their own copy. On more than one occasion Jann flew into London to berate the editors, only to find that those editors were gone and behind the desks sat strangers who regarded his authority with sneering disdain.

Sometime after the Rolling Stones landed in America to begin their tour, the *Rolling Stone* editor flew to the United Kingdom and pulled the plug on the British operation. On the return flight, Jann handwrote a long letter to his business partner. *British Rolling Stone* would have to be deep-sixed, the letter said, but he hoped their relationship would not suffer. It was easier said than done, he knew; the venture had cost Jagger some $40,000.

Now came a perfect opportunity to put the past behind them. *Rolling Stone* proclaimed the free concert "an instant Woodstock," while Greil Marcus hailed the band's brand-new album, *Let It Bleed*, as a perfect if disquieting entrée into the 1970s.

Originally, the Stones demanded that the concert be held at Golden Gate Park, the venerable site of 1967's Human Be-In. But bureaucracy and shoddy planning conspired to move the location twice in a three-day period. On Friday morning, less than twenty-four hours before Santana was due to begin the first set, a new site was found in the rolling hills east of San Francisco: the Altamont Speedway.

That Friday night Baron Wolman and John Burks arrived. Thousands more were there as well, encamped under eerie blue floodlight, smoking dope while engineers hastily wired the sound system and transplanted the four-foot-high stage that had been built for one of the earlier sites. Many thousands more huddled outside the raceway gates, which would open at seven the following morning. Scores of demolished stock cars sprawled like twisted carcasses on the far reaches of the track. Inside one of the cars, a Plymouth, two hippies loudly made love.

As Saturday dawn broke, Wolman strolled over to a hill to relieve himself. As he did, a rabbit sprang from the grass and darted away from Wolman. From nowhere appeared a Doberman. In its mad lope the dog overtook the rabbit and, in full view of Wolman, tore the little animal to pieces.

Shaken, Wolman zipped up his fly and retreated to the mobile home backstage.

At seven in the morning the gates were flung open, and tens of thousands of young Americans charged downhill, whooping like Apaches on a scalping expedition. Two hours later Greil Marcus appeared by the stage. He'd made good time here, to his surprise; the radio announcers were declaring impossible traffic jams all morning long, but the critic had gone 40 mph the whole way.

Marcus sat down and unwrapped the food he'd brought. In Woodstock spirit, he held up a sandwich, offering it to a stranger seated nearby.

The stranger looked at the sandwich, then at Marcus. He slapped the sandwich out of Marcus's hand. "I don't want your fucking food, you asshole," he snarled.

"Okay, okay," said the critic meekly as it dawned on him: *This is not, and will not be, Woodstock. We can't reenact it. Here people don't jam the back roads and frolic through the meadows with flowers in their hair, and here people don't share their food unless they're looking for a fight, and there, right in front of the stage . . .*

There stood the Hell's Angels, the concert's security guards. Their presence here was the idea of the show's chief organizers, the Grateful Dead, who'd been cavorting with the Angels ever since Ken Kesey had pacified them (so it seemed) with LSD over four years ago. Mick Jagger, always just out of his fans' desperate reach and wanting to stay that way, thought it was a fine idea—better than cops, certainly, and besides, the British Hell's Angels (admittedly not the real thing) had kept the peace at the Hyde Park free concert a few months back. The Angels agreed to police the stage in exchange for $500 worth of beer.

No severe objections arose from any quarter. In truth, the Hell's Angels were oft romanticized. The radical chic saw the Angels as their revolutionary musclemen; poets like Allen Ginsberg drew inspiration from their piracy. In

1966 a twenty-eight-year-old Southern journalist named Hunter Thompson published *Hell's Angels*, a book describing his years as an honorary member. Its opening words fed the fantasy:

> California, Labor Day weekend . . . early, with ocean fog still in the streets, outlaw motorcyclists wearing chains, shades and greasy Levi's roll out from damp garages, all-night diners and cast-off one-night pads in Frisco, Hollywood, Berdoo and East Oakland, heading for the Monterey peninsula, north of Big Sur . . . The Menace is loose again, the Hell's Angels, the hundred-carat headline, running fast and loud on the early morning freeway, low in the saddle, nobody smiles, jamming crazy through traffic and ninety miles an hour down the center stripe, missing by inches . . . like Genghis Khan on an iron horse, a monster steed with a fiery anus, flat out through the eye of a beer can and up your daughter's leg with no quarter asked and none given. . . .

Nonetheless, Thompson saw through the charred romanticism, believing that the Angels "will be among the first to be locked up or croaked if the politicians they think they agree with ever come to power." Then again, Thompson had nearly been beaten to death by the gang. From a distance, the Angels had irresistible appeal to writers like *Rolling Stone*'s book columnist, John Grissim, who had gushed only a few months back, "They embody the primordial energies of brute force, the excremental vision, and the freedom of the outcast. They are magnificent incarnations of the beast in all of us."

And now they were Law and Order. The thought did not settle well in Marcus's mind. He glanced up at the stage. Seated there by the Angels and by the equipment were the luminaries of this withering decade. Remnants of the Free Speech Movement like Denise Kaufman, Jann Wenner's old girlfriend. Timothy Leary, the acid priest, and Owsley Stanley, the psychedelic Great Provider. The West Coast's legendary musicians, its legendary promoters, its legendary groupies. The lionized organizers of Woodstock. All gathered here for this moment, this culmination, this extrusion from a five-year-long tunnel—all poised, this strange and giddy council, on a stooplike stage, surrounded by some of the most violent outlaws in America.

The music began at ten in the morning with Santana. Early into the band's second song, a hideously fat Chicano boy took off all his clothes and began to dance wildly. Marcus had not seen his like at Woodstock. There nudity came in gentle, willowy packages. Here at Altamont it blubbered forth like an immense walrus, joyously stomping on those seated nearby. Several Angels lunged from the stage, brandishing sawed-off pool cues loaded with lead. The crowd recoiled as the Angels bashed away at the fat boy, driving him back. As the Angels returned to the stage, so did the crowd shift forward. Marcus stood on one foot—there was no room for both— and begged those nearby to give him room; he wanted to get out. They did not heed him.

Again the Angels wailed into the fat boy, pummeling him to the ground. Blood poured from his nostrils. Santana left the stage as quickly as possible. Another fat naked person barreled toward the stage—a woman this time, but her gender entitled her to no clemency. The Angels bloodied her as well.

Up came the Jefferson Airplane, while back and forth charged the Angels, picking out heads to bash. Grace Slick petitioned for peace. For a time they heeded her. Then guitarist Marty Balin tried to restrain an Angel from beating on a black man. Balin was coldcocked, and lay semiconscious on the stage while his band played "Somebody to Love."

The Flying Burrito Brothers were next. Inspired by who could say what, they played better than ever before. There were no fights. Crosby, Stills, Nash and Young, heroes of Woodstock, took the stage. The quartet was nervous, their set perfunctory, while pool cues drove fans into the dirt like croquet wickets. Red Cross stretchers were passed across the stage. The Angels, their faces smudged with Owsley's acid, guffawed and guzzled beer. The stage was theirs and theirs only. One of them, wearing the head of a bear, clambered up to a microphone and blew into a flute. What came out resembled the shrieks of a beast being burned at the stake.

Baron Wolman took his last pictures at about four and made tracks. Jann would be furious that he left before snapping photos of the Stones. But Jann had also decided, after conferring with Gretchen Horton, that the omens did not portend peace and love. Even as he saw Mick and the boys off at the heliport, the *Rolling Stone* editor had decided to bow out of Woodstock West.

Seemingly miles distant from the bloodletting, John Morthland and Langdon Winner stood on a hill and tried to enjoy the music. It wasn't easy. The sound system was poor, and a rogue wind blew the vocals toward them, then away. If they squinted they could just make out the stage, but not the figures. For some reason, the music kept stopping and starting, as if the hand of God were skipping some great needle across a record. Now and again they could pick up the sounds of clamor and protest—"Come on, people, be cool." Then the music would return. It made no sense.

"It was clear that people wanted to have a good time," said Langdon Winner. "But they weren't." They were exhausted from the journey, then the wait, then the strain of trying to see and hear. It was cold, colder than the weather reports had predicted, and people began to set garbage on fire to keep warm. As the sun began to set, they dragged fence posts that had been cured in oil into the flames. An industrial stench wafted. Winner and Morthland began to feel sick. Back to the Garden? This was an urban slum.

Backstage, Marcus and Burks convened. The former had finally squirmed away from the mess near the front, found his car and driven to the nearby town of Livermore, where he called his wife from a pay phone. When Marcus told her of the ugliness he had witnessed, she scarcely believed him. "That's strange," she said. "On the radio they're saying everything's wonderful— great vibes, Woodstock West, everything's terrific."

Interesting, thought Marcus. So they're going to perpetuate the Wood-stock myth. All hail the golden calf. He returned to the scene of the lie and told Burks what he'd learned. The two began to think that perhaps *Rolling Stone* should not dignify this nonsense with full-scale coverage. Maybe a page-four column with the headline "Stones Play Concert" would pay suf-ficient homage.

Darkness began to fall. Still no Rolling Stones. Rumors swirled amid the tension. Marty Balin was in the hospital. Someone was going to bomb the whole raceway. The cops were coming. The Stones weren't going to play—they'd snuck out through the rear, leaving this dismal congregation of 300,000 at the bloodstained hands of the Angels.

But no! Answering the call of the dark, the Rolling Stones filed onstage. Around them the Hell's Angels formed a circle and walked backwards, forcing hundreds of Owsleys and Learys and journalists to fall off the stage, one on top of the next. Other Angels mounted their bicycles, gunned their motors and drove toward the crowd, forcing it back, then again, then again, producing no lasting effect. All the while the Stones tuned their instruments and Mick Jagger—an orange-and-black cape about his shoulders, his chest bearing the Greek letter *omega*, "the end"—paced and pranced and yam-mered, "All roit! All roit!"

"Jumping Jack Flash" erupted, the fans charged the four-foot stage and the Angels rained down upon them. Forced behind the stage, Greil Marcus could only see heads bobbing, figures flying in the air, like some Hieronymus Bosch nightmare ripping through the canvas. He saw the fat woman, nearly all her teeth gone. He saw the fat boy, bloody from head to toe. No longer was this morbidly interesting. This was horrible.

After a few minutes, waves of terror began to ripple through the crowd—acutely audible screams fluttering through the speaker systems. Hearing them from nearly a mile away, Langdon Winner gazed quickly about him, looking for exits, something the violence at Berkeley had taught him to do. Much closer, Greil Marcus decided he'd had enough. Mass executions could be going on for all he knew. He fought his way through the jungle of bodies, breaking into the clear only after many minutes.

The critic thus missed, by only a moment, the first stanzas of "Under My Thumb," during which an Angel brought his knife down into the back of an eighteen-year-old black Berkeley resident named Meredith Hunter— a diehard Stones fan, as it turned out—and stabbed him dozens of times and kicked blood out of his every pore and jumped up and down on his head while the Altamont masses stood frozen nearby. Marcus missed Keith Richards sputtering bravely into his microphone, "Okay, man, look, we're splitting, if those cats, if you can't—we're splitting, if those people don't stop beating everything in sight—I want 'em *out of the way!*" And like everyone else, Marcus missed the Angel's growling rejoinder: that if the Stones did not play, they were dead men.

Marcus stumbled near his car, and fell. Lying in the dust, catching his breath, Marcus listened to the final verses of "Under My Thumb." It sounded wonderful; the Stones were playing brilliantly, perhaps never better. Perhaps, it seemed, like their lives depended on it.

"The change has come; she's under my thumb."

A new decade had arrived. Paint it black.

———

Jann Wenner did not know what, or how much, his magazine should say about Altamont. But Ralph Gleason did. It infuriated him that the *San Francisco Examiner* and most other dailies were rendering the event as one of Peace, Love and Good Vibes. Four died, the media conceded, but four infants were alleged to have been born as well. It all evened out. Woodstock West, baby.

In his terse, nasal tones, Gleason urged Jann over the weekend to forget about whether or not his friend Mick Jagger's feelings would be hurt. Said Gleason, "We either go out of business right now or else we cover Altamont like it was World War II."

Jann took Ralph's words to heart. On Monday he met with Burks and

Marcus. They described to their editor what they had seen at Altamont. Both were depressed; Marcus was physically shaken, as if just now retrieved from the line of fire.

Look, let's forget about it, they told Jann. Or maybe we can't forget about it, but let's just not waste a whole issue on it. Let's move on.

Jann Wenner listened. Then he said: *No.*

"We are going to cover this thing," said Jann, his voice steady and resolute, "from top to bottom. And we are going to place the blame."

There was not much to be said after that. Lunch broke up. They had an issue to assemble.

Though the idea to cover Altamont like World War II had not been John Burks's, he made it his. This was a vintage Burks newsroom project. John Morthland and Langdon Winner were brought into the office. So was Lester Bangs, who had made the trip from El Cajon and saw much of the action at the front of the stage. Numerous other *Rolling Stone* staffers and friends of staffers had attended Altamont as fans; they were called, grilled by Burks and told to write down everything they remembered. Since Baron Wolman had left before the Angels ran completely amok, Burks and Charlie Perry began to collect the names of everyone at Altamont who'd brought a camera.

Bangs wrote a long essay describing the Angels' stageside reign of terror. Morthland interviewed the doctors and medical supervisors who sewed up the wounded. Accompanying Morthland was a *Rolling Stone* editorial assistant, June Auerbach, who interviewed Robert Hiatt, the doctor who tried to revive Meredith Hunter. In perhaps the tale's only blissful twist, Auerbach and Hiatt fell in love and later married.

Though Greil Marcus had no experience as a reporter, Burks dispatched him to the house of Alta Mae Anderson, the mother of Meredith Hunter. Mrs. Anderson was hospitalized, having suffered a breakdown, but her other children were there and willing to talk. What they had to say shocked Marcus. No one from the Stones had contacted the relatives of the deceased. No one said they were sorry. Meredith Hunter and his loved ones had been forgotten, swept under the Love Generation's magic carpet with the rest of the decade's sediment. Marcus relayed this to Jann Wenner, who told Marcus he would write the next of kin a check on *Rolling Stone*'s behalf.

That week John Burks located an eyewitness to the murder, who agreed to be interviewed anonymously. Burks pasted these and other viewpoints together. Jann did the final edit of the piece. The result was long, meandering and in places difficult to read. Like the event, the article was turbulent and frenzied. None of its three principals—Burks, Marcus and Jann—felt satisfied with the final product.

All the same, *Rolling Stone*'s Altamont story was a brilliant repudiation of the straight press's blind praise, a savage indictment of mythmakers and greedmongers. Blame was distributed in liberal doses: to Rock Scully, the Grateful Dead manager who suggested the Angels as Altamont's security force; to Sam Cutler, the Stones' operative who hired them; to the Angels; to the men who built the stage only four feet off the ground; to the hundreds of thousands of fans who allowed themselves to be bullied by a relative handful of hairy men on motorcycles; and to the Rolling Stones, the artful dodgers who declared to their fans, "Let It Bleed," and then escaped, their fine and flashy raiments unsoiled by Meredith Hunter's life leaking out upon the speedway.

All these things happened, and worse. Altamont was the product of diabolical egotism, hype, ineptitude, money manipulation, and, at base, a fundamental lack of concern for humanity.

Blame went everywhere, and some of it lingered at 746 Brannan. Among the tangled emotions in the Altamont article were guilt and self-revulsion. Jon Landau wrote it plainly, one full year before the disaster: "The Rolling Stones are violence." *Rolling Stone* printed these words, as it did just about any available verbiage pertaining to Mick Jagger's boys, not bothering to ponder the implications except, perhaps, to observe: in art there is violence, in violence there is beauty. Indeed. And as the Rolling Stones treated the Altamont masses to a first-time performance of "Brown Sugar," a song about rape and flagellation, several Hell's Angels carried bunches of yellow and red long-stemmed roses to the edge of the stage and flung the flowers into outstretched hands. . . .

———

On the thirteenth day of the new decade, John Lennon had his long hair cut off while his new wife, Yoko Ono, stood by and wept. Short hair, Lennon declared, was "more functional, and we need functional things."

Lennon would be thirty in 1970—suddenly old by Love Generation standards but, as always, a step ahead of his worshippers. Form must have function, else it must be shorn. Altamont decreed that Woodstock would not, could not, be recaptured. No longer would hundreds of thousands gather together in the mud and expect miracles from misery. As Sam Cutler, strung out to dry by the Stones after Altamont and subsequently hired by the Dead, put it: "It's the death of festivals. Bloody good thing as well."

In truth, San Francisco had been rushing kamikaze-style toward the disaster that became Altamont, hell-bent for an explosive finale. For every Luria Castel there appeared a Bill Graham, and for every Bill Graham a Los Angeles cynic like Don Kirshner, the man who gave rock & roll the Monkees and the Archies. The acid-dropping dandies who began everything, the Charlatans, had disbanded in June of 1969, six months after the Family Dog lost its revered Avalon Ballroom.

In the wake of the Charlatans rolled the bands who would be champions—the Airplane, the Dead, Quicksilver, Country Joe and Big Brother; but these bands were now America's, not just San Francisco's, and all this talk about a second wave of talent, then a third wave, was wishful. The Bay Area's soil still contained the minerals for sprouting greatness, as Creedence Clearwater Revival proved. But that same garden was cluttered with weedy imposters: Blue Cheer, Womb, Rejoice, Mother Earth and a host of others, bands anxiously passed on by record companies and *Rolling Stone* as the new guardians of the San Francisco sound.

The original Garden, the Haight-Ashbury district, now looked like a plundered graveyard. No band claimed to be from the Hashbury anymore; none, in fact, would be caught dead there. The prototype hippies had beaten a path, many in anticipation of the Summer of Love and the rest just after it. Their communes were now nestled in the countrysides of northern California, Oregon, New Mexico and Colorado.

The Haight was now what it once was, only whiter, uglier and far more dangerous. Those hippies who lingered in the neighborhood were hardly the old Hashbury's creative element. They loitered and panhandled; they rolled bums and were rolled themselves. Read the graffiti in one hippie crash pad: "I came to San Francisco with flowers in my hair—and I starved." Robberies jumped 300 percent in a year; people were stabbed over a loaf of bread. Cats did not prowl the neighborhood, it was said; the rats were too big for them. You could still buy acid in the Haight, but the new legions weren't Owsley clients—they were speed junkies and heroin addicts. Mere months after the Summer of Love, the womb of Good Vibes had become the nation's first teenage slum.

The most horrific symbol of a dream gone to seed lumbered forth from the Haight just after that blissful summer of 1967. While the Altamont planners were mapping their folly, a Los Angeles grand jury began its investigation of Charles Manson: a particularly intense Beatles fan who fancied himself a musician, with a particularly intense following of groupies.

These were girls on their way to the Haight, lost souls looking for something the Hashbury no longer provided. Come to me instead, Manson told the girls, and many of them did. Together they made love, roamed the southern California deserts and listened to the Beatles' *White Album*. In the lyrics to "Revolution #9" and "Helter Skelter," Manson and his family found a blueprint for a folly of their own. A revolution would come. Eagerly Manson's followers began it themselves in the summer of 1969.

The Tate-LaBianca murders made for sensational press, with the Establishment media casting Manson as the inevitable outgrowth of the long-haired LSD culture while the underground press deified poor persecuted Charlie. Seeing the matter as one that *Rolling Stone* was uniquely qualified to sort out, Jann Wenner announced at a staff meeting that he wanted to see his magazine do a major feature on Manson.

Jann assigned the piece in early 1970 to two Los Angeles-based writers: David Dalton, a British-born music journalist, and David Felton, a fine reporter who left the *Los Angeles Times* after seven years to become *Rolling Stone*'s Los Angeles editor. At the time, Jann envisioned a cover story with the banner headline "Manson Is Innocent!" When Felton and Dalton returned with their material, the headline instead became "The Incredible Story of the Most Dangerous Man Alive."

Felton and Dalton had been granted a two-hour interview with Manson, who wanted to promote his poor-selling album. The moment Felton laid eyes on Charles Manson in the Los Angeles County Jail, he thought the man scary and capable of murder. Dalton believed him innocent, even after two hours' worth of Manson comparing himself favorably with Jesus Christ, speaking affectionately of prison life and declaring, "I'm probably one of the most dangerous men in the world if I want to be."

Dalton changed his mind, however, when the two met Los Angeles County's chief prosecutor, Aaron Stovitz. Stovitz, for reasons of his own, outlined to the *Rolling Stone* reporters the prosecution's case against Manson in explicit, candid terms. It amounted to an incredible scoop.

With the Stovitz and Manson interviews, the description by Manson Family members of their racist philosophy and Dalton's remarkable photographs of the Family, *Rolling Stone* had a story as monumental as its Altamont investigation. But the writing was far better, and art director Bob

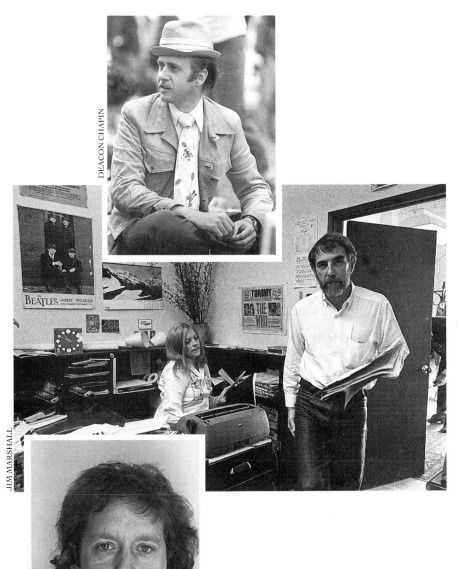

DEACON CHAPIN

JIM MARSHALL

JIM MARSHALL

The proud, the few, the unpaid of 1968:
Charlie Perry, longtime copy chief and
"Jann's first sucker" (above); secretary
Gretchen Horton and art director Robert
Kingsbury (middle); chief photographer
Baron Wolman (below).

Greil Marcus (above) became
Rolling Stone's first reviews
editor in 1969 and made music
critics Lester Bangs (right) and
Ed Ward (below) mainstays.

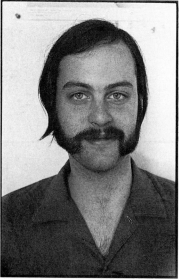

Ben Fong-Torres, the magazine's first music editor, in the Brannan office with fellow music writers John Morthland (center) and Langdon Winner (right).

Wenner and managing editor John Burks (center) discussing expansion possibilities with an architect, early 1970. A few weeks later, *Rolling Stone* relocated, but even the new offices weren't big enough for the two men. After a brief but emotional power struggle, Burks quit.

Rolling Stone's stars of the early seventies: senior editor Joe Eszterhas (left) and managing editor Paul Scanlon (right) with Wenner.

Associate editor Grover Lewis at Jerry's Inn – "a dreary bar with a Formica personality where the *Stone* coolies drink their Ripple," as one writer outside the circle put it.

Right: Associate editor David Felton, a.k.a. the Stonecutter, for his inability to meet deadlines.

Dr. Hunter S. Thompson: escorting
debutantes as a high school student in
1954 (far right) and on the campaign
trail with Senator George McGovern.

Above left: Reviews editor Jon Landau wrote, "I have seen rock & roll's future and its name is Springsteen," left *Rolling Stone* and became the Asbury Park, New Jersey, musician's producer/manager in 1975. Above right: Associate editors Howard Kohn and David Weir at the press conference following the release of their sensational Patty Hearst article in 1975. Bottom: Politics editor Richard N. Goodwin and Jann Wenner at the Elko, Nevada, think-tank conference of 1974. Goodwin's ground time with *Rolling Stone* was brief.

Kingsbury's spare design (which cast the cult leader in a malevolent yellow) was among his finest ever.

As with Altamont, *Rolling Stone* found its natural angle, exploring Manson's connection to the rock & roll world and how his alienation from Beach Boy Dennis Wilson and producer Terry Melcher may have incited Manson to violence. Furthermore, the Felton/Dalton article stated, the counterculture could no more absolve itself of Manson's crimes than it could of the Altamont fiasco:

> Charles Manson raises some very serious questions about our culture, whether he is entirely part of it or not. For actually we are not yet a culture at all, but a sort of pre-culture, a gathering of disenchanted seekers, an ovum unfertilized. . . . In the meantime we must suffer the void, waiting for the subversives in power to die, waiting for the old, dead, amoral culture to be buried. . . . Into this void, this seemingly endless river of shit, on top of it, if you will, rode Charlie Manson in the fall of 1967, full of charm and truth and gentle goodness. . . . This smiling, dancing music man offered a refreshing short cut, a genuine and revolutionary new morality that redefines or rather eliminates the historic boundaries between life and death. . . . [T]hat a number of lost children seem willing to believe him is indeed a disturbing sing of the times.

After the June 25, 1970, issue came out, Manson followers began to appear at the *Rolling Stone* offices, demanding an audience with Jann. Two young men made repeated visits; one carried a switchblade, which he slapped against his palm while Gretchen Horton assured them Mr. Wenner was gone for the day. Finally, she had them thrown out by a couple of the larger staffers.

Shortly thereafter, Horton received a card which read: "Gretchen, for a trip, try *Rubber Soul* #12." A chill ran down her spine as she recalled the twelfth song on the Beatles record: "Run for Your Life." Jann promptly flew Horton and her daughter to Seattle and hired Pinkerton security guards.

Later still, a freckle-faced waif took to visiting the office and chattering away in the lobby about poor Charlie while receptionist Judy Lawrence, noting the girl's pinwheel eyes, pretended to be interested. During one of these unannounced visits, controller David Lawson happened to be walking past with keys in hand.

"Can you give me a ride downtown?" the girl asked Lawson. Lawson said sure.

As they were driving off, Lawson introduced himself and asked the girl if she'd just been hired by the magazine.

"Oh, no," she said, and showed her teeth. "My name's Lynette Fromme. My friends call me Squeaky."

Lawson pulled over and let the future would-be Ford assassin walk the rest of the way.

———

The bottom of the Manson cover featured the headline "Our Continuing Coverage of the Apocalypse."

Dark drama unfolded everywhere; only the Who's deaf-dumb-and-blind boy Tommy could ignore the signs. In August of 1967, Yippie leader Abbie Hoffman had thrown dollar bills from the visitors' gallery of the New York Stock Exchange. Now the Weathermen were heaving bombs. The Jefferson Airplane once specialized in love songs. Now Grace Slick sang about revolution in the streets and on national television wore black makeup on her face and held high a black-gloved fist like the American sprinters in the 1968 Olympics. The Stones wrote "Street Fighting Man"; the Beatles, "Revolution." Each opted out of confrontation, but no matter. The two greatest bands of the sixties *acknowledged* conflict; they were *affected*. Tomorrow the world.

Joan Baez married former Stanford activist David Harris and urged girls to have sex with draft resisters: "Say yes," she said, "to guys who say no." For saying no, David Harris was awarded twenty-two months in federal prisons—four of those months spent in the Hole, dragged out once a week for his shower and otherwise as isolated as a living creature can be from America's continuing apocalypse.

Like cowboys and Indians in one of his beloved John Wayne movies, Governor Ronald Reagan and his troops did periodic battle with Berkeley and San Francisco State protesters. On May 15, 1969, Berkeley students were evacuated, by means of buckshot and tear gas, from People's Park, a condemned campus lot, an eyesore which students and city residents— some innocently, some in fervent hopes of confrontation—had taken it upon themselves to outfit with swings, slides and various forms of street sculpture. The fired buckshot injured over thirty-five students and split the chest cavity of a nonstudent, James Rector, killing him. That evening, at the governor's directive, three thousand National Guardsmen with bay-

oneted rifles marched through campus. Curfew was imposed; public gath-
erings of more than three people were broken up. People's Park was
permanently fenced in.

In February of 1970 Judge Julius Hoffman sentenced five of the Chicago
8 defendants to five years in prison for crossing state lines with the intent
to instigate a riot. All eight, plus their attorneys, were also found to be in
contempt of court.

Two months later President Nixon announced to a stunned nation that
the United States armed forces had invaded Cambodia. All across the nation,
campus ROTC buildings became tinderboxes. The first to burn was at Kent
State in Ohio. Responding, the President sent in the National Guard. Rocks
were thrown; guardsmen aimed their M-1s. Just a few days later, Neil Young
was singing about "four dead in Ohio."

There was no high road to take. The rocky road of revolution rose up to
meet the cold feet of Jann Wenner.

In May of 1968 he sent his message to the left: *Rolling Stone* is mine,
not yours or anyone else's. In the magazine's tenth issue, the editor—for
so long associated, however casually, with left-wing causes—denounced the
Yippies for trying to lure students and musicians to the 1968 Democratic
convention in Chicago, where violence would surely erupt. "The Yip
protest—in methods and means—is as corrupt as the political machine it
hopes to disrupt," Jann wrote. He added, "Rock and roll is the *only* way in
which the vast but formless power of youth is structured, the only way in
which it can be defined or inspected."

The young editor was well aware that *Rolling Stone*'s verdict in the matter
counted. Said Charlie Perry, "Jann struggled and suffered over opposing the
1968 Chicago Yip-In." Still, his editorial pulled no punches. In the end, his
suspicions about the bloody outcome in Chicago were well founded, as he
himself would point out in print.

Nonetheless, to some like former staffer Susan Lydon, "he showed his
true colors." While Warren Hinckle was encamping a huge *Ramparts* entourage in a Chicago hotel suite (running up a $10,000 hotel tab in the
process), Jann Wenner was in San Francisco, squealing about the mystical
powers of music. In the view of the left, saying that rock & roll was the
answer was ridiculous and downright cowardly. The 746 Brannan loft was
flooded with angry letters, while underground papers began, for the first
time but by no means the last, to denounce *Rolling Stone* as a capitalist shuck.

Charlie Perry's Berkeley friends turned on him. By association, he was no better than that pig Wenner.

A year later *Rolling Stone* pivoted distinctly to the left. The magazine's April 5, 1969, issue investigated a particular theme: "American Revolution 1969." Pages of articles dealt with unrest on university campuses—"the violent intersection," former FSM leader Michael Rossman put it in a guest article, "between the old and the new."

Most conspicuous about that issue, however, was the oddly reluctant tone in Jann Wenner's lead editorial. As if a gun was being pressed against his temple, he wrote, "Like it or not, we have reached a point in the social, cultural, intellectual and artistic history of the United States where we are all going to be affected by politics. . . . These new politics are about to become a part of our daily lives, and willingly or not, we are in it."

Jann Wenner, detractors would suggest, was the last person in America to recognize this. Until the April 5 issue, no one could accuse *Rolling Stone* of poisoning America's youth with politically volatile notions. True, the editors packed the magazine's pages with dope lore. But treatises on the history of Acapulco Gold cannabis and consumer tidbits relating to cigarette papers and plastic pot plants did not speak to a rioting nation. As far as anyone could tell, the Capitol had not been relocated to the Hashbury, jammed between the Print Mint and the Psychedelic Shop.

Still, Jann Wenner stuck to his belief that kids spoke through music, not with ballots or bricks. The new lifestyle would subvert the old order. Revolution began at the dinner table. Manifestos were bullshit, like gathering moss. As Dylan himself put it: "Don't follow leaders."

This rather loosely defined recipe for change seemed suspicious to the politically enflamed. Was *Rolling Stone* really interested in a revolution of substance? Or was Jann Wenner simply a younger, hipper Hugh Hefner with the same yen for hedonism espoused in the "*Playboy* Philosophy"? (The parallel between the two became even more irresistible in 1970, when Jann dispatched one of his staffers to scout locations for a possible "*Rolling Stone* Club," modeled after Hefner's members-only nightclubs.) Were music and dope tools for a movement or diversions from movements of any kind? This was a magazine, after all, whose subscription advertisement portrayed a wispy flower girl amusing herself with a reefer and a copy of *Rolling Stone*, while the headline made it plain: "If It Isn't Fun We're Not Interested."

The *Rolling Stone* worldview sounded especially ephemeral when preached over the din of political crisis. While the nation buried Martin Luther King, Jr., *Rolling Stone* published an obituary of "*Why Do Fools Fall in Love?*"

singer/songwriter Frankie Lymon; while America cried for Robert F. Kennedy, Jann Wenner fired bullets at the new Cream album. *Rolling Stone* responded to the rapid escalation of the Vietnam War with an article showing how soldiers were smoking good weed overseas. Nixon's election—a brutal blow to the counterculture—did not warrant mention, as the magazine was preoccupied with John Lennon's foreskin.

Now all this would change. The People's Park ordeal—a tragedy in the magazine's backyard—deeply disturbed *Rolling Stone* associates like Greil Marcus, Langdon Winner and John Morthland. The taking of the park by Reagan's troops said to them: *We do not want your contribution to this university. We do not trust you. You are the enemy.*

In an otherwise ordinary review of the debut album by British supergroup Blind Faith, Morthland drove Jann's "Like it or not" political concession right into the magazine's heart:

> The year 1969 has not been a very good one for rock and roll . . .
> Art theorists have hypothesized that artists are usually most inspired in times of crisis, that the forces of history push them to greater personal achievements. Perhaps the reason this does not hold true today is that while crisis is one thing, times are getting out of hand. With scientists calmly packing away quart bottles of nerve gas that can kill fifty people with one drop, military helicopters staging air attacks on their own populations, and atrocities bizarre beyond the imagination, the artist, too, must eventually feel the strain. Art suffers at the hands of Reality.

By the end of 1969, between Woodstock and Altamont, Jann's own convictions seemed stronger. Woodstock, he wrote on the occasion of *Rolling Stone*'s second anniversary, was a show of the counterculture's strength, but only a single gesture. He then stated, "If there is any hope left, I think that before the next two years are out, the culture we represent will make a serious effort at and succeed in taking for itself the political power it represents."

———

Just so it didn't take away his magazine in the process.

Through *Rolling Stone* he had fulfilled dreams, achieved stardom, won an identity. Now John Lennon knew who he was. They were friends, you could say. He and Yoko visited Jann and Jane, and together the four of them saw the movie *Let It Be*, which Lennon himself had not yet seen. Who in America would not have traded places with Jann Wenner that evening?

He had produced Boz Scaggs's first album—he was a *record producer*, just like Jon Landau. But his friend Landau didn't get asked to a Time Inc. "Meet tomorrow's leaders" luncheon. Jann did, and turned them down. *Time*, which ran an article on groupies just after *Rolling Stone*'s piece, never did him any favors.

He had been attacked, in print, by a Warren Hinckle publication, thus putting him in the company of presidents and popes. How it must have galled Hinckle to admit Jann's position among the music industry's "power elite"! And here was the old *Ramparts* muckraker, now a mere shadowboxer, past his prime. His media exploits went unmentioned by the press. No one lined up by the bar to hear what Warren Hinckle had to say anymore.

They came, instead, to twenty-four-year-old Jann Wenner. *His* magazine was on the move. By the end of 1969, *Rolling Stone* had nineteen employees; three months later it had fifty-five. Though *British Rolling Stone* hadn't worked out and *New York Scenes* flopped miserably, Jann was game for a new venture. At Baron Wolman's suggestion, he created *Earth Times*, a magazine devoted to environmental concerns. He also laid plans for a book company.

No longer could the Garrett loft accommodate *Rolling Stone*. When Ed Ward and John Lombardi began work in March of 1970, their desks were placed in the only space left: the hallway. Jann knew it was time to say goodbye to 746 Brannan. He called Charles Fracchia, who in turn contacted Ed Berkowitz, an MJB Coffee executive and one of Fracchia's investment clients.

Several weeks later, *Rolling Stone* deserted the Brannan loft, leaving its floor sticky with spilled sangria wine and marijuana brownie crumbs. The magazine had a new home: 625 Third Street, on the top floor of MJB Coffee's four-story facilities. Braced for further expansion, Jann leased the third floor as well. Straight Arrow's monthly payment to its landlord was $6,000—exactly $6,000 more than the rent at 746 Brannan.

———

It wasn't the rent that bothered Langdon Winner about the new offices.

Sure, there was plenty of room, and like everyone else, Winner far preferred the smell of fresh coffee beans to the reek of burnt lead type. But his studies at Berkeley taught Winner much about organization theory, and what he saw at 625 Third Street suggested a disheartening break from *Rolling Stone*'s communal past.

"In that first office there was sort of an open plan," said Winner. "It was just a warehouse, with Jann in a little office and Burks in a different corner, and otherwise fairly free-flowing and unstructured.

"Now, all of a sudden, you would come out of an elevator into this reception area. And if you were permitted past that area, you fanned left or right, and there were all these partitions. Now there was a hierarchy, spelled out in spatial form. One's value could be judged accordingly. And I in my own thinking associated that with the magazine's inevitable direction: away from movements and events, and instead oriented toward stars." The thought of this sickened the contributing editor, one of the many who helped build People's Park before its recapture by the state.

Burks and Marcus appreciated Winner's learned prose and gave him a long leash: he wrote a cover story on Captain Beefheart, dashed out a People's Park screed just before press time and wrote a variety of record reviews ranging from Paul McCartney to what could only be termed cultural oddities. Writing for *Rolling Stone* was a wonderful experience for Langdon Winner, certainly a nice diversion from grading term papers. But by the early months of 1970, other signs followed the move to Third Street that Jann wasn't going to throw his magazine to the revolutionary wolves. The "American Revolution 1969" issue had been followed by twenty-four covers having nothing to do with politics. The *Rolling Stone* editor had not expanded on the theme of his readership's "taking for itself the political power it represents." Quite the contrary. More and more frequently the word began to come down, by way of new reviews editor Ed Ward: "Don't talk about the politics of a record. Just write about the music."

Finally, almost a year to the day after the "American Revolution 1969" issue, *Rolling Stone* ran a long, venomous cover story on the Chicago 8 trial—a Burks project written by former *Ramparts* contributor Gene Marine. Just after the issue's release, Greil Marcus assigned Langdon Winner to cover a press conference in north Oakland, at the Black Panther headquarters. The featured speaker was radical French poet Jean Genet, who was touring the States on behalf of the Panthers.

Very early on in the press conference, Genet asked through his interpreter, "Is there anyone here from *Rolling Stone* magazine?"

Reporters eyed each other. Winner raised his hand.

Genet, bald and imposing, focused his sharp eyes on the young writer. "Your magazine has great power with the youth audience," he said. "But it is not living up to its role."

Genet went on to tear apart the Chicago 8 article. It was paternalistic toward blacks, said the poet, and "there was no political or revolutionary argument used." What little the magazine had to say about the Black Panthers was typically stuffed between stories relating to drugs and sex. How did *Rolling Stone* expect to enlighten its readers with such an uncommitted approach to politics?

There was silence in the room. All eyes were trained on Langdon Winner. After a few moments he rallied his courage and said, "Well, there are a group of us at *Rolling Stone* who are trying to get the magazine to cover political issues more closely. But we have some resistance to that from people who have a different view of what the magazine should be."

Replied Jean Genet, sternly but with a grain of sympathy, "My friend, those are only words."

———

Only words, perhaps, but the frustration beneath them was very real. Especially to *Rolling Stone*'s newer staffers, Jann Wenner's value to his own magazine was not entirely clear. He showed up late and promptly left again to dine with Timothy Leary's wife or Boz Scaggs or *Chronicle* gossip columnist Herb Caen or whichever record company fat cat happened to be in town. Often he was in New York or overseas. In his absence—as if in preparation for a royal entry—new furniture for his office arrived in crates: an antique oak circular desk, an antique bookshelf, a couch imported from London, all to be arranged neatly on the editor's new parquet floor.

Bills arrived as well, for these and other items. Those privy to Jann's expenditures were astonished. While his staffers were putting out a magazine every two weeks, Jann Wenner was charging limousine rides and expensive suits to *Rolling Stone*. Who did he think he was? Brian Epstein? Warren Hinckle?

In the meantime, the magazine's most hardworking employees—copy chief Charlie Perry and art director Bob Kingsbury—were putting in ninety-hour weeks, supervising *Earth Times* without additional pay. No doubt the new project needed supervision. Its editor, Stephanie Mills, had impeccable credentials as an environmentalist; she received national attention for her Mills College commencement speech in which she swore never to bring a child into a world as ecologically distraught as this one. Yet neither she nor her managing editor, Pennfield Jensen, had more than a dime's worth of publishing experience. The art staff was even less professional, to Bob Kingsbury's frustration.

What *Earth Times* seemed to do best of all was spend money and take up space. Gloom-and-doom stories like "The Story of Oil: Let Them Eat Ethyl" and "Nobody Loves a Fly" did not have magnetic appeal to readers. *Earth Times* died before its fourth issue, while *Rolling Stone* staffers were still trying to figure out why Jann had created it in the first place.

The editor seemed totally oblivious to his magazine, to his staff and to the times. The sweat he once expended to put *Rolling Stone* on the map was not apparent to new contributors like Jon Carroll, an *Earth Times* associate brought aboard *Rolling Stone* after the former's folding. Jann had hired Carroll, Ralph Gleason's former copy editor at the *Chronicle*, for the ill-fated magazine, saying, "Well, everybody says I should hire you, so I guess I should." After this, Carroll seldom felt the editor's presence.

"Jann had not been a factor in getting out the magazine," said Carroll. "If there was a time in *Playboy*'s history when Hugh Hefner just retreated to the hutch and screwed women with big breasts for eighteen months, that's what Jann was doing while I was there: hanging out with rock stars and taking a higher quality of drugs than his staff and not doing much of anything else.

"Here we were, believing we were involved in the greatest cultural revolution since the sack of Rome. And he was running around with starlets. We thought that Jann was just the most trivial sort of fool."

To Carroll and many other staffers, *Rolling Stone* was John Burks's magazine. Burks shepherded the articles, coached the writers, coordinated the design format with Kingsbury. His contributions were tangible and his coolheaded spirit most welcome. "John seemed like the man," said John Lombardi. "He looked like somebody you could trust and respect. And Jann was always this little elusive guy, skittering around, with motives you couldn't pin down. I thought Jann was an extremely intelligent guy, and I didn't like the sloppiness of John's editing. But as for the heart and soul, what made *Rolling Stone* a publication with a lot of potential for cultural impact . . . John Burks was far closer to it than Jann was."

Except to the magazine's music writers, Ralph Gleason seemed even further removed from *Rolling Stone*'s vitality than Jann. "He was considered an embarrassment by the staff," said Lombardi, "in terms of taste and thinking and writing ability. He seemed to us like an old guy trying to hang on. And there's nothing worse than an aging hipster."

At no other time had Gleason seemed more out of step with the staff's convictions than he was in the "American Revolution 1969" issue. Even as Jann Wenner was conceding that politics had changed the cultural landscape, Gleason was digging in his heels:

Politics has failed . . . It's all very well to talk about dying on your feet being better than living on your knees. Just don't ask me to do it. I'd rather be red than dead and I would also rather be alive than inside. The Beatles aren't just more popular than Jesus, they are also more potent than the SDS.

What do you think Dylan is doing up there in Woodstock? Counting his money? You don't resign from being an artist. Not until you're dead. No. He and the Beatles started something which is beyond politics, past the programs of the planners and out there in McLuhanland changing the heads of the world.

Out of it will come the programs. Out of it will come the plans. When the time is right.

A few months after People's Park, Gleason admonished all "grim, joyless anti-poetic ideologues" and assured readers, "The music will set you free. We know this. We have tried it and it works."

Staffers were aghast. What was this man talking about? Gently Burks would approach Gleason and urge him to write features, hopefully abandoning his "Perspectives" column along the way. But Gleason was a mountain that would not be moved. One did not edit his columns. One did not tell him what to write about.

Gleason's stubbornness exasperated copy chief Perry, who was quite fond of the *Chronicle* columnist and respected him as a music critic but joined the newer staffers in their distaste for Gleason's political treatises. Once, when Jann was out of town, Gleason turned in an overlong column a day after its deadline. Incorporated into the usual "The music will make the government tremble" musings was a confounding new wrinkle: sleep learning. Wrote Gleason, "I think America's children are sleep learning from Bob Dylan and the Airplane and the Doors and the Buffalo Springfield as well as from the Stones and the Beatles and Traffic and the rest."

Somewhat timidly, Perry called up Gleason. "The column's too long," he said. "I, uh, I have some cuts here."

Perry had in mind expunging from the text all references to sleep learning, but Gleason cut him off. "Why can't you run the whole thing?" he wanted to know.

To any other writer Perry would have felt comfortable saying, "Look, pal, *you gave us too much copy*." To Ralph Gleason he stammered, "Well, you know, we have to have an ad on that same page."

There was thoughtful silence on the other end. Then: "Can't you reduce the ad?"

Reduce the ad? Perry had difficulty containing his disbelief. "Ralph," he said, "if we reduce the ad, they don't have to pay for it."

"Well, then," said Gleason, as if the solution was obvious enough. "Drop the ad."

Gleason outranked Perry. The sleep-learning theory ran. The ad did not.

———

The younger employees also looked up to Greil Marcus, both for his veteran status and for his political leadership. In meetings at his house in Berkeley, Marcus would join Burks and Ralph Gleason in regularly haranguing Jann for his inattentiveness. At first, the editor seemed somewhat receptive to the criticism. "But after a while, he began to appear thoughtful," said Marcus, "which is not Jann's normal mode."

Marcus took no joy in his arguments with the young man he once thought so highly of. Jann Wenner, he knew, was not politically unattuned. It was the editor, after all, who stood by the policy of refusing to accept advertisements from the military—even when some staffers thought it might be an amusing idea. Jann even chided Marcus for having an account at the Bank of America, a financial institution with outspoken views on radicals. But it seemed to Marcus that the boy would not be denied his rightful spot at the debutante ball of rock & roll. The glamorous life, the John and Yoko life, afforded no time for tough questions.

The clashes between Jann and John Burks were, of course, more serious, as each argument implied a struggle for control over *Rolling Stone*. When CBS yanked *The Smothers Brothers Show* off the air for being too politically controversial, Burks thought a story was warranted. The editor nixed it.

"Why not, Jann?" persisted Burks. "It's what people are talking about. *You* watch it."

Jann Wenner waved the managing editor off. "It's not in our movie," he said.

On another occasion, the two clashed over whether or not *Rolling Stone* should make mention of the honorary degree bestowed upon Bob Dylan by Princeton. This time it was Burks who scoffed. "It's an *honorary degree*," he pointed out. "Those things are a dime a dozen. It says nothing about Bob Dylan."

Jann was beside himself. "If you don't see why we should publish this," he declared, facing off with a man thirteen inches taller, "then we're talking about two different magazines."

Burks stormed off. *An honorary degree.* This wasn't news. It wasn't even rock & roll. It was trivia.

———

Then the National Guardsmen arrived at Kent State, and all hell broke loose.

First the President announced that the United States would withdraw some 150,000 troops from Vietnam within a year's time. Two weeks hence, he informed a bewildered nation of an "incursion" by 8,000 U.S. ground troops into another country, Cambodia. That same day, April 30, he referred to student protesters as "bums." Four days and fifty rounds of ammunition later, four students lay dead on the campus of Kent State.

Outrage rippled across the nation's universities. Moderates and the politically indifferent became instant protesters. Campuses across the nation were trashed, then boycotted, then hastily shut down by administrators for the duration of the semester. Police buckshot flew in Buffalo; ten students at the University of New Mexico were stabbed with bayonets; eleven black students at Jackson State College were shot by Mississippi police.

Directly into the fray charged *Rolling Stone.* Burks postponed all planned features for issue No. 60 and fanned out his troops. John Lombardi was dispatched to Kent State. John Morthland was sent to track down the White House demonstrators who'd been visited at 4 A.M. by a restless Nixon. Burks instructed Jon Carroll to phone the White House and get an official response to allegations that Nixon was on drugs. Correspondents in New York, Texas, Georgia and elsewhere were contacted. Find the turmoil, Burks told them. The June 11 issue would resemble one great splatter painting of a nation at war with itself. Its cover title quoted Nixon: "On America 1970: A Pitiful Helpless Giant."

Jann, in the meantime, was puttering around Chicago and Lake Geneva. He was in New York's Stanhope Hotel, in a suite, cruising in style in a limousine, visiting Volkswagen account executives and the magazine's new high-profile distributor, posing for photographs in his custom-tailored English suit and being pre-interviewed for an appearance on *The Dick Cavett Show* by a woman who asked him, "How would you describe the philosophy of *Rolling Stone*?"—only to be told by the editor that well, *Rolling Stone* didn't really have a philosophy as such.

But that was changing, unbeknownst to him, at that very moment. Impassioned by Kent State, by the symbolic poignancy of Jann's absence and by Burks's decision to "detrivialize" the magazine, *Rolling Stone*'s staffers began to speak of the magazine as theirs, not Jann Wenner's. They drew up a manifesto, a list of "principles to be affirmed." The editorial staff would have more freedom and authority. Ralph Gleason's sociopolitical ramblings would not be published. Record reviews would not be sullied by Jann's whims. In essence, Jann Wenner would cede editorial control.

Gretchen Horton called up her boss in New York. "You'd better get home," she said. "The guys are having a war over here."

"What do you mean?" Jann asked. "What's going on?"

Over the phone she read Jann the list of demands. She could hear him crying.

———

In the reception lobby of *Rolling Stone*, Jann Wenner paced as he spoke. "We're not the *New York Times*," he said, his cadence even more nervous than usual. "We're just a little rock newspaper. We're not gonna turn into any big corporate bullshit. We're gonna do our own thing. We're gonna be better than *Billboard*."

Surrounding him was the *Rolling Stone* staff, their faces reflecting attitudes of worry and alienation and scorn. Vainly the editor attempted to rally their spirit. He quoted the Beatles. "We've got to get back," he said, pacing, punching the air. "Get back. Get back to where we once belonged."

The staff knew what Jann was really saying: No more politics. Jann's sentiments were shared by Ralph Gleason, whose continual misgivings about the *Rolling Stone* editor were more than offset by his unhappiness with the magazine's direction. Gleason had come to distrust Burks's editorial judgment. It was the managing editor, he believed, not Jann, who had lost sight of *Rolling Stone*'s mission.

"Get back," Jann repeated, several times over, finding comfort, it seemed, in the lyrics of his heroes. When the meeting broke up, John Burks marched into Jann's office and resigned.

Jann refused to believe that his managing editor was leaving. He told others that Burks was on a two-week vacation and asked Jon Carroll to step in as a sort of assistant managing editor. Carroll said that he would. Two weeks later, Jann fired him.

At about the same time, Jann fired Greil Marcus as well. Marcus had written a long and (considering the subject) unflattering critique of the new Bob Dylan record, *Self-Portrait*. The article had hardly been slipped in through the back door, as Jann had helped write passages of it. After the piece ran, however, his discomfort grew. It was bad enough that *Rolling Stone* was ranting about Nixon and the cops, but treating rock & roll legends like grubby street musicians was intolerable. Matters were not helped by the already frayed relations between the editor and his more politically sensitive associate.

At Jann's request, the two met to discuss how Marcus's role in the magazine could be redefined. By the end of the meeting, Greil Marcus was off the Straight Arrow payroll. Jann then commissioned a "second look" at *Self-Portrait*, one which described the album as "beautiful to listen to, an evolution in attitude and sound that works as well as anything Dylan has ever done."

A few weeks later, when Dylan's latest effort, *New Morning*, arrived at 625 Third Street, Jann sat with reviews editor Ed Ward and made it clear that Ward's review should be a positive one. Ward hadn't planned on trashing the album anyway, but the orders did not sit well with him. He wrote the piece to specifications but concluded, tellingly, "In the end, this is an album that, the less said about it, the better."

The departure of Burks depressed Ward and most of the other writers. John Burks had been their leader and their advocate; to many, he was their mentor. Clearly Jann had chased him off. Now with Carroll and Marcus axed, who was next?

Openly the editorial staff talked of confronting Jann. Excluded from these sessions was Charlie Perry. Though Perry had drawn up the manifesto and had at one point actually put his keys on Jann's desk in a dramatic threat to quit, no one disputed his loyalty to the editor. Absent as well was Ben Fong-Torres, who kept his own counsel throughout the mutinous talk. An affable yet intensely private young man, Fong-Torres thought the world of Burks, but especially loved *Rolling Stone* for its music coverage. He stuck to his reporting and avoided office politics like the plague.

If the conspirators snubbed Perry, they excused Fong-Torres, who was doing well just to be showing up at the office. His brother, a social worker, had recently been shot to death at point-blank range by Chinese gangsters. Though not given to histrionics, Ben Fong-Torres was understandably shattered.

———

While Fong-Torres grieved over the loss of his brother, Jann Wenner seemed arrested in a denial stage of his own. Even after firing Jon Carroll, he did not seek a replacement for John Burks. Instead, he simply skipped an issue, something that *Rolling Stone* had not done in two years.

Jann took Burks to lunch. The former managing editor had agreed to do some writing for the magazine, which Jann took as a hopeful sign. He spoke glowingly of the future, one word scrambling over the next as he listed new schemes.

"Look," Burks finally said. "I'm glad you've got all these plans. But make 'em without me, okay? *I'm gone.*"

Baron Wolman, there from the very beginning, was now gone as well. One minute they were sitting in Wolman's house playing Scrabble. The next minute Wolman was overturning the Scrabble board and yelling about how sick he was of Jann's competitiveness, how he always had to dominate things.

Now the former *Rolling Stone* chief photographer was writing Jann nasty notes, warning the editor not to use any of his old photos. Wolman was back in the Garrett Press loft, putting out a style magazine called *Rags*. Joining him were Jon Carroll and John Burks. The thought of it made Jann laugh darkly. Burks and Carroll always pissed and moaned about *Rolling Stone* not covering the revolution. Now they were covering . . . fashion.

Yet the editor's laughter trailed off. Mirth was hard to come by in 1970. His magazine was in sick financial shape. He laid off the receptionist and told staffers to cover the phone. John Lombardi, in his elegant South Philly way, told Jann what he could do with the phone.

His marriage was sick as well. Jane had taken up with musician Sandy Bull, a Chase Manhattan heir with a horrendous addiction to heroin. The Wenners, with Bull in tow, traveled to England for the much ballyhooed Isle of Wight Festival, where a drunken Jim Morrison lurched around backstage like the very embodiment of Festival Death. From there they traveled to London to attend Jan Hodenfield's wedding. Once there, Jann took Hodenfield aside and asked the groom-to-be if he knew where Bull could score some smack. Hodenfield told his boss he'd rather stay out of these matters.

Instead of returning to the States after the wedding, Jane and Bull hopped on the Orient Express. Jann followed them in another train. While he journeyed, the great guitarist Jimi Hendrix suffocated in his vomit and died.

Less than three weeks later, on October 4, Janis Joplin was found in her bed, lips bleeding, four dollars and fifty cents clutched in her hand— death by heroin. Now back in the office, Jann assembled an issue as fine as any Burks and Wolman had put together, with beautiful photos of Joplin by Jim Marshall and several comprehensive articles about the fallen singer. Yet the triumph brought no joy, only greater clarity to the pain.

Sandy Bull was living with the Wenners, leaving dirty needles everywhere. In the office Jann Wenner found no solace. John Morthland gave notice. *Rolling Stone* was no fun for him anymore; he wanted to live on a commune. Langdon Winner also quit, saying he didn't like the magazine's direction. He shook Jann's hand, wished him all the best.

Ed Ward left as well, fired after an argument over the redrafting of an article and the messy condition of the reviews editor's desk. He came to collect his belongings on the magazine's third-anniversary party. While the decimated *Rolling Stone* staff ate cake, Ward stuffed his records and telephone numbers in a cardboard box and a hard autumn rain pounded the office rooftop.

A year before, the *Rolling Stone* editor, flushed with power and ambition, declared his wish that his "third-anniversary letter from the editor" would be filled with high talk about the counterculture's political victories. But such was not to be. Jann Wenner had come crashing down to earth. He had no lofty message. Instead, he reprinted his editorial from the first issue, a humble return: "sort of a magazine and sort of a newspaper. . . ."

Inside *Rolling Stone*'s swank new office, the editorial staff looked like 1967 all over again. Aside from Jann and Ralph, there were now only three: Perry, Fong-Torres and Lombardi. And Lombardi would soon tender notice, deserting *Rolling Stone* for *Esquire*.

And the *Rolling Stone* editor would protest, saying that the magazine had big plans and John Lombardi was integral to those plans. "Get back," he would actually say, "get back to where you once belonged."

And when this did not work, he would actually turn on the stereo, put the record on the turntable and tell Lombardi to listen to the words, and with a confident smile would play "Get Back" and leave Lombardi to ponder the lyrics. And then he would return after the song's conclusion, bustling in, this nervy bowling ball of a man, and through his little boy's grin say, "Well?"

And John Lombardi would leave for *Esquire*.

This is how the seventies began for Jann Wenner.

PART 2

"A Goddamned Miracle Every Two Weeks"

Chapter Eight

JANN WENNER,
HIP CAPITALIST

*D*o you know what Chapter Eleven is?" Jann asked his new associate publisher, Alan Rinzler.

Rinzler said he didn't. "Well, listen to this," said the editor/publisher of *Rolling Stone*. "We get to keep the property, and we pay off our creditors thirty cents on the dollar or something like that. It's great!"

His voice tantalized with the same rah-rah charm that beguiled Alan Rinzler a year before. That was in 1969, when Rinzler—a New York editor at Macmillan who had published fairly unconventional books on photography and rock festivals—received his pudgy young guest and the large, silent companion who was introduced by Jann as "my bodyguard." (The companion was in fact an engineer for the Rolling Stones.) "He was very charismatic and charming," said Rinzler. "He had a sort of Huck Finn stumbling quality, but would then follow that with bursts of articulation and sheer youthful energy.

"Even at this point, he had visions of empires. As soon as he saw me, he said he had ideas for ten books, and he wanted to start a book division of the magazine. Then, perhaps the second or third time we met, he wanted me to come out west. And I laughed at him. I thought he was just really cute, but it took him a year to convince me he was serious. By the time he did, I was just fucked up in the romance of it. He really turned me on, actually."

Jann Wenner promised Rinzler the number two spot on the masthead, and stock options, and a book division all his own. "When I take this company public, we'll all be millionaires," he proclaimed. And so Alan Rinzler packed up his wife and children in July of 1970 and headed west, cruising giddily toward a dream that by his arrival was all but bankrupt.

Jann had boasted to Rinzler, "I have $100,000 in the bank," but this was not even close to the truth. *Rolling Stone*'s sickly condition was a secret known only to Jann and his financial confidants. Boldly he had assured *Newsweek* in early 1969 that the magazine was "comfortably in the black." But in fact *Rolling Stone* had been operating at a loss since its beginning, and by the end of fiscal year 1970 was over $250,000 in the red. Nearly half of the losses were incurred by "discontinued operations," meaning Jann's *New York Scenes* and *Earth Times* fiascos.

Charles Fracchia went back to his investors for another float, but the sum he accumulated fell far short of the mark. Jann dismissed him from the Straight Arrow board. The decision was not a pleasant one, as Fracchia's marriage and financial holdings were in tatters. But Jann had his own mess to attend to.

His wife, an equal partner in Jann's Straight Arrow stock, was globe-trotting with a junkie. His most valued lieutenants at *Rolling Stone* had disappeared. His makeshift publishing empire was in ruins. This time around, he could not curse the fates, his parents or Warren Hinckle. For his predicament Jann Wenner had no one to blame but himself.

Consumed by the magnitude of his failures, he wallowed in what he would later describe as a fundamental "crisis of the spirit." Often he cried on the shoulders of Rinzler, MJB Coffee executive Ed Berkowitz and Ralph Gleason. He spoke of giving it all up, of running away. An alarmed Gleason alerted board members to the distinct possibility that Jann Wenner might, without any notice, desert his magazine.

In the late summer of 1970, Robert Gutwillig and Richard Koff of *Playboy* met with Jann over lunch. Hugh Hefner was interested in buying *Rolling Stone*, they said. Only months ago, Jann might have laughed in their faces.

But anyone's money was good money, and talks progressed for over a month. In the end he turned Hefner down—partly because he wasn't satisfied with the offering, but also because Hefner wanted an employment contract which would commit Jann to remaining as *Rolling Stone*'s editor. Jann Wenner, in his jumbled state, could make no such commitment.

With Fracchia banished, Jann sought financial advice from Ed Berkowitz. Berkowitz lured San Francisco magnate Arthur Rock into the Third Street offices. Rock listened to Jann's plight and walked out five minutes later, saying he couldn't be of assistance. Later, however, Rock called Jann and said, "I have a friend who might be interested."

The friend was Max Palevsky, who as a driven young man from Los Angeles had designed a seminal computer and formed a successful electronics company, Scientific Data Systems. In 1969, Xerox bought out SDS for $100 million. Instantly the workaholic Palevsky became a tanned and toupeed playboy, a fixture in Vegas casinos and San Francisco soirees, a heavy contributor to liberal politicians and a dabbler in a variety of financial projects. For a converted hipster with money to burn, *Rolling Stone* offered considerable social cachet.

Palevsky agreed to invest $200,000 in Straight Arrow, a tremendous offering. The terms, however, were not so magnanimous. The investment stipulated that $50,000 would buy seven thousand shares of Straight Arrow stock, while the remaining $150,000 would accrue stock on an earnings-ratio basis—meaning how much stock the sum bought would depend on how well the company did in fiscal year 1971. Low profits for Jann meant more stock for Palevsky; if 1971 repeated 1970's pathetic economic performance, Max Palevsky would likely own the lion's share of Straight Arrow. The deal was complicated further by Palevsky's insistence that Jann's share of Straight Arrow stock be placed in a voting trust. Legal correspondence flew back and forth between San Francisco and Los Angeles. In the meantime, *Rolling Stone*'s financial desperation only grew.

Jann called an emergency staff meeting. The ad staff would be cut in half, typesetting would be done in-house and all employees would have to take a 10 percent salary cut, he announced. The news was not taken well. Many of them had been hired only within the last couple of months. They'd bought all that Hearstian talk about a *Rolling Stone* empire. And now they were being made to suffer for their boss's blunders, while Jann outfitted his office with antiques and parquet floors and zipped around in limousines and purchased ostentatious dwellings in Buena Vista Heights.

But the young editor vowed that the sacrifices would be short-term. He would reimburse the staff; *Rolling Stone* would see better days soon. And with that he dashed madly toward every money tree he could shake. His new distributor, Independent News, agreed to advance Jann $100,000 in exchange for a seven-year extension of a contract that, to put it mildly, took advantage of the magazine's predicament. Jann agreed to the terms, implying he would sign the contract extension, but in fact never did.

Next, Jann visited the offices of Columbia Records president Clive Davis and Elektra president Jac Holzman. He did not have to twist their arms. By now, *Rolling Stone*'s importance to the music industry was beyond dispute. Each executive advanced Jann for a year's worth of advertising.

Berkowitz purchased another $10,000 worth of stock. A handful of *Rolling Stone* staffers, under an employee purchase plan, invested an additional $30,000. On January 8, 1971, Jann's twenty-fifth birthday, Max Palevsky's check for $200,000 arrived. Jann would boast that Palevsky's money was no longer needed, that *Rolling Stone* was already solvent. He deposited the check anyway.

Even with the financial respite, Jann had more healing to accomplish. The damage to his staff's morale was considerable. Since the departure of Burks, most of the issues seemed utterly lifeless. Indeed, death—Hendrix's, Joplin's, the Haight's—seemed the only story worth reporting, and in its absence articles emerged from the very bottom of the grab bag: Pete Townshend blithering on about guru Meher Baba, a cover story on Polish rock bands, a wicked little stab at Dick Cavett presumably in exchange for Cavett's TV show's snubbing of Jann. "I'd look at those issues," said Charlie Perry, "and feel such depression, such a sense of diminished horizons and darkening skies. Frankly, we didn't know whether *Rolling Stone* stood any chance of survival."

Consequently, the staff had no reason to view Jann's trip to New York on December 3, 1970, as any sort of rescue mission. It seemed like just another opportunity for the editor to blow a wad of money. Traffic manager Dan Parker happened to be in New York at the time and caught a glimpse of the bill for Jann's ten days of limousine service: $5,000.

"Don't worry," the editor confidently told the former Garrett Press mailroom worker. "It'll pay for itself."

This time, he was right as rain. Jann returned to San Francisco on a midnight flight, cradling an interview transcript and grinning from ear to ear. Perry, who met him at the airport, saw the magazine's resurrection at that very moment. "Seeing how ebullient he was," he said, "I knew right then and there that we had a real scoop and that *Rolling Stone* would survive."

Jann had interviewed John Lennon, and what the great Liverpool musician had to say was staggering. The Beatles were finished, he proclaimed. This, insisted Lennon, was no great tragedy, for to hear him tell it now, the Beatles had never really dwelled beyond the pale of myth. He belittled his former band mates, particularly Paul McCartney, and claimed that Yoko Ono's "Don't Worry Kyoko"—a song largely comprising one long, hideous primal scream—was "one of the fuckin' best rock & roll records ever made. . . . It's as important as anything we ever did, and it is as important as anything the Stones or Townshend ever did."

With Ono at his side, the thirty-year-old Lennon sneered at Dylan and Joan Baez, cast aspersions on LSD and spoke of a womblike existence with his new wife. Each scathing judgment cut a vicious swath through the dream of the sixties. No other *Rolling Stone* interview would carry such resonance.

Jann and Perry drove straight from the airport to 625 Third Street. They hired typographers around the clock while Perry proofread the copy during a sleepless stretch of thirty-six hours. The presses rolled the following day, on December 16. Issues 74 and 75, containing the two parts of the Lennon interview, sold out. More copies were printed. Those sold out as well. Ralph Gleason, in his *San Francisco Chronicle* column, hailed his protégé's work as "a social document essential to our times."

Rolling Stone was alive.

———

Yet even amid the heroics of the Lennon interview, disturbing evidence suggested that the education of Jann Wenner, hip capitalist, was far from complete.

Lennon had granted the interview under one simple condition: Jann could not publish the text in book form. But when an excited Alan Rinzler saw the finished copy and declared that surely the Lennon interviews should be the first installment of Straight Arrow Books, Jann said nothing.

Well into the project, Jann sidled up to Rinzler. "Uh, I should probably tell you," he began, and stammered out his promise to Lennon.

"What?!" Rinzler, a man given to occasional histrionics, came unglued. "You can't do this to me! I've already made all the calls, I've got everything in motion—*I didn't hear that!* And I don't want to hear any more!"

Lennon Remembers was published in the fall of 1971, prompting an angry letter from the former Beatles songwriter:

As your company was failing (again), and as a special favor (*Two Virgins* was the first), I gave you an interview, which was to run *one time only*, with *all rights* belonging *to me*. You saw fit to publish a book of my work, without my consent—in fact, against my wishes —having told you many times on the phone, and *in writing,* that I did *not want a book, an album or anything else* made from it.

Jann sent a panic-stricken telegram to Lennon, saying, "Let's talk," and signing it "Love, Jann." Lennon rejoindered with a telegram that read, "Publish the letter, then we'll talk." Jann neither replied to the telegram nor published the first letter. Lennon's response was to withdraw Apple Corp.'s advertising from *Rolling Stone* for nearly a year.

Relations between the two eventually improved. It was Rinzler's fault, Jann would say. The devil made me do it.

Rinzler would forgive him. Jann Wenner, after all, was only twenty-five years old. He had so much to learn, all at once; so many dependents, so many lesser sorts who wanted a piece of him and so many enemies who would die for the chance to see him taste ashes. He was a kid, but great things were expected of him. If Jann Wenner fell short of greatness, he would be cast not as a boy but as a fool and a failure.

And yet Jann Wenner would not have it any other way. If riding high meant feeling the sting of frosty air, so be it. And if running *Rolling Stone* meant being responsible for fates other than his own, Jann would do what he could. He paid on time and gave out bonuses and his checks did not bounce. Success had made a fool of him, this was true. But how many people could wear the two hats required of the editor/publisher of *Rolling Stone* without appearing a bit ludicrous at times? How many would even dare to try?

He would suffer the barbs of the Burkses and the Marcuses, who never bothered to consider that people bought *Rolling Stone* to read about music, not politics, and that if *Rolling Stone* went the way of the revolution, its employees would soon be jobless. "You know," he told Charlie Perry during this period, "when I was younger I used to think that only ideologies could save the world. But now the most important thing seems to be running things well." Perry had to glance back to make sure he wasn't listening to some world-weary, middle-aged CEO.

His subordinates would never understand the maddening scope of his duties. Details rose up at every turn like walls of poison ivy. The subscriptions manager was a crook—he was siphoning off dollars and directing them into a phony account. A postal strike was crippling *Rolling Stone*'s new promotional campaign. The magazine's new Mexican edition was being run by a fraud who printed whatever he pleased. Each issue of the British edition (a reprint of the American version, not the publication co-sponsored by Jagger) had to be trotted past lawyers due to that nation's intricate libel laws. A distributor in Los Angeles was returning more copies than were being sold to him. He was scamming Jann, but how? It wasn't just lonely at the top; it was excruciatingly weird.

Yet it was becoming increasingly difficult to get the best of the *Rolling Stone* editor. The lessons were hard, but he learned them well. Jan Hodenfield, by 1970 the magazine's London bureau chief, would never forget the time Jann flew to London to interview potential new distributors for the British subsidiary of *Rolling Stone*. In an old wood-paneled office in venerable Hanover Square, a bushy-browed gentleman from Condé Nast received the two as if they were pets not yet housebroken. Jann permitted the man to patronize them until it was his turn to speak.

"Jann's performance was amazing," said Hodenfield. "He had all the figures down. He was on top of every single minute facet of distribution, things that were way beyond my experience and comprehension. But what I *could* comprehend was this old man, shrinking in his seat right in front of us. Jann just wiped him out. And from that moment on I always respected him. *He was just so good.*"

But like the girl with the curl, Jann Wenner could also stun colleagues with his awfulness. For someone so effective at direct, one-on-one appeals, his charisma altogether vanished in front of larger groups. Boy Wonder became Berkeley Dropout, his message dissolving into a quaking abyss of you-knows and blah-blah-blahs. Painfully aware of his limited speaking skills, Jann tended to fortify himself before manning the podium, which improved his spirits but not his oratory. After watching his distinctly sloshed boss slur his way through a speech at a distributors' convention, Dan Parker had to ask himself, "How in the hell did this man ever convince me to leave Garrett Press?"

His business sense blended hippie morality with a door-to-door salesman's flair for improvisation. Despite his own affection for three-piece suits, Jann's employees—including the advertising reps—could and did wear frayed jeans and beads and hair down to their shoulders for all he cared. He had no intention of running Straight Arrow like Time Inc. Nor, for that matter, would *Rolling Stone* chase the Establishment dollar. "Cigarette and cosmetic advertising will not be accepted," his advertising rate cards intoned—a stand that appeared rather bold until one tried to recall *any* tobacco or cosmetics company that had ever offered to do business with Jann's magazine.

The same 1971 rate card stated that *Rolling Stone*'s ad rates were based on a circulation of 250,000. In fact, the magazine's readership was nowhere near that high. It was not that Jann, in fudging on the rate base and other crucial demographic numbers, deviously sought to screw the system. He simply lacked the patience to go by the book. The book was a very slow read. It counseled prudence and bouts of outright self-denial. Its lessons were lost on someone of Jann Wenner's ferocious energies. The young publisher fretted over each cover, anguishing when one did not sell out on the newsstands. But the obvious solution—investing in a subscription drive to take the heat off newsstand sales—could not bring the immediate results he so craved. There was only time for *now*.

Jann's self-gratifying impulses were not easily reconciled with the magazine's economic hardships. Yet somehow he managed. Alan Rinzler and his wife had Jann over to dinner one night, and were astonished to look out the front window and see a chauffeured limousine parked outside. In London, Jann threw a party at a sumptuous penthouse suite for which the *cleaning bill* alone was nearly twice the monthly salary of his top British staffers. By 1971, one of the Straight Arrow board members was regularly supplying Jann with cocaine. He bothered less and less to conceal his fondness for the high-priced drug, snorting it at weddings and in hotel lobbies and, of course, on his desktop.

On one occasion, a drug dealer friend had Jann over for dinner and then dumped an enormous quantity of white powder on the table, railing out magnificent lines. Like a boy eating his way through a candy store, Jann grabbed two straws, one for each nostril, and snorted his way across the table before anyone else could get a chance. The dealer laughed knowingly as the *Rolling Stone* editor suddenly dropped both straws, recoiling and howling. It was sugar.

"He needed those trappings," said Rinzler. "He'd do all those drugs, and rent limos and hotel suites, and it made him feel better. The attitude was something like 'Even though we're hanging by our nails, we're wearing our best clothes.' "

It was an attitude Rinzler had to appreciate; without it his book division would surely have been scrapped. Straight Arrow Books may have come cheaply (Rinzler procured a distribution advance at no expense to *Rolling Stone*), but like most book companies, it was slow to realize even marginal profits. Without a great roster of authors, Rinzler contented himself with counterculture manuals and offbeat titles like *Swami Satchidananda, God Is Red, Chink, Kike, Mick* and *Wop*—not exactly high-yield endeavors.

The money had to come from somewhere else. An obvious answer was advertising, but here, too, glum new circumstances confronted Jann. The record industry was facing a slump in sales. Jann's decision to hike the per-page ad rate from $2,500 to $3,000 netted a nasty letter from Ralph Gleason and threats on the part of record companies to boycott *Rolling Stone*. Jann subsequently dropped the rate to $2,800 and resolved to end *Rolling Stone's* dependence on the music industry for ad revenue.

As a potential new source, Jann targeted Volkswagen, a lucrative company with a marketing approach far hipper than that of the Detroit automakers. For six months he wooed them. "Look," he told their account executive. "We're good. *Rolling Stone* has a demonstrated track record. We have an audience that believes in us. Talk to that kid on the street. Speak to some of the guys with long hair up in the media department."

But Jann Wenner was dealing with professionals now. Charm was no substitute for solid numbers. "We're broad-scale, mass-magazine-oriented," they told him. Jann's quest ended in failure when Volkswagen executives wrote *Rolling Stone* in March of 1971 and sardonically urged that Jann restrict his efforts to advertisers whose products were "perceived to be anti-Establishment."

Two months later, Jann launched a new advertising vehicle: local "flyers" to be inserted in the New York, Los Angeles and San Francisco copies of *Rolling Stone*. Instead of attracting advertisers in those regions, however, the flyers became an immediate cash drain. Jann sweated bullets. Looming over him was Max Palevsky's earnings-ratio deal. If fiscal year 1971 showed meager profits, Palevsky's $150,000 would buy a fearsome quantity of Straight Arrow stock.

His very parenthood of *Rolling Stone* at stake, Jann in the summer of 1971 took the hatchet to his budget. Gone were the flyers and their editors, including Jann's old secretary, Gretchen Horton, who had been in charge of the Los Angeles edition and who had once told a reporter that her boss "has a heart of pure gold." Article fees were slashed, hiring freezes established. Staffers began to mutter about the irony of their jet-setting editor laboring over every wasted paper clip.

Instead of using Palevsky's money for growth projects, Jann left it in the bank until the end of the fiscal year on October 31. The austere new budget, abandoned special projects, stock sales and advances from outside parties produced an astonishing result: Straight Arrow followed its dismal 1970 showing with a 1971 earning of over $400,000. Palevsky's $150,000 bought him a measly 7,610 shares.

And so Jann Wenner, hip capitalist, emerged from the economic crisis an enlightened man—a good-lifer given a mean dose of street reality. He and his staff had suffered to keep *Rolling Stone* afloat, without the help of the Woodstock Nation or any other communal vestige of the sixties. Jann and his loyal employees could depend only on each other, and owed the rest of the world not a goddamned thing. With a certain defiance, the editor addressed his readership on the occasion of *Rolling Stone*'s fourth anniversary —a birthday many had thought the magazine would not live to see:

> As long as there are printing bills to pay, writers who want to earn a living by their craft, people who pay for their groceries, want to raise children and have their own homes, *Rolling Stone* will be a capitalistic operation. . . .
>
> As attractive as it looks or may have looked, as lucrative and egoistic as the illusion is, we again disclaim for *Rolling Stone* the role as spokesman for anybody other than the people who write it and get it off the presses and onto the counters. We speak only for ourselves, hoping only that we do well in our own terms, as businessmen and journalists—that people will be interested in the same things we are, and at least respect our point of view.

The remarkable 2,500-word statement was explicitly worded, yet inevitably misunderstood. From the left came the usual catcalls of "sellout." From the right came gushing new admirers. The ultraconservative *Anaheim Bulletin* applauded the *Rolling Stone* editor for taking on "the bankrupt sort of modern liberalism," concluding: "He writes that this is fragmented; and we hope, along with him, that it is."

The editorial hung on the 625 Third Street bulletin board, where it was always good for a laugh.

———

Jann began 1972 with an itch for manifest destiny. He turned over his title of publisher to Porter Bibb, a former *Newsweek* executive and film producer. The move pleased Palevsky, who desired someone other than Jann running the business side of things. What Palevsky did not know was that Bibb knew even more about spending money than Jann did.

Both men were in the mood to talk expansively. "He was trying to put the best possible face on the magazine's business," said Bibb, "and I was trying to sell myself to him at the same time. So all we talked about was an upbeat future. We spent hours and hours talking about the idea that a magazine is not a magazine—it's a franchise: you've created an audience and now from a business point of view you have to try to see how you can develop the audience."

The man Jann sometimes referred to as "Porter Bigg" on the *Rolling Stone* masthead was a fount of new spin-off projects. *Rolling Stone* merchandise. A *Rolling Stone* book club. A *Rolling Stone* insurance company. A *Rolling Stone* travel club, sponsoring expeditions to Katmandu and the Khyber Pass. Television shows, newspaper syndication, a radio show. The acquisition of Sierra Designs Outerwear. Tomorrow the world.

A few of the ideas took. Jann put up money for "The *Rolling Stone* Radio Hour," for a new San Francisco magazine, for a well-appointed New York sales office on Fifty-sixth Street and Park Avenue and for "Project A," a top-secret scheme to shrink-wrap the magazine with assorted T-shirts and bumper stickers. ("This is the potentially most exciting idea now under consideration," the 1972 business plan gushed, "speaking to enormous revenues, the infusion of a new concept/element into *RS* and the future of publishing generally.")

Once again, however, the projects produced only immediate losses. By the spring of 1972 Jann had dug *Rolling Stone* into yet another financial hole, and stockholders clamored for his head. At a board meeting they confronted him. He began to cry. All his life he'd never been good at saving money, he confessed to them—his sisters had, but he hadn't. But in a cracking voice he pledged to change. As a dramatic gesture of this, Jann ordered the photocopier turned off and the supply cabinet locked.

The familiar summertime blues dropped down upon *Rolling Stone*. Writers spoke wryly of being put on the Wenner Plan, meaning taken off salary and paid as freelancers. All plans, including those for the heralded "Project A," were put on hold. Memos urged staffers to call collect or to limit their long-distance calls to three minutes. To help remind them, three-minute egg timers were put on every desk.

The sudden tightening of the purse strings vexed Bibb. "You can't go out in the normal throes of the magazine business and compete with everybody without spending money," he told Jann. But the editor lent no sympathetic ear.

Bibb paid a call on Larry Durocher, the former publisher of the *Cambridge*

Phoenix. The stocky, walrus-mustached man with deep roots in New England politics and a Boston accent to match had been recommended to Bibb by Jon Landau, who was writing columns for the *Phoenix* and *Rolling Stone* at the same time and had enormous respect for Durocher's abilities.

It became clear to Durocher that Bibb was out of his element with *Rolling Stone.* "He was wearing pressed dungarees and Gucci shoes with little buckles on 'em," Durocher said. "God, I thought he was the cutest thing I had ever seen. Now, Porter was terrifically bright. But he was not intimately familiar with the real internal workings of a small newsprint publication and really didn't have quite the feel at that time for the dynamic of it. The magazines he'd been involved in before had a certain weight and ballast of their own. They stayed upright when you walked away.

"Now all of a sudden he's walking around in a canoe with his Gucci shoes. And this situation didn't work well for a corker like Porter. He always tended to be one of these guys who couldn't quit selling when the sale was made."

Bibb invited Durocher up to San Francisco to survey the situation. A month or so later, the two met back in New York to discuss Durocher's assessment. "Let's take a walk," he told Bibb that evening.

As they strolled, Durocher delivered the bad news. The details were ugly, but Bibb wanted to hear them all. The walk took them from the magazine's sales office on Fifty-sixth up to Harlem and back again. It was light when they returned.

"Here you had this magazine that was a great critical success," Durocher later said, "but everything was just crumbling around it. Instead of taking the central premise and making it better and bigger, they started these satellite operations, and these activities were just sucking everything away from the central activity. And the central activity that they thought they had on autopilot going six hundred miles an hour was indeed hanging on a stall and really in trouble."

By the fall of 1972, Porter Bibb was told by Jann Wenner, "Things are not working out. *You're* not working out." His replacement was Larry Durocher.

———

"The things Larry did to turn the magazine around," said Tom Baker, *Rolling Stone*'s vice president under Durocher, "were not all that difficult to accomplish. Nor were they even that difficult to determine as the right things to do."

Yet for whatever reason, Jann could not solve *Rolling Stone*'s problems and neither could Rinzler and Bibb. Durocher, Bibb would concede, "was imbued with a different kind of enthusiasm. He was a very pragmatic, results-oriented guy coming out of the political world with a very can-do outlook."

Durocher's first task was to tear the magazine away from its current distributor, Independent News. Jann's contract with Independent was to expire on March 1, 1973, but in exchange for a $100,000 advance, he had agreed verbally to a seven-year extension of the deal.

The contract—negotiated by Jann "without advice or professional help," he wrote in a letter to Palevsky—was about as one-sided as an agreement could be. Shortly after signing it, Jann returned to Independent's office in New York with Alan Rinzler and literally begged for new terms. Rinzler later described the meeting for the *San Francisco Sunday Examiner and Chronicle*:

> Jann actually got down on his knees, cajoling, berating, pleading for five cents more a copy, for three cents more a copy, for two cents more a copy in our pockets, not theirs. He was sweating and his three-piece suit was too tight around the thighs as he jumped up and leaned halfway across the big cigarette-scarred desk.
>
> "Forty percent is outrageous. You took advantage of me. If I had known what you give other magazines, I would never have signed that contract. The returns clause is murder. You're going to bankrupt us, you're going to drive us out of business. Is that what you want?"
>
> We were up against the chief honcho of one of the nation's most venerable distribution companies. It was a rough business in the old days. Trucking wars. Lots of competition. He won. Now he's smiling benignly as he gently pushes Jann back into his chair. "What do you want, Jann, just tell me."
>
> "We want what's right and what's fair and . . ."
>
> "So . . ."
>
> "Forty-five percent."
>
> "And why should I give you forty-five percent?"
>
> "So I'll be happy."
>
> "What?"
>
> "So you'll make me happy."
>
> The man chokes in his face. "Hahaha." He can't believe it, he turns red with laughter. It looks as if he'll have a stroke on the spot, but he survives and we have to play out the contract.

Durocher was appalled by the terms of the agreement and immediately began negotiations with Independent's president, Harold Chamberlain, the man who had laughed in Jann's face.

"Chamberlain just hated Jann," said Durocher, "because Jann went in, made the deal, and then when he found out it was a bad deal he immediately started bad-mouthing Chamberlain. So in turn, Chamberlain did everything he could to torment Wenner. He just took delight in it. If there was an opportunity to give Jann money early or not give it to him early, he'd not give it early and wave a flag in his face. If Wenner complained about the distribution in this city or that, Chamberlain took great pride in not doing anything about it."

Over a period of time, Durocher sweet-talked Chamberlain out of the extension—"with the proviso," he said, "that I would write him a letter asking Independent formally to requote an offer. Of course, Wenner had no intention of using Independent again, but Chamberlain wanted the opportunity to write a letter to Wenner saying, 'I wouldn't distribute that piece of shit anymore.' " Durocher wrote the letter, Chamberlain rejoindered with his final barb and by the end of 1972 *Rolling Stone* had a brand-new contract with Select Magazines, the company that distributed *Time* and *Newsweek*.

The new distribution deal reaped immediate rewards. Durocher then turned his attention to the advertising side of the magazine's profit picture, and ran into another absurd logjam.

Since issue No. 8, *Rolling Stone* had a quarterfold format, which pleased newsstand dealers by taking up less space on the shelf. The quarterfold also gave *Rolling Stone* a distinct, compact look that staffers and readers alike found endearing.

But quarterfolding the magazine imposed a bizarre constraint that no one but Durocher seemed to understand. "One of the terribly shocking things I told Porter," said Durocher, "had to do with *Rolling Stone* projecting an ability to sell sixty and seventy pages of advertising an issue. And indeed, the magazine *could* sell that many pages of advertising an issue. But what Porter or anyone else at the time failed to realize was that the printing machines couldn't quarterfold more than eighty pages. When you try to fold any issue over eighty pages, it's like trying to quarterfold a baseball bat, and seventy-five miles of paper would fly around the pressroom."

The results of such a physical limitation were tragicomic. Said Durocher's subscriptions manager, David Obey, "The format dictated an absolute maximum number of pages that the magazine could have. So right around the fourth quarter of every year, when record companies would be releasing all of their product and wanting to place all these ads, we would actually have to *turn ad pages away* because we didn't have the room to put them in our magazine.

"So the cash flow would be nice in the fourth quarter, and Jann and everybody would start getting ambitious and start spending money. And then would come the doldrums of June-July-August and people would have to be cut back because ad sales were slim in the summer and there wouldn't be any money. We were constantly in the throes of this expand-and-contract cycle."

Durocher shattered the cycle by convincing Jann and the staff to convert to a flatfold. The new format not only allowed for larger-sized issues but also increased the printing speed and thereby reduced costs.

By this time Durocher had also pushed successfully for a hike in issue price and a switch from duotone to four-color. Each step, no matter how inevitable, required every particle of Larry Durocher's gift of gab. "We were very protective of the magazine," said Barbara Downey, a proofreader at the time. "Any change was a threat to the core of people who worked there. Any change was a violation, was selling out."

———

But Durocher took great care not to tamper with the essence of *Rolling Stone*. He would have been a fool to do so. For while he and Jann and Alan Rinzler and Max Palevsky were busy unknotting the magazine's financial snarls, *Rolling Stone* had somehow become the most dynamic publication in America.

It was, in fact, the beginning of *Rolling Stone*'s full flowering of greatness—"from late 1970," said Charlie Perry, "when we were down and almost out, to 1975."

Perry, the magazine's veteran copy editor, would count those years of his life as the ones most worth reliving. "It was exhilarating," he said, "like winning a marathon."

Chapter Nine

HUNTER

"A man is to be pitied who lacked the courage
to accept the challenge of freedom and depart
from the cushion of security and see life as it
is. . . ."

The sixteen-year-old boy who wrote
this sentence in 1955 knew something
about the cushion of security. He knew that his
friends had it and he did not. They were the sons of
Louisville, Kentucky's first families, and in their smooth
hands they held staggering fortunes from which dangled
Kentucky politicians and local police like oafish mari-
onettes. Theirs was a cushion of antique satin and down.
Princely indeed was their outlook as they toasted at their
steam baths at the downtown Pendennis Club, or galloped
across the Harmony Landing polo field, or sipped mint
juleps at the Louisville Country Club. What sensible young
buck among them would leave all this for the brutality of
"life as it is"? This was life as it should be. And it was
theirs by decree. They, and only they, would walk through
this hallowed dream.

The boy, Hunter Stockton Thompson, walked with
the blue bloods. They admired him, for he exuded a

powerful native magnetism no gold coin could buy. He was a tall, strapping boy, built like a swimmer, with brooding eyes set deep beneath his thick eyebrows—vaguely menacing, all the more so for his whirlwind mind, and thus a presence difficult to resist. But his parents were not Louisville liege lords. His father sold insurance and died when the three Thompson boys were very young. This left their mother no time for garden clubs. She worked as a secretary for the *Louisville Courier-Journal* while the boys' grandmother raised them.

"Hunter came from very solid middle-class stock," said a childhood friend, the future *Rolling Stone* publisher Porter Bibb. "And he percolated upwards, being very much the equal and in fact looked up to by the scions, the first families. And this gave him an enormous amount of power. But when the crunch came, when his friends went off to boarding school or got their new Corvettes, Hunter didn't have the goods. He was traveling in a world where everyone was filthy rich, and he didn't have a nickel."

All the Christian upbringing, the Southern manners and the exposure to the Confederate gentry's refinement could not conceal the rage exploding from young Hunter Thompson. "The Billy the Kid of Louisville," he would call himself. He broke into liquor stores, hot-wired bulldozers, stole searchlights from Sears. He tormented the aristocracy as their bolted portals tormented him. He vandalized their houses and spoiled their lawns with litter and tire tracks. Worse still, he dated their daughters, who found Hunter Thompson enormously exciting.

The fathers banned him from their households, but it did no good. Their daughters still managed to sneak their way into his long, athletic arms. He squired the Louisville debutantes, decked out in white tie and tails and a rebel's smirk. He wrote poems about them, just as he wrote vicious essays about their starch-collared, fat-assed daddies.

These he wrote for the Athenaeum Literary Association, the one social club that would have Hunter Thompson. The 150-year-old Louisville literary club met every Friday night, and all those present were required to wear a coat and tie. A member who missed two meetings was expelled.

For once, Hunter did not mind the social rigors. He loved literature, particularly that of F. Scott Fitzgerald, whose *The Great Gatsby* he would later proclaim "*the* Great American Novel, if there is such a thing." Writing for the Athenaeum's annual publication, *The Spectator*, gave him his first opportunity to channel both his talents and his rage in a way not deemed hazardous to society at large. He took the Athenaeum seriously, enough so to be an officer: the censor.

Even the boy's formidable criminal streak could not obscure his constructive potential. "Hunter was always appreciated by the authorities," said Bibb, "whether they were teachers or just older friends, as someone who had great talent and intellect and decency about him. Though he seemed hell-bent on self-destruction, people took an interest in him and tried very hard to set him straight."

But he pushed his luck too far. One night he went romping through the park with friends and harassed a couple as they kissed on a bench. The next morning Hunter awoke to find his mother having a discussion in the living room with two policemen. The charge, they said, was rape. They collared the Athenaeum censor and dragged him down to the Jefferson County Jail.

For thirty days he was held in custody while debutantes brought him sweets to eat in his cell. The school superintendent expelled Hunter Thompson, despite the fact that charges were dropped. The night he was released, Hunter stole a case of beer and tossed all twenty-four bottles, one after another, through the superintendent's living-room window.

It was obvious that the Louisville authorities had had it up to their jowls with Hunter Thompson. Yet he was granted a final chance when a local automobile dealer whose daughter fancied Hunter gave the lad a summer job driving supplies around in a truck.

"Hunter," said the man in a distinctly fatherly tone. "Now, I know you're a good kid. I know you mean well. And I know you're a good driver. But I have to tell you. This truck you'll be driving is brand-new. *You must not wreck it.*"

Well . . . he'd taken the alley at sixty many a time. Had that other truck not been parked there—had it been parked straight, rather than at an angle—then Hunter Thompson surely would have whizzed right through. As it was, the slice of metal removed from the truck was so, well, *clean.* It could have passed for a racing stripe.

But the Chevrolet dealer would not see it that way. No, indeed. His last Louisville advocate would turn on him like a rabid cur. Hunter Thompson drove the truck away from that hateful alley on a Saturday afternoon, parked at the dealership and walked briskly across the street to the Army induction center. Sorry, they told him, we've got a six-week waiting list. He muttered a few obscenities, then went next door. He took the Air Force's tests, blowing through them like third-grade multiplication tables. The master sergeant was impressed.

The following morning he returned to the Chevrolet dealer, hoping for clemency. None was forthcoming. Again Hunter Thompson crossed the street.

"How soon?" he asked the master sergeant.

"Twenty-four hours," came the reply.

The scourge of Louisville got stinking drunk that Sunday night with his friends. They got out their guns and sank a few boats docked on the Ohio River. The next morning he was on a plane bound for Kelly Air Force Base in San Antonio, Texas, chugging whiskey with the recruit seated next to him. When the plane landed, Hunter Thompson was carried down the ramp and deposited on the grass, where he lay vomiting while ranking officers hollered out his name.

There was no cushion in sight.

————

Airman Thompson wanted to "fly those fucking jets," but the Air Force had different ideas. He was routed into electronics school, and after that would be dispatched to some alien hellhole of a base, leagues away from adventure of any kind. Only the top student would get his pick of bases. Thompson, who claimed to his superiors that he harbored an innate fear of electricity, stood no chance of winning this opportunity.

Fortunately, a woman at the assignments desk took a shine to Thompson. She passed on to him an amazing secret: due to a procedural fluke, there were five base selections up for grabs that year, rather than the standard single selection. The four who stood behind the top student in line could take their pick. When the time came, Hunter Thompson made sure he was at the very front of the line. He selected Eglin Air Force Base in northwestern Florida, just off the beach.

Still, Thompson's outlook did not reflect the coastal sunny skies. The Eglin staff were as adamant as his superiors at Kelly about keeping him in electronics. You want out? they told him. Fine. Take a dishonorable discharge.

Again, good luck and a sweet inside tip saved Hunter Thompson. The sports editor of the base newspaper, the *Command Courier*, had been arrested in Pensacola for urinating in the streets. A new editor was desperately needed. Airman Thompson hastened to the base library, where he found a few yellowed texts on journalism. He memorized a list of buzzwords like "head" and "lead," then marched over to the Office of Information Services.

"The people in electronics were enraged when I got transferred," said

Thompson. "I told them, 'I've escaped, you fucks!' And they said, 'You bastard, this won't last long!' They kept trying to get me back."

But they failed. Hunter Thompson was a journalist now. He had a column all his own, which he called "The Spectator." He stood on the sidelines while the base football team scrimmaged, lounged on the beach under the pretense of covering skiing tournaments, went golfing while his fellows plowed through electronics manuals. Under the pen name of Thorne Stockton, he wrote a sports column and filed wrestling stories for a Fort Walton Beach paper, the *Playground News*.

Thompson's superiors watched him closely, waiting for a major slip. The sports editor, they agreed, was something of a discipline problem. He was cited for numerous uniform violations (favoring beach attire as he did), and more than once he left the base without bothering to ask for permission. Airman Thompson did not set a desirable example. "Sometimes his rebel and superior attitude seems to rub off on other airmen staff members," read an Eglin personnel memo. They threatened to send him to Iceland, but as yet he had committed no serious infraction.

This changed overnight.

Acting on the word of a reliable source, Hunter Thompson snuck into base headquarters while Eglin slumbered. There in the files he found the medical discharge issued just that day to the base football team quarterback, so that the player could sign with a professional team. It was the kind of scoop *Command Courier* writers seldom saw—the kind, perhaps, they had no business seeing, but this did not occur to the sports editor.

"I printed up the photostat at the last second, slapped it on the offset presses, without telling anybody," said Thompson. "And holy Christ."

The master sergeant who edited the *Command Courier* had a paternal fondness for his flamboyant sportswriter. He hated to see Thompson tossed in the brig. His tone was almost beseeching. "What's *wrong* with you, son?" he asked.

"Sir, I want to get out of here," said Thompson. "I'm just not fit for this place, you know?"

The master sergeant went to the wall for Hunter Thompson even as the higher-ups chorused for the airman's hide. A week later, the airman was honorably discharged.

———

Thus began, in the fall of 1957, the journalistic odyssey of Hunter S. Thompson. He convinced the *Jersey Shore Herald* in Jersey Shore, Pennsylvania, to hire him as its sports editor, though the paper had never employed one before. He and the editor got along so well that the latter set Thompson up with his daughter one night and loaned them his plush sedan, no doubt unaware of the Louisville boy's driving record. On that rainy night, Thompson and the editor's daughter drove out to a remote rural area to engage in some serious necking. While the two groped, the car dug itself into the mud. It took a surly Dutch farmer's tractor to tow the car out of the muck, and in the process the passenger door was somehow torn halfway off its hinges.

Thompson returned the daughter and the car late that night, drove back in his own car to his apartment and showed up at work the next morning, hoping against hope that the matter would somehow heal itself. Then he heard a clatter from the street. A crowd of staffers formed by the window and began to murmur. Thompson peeked over their shoulders. It was the editor in his car, driving toward the parking lot, the passenger door dragging against the concrete.

An eerie calm overtook Hunter Thompson. He knew what had to be done. He went back to his desk and picked up his coat and hat. He walked out the front door without saying a word. Then he dashed toward his car, gunned it to his apartment, packed up his austere belongings, threw them in the back of his 1949 Chevy and, with thirteen dollars in his pocket, drove to New York City.

He worked briefly as a copyboy for *Time*, then for several months at the *Middletown Daily News* as a general reporter. His tenure at the upstate paper ended abruptly after he kicked the office candy machine to death. He stayed in Middletown for a time, broke, living in a cabin and writing his first novel, *Prince Jellyfish*. When he failed to pay the rent, his landlord removed one of the tires from Thompson's car. The young writer rolled out his spare tire and fled the East Coast once and for all.

He made his way to San Juan, Puerto Rico, where he wrote travel articles and filed regularly for a bowling magazine. When money got tight, he modeled clothes. It was a life of daily improvisation—"running a lot of heavy gauntlets," he would later say, "with no real credentials and only the grease of human decency to get me through." Not every pensioner took him in, however. He petitioned the *San Juan Star* for steady work. The editor at the time, an Albany writer named William Kennedy, rejected Thompson, who then issued threats of a physical nature such that when Kennedy later took a liking to Thompson and invited him over for supper, Kennedy's wife wept with fear.

By this time it was 1960, and *New York Herald Tribune* editor Harold

Hayes was sufficiently impressed with Hunter Thompson's clips to hire him as a stringer. He began to brush with the sundry rapscallions of international journalism, drinking with them in strange Caribbean watering holes, listening to them talk of worlds he himself had only experienced through Hemingway novels. He deep-sixed *Prince Jellyfish* and began work on *Rum Diary*, a novel about the foreign correspondents whom he now called his friends. With an old Louisville friend and a girl named Sandy Dawn he'd met in Greenwich Village, Thompson procured a fabulous bungalow on Luquillo Beach, twenty miles away from the city. They commuted by old Vespa motorbikes and ate their meals by the beach. Hunter Stockton Thompson fancied himself unfathomably privileged, yet was somehow not surprised when his restless mind pulled him back to the States, all the way west to the stomping grounds of a hero of his, Jack Kerouac.

He bummed around San Francisco's North Beach and the wine country farther north before settling down in Big Sur. In the autumn of 1960, Big Sur teemed with artists and other odd collections of humanity. While Sandy made beds in a town hotel, Thompson sat by the edge of the Pacific and puffed on a pipe and put the finishing touches to *Rum Diary*. Though he never met Kerouac, he thought often of the seminal Beat novelist. "Kerouac turned me on to the idea that writing was fun," he said, "that you wrote about what you did." What Thompson did was scratch about for his own writer's identity even as he mimicked his idols: hitchhiking 3,700 miles across America in the span of six weeks, banging out distinctly Hemingwayesque observations for the *Herald Tribune* on his manual typewriter and constructing an intricate outline of *The Great Gatsby* to see how Fitzgerald had pulled off such a literary miracle.

With *Rum Diary* completed, Thompson prodded the *Herald Tribune* for new opportunities. Big Sur, for all its somnolent funkiness, was an intensely lonely place. Somewhat crazy to begin with, the young writer was driven to near-lunacy by the cacophonous sound track of waves slapping the rocks. By now he'd written two novels that would never see print, penned scores of articles which when patched together amounted to a formless body of work, and had roamed the free world like a sleepless fugitive. Now he headed south again. In Latin America he filed a few pieces for the *Trib*, and his work reached the attention of a new daily, *The National Observer*. The editors offered tremendous money, space on the front page and an expense account.

It was the last steady job Hunter S. Thompson would take for almost a quarter century—at which time the *San Francisco Examiner* columnist would write, "I have spent half my life trying to get away from journalism, but I am still mired in it—a low trade and a habit worse than heroin, a strange seedy world full of misfits and drunkards and failures." Yet Thompson was none of these as *The National Observer*'s South American correspondent. (He stood no chance of being a drunkard for very long, as the physicians who treated him for various indigenous maladies ordered him away from alcohol.) He wrote terse and ironic narratives often featuring the reporter as protagonist, just as Hemingway had for the *Toronto Star* after World War I. As a prose craftsman, the twenty-three-year-old Louisville journalist was not in the twenty-three-year-old *Star* correspondent's league. As a reporter of bizarre but telling events, however, Thompson matched Hemingway stride for stride.

In Aruba and Colombia he consorted with smugglers, lugging his cameras and his typewriter from one foul refuge to the next, submitting to their coconut whiskey and their requests for stories about Jackie Kennedy—"a lifelong acquaintance," he'd claimed, as a sort of passport. Rattling off serviceable Spanish, he covered political upheavals in Brazil and Peru, selling his pistol for food money, eating goat meat and leaves, contracting dysentery four times. In Bolivia he was bitten by poisonous insects and limped around La Paz, reporting on its sagging economy while the city lost all electrical power.

By the time his girlfriend Sandy had chased him down in Rio de Janeiro at the end of 1962, Hunter Thompson was a star, a chief correspondent in a white suit lounging on the Tropic of Capricorn. Repeated dosages of speed and cortisone and fear had caused most of his hair to fall out, but otherwise he had the world at his disposal. Other correspondents applauded his work. The *Washington Post* threw him a call in the summer of 1963. *The National Observer* knew they had a hot one. We'll give you the Caribbean, they told him. Or some other territory. Say what you want.

For now, at least, he'd had enough of the alleged glamorous life. "I want to go back to California," he told his editors at a Washington luncheon.

"Fine," they said. "Whatever you want."

So Hunter Thompson returned west with his new bride, Sandy, in 1964 and set up shop in San Francisco's Haight-Ashbury district. Fierce new winds blew across the Bay, he soon discovered. The Beats and the artists weren't the talk of the town anymore. Jack Kerouac's wild and wonderful Negroes had taken to the streets. Berkeley was ticking.

He watched with awe and excitement as Mario Savio and his lieutenants lashed the Free Speech Movement into the public consciousness. Thompson got on the horn to his editor in Washington. "This is a hell of a story," he insisted. The editor didn't agree. Rebuffed for the first time in ages, Thompson snarled, "Well, if you fuckers aren't going to cover something like this, fuck it. I'll just review books."

Which he did, for a few months anyway. His last piece submitted to the *Observer* was a wildly enthusiastic review of *The Kandy-Kolored Tangerine-Flake Streamline Baby*, a collection of odd pieces on a surging new American by an odd and surging young Southern journalist named Tom Wolfe. Thompson had not known at the time that Wolfe had been fired by the *Observer* and still had enemies in high places there. The review was rejected. Thompson suggested the standard anatomical impossibility to his editor, and quit his best gig once and for all.

Now it was 1965. Sandy would soon deliver their infant son Juan. Thompson, disgusted with the freelance life, now scoured the city for regular work. He could find none—not at the cab company, not at the grocery store. He grew his own vegetables and poached meat. That year he made the grand sum of $970.

To the rescue came Carey McWilliams, editor of *The Nation*. McWilliams called Thompson and asked him if he'd like to write a piece on something that interested him. Thompson had just the subject in mind. While roaming the Bay for work and action, he kept stumbling upon large packs of burly, hairy men gunning through the streets on Harley-Davidsons. They called themselves Hell's Angels, named after a World War I bomber squadron, and they seemed to live by some sort of violent creed, though it was hard to make out from a distance.

Hunter Thompson's phone was disconnected when the Hell's Angels piece ran. Laudatory notices of his work came in via U.S. mail. Six publishing houses sent him book offers. Each wanted a quickie, a sort of literary follow-up to the Marlon Brando movie *The Wild One*.

Thompson rejected this approach even as he signed a contract with Random House (who also agreed to publish *Rum Diary*). For about a year he hung tight with the Angels, gaining their trust, riding with them in the center of the storm on the BSA 650 Lightning he'd purchased with his book advance, wearing a tan sheepherder's jacket to distinguish himself from the clan but not managing to avoid constant harassment by the local authorities. Other writers and Berkeley radicals, imagining the Angels to be chic in their own brutish way, demanded that the liaison Thompson introduce them. At times he did. Most notably, he obliged Ken Kesey, who then turned Thompson and the Angels on to LSD and thereby set off a chain of unreckonable events.

Along the way, the writer showed the Angels a few of the pages he'd written. They were mildly amused, though one Angel wanted Thompson to remove the word "sodomy" from the text because the Angel's mother would be offended otherwise. He wrote as he rode, compiling half the manuscript in six months. The rest he wrote in four days, in a grubby hotel, on speed.

The quality of his work surprised even Thompson. Realizing that *Rum Diary* would not measure up to *Hell's Angels*, he asked Random House not to publish the novel. They ignored his request, so Thompson persuaded a Random House secretary to smuggle the lone copy of *Rum Diary* out of the building. In the meantime, a number of Angels waylaid Thompson after the writer refused to share his royalties, stomping him brutally and nearly crushing his head with a large rock. His honeymoon with the wild ones was over. As he would later confess: "Nobody with good sense would agree to live with those swine for a year."

But now it did not matter. The advance copies of *Hell's Angels* were generating enormous praise among literary circles. The book's first edition was sold out before the official publication date. *Esquire* offered a hefty serialization fee. And Hunter S. Thompson, the ultimate freelancer, the outlaw journalist, found himself on a thirty-five-day national promotion tour, doing as many fifteen interviews a day.

The time seemed ripe for another move. The Haight, by late 1966, was aswarm with bleary-eyed runaways and budding hip capitalists. Hunter Thompson decided to return to New York—to "whoop it up like Fitzgerald, be a famous writer," he said. Yet he only made it halfway. *Esquire's* money was slow to come, and Thompson discovered too late that his share of *Hell's Angels* earnings amounted to a paltry 5 percent. Enraged once again at the New York literary establishment, he settled down with his wife and son in Colorado, in an abandoned schoolhouse just outside of Aspen, in a blue-collar town called Woody Creek.

Random House sought to pacify its new star. Lucrative proposals were dispatched to his Woody Creek address. How about a book on policemen? On ghettos? Thompson opted for a project with the working titles *The Joint Chiefs* (his) and *Death of the American Dream* (Random House's). He sifted through the avalanche of freelance offers. As this year's fair-haired boy, Hunter Thompson could pick and choose, doing whatever he wished for whomever he wanted: *New York Times*, *Harper's*, *Playboy*, the *Boston Globe*.

Some assignments worked out; many did not. Editors who enjoyed reading *Hell's Angels* were nonetheless unprepared for the writer's hell-bent, semi-hysterical methods. He'd long since abandoned any attempt at Objective

Journalism—"a pompous contradiction in terms"—which did not sit well with the boys in the newsroom. His *Playboy* piece on the mass-marketing of Olympic gold medalist Jean-Claude Killy inspired one of the magazine's editors to write in a memo, "Thompson's ugly, stupid arrogance is an insult to everything we stand for." Thompson in turn denounced *Playboy* as "a conspiracy of anemic masturbators" and sent the Killy piece on to Warren Hinckle, about the only editor willing to give Thompson's predatory writing sufficient room to prowl.

Thompson regarded Hinckle as "the best conceptual editor I ever worked with." While others might have deplored Thompson's coverage of the Kentucky Derby—hardly coverage at all, for the writer spent most of his time brawling with drunkards and spraying Mace at fellow writers—Hinckle thought Thompson's rambling notes brilliant, and published them verbatim in *Scanlan's Monthly*:

> Pink faces with a stylish Southern sag, old Ivy styles, seersucker coats and buttondown collars. "Mayblossom Senility" . . . burnt out early or maybe just not much to burn in the first place. Not much energy in these faces, not much *curiosity*. Suffering in silence, nowhere to go after thirty in this life, just hang on and humor the children. Let the young enjoy themselves while they can. Why not?
>
> The grim reaper comes early in this league . . . banshees on the lawn at night, screaming out there beside that little iron nigger in jockey clothes. Maybe he's the one who's screaming. Bad DT's and too many snarls at the bridge club. Going down with the stock market. Oh Jesus, the kid has wrecked the new car, wrapped it around the big stone pillar at the bottom of the driveway. Broken leg? Twisted eye? Send him off to Yale, they can cure anything up there.
>
> Yale? Did you see today's paper? New Haven is under siege. Yale is swarming with Black Panthers. . . . I tell you, Colonel, the world has gone mad. Why, they tell me a goddamn woman jockey might ride in the Derby today.

Hinckle's vote of confidence in this reckless prose style overjoyed Thompson. It occurred to him, he later told a *Playboy* reporter, that "holy shit, if I can write like that and get away with it, why should I keep trying to write like the *New York Times*? It was like falling down an elevator shaft and landing in a pool full of mermaids."

The story was labeled "real gonzo" by fellow writer Bill Cardoso, and a new form—Gonzo journalism—was thus brought yowling into the world. The form was Thompson's, but Hinckle had much to do with its execution. After cartoonist Pat Oliphant turned down the assignment, Hinckle flew an obscure British artist named Ralph Steadman down to Louisville to illustrate the Derby. The pairing of Steadman with Thompson proved to be a masterstroke. Not only did the artist's grotesque caricatures suit the writer's maniacal style, but "The Kentucky Derby Is Decadent and Depraved" focused on their interaction—a Mutt-and-Jeff-stumble-through-the-apocalypse device Thompson would employ in many of his Gonzo writings.

Thompson's first foray into political journalism was published by *Pageant* in July of 1968. The subject was Republican presidential candidate Richard Milhous Nixon, a man roundly despised by liberals and the press, including Thompson:

> Richard Nixon has never been one of my favorite people, anyway. For years I've regarded his very existence as a monument to all the rancid genes and broken chromosomes that corrupt the possibilities of the American Dream; he was a foul caricature of himself, a man with no soul, no inner convictions, with the integrity of a hyena and the style of a poison toad. The Nixon I remembered was absolutely humorless; I couldn't imagine him laughing at anything except maybe a paraplegic who wanted to vote Democratic but couldn't quite reach the lever on the voting machine.

Thompson tailed Nixon in the spring of 1968, slogging behind the advance men in his mangy Aspen clothes, incurring their suspicions even when *Pageant* vouched for his pure intentions. When he got his interview with the candidate, Thompson was surprised. Nixon was a thoughtful, even *human* character—though as a politician, "still a devious monster." With Kennedy assassinated and Lyndon Johnson betraying the electorate, the veteran California politician had reemerged from the abyss: wiser, more relaxed and willing to spend ninety minutes being grilled by a speed-addled brute in a shabby ski jacket.

In an almost surreal episode, Nixon brain trusters Ray Price and Pat Buchanan agreed to let Thompson share a limousine with the candidate on a ride down New Hampshire's Everett Turnpike. The Boss was tired, Price explained; he needed some relaxing conversation. "They knew I was a madman," said Thompson. "But they also knew I knew sports." So for a leisurely hour they sat in the plush backseat, the two of them talking about the January 1968 Super Bowl: Richard Nixon, former hit man for the House Un-American Activities Committee, and Hunter S. Thompson, whose three heroes of the sixties were Bob Dylan, Fidel Castro and Cassius Clay. The politician confessed he'd like to be a sportswriter—this to a former sportswriter who was well on his way to developing a Nixonian addiction to politics.

The two would never speak again. But Nixon would remain foremost in the journalist's consciousness, a vulture perched just out of reach, its shadow forever upon him. "It is Nixon himself," Thompson would write four years later, "who represents that dark, venal, and incurably violent side of the American character almost every other country in the world has learned to fear and despise."

That same dark character clutched Hunter Thompson to its bosom in Chicago during the 1968 Democratic National Convention. Jann Wenner had urged his *Rolling Stone* readers not to go to Chicago, but Thompson was drawn there, and spent much of his time with the *Ramparts* entourage in Warren Hinckle's hotel suites.

He had attended the 1964 Republican National Convention at San Francisco's Cow Palace, wincing in disbelief as Arizona senator Barry Goldwater told the rabid throng, "Extremism in the defense of liberty is no vice." Yet even that grim encounter with national politics did not prepare him for Chicago. On the Saturday afternoon of August 24, 1968, Hunter Thompson stood on the corner of Michigan and Balboa, waving his press badges at policemen in an attempt to enter the convention hall. Thompson did not see the billy club until it was deeply lodged in his stomach. He fell moaning to the pavement, one of the sixty-five members of the media who would be beaten or arrested or both that week in Chicago.

Hunter Thompson never wrote about the atrocities of Mayor Richard Daley's Chicago convention. In another sense, however, he never stopped writing about it. The topics of depravity and violence, that two-headed gargoyle Fear & Loathing, enslaved his thoughts thereafter. Yet even the prospect of living in an America presided over by Richard Nixon or that rancid Daley ass kisser Hubert Humphrey did not dim his interest in politics. If anything, he required greater dosages. "There's a high in politics," he would later observe. "It's a combination of power and adrenaline that beats any drug I've found yet."

When he returned to Colorado after seeing Nixon narrowly defeat Humphrey, Thompson's foul mood was not soothed by the new influx of tourists and real estate hucksters now tearing up every cubic inch of Aspen.

He convinced a liberal-minded lawyer, Joe Edwards, to run for mayor of Aspen, saying he, Thompson, would manage the campaign. Incredibly, the unknown lawyer lost by a mere half dozen votes.

The experience gave Hunter Thompson a vicious adrenaline jolt. He decided to run for sheriff of Aspen in 1970—despite Chicago, despite his very public admissions of drug abuse, despite the fact that a friend had shaved Thompson's head while the latter was stoned and thought he was getting a normal haircut . . . or because of these things. His would be a different candidacy. He would run on the Freak Power ticket, going straight for the jugular, pledging to rename Aspen "Fat City" and sod its streets and put dishonest drug dealers in stocks and limit all public movement to that accomplished on foot or by bicycle.

The boy Louisville could not control was now thirty-one, and calm in his shrewd cognizance of what must be done. He would write about his campaign, publishing his screed in a magazine the apathetic hippie nonvoters of Aspen were sure to read—a magazine sure to make a difference for the Freak Power candidate.

That magazine was not *Scanlan's Monthly*. It was *Rolling Stone*. Warren Hinckle was enraged that his star journalist would take his story down the street to the office of that wise-ass little twit Hinckle once employed. Hinckle would pay twice what Wenner could afford. But Hunter Thompson was insistent. "By then I was a politician," he said, "pissed off, beaten up in Chicago." This was nothing personal, he said. Surely Hinckle would see the wisdom of the political strategy. This was not meant to be goodbye . . . but it was, as Hunter S. Thompson never wrote a major feature for Warren Hinckle again.

And so came the tall and wiry man—in wraparound sunglasses and matching black leather gloves and jacket with the misshapen wig on his bald head and the six-pack of Budweiser under his arm—to the fourth-floor office at 625 Third Street, walking in his jerky, crablike way to the office of Jann Wenner, who looked up at the writer he'd heard so much about, shook the visitor's hand and said, "Well, what have you brought us?"

"Thompson just launched into this rap," said John Lombardi, who witnessed the encounter. "And he must have talked for nearly an hour without stopping, drinking his entire six-pack, chain-smoking and taking his wig off and putting it on for no apparent reason and limping around the room— all the while talking about his plans to run for sheriff. He kept talking about the greed hogs and the fun pigs, and how he wanted to change the name of Aspen to Fat City.

"And Wenner is sitting in this high-backed Huey Newton chair he had, and he's listening to him, and he's sinking lower and lower in his chair till he's practically underneath his desk. Finally Thompson goes down the hall to take a leak. All this time nobody had said anything."

Jann Wenner looked up at Lombardi from his reclined slump. "Look, I know I'm supposed to be the spokesman for the youth generation and everything," said the editor of *Rolling Stone*. "But what the fuck was *that*?"

It was the future of Jann Wenner's magazine. And the future emerged from the bathroom and withdrew a huge syringe from his leather jacket, and lifted his shirt and jammed the syringe into his navel, and looked up at the gaping visages of the *Rolling Stone* rank and file. And burped.

Chapter Ten

GREATNESS

e've got to get back, get back, get back to where we once belonged," Jann Wenner told his demoralized staff in the hard days of 1970. But when *Rolling Stone* got back, there was nothing waiting for it.

Ralph Gleason continued to write of music's transformative powers, claiming that "the great musicians are . . . the true shamans, the religious and the secular spokesmen, the educators and the poets." Yet where were these great musicians? The Beatles, Dylan and the Rolling Stones had receded from pop culture like giant stars mysteriously dwindling from the constellation. Jimi Hendrix and Janis Joplin were dead; by the summer of 1971, Jim Morrison of the Doors would join them in the soil. "The truth of the matter," wrote Jon Landau, "is that the names of the Sixties have become anomalies. No one looks to them for direction, no one copies them and few are still influenced by them."

At the same time, Landau acknowledged, "every era requires strong innovators and personalities to give glory to the movement . . . heroes." Who would step forward in the seventies? Mortals, it appeared. Bands openly derided in *Rolling Stone* like Led Zeppelin, Grand Funk Railroad and Blood, Sweat and Tears. Self-referencing singer/songwriters like James Taylor and Joni Mitchell. Not a hero among them.

There would always be an audience, and always good music being made. But rock & roll's "magic that will set you free" now came in the form of flash paper and coin tricks. And perhaps this was sufficient. Perhaps this generation had seen enough of its supermen quarreling like brats deprived of their afternoon nap or dying alone like winos by the bayou. Perhaps now, after five halcyon years, it was time for the Love Generation to wake up and smell the coffee.

———

But what would this do to *Rolling Stone*?

John Burks left the magazine in the summer of 1970, convinced Jann Wenner had made a deal with financiers who demanded in return that *Rolling Stone* be reduced to its original formula: no politics, just rock & roll. In one breath, the editor would scoff at these claims; in the next, he would describe Burks as a man who "didn't know very much about rock and didn't like it very much," and who was therefore "incompatible" with *Rolling Stone*'s interests.

Of the two dozen or so contestants interviewed by Jann and John Lombardi to replace Burks, the man who ultimately prevailed was a friend of music editor Ben Fong-Torres. The friend, Paul Scanlon, was told that his chief duty would be "to write about rock & roll music in northern California." Scanlon assented quietly, as combativeness was not his style.

What the new managing editor had not told Jann was that he, like Burks, had only a casual interest in rock music. His background at *The Wall Street Journal* and the *Palo Alto Times* had been news and sports, not the counterculture. Scanlon had fallen in love with *Rolling Stone* since its first issues, while he served in the Army—yet not for its endless championing of Dylan, the Beatles and the Stones. What attracted Scanlon to *Rolling Stone*, he said, was "the cultural/political stuff it did—the kind of stuff no one else was doing, or could do." The few rock stories that caught his eye were those with a keen news slant, like the article about a riot at a Sly Stone concert which left the dim-witted body counting to the dailies and instead focused on the riot's causes stemming from inadequate concert planning.

Scanlon's appreciation of *"Rolling Stone*-type stories" was similar to that of Burks, whom Scanlon had known and admired when they both attended San Francisco State. In style, however, the two shared little. Scanlon wore a tie, kept his own counsel at editorial meetings and quietly apprenticed himself by scanning back issues of *Esquire*, whose editor at the time was the *New York Herald Tribune*'s legendary Harold Hayes. While he learned the ropes, Scanlon was content to let copy chief Charlie Perry and associate editor John Lombardi run the show.

Lombardi, who had been instrumental in Scanlon's hiring, was by now itching to depart *Rolling Stone* for *Esquire*. Before he did, however, he lured to *Rolling Stone* two writers who helped shatter once and for all the perception of the magazine as a rock & roll tabloid.

The first was Hunter Thompson. Lombardi, while editing Philadelphia's underground paper *The Distant Drummer* in 1967, had published Thompson's savage obituary of Lionel Olay, "the ultimate freelancer." Lombardi renewed the tie after Burks recruited him in 1970, though at first Thompson was unreceptive. "A bunch of faggots and hippies," snarled Thompson at the mention of *Rolling Stone*, which, he recalled, had stayed home and urged others to do the same while Thompson and some sixty-five other journalists were beaten and/or arrested in Chicago in the summer of 1968.

But Lombardi's urgings, plus the Aspen sheriff's race of 1970, brought Hunter Thompson into the magazine's fold. Lombardi edited the Aspen piece, spreading out the writer's fits and starts of prose on the parquet floor of Jann's office, moving the paragraphs around like chesspieces while Thompson stood over him, mumbling his appreciation as he scarfed down Budweisers and marshmallows. Several months later, the candidate carried the city of Aspen but was pummeled in the suburbs ("the Spiro Agnew vote"), a narrow defeat in the final tally. Thompson's loss was Jann Wenner's gain. For the next five years, Dr. Hunter S. Thompson wrote for no one but *Rolling Stone*.

———

The other Lombardi protégé, Grover Lewis, had certain things in common with Thompson. He was a Southerner, a Texas newsman who had roamed his native nation-state as young Thompson had wandered both seaboards. With his boyhood companion Larry McMurtry, Lewis witnessed a sloe-eyed country boy named Elvis Presley get stomped by oil field roughnecks outside a Wichita Falls roadhouse in the mid-fifties. A few years later, he and McMurtry began their writing careers at North Texas State by publishing a controversial campus magazine, *The Coexistence Review*. Fresh out of college, he covered the Kennedy assassination at close range for the *Fort Worth Star-Telegram*, spending three years at that paper and another three at the *Houston Chronicle* before moving to San Francisco at the beginning of 1969.

Lewis, like Thompson, came to the Bay as a reporter, not a hippie. As the San Francisco correspondent for *The Village Voice*, he consistently filed stylish, brilliantly reported pieces that caught John Lombardi's attention. Lombardi was particularly taken with Lewis's Altamont article—far superior, Lombardi thought, to the *Rolling Stone* analysis that involved over a dozen reporters, and with an infinitely more metaphorical ending:

> When we reached the Alameda County line, about a mile north of the amphitheatre, I spotted a teenage girl wrapped in a poncho sitting alone on the shoulder of the highway. Something about her posture made me get out of the barely moving car to see if she needed a ride. She didn't raise her head at the question. "Man, I don't need a ride," she said in a thick, stoned slur. "I need to go to a hospital." Involuntarily, her hand twitched out from under the poncho. Apparently she'd lit a cigarette some time back, and then forgotten about it. Her fingers were on fire.

Lombardi paid a call, telling Grover Lewis that his own job would soon be up for grabs and suggesting that he give it a whirl.

As fate would have it, Lewis was assigned by *The Village Voice* to do a piece on *Rolling Stone*—an article, the *Voice* editors had in mind, that would portray Jann Wenner's magazine as a financially crippled beast hobbling from one issue to the next. Yet Lewis arrived at the Third Street office on October 27, 1970, to find *Rolling Stone* weathering the personnel and fiscal crises admirably well. His piece reflected this and was rejected by the *Voice* for being too soft. Lewis, who had never been terribly satisfied with his employers anyway, began to consider Lombardi's offer.

That winter, Grover Lewis returned to Texas to play a minor role in the Peter Bogdanovich-directed movie *The Last Picture Show*, based on Larry McMurtry's novel. Before leaving for Archer City, Lewis asked Jann if he'd be interested in an on-location report. Jann said sure.

The resulting opus, "Splendor in the Short Grass," was the most gorgeously fashioned article *Rolling Stone* had yet published (it ran in the magazine's September 2, 1971, issue), one of the finest pieces it would *ever* publish. The hilarious and affecting backstage conversations between Bogdanovich, Cloris Leachman, veteran Ben Johnson, newcomer Cybill Shepherd and the bemused West Texas townsfolk were rendered delicately by Lewis, a man of this country:

> The shuttle plane, an 18-seater De Haviland-Perrin, seems infernally slow after the rush of the Delta jet from San Francisco; its engines are loud, too, and it bucks around in the brown overcast between Dallas and Wichita Falls like a sunfishing busthead-bronc. Fitfully, I'm riffling through the pages of an underground sheet called Dallas Notes—"Narc Thugs Trash Local White Panthers"—but the lonesome countryside below keeps drawing my mind and eye away from the real-enough agonies of Big D's would-be dope brotherhood. Somewhere down there slightly to the south, a pioneer Texan named William Medford Lewis—my paternal grandfather—lies buried in the Brushy Cemetery, hard by the fragrant dogwood trails of Montague County where he and I once tramped together in less fitful times. Beside him, that fierce, pussel-bellied old man I remember above all other men, lies his next-to-youngest son, Cecil—a ghostly wraith-memory of childhood, a convicted bank robber and one-time cohort of Bonnie and Clyde who was paroled from the Huntsville pen in 1944 just in time to die 56 days later in the invasion of Sicily—and beside Cecil, in turn, lies my grandmother, who once lifted an uncommonly sweet contralto in whatever Pentecostal church lay closest to hand.

Among those floored by "Splendor in the Short Grass" was Hunter Thompson, who whipped off a two-page letter to Lewis immediately after reading the piece, declaring he'd just gotten "a first-class morning high off it" and that the two of them would have to confer sometime on higher literary matters—"the importance of getting a genuine wind sound into writing, and also water movement, etc."

Upon handing in the article in March of 1971, Lewis promptly took over Lombardi's duties. With Scanlon and Charlie Perry, he scoured the horizons for new talent while contacting the agents of writers like William Burroughs and persuading them to submit pieces to *Rolling Stone*.

A new literary sensibility crept into the pages of the magazine issue by issue—typified, perhaps, by the sign on Lewis's desk sporting the Muddy Waters lyric: "I Do Not Write No Rock & Roll." This was not entirely accurate, as Lewis—like every *Rolling Stone* editorial staffer besides Hunter Thompson—would be called upon to write about music during his tenure.

Nonetheless, between Ben Fong-Torres's music features at the front and Jon Landau's record reviews section at the back, a different breed of *Rolling Stone* journalist reared its war-painted head.

———

Joe Eszterhas was one of the breed. A burly, macho Hungarian émigré, Eszterhas spent his childhood years in postwar American refugee camps— surrounded, as he would write in *Rolling Stone*, by "the victims of Soviet prisons, the haggard, hollow men who chain-smoked cigarettes with rheumatic fingers ..." As a reporter for the *Cleveland Plain Dealer*, he won notoriety when he obtained the damning exclusive photographs of the Mylai massacre. Disgruntled with the paper's handling of the event, Eszterhas published a highly critical 15,000-word article in *The Evergreen Review* called "The Selling of the Mylai Massacre." The *Plain Dealer* fired Eszterhas in September of 1971; the reporter took the case to court and lost.

Several months before then, Joe Eszterhas headed west and visited the offices of *Rolling Stone*, coveting a staff job. The receptionist would not let him see anyone. Eszterhas bought some fifty back issues and left. Later, however, Paul Scanlon noticed an Associated Press story in the *San Francisco Chronicle* about a biker riot in a place called Polish Hall in Cleveland. Scanlon located the writer, who confessed he'd copped the whole story from an article written by a *Plain Dealer* reporter named Joe Eszterhas.

Scanlon called Eszterhas and asked him to write a news feature on the riot. "Maybe three days later this piece comes in," said Scanlon, "about three thousand words long, absolutely perfect. I think I changed maybe a half dozen words. I thought, Shit, this guy's terrific."

> The Breed came here on a bleak, rain-swept afternoon, the first Saturday in March—Cochise and Tiny and Hammerhead and Big Bill and their old ladies—meeting at the abandoned old barn outside of town, in Brunswick, where they nailed a ketchup-smeared mannequin to the wall, stripped a mama down to her black panties, and opened their kegs of beer. It was cold and they built a bonfire, piling together a clump of the old owner's canceled checks, pissing on that dead man's faded debts, beginning their party.

"The Biker War at Polish Hall" went all but unnoticed in an issue that included Fong-Torres's expansive cover story on the Jackson 5, Hunter Thompson's even longer investigation into the murder of Chicano reporter

Ruben Salazar and an inventive short story by a Stanford physics student Grover Lewis had come across, Michael Rogers. But Scanlon sensed he had a hot one with Joe Eszterhas. He assigned the writer to do a feature on the anniversary of the Kent State killings, on which Eszterhas had written a book the year before. The results were again spectacular.

Scanlon petitioned Jann to hire Eszterhas. "We don't have any money," Jann protested. But the new managing editor and Grover Lewis, who loved the Polish Hall piece, went to the wall for the former *Plain Dealer* journalist. Joe Eszterhas joined the roster in the fall of 1971.

By this time, *Rolling Stone* had achieved a literary pinnacle by winning the 1970 National Magazine Award for the Altamont and Charles Manson pieces—articles, said the judges, which "challenged the shared values of its readers." Burks, John Morthland, Greil Marcus and the other Altamont reporters were not around to bask in the honor.

———

But Manson co-writer David Felton was. In fact, the witty Los Angeles journalist was by the summer of 1971 a full associate editor at *Rolling Stone* and plodding away on another dangerous assignment: an investigation into the violent cult of a slightly built little man named Mel Lyman who extolled the virtues of *feeling of any kind*, especially pain and suffering.

The piece would take over half a year for Felton to complete (and indeed he did not manage to complete it—the last section of the article was provided by Grover Lewis). For Felton, this was speedy. His torturously slow pace was legendary at the *Los Angeles Times*, where he was known as the Stonecutter. A commonly told story had Felton assigned to do a piece on the January 1 Rose Bowl, which he of course failed to complete on time. The editor granted him clemency of major proportions: Felton would have a full year, until the *next* January 1 Rose Bowl, to finish the article.

Months crept by. December approached, arrived, slowly passed. Still no article. The New Year was dawning when the editor, at wits' end, charged over to David Felton's desk.

Felton, his face racked with tension, looked up from the typewriter at his deadline-crazed editor. It is said that he lamented aloud, "If *only* I could come up with the lead . . ."

It was not in the cards for David Felton to work on a daily paper. Certainly no city desk editor would cajole and browbeat a reporter as Jann Wenner did David Felton. The actual writing of the two-part Lyman piece took a month—a solid thirty days of Doggie Diner take-out hamburgers and Jann standing over his writer, saying, "All right, David, it's time for your prescription," handing him capsules of speed and Ritalin, which Felton would take . . . only to doze off at his desk and then, perhaps an hour later, be resurrected by the sudden onset of the drugs. This was not how the venerables at the Columbia School of Journalism trained their smooth-skinned legions.

On the other hand, no newspaper in the land would have yielded enough space for the magnificent 40,000-word journey into the dark soul of the Lyman cult—culminating, after dozens of interviews with his lost wild followers, with the Interview:

> "Most people who are non-violent don't even know what violence is," said Mel. "I think people cheat themselves out of a lot of wonderful experiences. And after all, the way you grow is through experience."
>
> Yes, I argued, but you can't have a society with people hurting each other for the sake of their own experience.
>
> "Sometimes you have to take that chance. I'm *glad* I tried to attack that cop."
>
> Mel shrugged. "We haven't *killed* anyone."
>
> OK, I said, but then you have Kweskin going around saying, "We haven't killed anyone—yet." What's that supposed to mean?
>
> He turned back to the pool and started drumming his lips with his fingers. At first he spoke almost to himself. "Let me see if I've killed anybody yet . . . my mind must be getting tired . . . it's getting late." He rubbed his eyes.

After the last word was on the page, Jann Wenner called Felton into his office. "Now, see, David," the editor said, grinning, "there's no reason why the way you've been working the last few days shouldn't be your normal speed of writing."

"Normal?" Felton took a step back, regarding his boss with terror. "You expect me to do this *normally*?"

This was, of course, impossible. Waiting for David Felton to meet his deadline was like watching a glacier melt. "He would sit there by his typewriter for hours," said Barbara Downey, then a copy editor. "Then he'd type: 'Newsprint.' And under that: 'David Felton.' And it would sit there for *days*. Then he'd type the headline; then 'by David Felton,' and maybe the lead. And then it would *sit* there. Days! Weeks, possibly! Of course, when it finally came out, it would be *the most brilliant* . . ."

"I always had the impression," said Charlie Perry, "that he was trying to ingest the material so that the subconscious would write it. So he'd just be sort of sitting there, waiting for it to come out." In an effort to aid the process, Perry once held Felton out a window so as to impress upon him the virtues of punctuality. Word of Perry's strong-arm techniques reached Hunter Thompson, who bumped into the copy chief at the office a few days later.

Thompson reacted as if he'd stepped on a snake. Perry, a little bewildered, smiled. "How's it going, Hunter?" he asked.

"It's doing good, it's almost finished, I'll have it to you soon," Thompson stammered, and vanished down the hall.

Thompson, unlike Felton, was a writer with a guilty conscience. Always in agony at the deadline hour, Hunter Thompson was especially morose at the prospect of completing his investigation of the Ruben Salazar murder. The story was ugly, redeemed by no trace of humor. In his desperation to avoid writing the piece, Thompson did something he had never done before and would never do again: he sought refuge in another writing project.

He collared his friend and Chicano politics mentor, attorney Oscar Zeta Acosta, and the two hopped in a rental car and drove out to Las Vegas to cover a motorcycle race for *Sports Illustrated* ... then, for the hell of it, barged in on the National District Attorneys' Drug Conference. Upon returning, Thompson checked out of the junkie-riddled Hotel Ashmun, where he'd been investigating the Ruben Salazar murder, and holed up at the Ramada just outside of Pasadena—writing the Salazar piece by night and then, for comic relief, conjuring up by dawn's approach the fevered tale of his and Acosta's misadventures in Vegas:

> We were somewhere around Barstow on the edge of the desert when the drugs began to take hold. I remember saying something like "I feel a bit lightheaded; maybe you should drive...." And suddenly there was a terrible roar all around us and the sky was full of what looked like huge bats, all swooping and screeching and diving around the car, which was going about a hundred miles an hour with the top down to Las Vegas. And a voice was screaming: "Holy Jesus! What are these goddamn animals?" ...
>
> It was almost noon, and we still had more than a hundred miles to go. They would be tough miles. Very soon, I knew, we would both be completely twisted. But there was no going back, and no time to rest. We would have to ride it out.... I was, after all, a

professional journalist; so I had an obligation to *cover the story*, for good or ill . . .

But what *was* the story? Nobody had bothered to say. So we would have to drum it up on our own. Free Enterprise. The American Dream. Horatio Alger gone mad on drugs in Las Vegas. Do it *now*: pure Gonzo journalism.

There was also the socio-psychic factor. Every now and then when your life gets complicated and the weasels start closing in, the only real cure is to load up on heinous chemicals and then drive like a bastard from Hollywood to Las Vegas. To *relax*, as it were, in the womb of the desert sun. Just roll the roof back and screw it on, grease the face with white tanning butter and move out with the music at top volume, and at least a pint of ether.

"I was assigned by Jann to edit the Salazar piece," said Felton, who at this point still lived in Los Angeles. "So Hunter came over to my house to talk about the article—but instead he had these *pages* in his hand, and he was *very excited*."

"Fear and Loathing in Las Vegas," read the headline, with the subhead: "A Savage Journey to the Heart of the American Dream." The listed author was Raoul Duke—a device Thompson had employed in the past to allow for the insertion of particularly outrageous verities or vicious swipes at public officials. As for the story itself . . . well, it appeared to revolve around the folly of, in the author's words, "laying a sixties trip on Las Vegas in 1971." Yet in the end, "Fear and Loathing in Las Vegas" was about the lunatic pleasures of Gonzo journalism.

Thompson handed the first nineteen pages over to Jann Wenner. The editor returned the copy later. His voice was unsteady, his elation barely contained. "Keep on going," he said.

Paul Scanlon read the manuscript and fell to his knees laughing.

Charlie Perry, upon reading the first installment, believed Thompson's savage missive to be the final stake in the heart of the sixties. "I remember each of the editors got a chance to read the manuscript," he said. "Each had about a day to go through the thing. We all had the exact same experience. As soon as you finished it and went home, life was incredibly dramatic. You expected disasters to come rolling out of alleys, water to be boiling over. After reading it, nobody with a straight face could talk about psychedelics as being essentially a religious experience."

Along the way, Thompson turned in his motorcycle-racing piece to

Sports Illustrated. The article was ten times longer than required, and aswirl with fear and loathing. It was "aggressively rejected."

Thompson set out with Acosta to complete the *Rolling Stone* assignment—half reporting, half method-acting, simulating bizarre incidents and charging things like drugs and flutes and Gerber Mini-Magnums to the expense account. He discovered, too late, that such items were coming directly out of his pocketbook, and fired off a complaint to Felton:

> You scurvy pigfucker. I was just about to send you some mescaline when I talked to Jann & found out that all my daily expenses on the Salazar/Vegas stories were disallowed—for reasons of gross excess and irresponsible outlay. That $500 you sent wasn't for my expenses at all; it was my fucking *June retainer*, which means I was spending my own money all that time. . . . You treacherous pig. . . .

Thompson would later avenge this injustice by selling the "Fear and Loathing in Las Vegas" book rights to Random House, not Straight Arrow Books. In the meantime, he gunned out the final pages, after which the completed text was mailed to Ralph Steadman in Kent, England. Steadman mailed back incredibly vile visual representations of Hunter Thompson's narrative. The two installments of "Fear and Loathing in Las Vegas," each with a Steadman cover drawing, splattered across the November 11 and 25, 1971, issues.

It was like selling tickets to the apocalypse. The issues jumped off the newsstands. A superstar was born.

———

There were others as well. From Waukesha, Wisconsin, came Tim Cahill, a failed swimmer in college and aspiring Great American Novelist, who was scrubbing pots in a San Francisco hotel kitchen when Grover Lewis, through a mutual friend, asked to see Cahill's stuff. His portfolio consisted of a couple of *San Francisco Examiner* articles, though in fact Cahill had even less journalistic experience than these clippings implied.

The writing was rough, but good enough for *Rolling Stone*. The magazine, said Lewis, was looking for "an editorial drudge." By this the associate editor meant someone to write "Random Notes." Under Paul Scanlon's dedicated tutelage, however, Tim Cahill eventually rose from an "office mascot" who turned in unreadable tangles of prose to a New Journalist of his day, breathing that rarefied ozone with the likes of Thompson and Lewis.

From the *New York Post* came Timothy Ferris. Like Felton and Eszterhas,

Ferris had toiled for years in the creative bondage of the newsroom, filing short and rigidly defined snippets, his quirky brilliance poking through only, it seemed, by accident. But Ferris put in a call to *Rolling Stone*, and soon found himself doing strange profiles on deceased bluesman Robert Johnson, broadcaster David Brinkley, political prisoners and Raquel Welch. (In 1973 he would meet a relatively obscure astronomer named Carl Sagan, virtually introduce Sagan to pop culture and soon spin off into a dazzling orbit of his own as one of America's most accomplished science journalists.)

Though Jann Wenner discovered none of these writers, he used their talents as no editor had before. Thompson, Lewis, Eszterhas and Cahill found their voice at *Rolling Stone* simply because Jann gave them the freedom to do so. Obscene language was allowed; a vicious snubbing of objectivity was encouraged. Despite Jann's earlier, more constricting interpretations of the *Rolling Stone* charter—to write about music, and "the things and attitudes that the music embraces"—he now allowed his writers to kick away the barriers. Grover Lewis wrote about film and introduced a fiction department into the magazine. Joe Eszterhas developed an interest in police corruption. Tim Cahill gradually found his voice writing about fringe groups and alien worldviews. Hunter S. Thompson sought out "bad craziness" in all its disparate forms.

Yet the vastness of the territory they staked out proved the Manifest Destiny of the Wenner Charter. The "things and attitudes that the music embraces" certainly included investigations into the murders of small-time dope dealers by narcotics cops. Profiling Robert Mitchum, the maverick actor arrested for marijuana decades before it became fashionable, was undoubtedly in keeping with the *Rolling Stone* spirit. Cultists, gurus and other refugees of the underground? Clearly fair game.

Young writers like Cahill were afforded the opportunity to cut their teeth on more routine articles before ambling into weirder dimensions. "At first I didn't know where I'd fit in," he said. "I came in and Felton, Hunter and Eszterhas were already there and doing well. So I became kind of a utility infielder. Anything that needed to be done, I'd go out and do it. Want me to interview a doorknob, I'll get the story. Since I knew nothing about journalism, I needed a mentor, and that was Paul Scanlon. At the same time, I had complete freedom to try anything."

Indeed, the laissez-faire editorial attitude suggested to writers a *responsibility* to bend all conventions. Jan Hodenfield's younger brother Chris, who started writing for the magazine in 1970, began his 1972 Alice Cooper cover story with a detailed description of Cooper's pet boa constrictor devouring a mouse. "You were not only allowed to write in an explosion, shooting off fireworks in the sky," he said, "but they almost expected it of you. Your explosion was *appreciated*."

"All the news that fits" became the *Rolling Stone* motto, and only partly as a snickering rejoinder to the *New York Times*'s buzzphrase. Jann's new stars did not compete for space in the magazine because, as Cahill said, "there was an *infinite* amount of space." If Thompson's Salazar investigation, "Strange Rumblings in Aztlan," suddenly bloated to 19,000 words (as it did), then that was fine. Minor features were bumped or pages were added—and if Thompson's verbiage didn't completely fill the added space, the production department would call for a house subscription ad and thereby seal the void.

"One piece I wrote came in three times the contracted length—something which I never even bothered to tell anyone about," said Timothy Ferris. "Jann later told me that when he first saw the length of the piece, he was tempted to reject it then and there. But instead he read it, and ran it without any cuts at all. Which was the great thing about *Rolling Stone*."

These indulgences did not come without a price. Writers like Ferris, Cahill and Chris Hodenfield often found themselves, without warning, taken off salary and asked to freelance—that is to say, put on the Wenner Plan —when money got tight in the summer. "But what could you do?" said Hodenfield. "*Rolling Stone* was the only magazine you'd really want to write for. And Jann knew that."

To get more bang for his buck, Jann saddled a number of his writers with editorial chores. If the extra duties were burdensome at times, they also helped to broaden the magazine experience of promising neophytes. "Jann had an extraordinary acumen," said Ferris, "for picking people out of positions like mine who were newspaper reporters and didn't have anything on a résumé that would indicate their capabilities."

Jann hired Ferris to head the New York bureau in 1971. Though he had no background to bring to his new responsibilities, he was "a wonderful editor," said Chris Hodenfield. "It was when I went back to New York and worked under Tim that I really developed as a feature writer."

In turn, Ferris's copy was handled by L.A. bureau chief David Felton, another novice editor who nonetheless employed his own writer's faculties to get to the guts of a story. "He edited a piece I did on political prisoners," said Ferris. "And in its original form, I had a preface in which I made some emotional statement about the outrage that 'we,' *Rolling Stone*, felt about this issue. And Felton just very gently said, 'You know, the presumption is that that's why we're running the piece to begin with.' That one remark was a year's worth of education."

Ferris made a sign and hung it by his desk. It read: "David Felton Is Always Right."

The effect of using lifelong writers like Lewis, Felton and Ferris to assign and edit copy was to embed the mind-set that *Rolling Stone* was a writer's magazine. Domineering presences like Hunter Thompson and Joe Eszterhas took their rope and thundered off with it. Others followed.

"One of the things that from an editorial standpoint Hunter taught me," said Felton, "was that you should have more respect for writers who were different, that it wasn't unfair to do so, that nothing was gained from imposing a rigid style. That was a good lesson, since I had come from a tradition at the *L.A. Times* where the editor had all the power and writers really had no say. But Hunter was so belligerent and stubborn—I mean he just *insisted* on more freedom for individual styles."

That *Rolling Stone* was no longer simply a music magazine—that it was *different, literate*, maybe even *important*—was a revelation quickly spreading. Once known for its profiles of the rock & roll elite, *Rolling Stone* was now securing interviews with heavies like Brinkley and Woody Allen. Marlon Brando, normally reclusive, respected *Rolling Stone* and agreed to speak with Chris Hodenfield. Jane Fonda was less familiar with the magazine, but after reading a few back issues forwarded by Jann, she consented to an interview as well.

Though such a scheme promoted creativity, the leeway afforded writers came at the direct expense of the sanity of *Rolling Stone* accountants, production workers and Jann. The production staff, aggravated by his eleventh-hour copy submissions and his arrogant refusal to proofread his galleys, designed a dart board with Hunter Thompson's face on it. Felton's tardiness was so disruptive that Jann and the entire staff conspired to make up phony deadlines in hopes of getting Deadline Dave's copy by the required hour. Somehow, the Stonecutter always uncovered each scheme, subverting all deadlines real and contrived.

"I'll talk about good work habits when people around here start doing good work," a Felton memo sneered.

Joe Eszterhas, known to crank out fifty thousand words over a weekend, did not suffer from Felton's creative block. Nonetheless, copy editors came to despise him for his unwillingness to give an inch on editorial revisions. When art director Bob Kingsbury deleted a comma on a pullout quote for space purposes, Eszterhas blew a vessel. "I *wrote* that comma!" he hollered.

Yet Jann tolerated such abusiveness. After the doldrums of 1970, the air was electric again, and if sparks flew into a few humorless eyes—well, get safety goggles. As for the *Rolling Stone* editor, he was in his element as never before. He personally assigned the major pieces and did much of the line editing on them himself—more often than not, to the great satisfaction of his egotistical superstars.

He converted the spacious parquet-floor office that was once his into the Raoul Duke Room, where editorial conferences were held. There he assembled his lieutenants and presided over the creative jousting. Felton, through his cigarette holder, tossed out brilliant headline ideas and feature topics that bordered on the otherworldly. Eszterhas stood and blustered, emphasizing his point by flinging his buck knife into the teakwood tabletop. Lewis, his glances almost indecipherable behind his thick glasses, took his jabs at Eszterhas in an Old Testament baritone. Perry argued linguistic fine points. Scanlon and Fong-Torres sat like mustachioed poker dealers.

And Jann Wenner, gavel in hand, legal pad before him, led the proceedings—part CEO, part group therapist. "Running a meeting was one of his great talents," said Scanlon. "And he'd drag them on forever if he felt like it."

Jotting down ideas, vetoing others with the bang of a gavel. Berating. Coddling. Playing one writer's ego against another's. His vaunted instincts never seemed sharper—every launched missile found its target. These were men who lived by the Dylan lyric "Don't follow leaders." And twenty-five-year-old Jann Wenner had their respect. He led them.

———

In December of 1971 he led them to Big Sur's Esalen Institute for a full-blown editorial conference. The San Francisco editors were there; so were Jerry Hopkins from Los Angeles, Timothy Ferris from New York, Hunter Thompson from Woody Creek, London bureau editors Andrew Bailey and Robert Greenfield, and from Boston, Jon Landau and a new contributor, Timothy Crouse.

Pointedly not invited to the affair was the publisher at the time, Porter Bibb, or any other *Rolling Stone* "business type." It also became obvious, once the participants shed their clothes and rolled into the gigantic Esalen hot tub, that women had been excluded as well.

Save one. Photographer Annie Leibovitz was there, amiably nude with the boys in the tub. Jann had brought her along to photograph the event for posterity's sake. Yet Leibovitz's place among the *Rolling Stone* elite was hard earned and much deserved. Like many of those splashing around her, she had come to the magazine only in the last year. Yet her star was rising fast, and within a breathless span of time it would rise higher and faster than all save that of Hunter Thompson.

She was vintage *Rolling Stone*: a nobody, a gangly bespectacled twenty-year-old dropout from the San Francisco Art Institute, an Air Force brat who showed up with a handful of prints at the *Rolling Stone* offices and was quickly put to work by Bob Kingsbury. Cover shots came after six months: Grace Slick for the November 12, 1970, issue, Rod Stewart a month later. But her big break came when she found out that Jann was flying to New York in December for what became his milestone interview with John Lennon.

Though painfully insecure, Leibovitz could not miss this opportunity. She marched into Jann's office. "Jann," she told the editor, "if you hire a photographer back East, it's going to cost you $150 a day. I can fly youth fare, stay with friends and eat their food."

Her fee for the Lennon cover, plus negatives, was a princely $100. But the sacrifice paid off. Kingsbury relied heavily on her, as good photographs had always been hard to come by, particularly so after Baron Wolman's departure. The kindness of veterans like Grover Lewis helped see her through the early days. "She was so big, and her face looked so old for her age, that it was easy to forget that she was actually a very scared kid," said Lewis. "And by scared, I mean she needed encouragement just to get out of the car and set up the equipment."

Before long, she learned to turn her insecurities to her advantage, using her "bumbling teenage photographer act" (in the words of one of her art directors) to ingratiate herself with the subjects. In truth, said Ben Fong-Torres, "it wasn't really an act. She'd be nervous before the assignment, during the shoot and even looking at the prints. She was just constantly a case of nerves about her work, but that endeared her to her subjects. The artists would respond to her warmly and that would make a good picture—or they'd get nervous and freaked out and *that* made a good picture. She was innocent in a way that allowed her to get into people and discover their core. And that meant she got the better picture."

As Annie Leibovitz suffered over her art, so too was the *Rolling Stone* budget made to suffer. She shot more rolls of film than most photographers, and had a befuddling tendency to lose cameras and abandon rental vehicles. "Look," she told one of the finance officers who confronted Leibovitz on her budget-shredding ways. "What am I supposed to do? I'm in my car, I'm driving to the concert, I see Mick Jagger just stepping out of a limousine and the people are surrounding him and there's no place to park. If I don't move, I don't get those pictures. What's more important? *The sole purpose for me being there is to get those pictures.*"

It was the kind of logic that infuriated numbers men. Like Hunter Thompson, Grover Lewis, David Felton and Joe Eszterhas, Annie Leibovitz was all over *Rolling Stone*. The two could scarcely be separated.

And so Leibovitz was there as well at Big Sur, partying late into the night with Felton and Thompson, who would park his car up against his door so that Jann would not disturb him during his daytime sleep. The Gonzo journalist was the star of the conference, and he did not disappoint. One night he was stopped by highway patrolmen while driving mescaline-addled with Leibovitz and Felton as his passengers. Challenged to close his eyes and touch his nose, he tried—and missed.

On the very precipice of being arrested, Hunter Thompson tried a final ploy to prove his sobriety. He flipped the sunglasses off the back of his head with one hand and caught them behind the back with another—"the first time I'd ever managed to do that," he later said, "and the last." It was enough. The patrolmen sped off.

By day he basked in the attention, walking around in a bloody T-shirt and convincing Scanlon and Jann that he'd taken to injecting rum into his stomach. The act was applauded wildly; no one wished to see it end. "Everyone egged Hunter on," said Robert Greenfield. "It reminded me of the Isle of Wight, when the other three guys in the Doors would try to drive Jim Morrison crazy onstage, incite him somehow so that he'd do something to get the crowd going. It was the same way at Big Sur. Everyone was involved in the process of trying to drive Hunter crazy. He had complete license in this group."

Before long, the Hunter Thompson Show got out of hand. Grover Lewis was conversing with Jann when Thompson sidled up and demanded the editor's immediate attention—and when he did not get it, began yelling wildly and slinging furniture around the room, like an insolent, jealous child. Worse, his mad ways were infectious. "There was almost a macho thing of who could keep up with Hunter, be the craziest, do the most drugs," said Alan Rinzler. The nights got louder, the hot-tub sessions more raucous. Finally, inevitably, the knock came on Jann Wenner's room one morning. Esalen wanted *Rolling Stone* to vacate—now.

This was no great loss, as the conference had been more of a bacchanalian social mixer than anything else. Each day of Jann's brainstorming and forecasting had been, according to Paul Scanlon, "the most excruciating eight or nine hours I ever went through." Ferris puffed on his cigars and Eszterhas on his pipe, Thompson drank his six-packs and Leibovitz took her pictures—photographs which would later be waved about by angry female staffers as evidence of *Rolling Stone*'s blatant chauvinism.

From the endless sessions came a single brilliant idea. Hunter Thompson proposed that *Rolling Stone* cover the 1972 presidential campaign "like it was a fucking Rolling Stones concert tour." Thompson himself was en route to Saigon to file a story, but surely someone among them had the balls to do the job.

No one volunteered. Indeed, if anyone thought Thompson had a hot notion (and many would claim, much later, that they had), that advocate held his tongue. No one encouraged the idea except Timothy Crouse, a newcomer who was paid little mind. Crouse, a shy, studious-looking young Bostonian, whose father had scored *The Sound of Music*, had been filing music and a few political features for nearly a year, but his steady contributions were lost in the shuffle of superstars.

After a generally indifferent discussion, Thompson issued his declaration. "Fuck you bastards," he said. "I'll do it myself."

He turned to Timothy Crouse. "And you can go with me," he said.

————

A couple of weeks later, Dr. Hunter S. Thompson arrived in the nation's capital, towing a U-Haul full of books behind his supercharged Volvo. The Gonzo journalist was playing in a different league now, where there would be no place for his rum-syringe trick. He would be in the company of the nation's most seasoned reporters—"players," he liked to say; and if on paper he and *Rolling Stone* had nothing to lose, the thirty-three-year-old Louisville rebel had something to prove. He wanted to be taken seriously.

Besides, he was a partisan. As providence would decree, Thompson openly and shamelessly endorsed South Dakota senator George McGovern—a virtual one-issue antiwar candidate—from among the Democratic pack, and became one of the handful of reporters to cover that improbable campaign from the New Hampshire primary to the convention. In December, McGovern was much like Thompson: a minor character, an outsider playing a game stacked heavily in favor of insiders, a man not given to ass kissing.

Like McGovern's early campaign speeches, Thompson's first attempts to describe the surging madness of the political process were earnest but only marginally effective. Still, Jann Wenner—who, if cool to the idea at Big Sur, thereafter threw his support behind his star writer—had a Puritan's faith. Over the objections of the other editors, and in direct contradiction of his own views a mere eighteen months before, Jann ran Thompson's political coverage at the very front of the magazine, issue after issue.

Resigned by now to Thompson's inability to write anything except at the very last minute, Jann supplied him with a "mojo wire"—a telecopier machine much like the one Thompson had been ogling at Max Palevsky's Palm Springs compound. Just as the issue would be going to press, the Third Street mojo would come burbling to life, vomiting out a tremendous barrage of pure screed. Usually the first page to exit the machine would be headed not "Page 1" but rather "Insert Q"—the Gonzo journalist's way of buying time.

The pages were, in fact, never numbered, the copy blocks governed by some cryptic sense of order. For his sins, David Felton, the Stonecutter, was charged with editing most of the campaign articles. As John Lombardi had before him, as others would since, Felton would lay the pages out on the floor, shifting them around, building a skyscraper from scrap metal.

"Every hour or so, the copy would pump out of the mojo," said Felton. "And then I'd have to check to see if what he'd written that hour had anything to do with what he sent the previous hour. He'd be all wired up, and this would go on for two or three days, and I couldn't sleep—I'd have to use the time to make sense of what he'd given me, so I wouldn't get any sleep for something like a week.

"At one point, I just broke down and cried. I said, 'Why am I doing this? Nobody should have to do this.' "

The agony did not end with Felton. A whole production crew would be subjected to eleventh-hour hysteria, cutting and pasting and cursing the name of Hunter Thompson as few had been cursed since the day of Lee Harvey Oswald. During one incredible string, eight of ten issues were sent to the printer incomplete due to Thompson's habits.

"We can no longer go through this deadline scene as we have now with every one of your reports," wrote Jann to Hunter Thompson. But the admonition was more for the benefit of the dozen or so infuriated staffers to whom the memo was blind-carboned than for Thompson, who continued to drag *Rolling Stone* along his razor edge.

His expense forms were illegible and padded with prohibitive items. His articles flippantly described matters that never took place: McGovern campaign director Frank Mankiewicz attacking Thompson from behind a bush, Thompson stealing a carpet from the Ritz Carlton, NBC anchorman John Chancellor tripping on LSD. These dangerous antics only seemed to amuse the *Rolling Stone* editor, who delighted in letting his authority hover over

Hunter Thompson like the sword of Damocles. "It was most amusing to see those two interact," said Grover Lewis. "They played off each other's strengths and weaknesses like a vaudeville team."

Jann was less charitable toward Tim Crouse, riding him and flaying him like the family mule. For this behavior there seemed no rhyme or reason. Certainly he was easy prey for the fast-talking editor, as Crouse had a terrible stammer and was easily flustered. It was as if Jann harbored an almost primal need to drag Crouse, the son of a celebrity, through the sludge. "The way he treated Timmy was shameful—an act of complete cruelty on Jann's part," said publisher Larry Durocher.

The editor told Crouse he was on the campaign trail for one reason and one reason only: to look after Thompson—"to carry my whiskey," in the words of Thompson, who would have none of this bullying. Often Thompson sent the young reporter out to interview campaign officials and pry information from other reporters. Despite Jann Wenner's wishes, Tim Crouse was undergoing a valuable apprenticeship.

"He became my left hand," said Thompson. "When his stuttering got in the way, I'd say, 'Goddamnit, go interview that sonuvabitch, and *don't stutter!*'

"And by the end of the year, he did not stutter."

Before this came the Wisconsin primary—the breakthrough for McGovern, for Thompson and for Crouse. McGovern trounced the favorite, Edmund Muskie, and Thompson darkly reported that this defeat was clearly a sign of Muskie's addiction to a little-known West African drug called Ibogaine. Editors from respected newspapers and magazines bought the hoax and demanded that their reporters chase down this Ibogaine lead.

In the meantime, McGovern singled out Thompson at a campaign stop to congratulate him for a recent article he'd filed. Other reporters took notice. In two consecutive columns, *Newsweek*'s Stewart Alsop quoted the *Rolling Stone* correspondent's assessment of Hubert Humphrey as "a treacherous, gutless old ward-heeler who should be put in a goddamn bottle and sent out with the Japanese current." Alsop lectured Thompson for the ferocity of his remarks, but other reporters exhibited a certain wry admiration for the Gonzo journalist. After all, how many among them hadn't wanted to compare Nixon to Hitler and to label Humphrey "a brain-damaged old vulture" who "should be castrated"? Where their editors had instructed them to tiptoe through the political tulips, Jann Wenner had apparently given Hunter Thompson the green light to cut a defiantly wide swath.

Autograph seekers began to dog Hunter Thompson. But the real upset in Wisconsin belonged to Timothy Crouse, who had covered the McGovern campaign in that state while Thompson shadowed the front-runner, Muskie. Thompson told Jann that Crouse should write the analysis of the victory. Jann rejected this. The editor assured Crouse, on the telephone, that he would be fired if he wrote the article instead of Thompson.

Crouse wrote the article anyway. With space aching to be filled, Jann ran the report; then, as promised, jerked Crouse away from the campaign trail. But the *New York Times* praised the Bostonian's thoughtful, well-researched analysis so lavishly that Jann Wenner had little choice but to swallow his pride. Crouse returned to action.

The two made a fine Mutt and Jeff team, both on the trail and in Thompson's articles. It was Crouse who filed on the campaign's most significant preconvention event: the attempted assassination of George Wallace. And it was Crouse whose remarkable dissection of the campaign press corps formed the basis of *The Boys on the Bus*, among the most important books that rose from the ashes of the '72 saga. But it was the Mad Doctor and none other who was seen on the floor of the Republican convention, surrounded by a chanting gaggle of Nixon Youth while he wore his McGovern button and shook his fist up at the NBC booth, screaming himself hoarse at anchorman John Chancellor: "You evil scumsucker! You're *through!* You limp-wristed Nazi moron!"

Eager to get in on the act, Jann flew to Nebraska to be introduced to McGovern by Thompson, then later attended the Democratic convention in Miami. He'd hoped to acquire a pair of futuristic jet packs so that he and Thompson could fly from building to building like dope-maddened Supermen, but the Secret Service nipped this idea in the bud.

Timothy Ferris, who was assigned to help cover the Miami convention, was not surprised to see Thompson charging Hawaiian shirts and Bermuda shorts to his expense account and wandering the beach in search of a marijuana dealer. The Big Sur conference, after all, had prepared him well for the Gonzo journalist's proclivities. But nothing in that brain-cell-depleting week had suggested that Hunter Thompson was a fiercely dedicated reporter, obsessed like the best newsmen with nailing down an exclusive story.

Ferris found that Thompson did nothing halfway. The Washington Hilton, where the journalist set up *Rolling Stone*'s "National Affairs suite," grudgingly relaxed its rules to allow Thompson to swim laps in the pool at midnight. Ferris often joined Thompson in a lengthy regimen that began in the Hilton's weight room, then the pool and sauna, and concluded at the hotel bar.

On one such evening, the two sat at the bar, quietly nursing their drinks, when Thompson began to shudder violently. Ferris eyed him with alarm. "Jesus, Hunter, what's wrong?" he asked.

Thompson's convulsions ceased. He shook his head. "I was just imagining," he said, "what it would be like to do all this in reverse."

———

As the days darkened for the Democrats, Hunter Thompson found his apocalyptic edge. For all his Ibogaine ruses and rowdy entrances to press conferences, Thompson proved that the campaign trail was not just legitimate stomping ground for *Rolling Stone*, but in fact a process the magazine could unravel as few publications could or would. It was Thompson who described the almost surrealistic splendor of the press corps: shepherded mindlessly from one choreographed "event" to the next, betting on victory margins like fat Romans wagering how long it would take for the lion in the pit to devour the Christian, taping their thousands of hotel keys to the interior of the press corps plane, which then, during every takeoff and landing, "jingled like a giant tambourine. . . ."

Rock & roll, of a certain order. Jon Landau had called out for heroes to emerge, and Hunter Thompson declared unabashedly that he had found one in George McGovern. While the press corps scratched away at the senator's mild-mannered veneer, tarnishing his credibility, Thompson took what appeared, somehow, to be a high road:

> There is almost a Yin/Yang clarity in the difference between the two men, a contrast so stark that it would be hard to find any two better models in the national politics arena for the legendary *duality*—the congenital Split Personality and polarized instincts— that almost everybody except Americans has long since taken for granted as the key to our National Character. . . .

The media conspiracy of silence surrounding McGovern's ill-fated vice presidential nominee, Thomas Eagleton, embarrassed and angered Thompson. These same reporters had spent months ignoring the South Dakota senator and then, after Wisconsin, had played him up like an overnight sensation, only to shoot him down in the wake of the Eagleton scandal though they themselves had for years lacked the courage to expose the Missouri senator's mental-health problems.

McGovern's blunder sickened Thompson, but far more galling was the American public's drowsy-eyed gullibility:

> If the current polls are reliable—and even if they aren't, the sheer size of the margin makes the numbers themselves unimportant— Nixon will be re-elected by a huge majority of Americans who feel he is not only more honest and more trustworthy than George McGovern, but also more likely to end the war in Vietnam.
>
> The polls also indicate that Nixon will get a comfortable majority of the Youth Vote. And that he might carry all fifty states.
>
> Well . . . maybe so. This may be the year when we finally come face to face with ourselves; finally just lay back and say it—that we are really just a nation of 220 million used car salesmen with all the money we need to buy guns, and no qualms at all about killing anybody else in the world who tries to make us uncomfortable.
>
> The tragedy of all this is that McGovern, for all his mistakes and all his imprecise talk about "new politics" and "honesty in government," is one of the few men who've run for President of the United States in this century who really understands what a fantastic monument to all the best instincts of the human race this country might have been, if we could have kept it out of the hands of greedy little hustlers like Richard Nixon.
>
> McGovern made some stupid mistakes, but in context they seem almost frivolous compared to the things Richard Nixon does every day of his life, on purpose, as a matter of policy and a perfect expression of everything he stands for.
>
> Jesus! Where will it end? How low do you have to stoop in this country to be President?

George McGovern was crushed in November, but Hunter Thompson was not dragged down with him. Greatness was not so easily quelled. The journalist looked ahead to 1974, when there would be a U.S. Senate race in his state of Colorado. McGovern's campaign manager, a young man named Gary Hart, had already announced his intention to run on the Democratic ticket.

Well, why stop now? The former Freak Power candidate began to make a few calls. He'd give that neophyte bastard Hart a run for his money.

Chapter Eleven

THE ENDLESS
BOOGIE

Ever since his days at Garrett Press, *Rolling Stone* traffic manager Dan Parker spent his lunch hour at Jerry's Inn, an old warehouseman's bar catty-corner from 625 Third Street. The longhairs at *Rolling Stone* liked to mount the office roof and fire up reefers, but Parker's taste ran to whiskey. And so it was his custom to dine at Jerry's every noon, enjoying a couple of pops with the Garrett boys so as to take his mind off the madness being wrought daily across the street.

But the madness pursued him. Before long, managing editor Paul Scanlon and associate editor Grover Lewis began to show up at Jerry's Inn. They, too, sought refuge from the office hysteria, the endless phone calls and deadline pressures. "Escaping the Drongos," they called their forays.

Soon the escapees swelled in number—Joe Eszterhas, Tim Cahill, Ben Fong-Torres, the administrative and business and mail-room crews—until there was hardly anyone left to escape *from*. Honorary members were added. Oscar Zeta Acosta, the Chicano attorney who often turned up in Hunter Thompson's stories, became a Jerry's fixture. So did the Owl, an almost midget-sized cocaine dealer whose clients included most major Bay Area bands as well as various *Rolling Stone* staffers. Before long there appeared outlaw lawyers, crazy professors, dope-seared musicians and assorted other mascots. Dan Parker knew a trend when he saw one, and found a new watering hole.

By late afternoon, the booths at Jerry's would be stuffed with *Rolling Stone* minions: interviewing, drinking Rainier ale ("green death," they called the brew), snorting lines of cocaine off the tabletops, running up prodigious tabs and trafficking in lurid office gossip—specializing, of course, in wicked rumors about their fearless leader.

Jann Wenner seldom paid a visit to Jerry's Inn. The territory was distinctly not his, the events clearly beyond his control. All the same, the editor was well aware of the activity across the street. "Jerry's *became* the office," said receptionist Judy Lawrence, the Alabama-bred Mouth of the South and self-appointed *Rolling Stone* Director of Rumor Control. Jann took the threat seriously, enough so to consider buying another bar himself in hopes of driving Jerry's Inn out of business.

Bar owner Jerry Franceschi was happily oblivious to this. He and his brother Ken kept personal tabs for Paul Scanlon, Grover Lewis, Joe Eszterhas, Hunter Thompson and the other members of what he thought were the Rolling Stones. "Very good boozers," Jerry Franceschi would note approvingly. "They can put 'em away. They don't play with the drinks."

———

Surely they were Privileged Ones. Their "little music magazine," as their boss often called it, was known the world over. What other magazine was so important that Dr. Hook would sing a Top Forty song about wanting to be on its cover? And what other magazine would have the arrogance or sense of humor (take your pick) to put that very band on the cover?

What other magazine had, as Tim Cahill put it, "at least one article per issue that was like a pitchfork to the solar plexus"? What "little music magazine" would shrug off advertising boycotts by David Geffen, Carole King and Elton John? For that matter, what music magazine—big or little—would commission Tom Wolfe in 1972 to write a massive story on *astronauts*?

This was success on its own terms, far from the Darwinian travails of

New York. And the shareholders of this success were bound only by an amorphous charter, one reinterpreted with every new issue. Yet this independence was their addiction. Working for *Rolling Stone* meant a daily dose of its self-styled fast track. The employees even had a name for it: the Endless Boogie. The lunacy it engendered was all but impossible to abide, yet how was one to turn one's back on it?

"There was a *Rolling Stone* character type," said Abe Peck, one of the magazine's music editors. "The place attracted people who were willing to give their all because they believed that this magazine somehow represented an articulation of their worldviews. People who joined *Rolling Stone*, including myself, were willing to be consumed by the magazine. We were like moths to a flame."

By and large they were young, with structured beliefs but unstructured lives. They were single, or would be after a few months on the job. They were intensely loyal to *Rolling Stone* as a magazine, and susceptible to the notion of *Rolling Stone* as one feverish, feuding, endlessly boogying family.

The *Rolling Stone* family was a tribe altogether alien to the traditional family system. Each spoke an entirely different language. When the wife of associate editor David Weir had a baby, the staff came up with what it thought was the perfect shower gift: a coke spoon.

Working for a magazine where staffers frequently drank, drugged, slept and lived together seemed either appealing or perilous, depending on the individual's own personal stability. Jon Landau, often prodded by Jann to forsake Boston for San Francisco and become an executive editor, resisted the offer—partly to avoid being accountable to Jann, but also due to his leeriness of the magazine's social web. (Ironically, Landau later married senior editor Barbara Downey.) The same held true for New York bureau editor Timothy Ferris. "Most of the people brought in by Jann didn't seem to know anybody much except for their co-workers at *Rolling Stone*," he said. "They'd hang out together in the evening, and this struck me as kind of sick and claustrophobic. In that kind of limited social circle, you're ripe to have your heart broken *however* it happens—whether by Jann or by someone else in the circle."

"It was a goddamned miracle every two weeks," said John Crowell, the magazine's mail-room chief. God only knew how anything was accomplished at 625 Third Street. There was always someone yelling, someone fighting, someone crying. There was never a moment's clemency.

There was Crowell, being dragged off by federal investigators after a large unaddressed package of cocaine was delivered to the mail room.

There was Alan Rinzler, the head of Straight Arrow Books, hearing someone say of Jonathon Cott's entrance, "Cott's here"—and actually hearing the words "Cops here!" and immediately flinging the marijuana off his desk and out the window. There was Rinzler on the phone, yelling, summoning righteous rage by standing on his chair, then on his desk, fulminating like Moses.

There was Charlie Perry on *his* desk, then bounding over to the next desk, then the next, neatly scooping up copy, not touching the ground for an hour at a time.

There was the business manager in his cubicle, doing levitation exercises. The "Random Notes" editor in his, doing push-ups. A photo assistant in the darkroom suddenly consumed by deadline demons and barricading himself inside. An art director designing his last cover, then slashing it to pieces with an X-acto knife.

There were the *Rolling Stone* carpenters, forever putting up walls and tearing them down according to Jann Wenner's whims—appointed for life, like Sisyphus. Associate art director Barbara Ziller told Jann she couldn't get any work done with all the racket and demanded her own office. She marched back to her desk, and before she knew it, the three carpenters materialized, banging away with their hammers, building walls around her desk. Ziller got up and left 625 Third Street and never returned.

There was Hunter Thompson, visiting his bedlam on the unsuspecting: shooting off Roman candles, spraying fire extinguishers, painting his face corpse white, snarling at the accountants for refusing to let him deduct a leather jacket as a business expense. On one occasion he showed up in a rental vehicle, but by afternoon's end he could not for the life of him recall where he had parked it. The police were eventually summoned, creating wholesale paranoia and drug flushing.

There was receptionist Judy Lawrence keeping the wolves at bay—the uninvited guests who barreled out of the elevator, claiming they were God or Todd Rundgren. Her desk was equipped with a security buzzer, which she punched for all it was worth the afternoon Buddy Miles and his thugs came to visit. The drummer's eyes were glassy. He'd gotten a bad review.

"Where's Jann?" he hollered, and reached for Lawrence.

Dan Parker was the first to respond to the buzzer. Parker, a big, solid Texan, approached Miles, who picked up the traffic manager and threw him against the water cooler, which had to be repaired later.

"I'm pissed off!" Buddy Miles yelled, and commenced to weep even as Scanlon entered the room and was slapped down like a paper doll by Miles before a SWAT team entered the building and escorted the burly drummer down to the street. Miles never laid a hand on Jann Wenner, whose disappearing act that afternoon was noticed by all.

There were other threats as well. Charlie Perry called a dope smuggler's book "self-infatuated," and received word that he was a dead man. Ben Fong-Torres was informed, after writing an unflattering portrait of Ike Turner, that a man was claiming to police that he'd been hired by Turner to break one of Fong-Torres's legs, and one of Jann's for good measure.

Assaults came from within. A photographer twice pointed guns at Alan Rinzler. Rinzler himself attacked an art director after squabbling over a book design. One of the business personnel instructed a particularly attractive receptionist to have sex with him, and was later apprised, positioned uncomfortably against a wall with Grover Lewis's fists wrapped around each of his lapels, that people didn't behave like animals at a gentle workplace like 625 Third Street.

Bad Craziness, they called it, and most of it seemed to be due to the fact that—as Barbara Downey put it—"we always operated on a sleep deficit." Nothing worth doing at *Rolling Stone* was done until the last possible instant. Thompson and Felton were by no means the only culprits. Tim Cahill's cover story on the marketing of Olympic swimmer Mark Spitz was, he said, "written in seventeen hours straight, with them taking each page as it came out of my typewriter and running it over to the printer." Ben Fong-Torres was so late on a story that an art director was moved to heave a plateful of spaghetti at him. Annie Leibovitz was asked to take a picture of a Coca-Cola can and took two days to get it right. Even the work of disciplined writers like Tom Wolfe came in at a furious rush, prompting a series of aggravations and invectives—the very essence, it seemed, of the Endless Boogie.

New employees would show up at nine in the morning to find they had the whole office to themselves. Much of the work got done at night—often all night. The production staff, said Dan Parker, "did absolutely nothing until three days before going to press. And then we'd put together 112-page issues in three days, twenty-four hours a day. And that's the reason we had such a huge staff of pasteup artists, because it all happened at once."

Visiting art directors, like *Ramparts* veteran Dugald Stermer, were appalled by the shoddy organization. "They were way overstaffed," he said, "with researchers everywhere and picture editors coming out of the woodwork. I suspect that was because Jann would say, 'Let's use a picture of John Lennon picking his nose,' and they had to get forty pictures of Lennon picking his nose, and then Jann wouldn't like any of them. When you're constantly ripping everything up at the last minute, you have to have assistants to assist the incompetence."

As the last stop on the *Stone* Express, the production staff suffered most intensely for every photo finish. "I used to sit there," said Barbara Ziller, "and think, This has got to be some kind of strange experiment, conducted by psychiatrists, to see how much stress a person could take." Drug use was heavy among the art staff, but never for recreational purposes. These were speed seekers, caught in a frantic cycle, and every single one of them might have been driven to padded rooms were it not for the good humor of Cindy Ehrlich, the production director, who wore a nurse's uniform during deadline periods and personally chased Jann Wenner out of the art room whenever he dared to enter and compound their misery.

The editor always seemed to lurk beneath the hysteria. Beyond the leeway Jann gave his foot-dragging writers, he was himself fond of acting at the last minute. In particular, Jann liked to toy with the masthead: moving names up and down like flags on a pole, changing an "associate" editor to an "assistant" or (worse yet) "contributing" editor if that individual had fallen from grace. Everyone had laughed when Charlie Perry gave a *Rolling Stone* editor a trophy whose plaque read: "Masthead Editor"; but thereafter they continued to refer to the masthead, hoping to divine what Jann Wenner thought of them that fortnight.

Staffers especially dreaded his tendency to switch covers just as the magazine was being put to bed. If "the cover of the *Rolling Stone*" was worth singing about for Dr. Hook, it was certainly worth the editor's obsession —for the cover dictated not only stance but sales as well. "Jann told me once that they were going to put a religious theme park on the cover," said art director Bob Kingsbury. "He didn't know where the park was going to be built, but fortunately I found someone who did. So after a full day, we found out the location and got someone to take shots of the park.

"Then Jann says, 'We're gonna change the cover.' So I spent another day arranging for *that*, when I ordinarily would have been working on layout. The next day, new cover. It's gonna be Liza Minnelli, he tells me. 'She's gonna be married, she's in Chicago, find out where.' So I called her agent in L.A., found out where she could be reached, located a photographer . . . and then Jann says, 'No. No photographs.' He now wants Norman Rockwell to do the cover.

"I said, 'Jann, I've got a four-hundred-dollar budget!' He said, 'Call him up anyway.' I went back to my office, not knowing what to do. Paul

Scanlon told me not to worry about it, to forget about calling Rockwell. A good thing, too, because the next day he changed the cover again. *Five times in a fucking week.*"

More celebrated was the Peter Frampton episode. Jann commissioned two different covers by two different photographers: one of the singer/guitarist standing windblown on the beach, the other of him in a shirtless, pretty-boy pose. The latter photo, said art director Roger Black, "made Frampton look like sort of a gay sex object, and it was pretty weird. Jann loved it, and it was incredibly embarrassing to the staff that he liked it so much."

His lieutenants begged Jann to run the beach photo. The editor wasn't persuaded. He had Black go to a shopping mall and randomly poll passersby as to which photo they found more appealing. Results favored the beach photo, so Jann relented.

But not for long. The day the cover was due to be shipped to the printer, Jann buttonholed Dan Parker. The traffic manager was aghast. "Be reasonable, Jann," he said. "There's no reason why we should change at this point. It's gonna cost us too much money, we're not gonna make our deadlines, we're gonna hold the press up—"

The editor cut him off, acknowledging the folly. That night, however, at two in the morning, Parker got a call.

"I understand your reasoning," said Jann. "And I don't care. I want the other cover."

Parker suppressed a mouthful of obscenities and assented. He personally delivered the new cover to Jann's house at about five in the morning.

As a result, early shipments and later shipments sported different photos of Peter Frampton. The cost for the switch itself ran to perhaps $15,000 —enough to hire an additional associate editor. To prove that the gamble had been worth it, Jann had sales figures compiled for each of the two covers. The figures showed little difference, but overall the Frampton issue sold extremely well, as word of the editor's last-minute boldness had been leaked to the media, giving the issue valuable advance press.

Dan Parker would remember the incident for several reasons. Not least of these was the sight of Jann Wenner at his gorgeous Victorian house on California and Octavia, hunched over an immense brandy snifter filled with cocaine. The editor's indulgences were legendary, but not altogether appreciated by his staff. Depending on a hungover or coked-out Jann Wenner was tempting fate. "He'd go out and party with someone, and the magazine would suffer for days," said an art director.

One doctor who examined Jann in the mid-seventies wrote to the editor, begging him to go easy on the booze and quit cocaine. Business associates always lived in fear that Jann would overdose, be arrested or commit a series of irrational acts that would plunge the company into bankruptcy. No one on the staff could prove that it was drugs that caused Jann to tear up covers at the last minute, or to commission expensive art by the photographer Hiro and then completely forget that he'd done so. But his associates weren't ignorant of the editor's habits and how those habits altered his personality. The staff had painted a coke spoon on the decorative stone that marked Jann's office parking space. Oftentimes the stone seemed to hang around the magazine's neck.

On one occasion, after Jann had taken a cover home and dawdled excessively with the headlines, Paul Scanlon raised the matter at an editorial meeting. Jann was contrite, admitting he'd been going at it rather hard, but promising that today marked a new day, that he'd clean up his act. Joe Eszterhas was not convinced. He jammed the blade of his buck knife into the teakwood table, demanding greater assurances, reminding Jann that they'd all heard him apologize before.

"Here was this very fierce guy just hitting on Jann," said Charlie Perry. "And there is no question at all that Joe was right and that all the things he was saying were true. And Jann's self-esteem sort of crumbled and his hands began to shake.

"He had come prepared, apparently, because he fumbled this cigarette out of his pocket, and it wasn't a cigarette—it was a cigarette paper filled with coke. He snorted it right there in front of us."

Paul Scanlon and Charlie Perry traded shocked stares. Scanlon snapped the pencil he was holding.

———

Rolling Stone's staff, Jann Wenner told a reporter, was "part of the drug culture." Yet it seemed that the only person at 625 Third Street who had the time and money to overindulge in recreational drugs was Jann. The others had too much work to do.

This always came as a crashing disappointment to new employees. They'd expected an office full of rutting, hallucinating hippies, not the grim asylum 625 Third Street sometimes appeared to be. "There we were, in rock & roll heaven," said one staffer who was there only briefly. "And no one was rocking out."

Those who came in from the cold and expected hearty slaps on the back were in for a surprise. At editorial meetings, said one new staffer, "I was made to feel that I was in kind of a mandarin-like atmosphere, and that I shouldn't say a word for the first two years."

Albany Knickerbocker News reporter Jim Kuntsler, after writing a favorable article about Jann, was hired by the editor to be the magazine's "Random Notes" editor. Jann took an immediate shine to the brash Easterner, calling him Nox (for "obnoxious"), as his English teacher at Chadwick had once referred to him. Kuntsler thought he had it made.

"Like a lot of people in my position," he said, "I was seduced by the idea of getting a real glamour job. What I realized after I got to *Rolling Stone* was that it was run like the Nixon White House. People communicated by memorandum, everybody would disappear into their little pigeonhole all day, and there was this whole alcoholic aroma that hung over the office. I realized after about two weeks there that this was not some sort of little hippie paradise I'd landed in—it was really an office full of sort of semi-alcoholic overachievers. I mean, it was not laid back and mellow *in the least*."

Even the sublime could be self-conscious, as no one proved more brazenly than Eszterhas. The once humble *Cleveland Plain Dealer* reporter underwent a transformation at *Rolling Stone* that bordered on the comical. He took to smoking a pipe, defending his copy to the last asterisk and, of course, waving his Buck knife at editorial meetings.

"The great image I have of Eszterhas," said one art staffer, "came when I was sitting there by my window, waiting for something to do. I was staring out into the parking lot, and he pulls up in a Saab and gets out. And he has a turtleneck on, and this pipe in his mouth, and his closely shaved beard like Hemingway's. He pulls out this full-length brown German leather coat that he has no reason to wear because it's not even cold. And he puts it on, and it's cut in a trench-coat style, so it's *full*—I mean, it's a lot of leather on this guy—and ties the belt around him, then checks out his reflection in the mirror on the side of the car. Then he takes his briefcase out and he checks the fit of the briefcase in his hand, and the fit of the pipe in his mouth. He looks himself over, and then he comes in the office, and he's set to go for another day."

Yet even Eszterhas was not as vain as his employer, Jann Wenner, a man so conscious of his looks that he denied a staff photographer a press pass because the photo she'd taken of him made him look fat. Unfortunately, the camera did not lie. Endlessly Jann wrestled with his weight. He tried a variety of reduction programs, including one which prescribed periodic injections of Swiss sheep urine. Nothing really worked. As his wife, Jane, told a friend, "Jann is the only person I know who can spend twenty thousand dollars a year on coke and gain twenty pounds."

If his employees were the moths, then Jann was the flame. Routinely he scorched their wings and they fled, unable to stand the heat of his capricious ways. At the office they spoke of "Waiting for Godot to Leave," and anonymous notes bearing the inscription "Jann Is the Wenner of Our Discontent" found their way onto various desks. "He was one of those men," said Dan Parker, "whose presence in the room you could actually feel." Indeed, whenever carpenter Ron Nagle felt Jann's presence, he habitually dropped his hammer.

One moment he was praising John Lennon's primal-scream therapist, Arthur Janov (who also treated Jann), saying, "It's the official position of this magazine that Janov is where it's at." The next moment he would be ordering Tim Cahill to tighten the screws on his previously objective piece on promoter Bill Graham—"to be something of a hatchet man," said Cahill. Cahill he would stand behind. Critic Lester Bangs he would not, and banned Bangs from *Rolling Stone* after a slam of a Canned Heat record drew a fiery reply from the band's manager . . . though later an interviewer would remind Jann of the thin ice *Rolling Stone* treaded with negative record reviews, inspiring the breezy reply: "Fuck 'em."

Often, and with some justification, Jann Wenner crowed publicly about *Rolling Stone*'s autonomy. Yet when money got tight, he told his music writers to accept airplane tickets and hotel accommodations offered by record companies rather than charge expenses to *Rolling Stone*. "Just be sure the story's unbiased," the editor would tell Ben Fong-Torres, who had learned much about bias simply from watching his boss. It was Jann, after all, who had ordered Fong-Torres to do a full-blown *"Rolling Stone* Interview" on Art Garfunkel rather than a simple profile, which the music editor thought was more appropriate. But Garfunkel, a tennis buddy of Jann's, got preferential treatment . . . and in fact was given the chance to revise the interview transcript—"and of course he slashed away like crazy," said Fong-Torres.

It was Jann, not one of his music writers, who covered the press conference announcing the breakup of Loggins and Messina. The editor took a personal interest in the matter, as Jim Messina was a good friend of his. After the conference, he repaired with his wife to Messina's Mother Lode Ranch in the Ojai Valley, where he lobbed a few questions at his friend "Jimmy—always known as Jim on his albums," as Jann wrote. Predictably, the interview was "full of all kinds of puff," said Fong-Torres, who fought to excise what he could.

When not invited to a party thrown by Paul McCartney, the editor repaid the snub by inserting a barb in a McCartney cover story. Only a year before, Jann had fired a writer for following his orders and asking McCartney if it was true that wife, Linda, was cheating on him.

It was hard to keep up, hard to ferret out his will from among the lightning impulses. Obsessions came and went. In early 1973, Maria Schneider, Marlon Brando's saucy object of desire in *The Last Tango in Paris*, became a Wenner houseguest, a companion of Jane's and, naturally, a subject for a major *Rolling Stone* feature, possibly even a cover story. By the middle of 1973, Jann had plans to write the story himself and even shoot some of the photographs. Not long afterward, Maria Schneider vanished from the Wenners' lives, and thus from the *Rolling Stone* feature inventory.

When in doubt, staffers learned to put presumption in favor of celebrity, for Jann certainly did. The rule rather than the exception was to show musicians respect, as critics like Lester Bangs learned too late. Columbia boss Clive Davis was to be referred to by *Rolling Stone* writers as "Mr. Davis." Also by decree, all celebrity names listed in "Random Notes" were to be boldfaced. Ben Fong-Torres knew how to make the best of this. He boldfaced "God" and "Allah" whenever the names appeared.

What staffers did not always realize was that Jann's infatuation with celebrity could come at their direct expense, without any warning at all. Associate editor Robert Greenfield certainly learned this the hard way. Greenfield covered the bawdy, storied Rolling Stones tour of 1972, having won the complete confidence of the Stones (later reflected in Greenfield's book about the tour, *S.T.P.: A Journey Through America with the Rolling Stones*). Things were going fine until Truman Capote and Princess Lee Radziwill began to show up at the concerts with *Rolling Stone* press passes. Before Greenfield knew what to say, he received word that Jann wanted one 15,000-word feature from him, after which Capote would cover the tour. The explanation was simple enough: it was summertime, and the magazine could no longer afford to pay Greenfield's expenses.

The associate editor was not pleased by this news, but nonetheless undertook to write his opus. To his horror, the 15,000 words were reduced to 1,500 words of captions for Annie Leibovitz's photos. In the meantime, Capote—who was casually treating Stones personnel to dinners and forwarding the bills to *Rolling Stone*—never filed a word.

"Truman and his guests were living *big* on the road," said Greenfield. "They had *suites*. And this is with *Rolling Stone* having no money, right?

Jann took me off, a guy just willing to do hard work, and gave it to Capote, and got nothing for it."

In fact, Jann did get something. He got to meet Truman Capote.

Often Jann communicated his desires by a swarm of memos, many completely contradictory, others so niggling or preposterous as to warrant no attention at all. The masthead, at least, could offer clues as to how Jann felt about his underlings, but even that proved too cryptic. Associate art director John Goodchild thought he'd found the answer. He drew up a "Karma Chart," graphing—with alarming accuracy—the rise and fall of key staffers. Many were amused by the Karma Chart, but few heeded it. Each refused to believe that his or her savage love affair with *Rolling Stone* and Jann Wenner could have so predictable a doom.

Yet no one could deny that the editor tended to fall head over heels for a prospective employee, hire him or her with great fanfare, then later turn on his "flavor of the month" (as critic Dave Marsh termed it) and find some way to force the individual out. Jann had certainly been high on Timothy Ferris, telling him at one point that he'd like Ferris to be his next managing editor. A few months later, Ferris was taken off salary even as his star was rising in literary circles.

(A jolted Ferris called Hunter Thompson just after Jann delivered the news. Hunter wasn't home, said Thompson's wife, Sandy, who also mentioned that the Thompsons were having financial problems as well—down to their last four hundred dollars.

(Later that day, Ferris located Thompson at the Watergate Hotel. Thompson asked how Ferris was weathering the bad news. "Well, okay," said Ferris. "It'll work out in the long run. But what pisses me off is that Jann won't pay me severance."

(Thompson did not hesitate. "If you need any money," he said, "I could lend you four hundred.")

Often Jann's problem was not who to fire, but how. The editor was not known for his bravery. He openly contemplated firing production director Cindy Ehrlich while she was in the hospital. He repeatedly mispronounced a staffer's monosyllabic last name until the staffer got the message that he was being written out. Concerned on one occasion that an employee might take his dismissal violently, Jann locked his office door and slipped the termination under his door for his secretary to deliver.

Since the editor had his difficulties delivering the bad news straightforwardly, speculation about when a person was likely to be fired became office sport. "You are on the shit-list," one in-house quiz had it, when:

—You're given a "promotion" with no increase in salary.

—You hear that Jann's been bad-mouthing you. [No. Jann bad-mouths everybody.]

—Your office is torn down so that the department will be "more spacious."

—The receptionist asks if you have an appointment with someone here. [No. You're just a face in the crowd, which is a plus.]

—You come back from vacation and several people ask you if you found a job.

—Your office is moved regularly. [No. This is a sign of stability.]

How to retire art director Bob Kingsbury became particularly problematic for Jann. Kingsbury's contribution to *Rolling Stone* was illustrious. His clean, sculptured graphics were single-handedly responsible for giving the magazine a look demonstrably different from those of other underground papers. He worked slavishly long hours and seldom seemed affected by the hysteria around him. On Jon Goodchild's Karma Chart, a single straight line was drawn across the graph: The Kingsbury Constant.

But Bob Kingsbury's value to *Rolling Stone* began to diminish immediately after the magazine switched to four-color at the beginning of 1973. Perhaps Kingsbury could have mastered four-color as he had the duotone process, given a week or two of apprenticeship, but the magazine never had that much time to spare. There were other problems as well. Kingsbury, at forty-five the oldest staffer, was slowed down by poor eyesight and creatively hindered by what some saw as an antiquated view of graphics. In the meantime, said Barbara Ziller, "Jann was getting a lot of pressure from a lot of people to make the magazine a lot slicker, and Kingsbury was a perfect target."

Or was he? After all, Kingsbury was married to Linda Schindelheim, Jane Wenner's sister-in-law. The Schindelheims and Kingsburys owned a considerable block of company stock. Jann had enough problems with his own vacillating marriage and the implications it held for control of Straight Arrow Publishers, Inc. He didn't need to add to them by alienating the Schindelheims.

Jann found a way out by appointing Kingsbury "Art Director of Special Projects" and filling the vacancy with Mike Salisbury, a renowned designer from Los Angeles. Kingsbury was moved to a new office, given a variety of often menial tasks and assigned leper status.

"My marriage was falling apart at the time," said Kingsbury, "and this was tied in to my job in all sorts of complicated ways. I was trapped. If I quit my job, I lose my wife. If I stay on, I feel miserable about being here."

Arguably, Jann Wenner was showing his compassion by keeping Bob Kingsbury on the payroll until it was no longer affordable to do so. His humanity was not so easily discerned, however, in the case of Grover Lewis.

Lewis and his boss had never exactly been pals. The Texas newsman considered the Berkeley dropout a brat and a groupie. Lewis was only slightly amused when Jann seemed flattered that people called him Citizen Wenner—a nickname Lewis had sardonically coined. He was amused even less by Jann's reverential treatment of rock stars when a little bit of journalistic detachment might have been warranted. And Lewis was downright incensed when the editor changed a passage in a Lewis story, whereby a passing reference to Tom Wolfe became "the great writer Tom Wolfe."

He was particularly rankled by Jann's cavalier treatment of freelance writers. Lewis had been charged with establishing a fiction department and purchasing short stories. He procured six manuscripts, promising each author $200, payable upon publication. The manuscripts gathered dust for over a year. Inquiring writers wanted to know when they'd see their money. Lewis asked his boss the same question. No reply was forthcoming. Finally, nearly two years after some of the stories had been contracted for, Jann rendered his decision. None of the stories would be published, and none of the writers would receive a dime. Infuriated, Lewis took the matter up with research assistant Sarah Lazin, who eventually coaxed Jann to authorize $70 kill fees for each author.

By this time it was March of 1973, and Lewis was already thinking of leaving *Rolling Stone*. Two months before, Lyndon Johnson had died, and at Jann's behest Lewis had contacted Texas writer and LBJ historian Ronnie Dugger. *Rolling Stone* wanted a major piece on LBJ's burial, Lewis informed Dugger. Dugger said he was sorry but he didn't have time in his schedule.

Jann would not take no for an answer, insisting that Lewis press Dugger. Dugger finally relented and wrote the article under intense deadline pressure. Paul Scanlon read the piece and told Lewis to notify Dugger that the article had been accepted. The following day, the LBJ piece was killed. Profoundly embarrassed, Lewis wrote in a memo that the incident "casts a slur on my personal and professional integrity as an editor of *Rolling Stone* or any other imaginable publication."

The associate editor made no attempt to hide his contempt for Jann

Wenner, who once asked David Felton, "Why does Grover hate me?" Unlike Felton or Charlie Perry or even Hunter Thompson, Lewis would not look past the editor's foibles.

For that matter, Grover Lewis had foibles of his own. He was, by his own admission, "from the hard-drinking Texas reporter tradition." But not all hard-drinking Texas reporters had to be picked up off the floor of Jerry's Inn and driven home in the *Rolling Stone* van. Lewis's fall-down episodes became more numerous by the beginning of 1973, when the short stories and the LBJ piece were killed. Some of the other editors suspected that Lewis's increasing reliance on quotations rather than his own shimmering prose was a direct result of his drinking.

On the other hand, as Hunter Thompson put it: "Hell, *I* was a drunk! *Jann* was fucked up. How could you single out Grover?"

Said Charlie Perry, "He was a lot more productive than Felton, for example. And he had a professional attitude. I mean, he *would* get drunk sometimes, certainly, but he was the kind of guy who would write at least a thousand words a day—and terrific words, too. He was carrying his weight."

But Grover Lewis's unpleasant attitude toward Jann made his drinking less forgivable. Jann wanted Lewis out. Lewis himself wanted out, and had in fact been shopping for a contract to do a biography on controversial Texas politician John Connally. His highest offer was $35,000. Jann got wind of it and offered $40,000. Lewis accepted, and a contract was drawn up and signed on June 12, 1973. Lewis gave up his apartment lease in San Francisco, put down money in San Antonio for a house and a new car and set a wedding date with his fiancée, *Rolling Stone* secretary Rae Ence.

The ink on the contract had not been dry for long when Jann called up Alan Rinzler. "Alan, I don't want you to do this book," he said. He added that Grover Lewis was a drunk and Jann wanted nothing to do with him.

Rinzler took the contract over to Straight Arrow vice president Tom Baker. Baker examined it and looked up at Rinzler. "Well," he said, "it looks like we've got a deal here."

"Yeah," Rinzler agreed, taking the contract back. "But we're not going to honor it."

Rinzler delivered the news to Lewis in an act he would later describe as "one of the worst things I ever did as a person." It was two days before the writer was to be married. Several days after the wedding, Jann wrote Lewis. "We are all deeply sorry that Straight Arrow Books was unable to go through with the Connally biography," the letter began, and ended with "Good fortune and good years in the married life."

In an attached note, Jann asked Lewis to return to the *Rolling Stone* office a special typewriter he'd presented to the writer as a gift.

Lewis did not return the typewriter. Instead, he filed suit. The case took nearly a year before it went to arbitration, with Jann protesting his innocence even after the presiding judge warned him that if a settlement wasn't reached, he was prepared to side with Lewis. "Screw it! I won't settle!" the editor said to his attorney during recess. Rinzler bore down on his boss. Grover Lewis was awarded $13,000. He kept the typewriter as well, using it only for occasions when nasty letters were called for.

———

Even with Lewis, however, Jann could not say, "You're fired." In the same letter in which he acknowledged being "unable" to publish the Connally book, he offered Lewis a feature assignment "to bring in some of those fast, big bucks." Lewis, at this bitter stage, wasn't interested.

But others were, and would be. Immediately after removing Tim Cahill from the payroll—even after a number of editors volunteered to take pay cuts to keep Cahill salaried—Jann got wind that the writer was planning to hitchhike across the United States and promptly contracted him for an article on the subject. When Cahill returned from his travels, he was rehired with a substantial increase in salary.

When music editor Abe Peck accused Jann of being a tyrant, of making people's lives miserable, Peck was promptly fired . . . and then contracted to write a book on the history of the sixties, for more money than he'd been making as music editor.

It was Jann Wenner's strange way of imposing his authority and apologizing for the need to do so. He would change covers without regard for the suffering it would bring his production staff. After seeing them in tears, however, he would buy them massages at Kabuki Springs. He would take writers off salary with neither warning nor explanation. But when they had a sick mother or a child needing special education, Jann would take out his checkbook without hesitation. It was also very much like Jann Wenner to award Dan Parker a $500 bonus and then to scream at the business staffer who deducted taxes from the sum. The editor's monumental gestures were not meant to be deductible.

Among these brilliant, erratic talents, Jann Wenner had one thing the others did not have: "a gift," as one staffer put it, "for telling other people what to do and getting them to do it." This was no casual skill. When Cindy Ehrlich stole a copy of the company payroll in an effort to prove the inequities in the salary structure, the editor had several choices. He elected to laugh about it and act on Ehrlich's suggestions. His tirades over this missed fact or that bungled caption were often justified. "And just as he could be overly negative about something," said Ben Fong-Torres, "he could suddenly soften up and see your side of it."

The reins were loose but forever in his hands. "He let you feel like it was partly your magazine," said Barbara Downey, "until it really came down to a crunch. Then it was *his* magazine." This meant giving David Felton five months to write a two-part cover story on Richard Pryor and Lily Tomlin and nearly a year for another story that never ran. But when Felton disappeared for several days and left his office door locked, the editor felt it was time for a message. He had the writer's office broken into, his belongings boxed up and the boxes transported to a warehouse.

The man was himself a mystery to the staff. For someone who seldom read books, he certainly brought a wealth of current knowledge to editorial meetings. Though employees came and went, he made a point of knowing them, even compiling haphazard dossiers which he kept in his files.

He chewed his nails to the bone, consumed food and drugs in unbelievable quantities, flirted one minute and hollered the next. He feared the Next Great Earthquake, kept documents stored in a nuclear-safe vault in Monterey County and was married to a woman who so loathed driving that Jann often sent a car over just to get her out of the house—"limo therapy," some called it. He was a man of strange phobias, a kid, dancing from the shadows into the light and back into the shadows again. How could he be so uncannily aware of things? How could he prevail over his demons? How could his vision be so unmottled?

———

At his Victorian house, a wonderful edifice duly noted in home & garden magazines, he threw a party. They all came, the dancers in this Endless Boogie, and drank champagne and took mescaline and sat in the backyard around their leader. He hardly looked like their father, but Jann Wenner liked to think of *Rolling Stone* as his family. It was a concept he promoted, and not just to breed company loyalty. It gave them all purpose, a reminder that the suffering was shared, that the triumph was not only his, that he and they were a part of each other, that he was not alone.

David Felton arrived at the party, as he often did, with the family's child, wrapped in swaddling clothes, cradled in his arms. It was a canister of nitrous oxide. Together they laughed.

Chapter Twelve

THE BIG LEAGUES

On the evening of June 17, 1972, Hunter Thompson was sitting in the bar of the Watergate Hotel—preoccupied with his usual medley of Sauza Gold tequila shots and football conversation—when a pack of burglars led by G. Gordon Liddy broke into the Democratic National Committee headquarters.

Only a few months before, a young reporter from the *Washington Post* named Carl Bernstein had sent his résumé to *Rolling Stone*, hoping to join the likes of Thompson, Timothy Crouse, Joe Eszterhas, Grover Lewis and David Felton. Jann Wenner passed on the chance to hire Bernstein.

The Watergate story thus became Bernstein's and the *Washington Post*'s, not Thompson's and *Rolling Stone*'s. But Thompson had loftier concerns on his mind. There was, for starters, the U.S. Senate race in Colorado. He'd received hundreds of letters from people offering to work on his campaign. Running for high office seemed like the next logical step on the depraved Jacob's ladder he called his career.

On the other hand, it was hard to picture the Gonzo journalist breaking bread with the likes of Barry Goldwater. It was compromising enough that, during a debate with the Aspen sheriff in 1970, the Freak Power candidate had been made to promise that he wouldn't eat mescaline on the job. He'd probably be collared and dragged off to a brig in the Capitol basement the moment he appeared on the Senate floor in his ski jacket to denounce the sundry greed hogs and fun pigs of the Western world.

So Gary Hart, God save his twisted soul, could *have* the Colorado seat. After George McGovern's landslide defeat, Thompson was inclined to view the 1976 election as "a final affirmation of the Rape of the 'American Dream,' " with Nixon passing the torch to that loathsome media attack dog, Spiro Agnew. Then came Watergate and a feeding frenzy of investigative journalists, congressional investigators and special prosecutors. By early 1974, even the apocalyptic Dr. Thompson had to raise an eyebrow.

As he wrote in a memo: "Agnew is gone, Nixon is on the ropes, and in terms of *realpolitik* the Republican party is down in the same ditch with the Democrats—they are both looking *back* into their own loyalist ranks for names, ideas & possibilities: the GOP has been stripped all the way back to 1964, with Goldwater/Reagan vs. Rockefeller & maybe Percy on the outside . . . but in fact Nixon's mind-bending failure has effectively castrated the aggressive/activist core of the GOP (all the Bright Young Men, as it were), and barring totally unforeseen circumstances between now & Nov. 1976, the GOP looks at a future of carping opposition until at least 1984."

That was one side of Hunter Thompson—the side that presumably gave him impetus to climb out of bed every afternoon. Tugging at his soul, however, was the belief instilled since Chicago in 1968: "that *all* career politicians should be put on The Rack—in the name of either poetic or real *justice*, and probably for the Greater Good."

The more optimistic side prevailed. In early 1974, Hunter Thompson proposed to his friend and editor Jann Wenner that the two of them round up some of the finest liberal minds in the country, hole up for a weekend and "put something together that will force a genuine alteration of consciousness in the realm of national politics."

That was big talk, but Jann Wenner was ready to hear it. *Rolling Stone* had been poised on the brink of greatness, and the widely heralded 1972 campaign coverage of Thompson and Timothy Crouse provided the needed shove. Now Dan Rather and *New York Times* editor A. M. Rosenthal were chorusing *Rolling Stone*'s praises. Joining their sentiments was the prestigious *Columbia Journalism Review*, which said of Jann's magazine, "In a very real sense, it has spoken for—and to—an entire generation of young Americans. It has given an honest—and searching—account of one of the deepest social revolutions of our times."

Those ringing words were published and read by Jann just as Thompson was launching his auspicious proposal. But the editor had additional reasons for liking the idea of a highbrow political conference. No matter what John Burks or the other bygone rabble of 1970 might say, the editor was as disgusted by Johnson and Nixon as the next liberal. Fully eighteen months before McGovern won the Democratic nomination, Jann was singling out the senator as "a righteous cat." He felt far more comfortable in the realm of partisan national politics than with the impractical yammerings of the radicals.

By no means was he a sophisticate. "What we need," he told one of the many interviewers who solicited the worldviews of the *Rolling Stone* prodigy in 1970, "is a good business executive, well-motivated, who can run the business of the country. We don't need a leader to set our foreign policy. Our foreign policy should be, 'Let's take care of our own problems.'"

As publisher Larry Durocher would say: "I would bet you a hundred dollars Jann doesn't know how a bill gets through Congress. I'd bet you a thousand dollars Jann couldn't define the term 'initiative petition.' He just had no fundamental understanding of how the whole thing worked."

Durocher, like many, suspected that Jann's interest was in politicians, not politics. But Jann was also interested in Hunter Thompson, which was the other reason why the conference appealed to him. The editor had been trying, without much success, to keep his star writer tied to *Rolling Stone*. He'd proposed story after story: the mayor's races in New York and Los Angeles, wrestling, truckers, Texas. Each was assigned; none was written. It was no secret that Hunter Thompson was the magazine's most marketable commodity. The Gonzo journalist had a hold on *Rolling Stone*'s readers no other writer could duplicate. Joe Eszterhas's three cover stories in 1974, for instance, were among the four worst-selling issues that year. By contrast, Thompson's articles generated an average of five-hundred letters each.

Jann dangled one offer after the next. In truth, Hunter Thompson was in no shape to contemplate a new assignment. "He was so exhausted," said Paul Scanlon. "For the '72 campaign, he filed something like 95,000 words against deadline, and it was rigorous. For all of his Dr. Raoul Duke shit, when he got down to doing it, he did it, and it wasn't fucked up when he did it either."

So all this highfalutin talk of organizing a think-tank session was most encouraging. Jann agreed to finance the affair, which Thompson decided should take place as far from the media loons as possible. He had just such a place in mind: Elko, Nevada, a town of 8,617, described by Thompson as an "atavistic sanctuary with nothing to recommend it except the world's largest dead Polar Bear and the biggest commercially available hamburger west of the Ruhr."

And so they convened on February 21–24, 1974, in the Elko Stockmen's Motor Hotel: Jann Wenner, Hunter Thompson and seven alumni of the McGovern/Kennedy/McCarthy school of liberalism. During that cold weekend, the men vocally mulled over, as Thompson put it, "some of the critical and unavoidable questions that *any* presidential candidate will have to deal with, in order to be taken seriously in '76." In a broader sense, he added in his Elko preamble, "I think we should also take a serious look at the health/prognosis for the whole idea of Participatory Democracy, in America or anywhere else . . . because unless we're honestly convinced that the Practice of Politics is worth more than just a short-term high or the kind of short-term money that power-pimps pay for hired guns, my own feeling is that we'll be a lot better off avoiding all the traditional liberal bullshit and just saying it straight out: that we're all just a bunch of fine-tuned Political Junkies and we're ready to turn Main Street into a graveyard for anybody who'll pay the price & even pretend to say the Right Things."

No stone was left unturned: income distribution, natural resources, foreign policy, the failure of the free press, racism. . . . Each participant brought a position paper, ranging from McGovern strategist Rick Stearns's analogy between the American political system and Plato's cave to Jann Wenner's less learned observations: "We need a statement and a program that can be brought to the people for public debate. . . . Language must be simple, basic and profound. To restore the confidence of the people, we must go directly to them."

Not much was decided at Elko, except to combine their ramblings in book form and to meet again in the summer. Thompson walked away from the conference disgusted, calling the affair "gibberish" and "liberal elitism at its worst." After reading the transcript of the meeting, he suggested in a letter that Jann "view the whole gig as a tax write-off" or publish the book for whatever "dubious measure of 'prestige' " it might garner.

The Elko attendants never reconvened, and the transcripts of that first meeting never saw the light of day. Yet the very fact that the editor of *Rolling Stone* would sponsor such an event was remarkable to many—including Hunter Thompson and another Elko participant, Richard N. Goodwin.

Goodwin was a major catch for Jann Wenner: a political veteran, a *player*, a man of great controversy and fabulous connections. He'd graduated first in his class at Harvard Law School in 1958; served as Supreme Court Justice Felix Frankfurter's clerk just after graduating; investigated TV quiz-show payola scandals for the House in 1959; was tapped later that year to be Senator John F. Kennedy's speechwriter; and thereafter leapfrogged from one Democratic administration or campaign to the next, acquiring loyalists and vicious detractors who cited him for arrogance and opportunism. But even his worst enemies had to admit that Dick Goodwin, bastard or no, was a political genius.

Having just completed a book, Goodwin had time on his hands and a willingness to try something new. Jann's offer was expansive: he wanted Dick Goodwin to be *Rolling Stone*'s politics editor, to set up shop in Washington and to coordinate a news bureau there. Goodwin would be in charge of a "Politics" section in each issue. If all went well, the section might spin off into a magazine of its own. In the meantime, Goodwin would receive a handsome salary, part of the rent on a house in Georgetown, an office and a free hand to develop the Washington bureau.

Publisher Larry Durocher was disturbed when he heard of the deal. He and Goodwin had crossed paths frequently in New England politics, and while Durocher had enormous regard for Goodwin's intelligence, it was the publisher's view that "*Rolling Stone* readers would never read Goodwin's political pages. What they wanted to read was cultural politics, the kind of stuff Hunter Thompson and Timmy Crouse wrote.

"But along came Dick Goodwin, and Jann once again got starfucked. He walked into the room and said in a sense, 'What does it cost me to kiss your ass?' And Dick Goodwin looked him in the eye and said, 'Well, jeez, I'm awful broke and I'm always destitute, and whatever money I have I always piss away, including money I have access to until I get fired for pissing it away.' And so *eyes open* Jann walked into that deal with Goodwin."

But Durocher could not bend all his attention toward ousting Goodwin from *Rolling Stone*. He had to keep at least one eye on another Wenner acquisition, John A. Walsh.

For some time Jann had been nurturing a creeping dissatisfaction with his managing editor, Paul Scanlon. The man Ralph Gleason called "Jann's Irish bleeder" was an effective buffer between Jann and his writers, often absorbing the editor's rantings without so much as a counterpunch. That made him quite different from John Burks, or, for that matter, Joe Eszterhas, whose size and swagger and Buck knife intimidated Jann greatly.

This very lack of flamboyance also made it easy to overlook Scanlon's crucial role at the magazine. Like Felton and Perry, he was a tastemaker, a man who knew good writing and how to advance literate "Rolling Stone stories." Unlike his associates, Scanlon was involved daily with grooming writers, building a stable of talent and going to the wall for them. The result, said Durocher, was that "Scanlon had just become a doormat. Wenner would kick him down and Scanlon would get up. But he always got the job done, always got the paper out."

Yet by the middle of 1973, Scanlon—always reclusive and never one to break his neck returning phone calls—had become, in Jann's eyes, down-right unaccountable. The managing editor was spending more and more time at Jerry's Inn, doing much of his editing work there. Scanlon appeared demoralized, noting no doubt that his name on the masthead now appeared below two editors he outranked, Eszterhas and Fong-Torres—a telltale sign. But it was not Paul Scanlon's style to confront Jann with a stream of bilious ultimatums. Instead, he simply withdrew.

Jann had dangled Scanlon's job in front of several people, including Timothy Ferris and Jon Landau. In the meantime, Scanlon's close friend Joe Eszterhas took it upon himself to conduct editorial meetings when the managing editor went on vacation, and at the same time suggested Scanlon's replacement to Jann, a man he'd written a few freelance pieces for: *Newsday* sports editor John Walsh.

Walsh had everything the *Rolling Stone* editor wanted: impeccable news-room credentials, imagination and a Rolodex bulging with the names of top-flight journalists. Jann put in a call to Durocher and asked him to interview Walsh.

"Why do I have to talk to him?" Durocher wanted to know.

"Well," said Jann, "he's Irish, you're Irish . . ." His voice trailed off.

"Have you already offered him a job?"

"Yeah."

"What happened?"

"Well, he doesn't want the job," Jann stammered. "He's heard I cheat people, he's heard I do this and that . . . Anyway, he knows a couple of people you know and . . . well, look, just make one of your deals with him. Make a deal so that if he comes and I do whatever he thinks I'm gonna do to him, he'll come out all right."

Durocher made the call to Walsh. The *Newsday* sports editor explained that he'd heard that Jann was a difficult man to work for, a man given to prolonged honeymoons and then sudden, inexplicable divorces. Durocher nodded to himself. They were talking about the same man all right.

He persuaded Walsh to meet for drinks. "Why don't we meet in Manhattan?" Durocher suggested. "I've got to commute out there anyway."

Walsh hesitated. "Could you maybe come out here to Long Island?" he asked.

Durocher was taken aback. "Uh, well, I could, John," he said. "But it'd be more convenient if you could hop in your car and—"

"I don't have a car," said Walsh.

"Really? How come?"

"I don't have a license."

"Jeez," muttered Durocher. "Thirty years old and you don't have a license?"

"Well," said Walsh, "I'm legally blind."

"You're *blind* . . ."

Immediately after they hung up, Durocher got on the horn to Jann. "What the hell are you doing with this guy?" he demanded. "Next time would you please give me a little tip about a guy's handicap before you send me off to talk with him, for Chrissake?"

"You're always telling me it doesn't matter what color a man is," Jann replied huffily.

"Color?" The New Englander was confused. "What are you talking about? Is the guy black?"

"No," said Jann. "He's an albino."

"Well, that's not a handicap. That's not what I'm talking about. Jann, he's blind!"

There was a moment of silence. Then: "He can't be blind!"

"Jann. I have it from a fairly reliable source."

Walsh was eventually hired and given a sweetheart deal that guaranteed him eighteen months of salary. His entry was preceded by the demotion of Scanlon to senior editor—an act that Scanlon was almost literally the last person on the staff to find out about—and subsequent boasts by Jann that he'd netted a big fish, a man who would kick *Rolling Stone* up a whole new flight of stairs. "We'd been hearing about him a long time before he actually showed up," said associate editor David Harris. "Walsh was supposed to be the latest savior, this great ace Jann had found."

Even when the staff blanched at the initial sight of the rather straight-looking *Newsday* editor, Jann's enthusiasm did not abate. The *Rolling Stone* editor desired a new look for his magazine, a newsier format, something more in keeping with *Time* and *The New Yorker*, and he encouraged Walsh to experiment. A back-of-the-book section was developed, featuring a drinking column by Charlie Perry among other regular items, and the front of the book was expanded to include "Loose Talk," a box of zippy quotes by various celebrities. For feature assignments, Walsh often reached for his fabled Rolodex and brought in East Coast writers, sometimes with excellent results—most notably Rob Ross's jolting exposé of Freelandia Airlines, a critically heralded "not-for-profit" travel club that was in fact bilking its members to the tune of millions of dollars.

Walsh cultivated a good relationship with Jann, taking him to a Giants baseball game and explaining to the fascinated editor the meaning of a double play. He also handled the Paul Scanlon problem deftly by assuring his predecessor that he wanted Scanlon to stay with the magazine. The rest of the *Rolling Stone* staff was not as easily charmed, however, and resisted his every innovation. By spearheading a scheme that moved production facilities to St. Louis, which entailed firing the entire *Rolling Stone* production staff (minus Cindy Ehrlich, who became the "Random Notes" editor), he infuriated the magazine's rank and file. Walsh also drew the ire of the music editors by suggesting sweeping changes in the music coverage. Fong-Torres wasn't sure the *Newsday* sports editor knew enough about rock & roll to be up to such a task. Walsh certainly earned no points with Jon Landau when the managing editor made it clear that he intended to have the reviews editor removed from his position.

"He was trying to professionalize the magazine," said one staffer. "We were like tops spinning out of control, growing enormously—very visible on the national scene and yet still being run like this little hippie alternative weekly in somebody's basement. He was bound to step on people's toes."

Had Walsh proved a charismatic authority, he might have won the staff over to his structural maneuvers. Unfortunately, many of them found his judgment appalling. Even those who genuinely liked and respected Walsh —and many did—wondered what he was doing at *Rolling Stone*. He seemed hopelessly out of step. His first supporter, Joe Eszterhas, thought Walsh was making dull assignments and said so. Charlie Perry was seldom amused by the "noncomic pun" headlines Walsh conjured up.

Walsh wrote fan letters to fellow albinos Johnny and Edgar Winter, invited them to the office and took to wearing a "White Power" T-shirt. Photos of the Winters seemed to crop up unsuitably often, including a nude shot of Johnny Winter and a female, which struck many as beyond the pale of good taste.

Then there was Walsh's "secret project." The managing editor had a big story in his hands and would tell no one, not even Scanlon, about it. Editors huddled at Jerry's Inn: What was Walsh up to? Perhaps the fellow really did have a bombshell on his hands. Perhaps Jann knew what he was doing, after all, when he hired Walsh.

Word finally leaked out. The secret project was a story about J. Edgar Hoover being gay. Scanlon was astonished. "That's the oldest story in the world!" he told Michael Rogers. "What are we doing that for? It's not doable, and it's thirty-five years old anyway!" The piece never ran.

A story that did run was a profile of the children of Watergate burglar E. Howard Hunt, written by Washington freelance journalist Julia Cameron. The idea was Jann's, but Walsh shepherded the project along and would later describe the article as one of the accomplishments of which he was most proud. Larry Durocher saw it differently. The publisher believed that the article, in which the jailed burglar's children spoke bitterly of their father, was "a terrible thing to do," a cheap shot unbefitting a respectable publication regardless of its political persuasion.

For perhaps the only time in his life, Durocher was in agreement with William F. Buckley of the conservative *National Review*. Buckley, the Hunt children's godfather, wrote Jann—who was due to appear on Buckley's TV show, *Firing Line*—after the article appeared. "You are a sham as a journalist," wrote Buckley, "and a failure as a human being." He also withdrew Jann's invitation to appear on his show.

Jann hastily wrote back, claiming that he was out of town when the article was published. The Buckley missive he pinned to the office bulletin board—delighted, it appeared to Durocher, to be getting a letter from the great Buckley, no matter what it said. "Now that's what you call terminally starfucked," Durocher sighed.

Though John Walsh had made a career out of reading the printed page, his poor eyesight remained an obvious handicap. Staffers began to notice the unread manuscripts piling up on Walsh's desk. Assistant art director

Lloyd Ziff grew impatient waiting for Walsh to examine the art for each issue, and finally began to go around the managing editor and get approval from the associates.

Walsh did score a coup in nursemaiding Hunter Thompson through "Fear and Loathing at the Super Bowl," though the piece was tedious and (even by Gonzo standards) meandering. (Among Thompson's sources were a few Oakland Raiders who felt more comfortable sharing their views after the journalist treated them to cocaine. Thompson later insisted that *Rolling Stone* reimburse him for the coke as a legitimate business expense. The accountants said no, but Walsh interceded on Thompson's behalf.) His single greatest achievement, however, had nothing to do with any particular story. By hiring *Forbes* staffer Marianne Partridge as his copy chief, Walsh broke the gender barrier at *Rolling Stone* and changed the dynamics of the office forever.

———

Jann Wenner was hardly a standard-issue chauvinist. If a woman, an albino or a hippie leftist could get the job done, so be it. (Unless the person was unattractive. The editor, who enjoyed reading articles that described his appearance in flattering terms, believed that physically unappealing people were ineffective leaders. He refused to include one of his top female staffers in a publicity photograph because she wasn't suitably attractive. The woman went home crying that day. Yet even this mean streak was gender-blind. Years later, Jann would refuse to hire a well-qualified male candidate for the post of assistant managing editor. "He's ugly," the editor said, and that was that.)

All the same, the photographs at the Big Sur conference of 1971 said it all. Of the eighteen who attended, the only female among them was Annie Leibovitz, who was there to take pictures of the men. Back at the office, women were answering the phones, ordering the supplies and typing the memos. They were Jann's "chicks," entrusted to remind him when Jane's birthday came, to buy gifts for his friends and family, to keep him from smoking too many cigarettes, to make his coffee . . .

One day editorial assistant Sarah Lazin refused to bring Jann his coffee. Jann fired her. Walsh advised Lazin to ignore him. She did, and the editor never brought it up again. But he still expected the "chicks" to bring him his coffee. One woman found her own way of getting even. She regularly spat in the cup before presenting it to her boss. Jann did not seem to notice the difference in flavor.

As the male editors of *Rolling Stone* mirrored the various attitudes and values of Jann Wenner, so too did Jane Wenner reflect the predicament of the magazine's females. The editor's wife was a valued confidante who often helped him make cover and personnel decisions. Yet her role was strictly advisory, despite her equal partnership in Straight Arrow Publishers, Inc. Unlike her focused, exceedingly ambitious husband, Jane, with her obvious artistic talent, required constant nurturing. She received far more of this from Max Palevsky, who attempted to find work for her in films, than from the oft-preoccupied Jann Wenner.

She seemed a lonely woman to her friends, and remarkably unsure of herself for one so witty and beautiful. Seldom did she show up at the office; and once when she did, carrying an armful of shopping bags, Jann loudly berated her for parading their wealth in front of his staffers. At a party, Jann introduced his wife to Timothy Ferris in a manner Ferris found rather telling: taking Jane's hand, inserting it into Ferris's and then pumping their clasped hands with his own, as if Jane Wenner could not perform this primitive gesture without her husband's assistance.

Viewed strictly as a workplace, *Rolling Stone* had for some time owed its stability to women. Advertising director Laurel Gonsalves had performed valuable administrative functions for years; receptionist Judy Lawrence and production director Cindy Ehrlich were indispensable staffers and, in the words of art director Mike Salisbury, "cracked the whip and ran the show." Yet the real levers of power were well out of reach. In a sense, the women of *Rolling Stone* could do no better than to press their faces up against the window of the Raoul Duke Room and imagine what it must be like inside that hallowed incubator. Each of them could understand the frustration of Sarah Lazin, who lived with Paul Scanlon and heard him describe every evening a spectacular world to which she was denied access.

It was difficult for a female employee to contemplate the *Rolling Stone* experience without thinking of opportunities withheld; of the business manager who habitually brushed up against their backsides; of the accountant who urged staffers to lean out their windows so as to witness a woman performing oral sex on him in the parking lot; of the prohibitively macho conversations Scanlon, Eszterhas and Cahill had at Jerry's Inn about Hemingway and other suitable role models; and of the reaction several male staffers gave to the hiring of Partridge: "What does she look like? Does she have good legs? Does she have big tits?"

The new copy chief, to the likely dismay of some, did not look or act like Betty Boop. Marianne Partridge was a brilliant, bullheaded, ambitious woman who commanded instant respect. Her résumé included stints at the *New York Times, Forbes* and *The Saturday Evening Post*, where she apprenticed under another talented editor, Deborah Harkins.

With her discovery that women at *Rolling Stone* were being treated like serfs, Marianne Partridge discovered something else: many of the women were extraordinarily well educated and intelligent. Paul Scanlon's assistant, Sarah Lazin, had a master's degree in history; Joe Eszterhas's secretary, Christine Doudna, had a master's in English. The assistant to the subscriptions director, Harriet Fier, had only recently been working the night shift on the switchboard despite graduating Phi Beta Kappa at Smith College. These weren't office bimbos. They weren't even "chicks." They were dormant resources buried under a heap of paper clips, coffee filters and flatulent male egos.

Walsh charged Partridge with professionalizing the editorial staff, an idea way overdue. As Walsh put it: "Someone would say, 'We need this done,' and everyone ran over there to do it, and then someone yelled, 'Hey, we need this done,' and everyone would scramble over there and do it. Now, there's a lot of good that comes out of such an informal system. But we had to do some structuring, and Marianne was a key candidate."

For all of eleventh-hour spontaneity's aesthetic charm, too many errors slipped through and into the pages of *Rolling Stone*. Names were constantly misspelled, even well-known ones. The magazine never seemed to stay out of legal trouble for very long. Thanks largely to Charlie Perry, *Rolling Stone* was grammatically well scrubbed, but neither Perry nor anyone else had the time to check out whether what *Rolling Stone* was printing was factually wrong or even plagiarized.

Had anyone done so, they might have found some surprises, particularly in the copy of Joe Eszterhas. Jann, Scanlon and Grover Lewis knew the reporter had fallen out of favor with the *Cleveland Plain Dealer* when the latter supplicated them for a job at *Rolling Stone*. Incredibly, they did not know that Eszterhas had been sued while at that paper for printing "calculated falsehoods" about the family of a man who was among forty-four killed in the collapse of an Ohio River bridge in 1967.

In investigating the traumatic aftermath of Melvin Cantrell's death, Eszterhas visited the home of the deceased. Though the widow was not home, the reporter nonetheless wrote, "Margaret Cantrell will talk neither about what happened nor about how they are doing. She wears the same mask of non-expression she wore at the funeral." Furthermore, as Eszterhas later admitted in depositions, he significantly exaggerated the abject conditions of the Cantrell household in his article. The U.S. Supreme Court held 8–1 against the *Plain Dealer* in December of 1974 and awarded the Cantrells $60,000.

The court did not find malice in Joe Eszterhas's misrepresentations. It seemed that in his zeal to drive home a point, the reporter could not resist embellishing. It was a temptation he did not pass up at *Rolling Stone* either.

Always at home with tough, mangy subjects, Joe Eszterhas developed an obsession with the violent and shadowy world of narcotics officers. He won the confidence of the Bay Area's most prominent criminal defense attorneys, who shared with him reams of material about the fascistic narcotics law underworld. His several features on the subject were among the most vivid and scarifying articles ever published in *Rolling Stone*.

Nonetheless, Paul Scanlon and Sarah Lazin were surprised when they visited a bar described in "Nark, a Tale of Horror." They thought they'd check out the place where the bartender "struts with a military posture, goose-stepping back and forth to the jukebox, playing Frank or Matt Monro." The name on the building was right—LaRocca's—but nobody was playing Frank or Matt Monro, as the bar had no jukebox.

Fully a year later, *Rolling Stone* put another Eszterhas "Nark" story on the cover: "Death in the Wilderness: The Justice Department's Killer Nark Strike Force." The story examined the apparent murder of a low-rent pot dealer in Humboldt County, California. The article won immediate acclaim and resulted in a Justice Department investigation. The prose was taut and ground-level, the mood nightmarish. Everything about "Death in the Wilderness" was vintage Eszterhas.

Except for the research. As only a few staffers learned, a freelancer named John Ross had personally submitted to Eszterhas a piece he'd written about the Humboldt County murders. The senior editor promised to get back to Ross about whether *Rolling Stone* would publish the article. A few days later, Eszterhas told the freelancer that his piece wouldn't do . . . but that Eszterhas would pay a hundred dollars for Ross's article, plus all research, as background information for an article Eszterhas might one day write. Ross, observing that Eszterhas already had a photocopy of his article, reluctantly consented.

An accountant at *Rolling Stone* who later examined both "Death in the Wilderness" and Ross's original piece was astounded to discover that Eszterhas had relied almost exclusively on the freelancer's research. He'd claimed five days' worth of expenses—which seemed like an awfully short period of time to research such a massive project—but included no receipts in his expense report. It all looked very dubious to the accountant ... except, of course, that the prose was vintage Eszterhas. The writer had applied all sorts of florid images to events which he'd never witnessed. It was as if Joe Eszterhas had usurped not only the research but the story's actual events as well.

After "Death in the Wilderness" made its splash, John Ross sought legal counsel. He was advised that he had no case. After all, he'd accepted a hundred bucks from Eszterhas. Perhaps the *Rolling Stone* senior editor had gone too far in using all of Ross's information without giving him an iota of credit, but it wasn't outright plagiarism. Eszterhas had taken the work of a hippie journalist and made it *passionate*. Cream rises, kid.

———

Marianne Partridge took Christine Doudna, Harriet Fier and Sarah Lazin away from their menial jobs and put them to serious work. Doudna became Partridge's assistant copy chief; Lazin and Fier oversaw a research department modeled on *The New Yorker*'s venerable fact-checking system.

The new female front line attracted abuse from all sides. "No broad's gonna edit my copy," Joe Eszterhas snarled. Ralph Gleason sent paragraphs riddled with obscure data to Lazin and taunted her: "Now, fact-check *that*." Charlie Perry, discovering that much of his duties had been usurped by a brace of feminists, remained his gentlemanly self but could not altogether hide his disdain. He saw them as a cabal. God only knew what they talked about at their weekly consciousness-raising group, though he had his suspicions. They seemed intent on promulgating views Perry considered every bit as strident as those of the John Burks contingency. One article ridiculed buying dolls for girls; a piece on Saigon by Laura Palmer made them ecstatic—"as if," said Perry, "no woman reporter had ever covered a war, and as if it mattered a damn that she was a woman." In a similar vein, they applauded a prominent photograph of comedienne Lily Tomlin flashing her armpit hair, and groaned loudly over the thorough make-over given Phoebe Snow on a cover shot. On the office Christmas tree, they hung photographs of naked men, "evidently expecting us to feel exploited by porno," said Perry, "but the men were just puzzled and amused."

Partridge's feminists occasionally tripped over their own stridency. When Ben Fong-Torres turned in a piece on Motown's "girl groups," the copy chief's assistants dutifully changed every reference to "women's groups." "It was humiliating," admitted Partridge.

Yet the *Rolling Stone* women could be forgiven their occasional heavy-handedness. The real cabal, however unconscious, was the magazine's male oligarchy. Few missed the point when Partridge put a sign on Jann's office door that read: "Boys' Club." She was serving notice: those doors would be busted open. The copy chief positioned her large round table where she could see people enter and leave Jann's office, and where they could see her. "As far as office power politics are concerned," said Jim Kuntsler, "she was certainly geographically located to be at the very nerve center of the magazine. Marianne was very savvy in that way."

Her assistants, the magazine's former "chicks," underwent a dramatic transformation. "I got really interested in learning how to be an editor," said Lazin. "I started to see this as a longer-term career rather than just a job and a groovy place to be." Before too long, male writers began to seek out Partridge and her staff for advice. The copy and research departments became crucial cornerstones at *Rolling Stone*, and thus a very noticeable feather in managing editor John Walsh's cap.

Yet his brainchild may well have contributed to Walsh's doom. Compared with the combative, often histrionic Partridge, the managing editor appeared ineffectual—rendered ceremonial and impotent, it seemed, by the copy chief's shadow government. As a result, few rallied behind him when Walsh suffered his first major clash with Jann Wenner.

———

The subject was Dick Goodwin. Jann was thoroughly taken by the new politics editor, who in turn knew that the surest way to hold the editor's attention was to drop a dazzling name here and there. An accomplished storyteller to begin with, Goodwin enjoyed jerking Jann's chain with a well-timed "As Jackie used to say . . ."

It seemed that the two were speaking the same language when Goodwin laid plans for the magazine's new Washington bureau. *Rolling Stone* was in the Big Leagues now, a realm occupied not by tawdry old rockers but rather by the people who ran America. Things would have to be first-class all the way. *Access* would not come cheaply.

Or so believed Goodwin, who exhibited his sense of style by procuring, in the summer of 1974, a rather auspicious early headquarters for the Washington bureau. An award-winning Boston journalist named Joe Klein had been recruited by Goodwin. He recalled their first meeting:

"Goodwin asked me to come down to Washington on a trial basis," said Klein. "He gave me an address in Virginia. So I loaded all my stuff, all my earthly possessions, into two suitcases, landed at the National Airport, got into a taxi, gave the address to the cabdriver, and eventually we pull up to a *mansion*.

"The cabdriver said to me, 'This is the Kennedy house. You one of them?' And a little Hispanic maid trundled out and said, 'Oh, Mr. Klein, Mr. Goodwin is waiting for you down by the pool.' I go through the house—I mean, this is Hickory Hill! This is the first Washington bureau—and I go down to the pool.

"And there's Goodwin. He's treading water, and he's smoking a cigar. And he said to me, 'Tax reform.' That was my first assignment."

Later, Hunter Thompson showed up at Ethel Kennedy's mansion. So did a number of the Kennedy children, who wanted to meet the Gonzo journalist, and there followed a regimen of heavy drinking and rambling discussions about everything from drugs to shoe imports. Hearing rumors of wild activities at Hickory Hill, Jackie Onassis was moved to call and check up on Caroline.

The following Monday, Goodwin and Klein repaired to the nation's capital and leased an office at 1700 Pennsylvania Avenue, next door to the Executive Office Building. The new staff fanned out, stroking liaisons, buying fancy lunches. "In a matter of weeks," said Klein, "it became clear to me that Dick was taking this for all he could get."

Jann Wenner wanted access, so Richard N. Goodwin made the necessary arrangements. One extravagant dinner party followed the next. The editor pressed the flesh, but in these rarefied climes he fared poorly. At a dinner set up to discuss foreign policy, the dignified guests conversed vigorously while Jann in his madras shirt sat on top of a stereo speaker, legs crossed, flipping through a copy of *Foreign Policy* and pretending to look interested.

Larry Durocher viewed Jann's courtship of the Power Elite with extreme distaste. The publisher was well aware that the editor's fumbling attempts to seize influence were causing great mirth in Georgetown circles. People were laughing at Jann Wenner, and by extension, Larry Durocher.

"Jann was so much more than most of these shmucks he wanted to meet," he said. "Something I've known about politicians since I was a kid is that most of them are starfucked by anybody who has done anything on their own without the help of the government. And so to Jann they had that aphrodisiac of power and fame; and to them, they say, 'Look at Wenner, he's got a bucket of money and a car, and the government doesn't even pay for the driver!' And they and Jann looked at each other like two icebergs passing in the night, just seeing the tips of each, thinking, God, it must be grand. And neither one realizing that the other one feels the same way."

Durocher and Walsh were allied in their view that Dick Goodwin was taking *Rolling Stone* to the cleaners. Yet that was nothing new; Jann was always finding ways to drain the coffers. What disturbed the publisher and the managing editor most was Goodwin's writing. Even his most insightful essays were turgid and academic, written like position papers. Dick Goodwin's stuff was fine for some obscure think-tank journal. In the pages of *Rolling Stone*, his political essays were, in Durocher's words, "thoroughly destructive."

Jann would hear none of this. He found the Goodwin lifestyle intoxicating. The *Rolling Stone* editor had by now hired two publicists: Bryn Bridenthal, who pushed *Rolling Stone*, and Anne Wexler, who pushed Jann Wenner. He had abandoned his earlier, infuriating (to his lieutenants) habit of addressing audiences with the line "We're just a little rock & roll newspaper from San Francisco." Now *Rolling Stone*, the publicity sheets intoned, was "a biweekly general interest magazine covering contemporary American culture, politics and arts, with a special interest in music."

And Jann Wenner, according to that demon idol *Time*, was "a brilliant, brash autocrat with an eye for lucrative markets and talented writers." That eye now flickered like a corona at the mention of politics. He lent his hand to the campaigns of California gubernatorial candidate Bill Roth and aspiring senator Tom Hayden (who was listed on the *Rolling Stone* masthead as a contributing editor). Rumors about his own political ambitions galloped throughout the 625 Third Street office.

After a Straight Arrow board meeting, Jann addressed finance officer Tom Baker. "You know," he said, smiling, "meetings like this make me feel so good. When I see all these good people we have, it really makes me think about being President."

President? Of . . . He didn't mean . . .

Sometime later, Anne Wexler said to Baker over lunch, "Well, are you ready to be Secretary of the Treasury?"

Baker dropped his fork. "What?"

Wexler smiled privately. "Just thinking," she said.

The apple still needed polishing, however. When a reporter for the *Columbia Journalism Review* came to San Francisco to interview Jann, the editor was nowhere to be found. Bryn Bridenthal took the reporter across the street to Jerry's, hoping to soothe his annoyance. Three hours later, Jann showed up and proceeded to snort a white powder out of a plastic bag. The reporter, no doubt insulted by the three-hour wait, duly reported the snorting. Jann blew up at Bridenthal for allowing this to be printed, and later told reporters he was just "putting the guy on."

———

Throughout the magazine's internal jousting, the demise of President Richard Nixon proceeded like a forest fire in dry August. Like much of America, the *Rolling Stone* staff monitored Watergate with awe and curiosity, viewing the Senate hearings on the television set by Jann's office and catching the evening news at Jerry's Inn.

Of course, the magazine also covered Watergate. Timothy Crouse did his usual excellent behind-the-scenes work, and Annie Leibovitz captured the sagging administration so masterfully that even the *Rolling Stone* business staff was moved to admit that she was worth all the lost cameras and abandoned rental cars. The bigger problem was Hunter Thompson.

Plans had been made for Thompson to write a book about Watergate —hopefully about the impeachment of Nixon. If anyone belonged to this moment, surely the only journalist in America to liken the President to Hitler did. Yet the ascendancy of the Watergate Journalist—led by *Washington Post* reporters Bob Woodward and Carl Bernstein—seemed to come at the direct expense of Hunter Thompson, who noted ruefully, "There was not a hell of a lot of room for a Gonzo journalist to operate in that high-tuned atmosphere. For the first time in memory, the Washington press corps was working very close to the peak of its awesome but normally dormant potential."

Thompson made this observation in his colossal "Fear and Loathing at the Watergate" article, which he filed under the usual deadline madness, with crucial assistance by Crouse and Partridge. It was a hilarious, astute piece of Gonzo, but in the context of a whole swarm of brilliant Watergate analyses, it fell short. The *Rolling Stone* editors were disappointed, and publications like *Time* gave the article derisive notices.

Still, Jann had high hopes for Thompson's Watergate coverage. After the *United States* v. *Nixon* Supreme Court decision forced the President to hand over damaging tapes to the Watergate special prosecutor, Nixon's downfall seemed a certainty. By the beginning of August 1974, it was no longer a secret: the President either would be impeached or would resign.

He resigned on August 9, 1974. Following the announcement, Jann was explicit in his orders to John Walsh: "I want to do an issue on Nixon, and I want Hunter to write the cover story."

The managing editor hedged. Getting Thompson to meet any deadline was a shaky proposition. Forcing him to kick out a historic screed on the spur of the moment—

"Just do it," snapped Jann Wenner.

Walsh went to work. He reached Thompson by phone, pled and cajoled as best he could ... but Hunter Thompson parried each with a plea for more time, another excuse, a lead that hadn't yet panned out, simply no time ...

When it became clear that Thompson's Watergate story would not be filed on time—that it would not in fact be filed in time for the *next* issue —the *Rolling Stone* staff went into furious motion: raiding the Leibovitz photo file, clipping old Nixon-related articles from bound volumes of back issues, weaving a patchwork ensemble and hurling it into the yawning void left by Hunter Thompson. David Felton, as he so often did, came up with the succinct title of the issue: "The Quitter."

The retrospective issue was magnificent, but fatal for John Walsh. Not long after it was put to bed, Jann Wenner took his managing editor out to dinner at the same restaurant where he'd hired him and gave him his walking papers.

Larry Durocher did not attend to this development. He was mulling over Jann's recent acquisition of Rich Irvine, a Walt Disney executive and cohort of Nixon press secretary Ron Ziegler, as president of Straight Arrow Publishers, Inc. It did not seem likely that *Rolling Stone* would be big enough for the both of them—or, for that matter, big enough for *anyone* and the increasingly willful Jann Wenner. Durocher tendered his resignation in October of 1974.

One by one, Jann was shedding his business mentors. Max Palevsky had resigned as chairman of Straight Arrow Publishers, Inc. in the middle of 1973, convinced that Jann was duplicitous and uncontrollable. Jann asked Palevsky to stay on, but would not accept the rather stern conditions set forth in the new contract.

The alienation of Straight Arrow Books associate publisher Alan Rinzler from *Rolling Stone* was more protracted and emotional. Starting with nothing, Rinzler had built the book division into an innovative, if erratic organ. Though less respected by staffers than Jann (most likely because he so often served as Jann's hatchet man), Rinzler seemed so aligned with the editor's tastes and values that Larry Durocher figured Rinzler would be a natural successor should anything happen to Jann.

But Straight Arrow Books had become Alan Rinzler's personal fiefdom. He routinely vetoed Jann's ideas, developing a catalogue that fit *his* personality, not *Rolling Stone*'s. In the meantime, he'd long since outlived his usefulness as a business aide, and at the same time developed a creeping sympathy for the editor's detractors. Oh, the Wenner charm was still there. But Rinzler had seen too many broken hearts, heard too many broken promises. Like Durocher, it astounded him that Jann Wenner would not grow up. Also like Durocher, he'd given up waiting for it to happen.

"I can see in your eyes how cold and unfriendly I've been lately," the editor wrote his associate publisher in a memo, "but please understand it as a result of my own personal unhappiness and inherent difficulties in being able to handle human relations and sometimes even love and nothing to do with you as a person or with your work, both of which I secretly admire highly . . ."

Jann Wenner kept the secret well. By the middle of 1975, Alan Rinzler had no ties to *Rolling Stone*. By the end of the year, Jann would demolish the division Rinzler had raised from the crib, electing to parcel off this or that title rather than sell the division, even when attractive offers were made. His financial officers, noting the modest numbers yielded by Straight Arrow Books, went along with him. Years later, vice president Tom Baker would look back on the decision as the most regrettable he participated in while at *Rolling Stone*. "It was something to build on, something that could truly have been great," he said. But it was Alan Rinzler's, not Jann Wenner's. To the scrapyard it went, without ceremony, another puzzling little corpse.

———

Jann Wenner could not afford the Big Leagues.

Dick Goodwin was breaking him. Some $600 a month for rent, plus salary, plus the 1700 Pennsylvania Avenue office, plus all those unfathomably pricey dinner parties, one of which Jann flatly refused to pay for, provoking Goodwin to declare that if the editor did not do so, then he, Richard N. Goodwin, would represent the caterer in a suit against Jann Wenner.

The two had discussed at length a satellite project. *Politics*, they would call it: a "non-boring *New Republic*" with pop art, according to Jann; "an investigative and interpretive journal devoted to exploring, in concrete detail, the forces, interests, and individuals involved in the acts of government," according to Goodwin. Goodwin was very keen on the subject and drew up a list of possible articles, ranging from over-the-counter drugs to multinational labor.

Many of the articles were assigned, and some later used—though in *Rolling Stone*, not *Politics*. After a spate of advance press, Jann abandoned the project and waited anxiously for his six-month contract with Dick Goodwin to expire. Just before it did, he dispatched Joe Klein over to Goodwin's house to pick up a *Rolling Stone* tape recorder Goodwin had absconded.

Klein knocked on the door. Goodwin poked his head out just slightly. Klein told Goodwin why he was there.

"Screw it," Goodwin muttered, and closed the door again.

Joe Klein continued to write for *Rolling Stone*: covering the George Wallace campaign in 1974 when no other magazine took Wallace seriously, traveling with George McGovern to Cuba to meet Fidel Castro, then dogging Jerry Brown and Tom Hayden. Klein had made it to the Big Leagues along with Jann Wenner and *Rolling Stone*—a far, far better thing than his days at Boston's *Real Paper*, slogging about with little pay and minor league credentials.

Yet as Klein would say later: "It didn't really ever work out perfectly between me and Jann, because I'd always thought of politics as a process. When Jann said politics was the rock & roll of the seventies, it was clear he thought of politicians as rock stars."

Hunter Thompson, too, was a rock star of the seventies, playing in the Big Leagues by himself, unaccountable to Jann Wenner or to any other living thing. He was a celebrity, his autograph much in demand. Cartoonist Garry Trudeau created the "Doonesbury" character Duke from the Gonzo journalist's persona—at first to Thompson's amusement, and later, as the scenarios became more personal, to his great anger.

But such was superstardom. Thompson began to speak on campuses— seldom, in fact, giving a prepared speech, preferring instead to field questions (and drugs) hurled from the audiences. Often the questions would be ludicrous references to his Gonzo lifestyle, provoking replies like "Christ, isn't there anybody here with any intelligence?" Often he would leave the stage to boos.

"It was painful to see him becoming a prisoner of his image," wrote student journalist Steve Cummings after a particularly grim "lecture" at Duke University in the fall of 1974. "All we can do, though, is wish him well as he battles the Great American Success Machine, an enemy as corrupt as the Hell's Angels, as elusive as an LSD vision."

The process of confronting an empty page with a typewriter had never been an easy one for Hunter Thompson. Now, with the distractions of success, it seemed impossible. The Watergate book fell through. A proposed novel, *Guts Bull*, amounted to a few cassettes' worth of incoherent dictation.

Jann sent Thompson to Zaire to cover the Ali-Foreman boxing rematch. He never filed the story—did not attend the fight, in fact, preferring to watch it on a television by the hotel swimming pool.

In March of 1975 he landed in Saigon to cover its fall for *Rolling Stone*. Thompson didn't know that just prior to his departure, Jann collared Tom Baker and made an unusual request: he wanted the Straight Arrow vice president to purchase a life insurance policy on Thompson, such that if their star writer was killed in Saigon, "*Rolling Stone* would make a lot of money," said Baker.

Baker was flabbergasted. "I didn't know if you could buy a life insurance policy on a guy and not tell the guy," he said. "It sounded strange. But that's what Jann wanted, so I called the insurance guy I dealt with, and he did quite a bit of running around. And I think we did wind up with some kind of policy—an accident policy, moving into a war zone."

Into the war zone moved Hunter Thompson; he lived to tell the tale. But aside from a few disjointed paragraphs spewing out of the mojo that seemed to have more to do with the lack of ice cubes at the Saigon hotel than with the fall of that tortured city, he did not file. Jann Wenner advanced Hunter Thompson no more money, leaving the writer broke and furious in Southeast Asia.

Meanwhile, the Big Leagues beckoned. The editor would have to find a new slugger.

Chapter Thirteen

THE UNIDENTIFIED MAN

He did.

Howard Kohn was hardly a mirror image of Hunter Thompson. He was a Michigan farm boy, a Missouri Synod Lutheran from the Saginaw Valley bean fields, bred in a house with no television and telephone, a quiet and studious non-*Rolling Stone*r if there ever was one. Like Thompson, however, Kohn longed as a child to escape the bonds of his simple, languid environment. He knew there was a life beyond the udders of cattle and the rich brown dirt that sustained the Kohns. He knew this because he read the newspaper.

At the University of Michigan he began to write for newspapers, sometimes three at a time. The farmer's perseverance he now applied to investigative journalism. One story after another he blew wide open: college athletic scandals, Vietnam pilots protesting the war by unloading their bombs into the Pacific Ocean, stories about racism his editors were too timid to print. By the age of twenty-two, Kohn had already won more prizes than most journalists would in their lifetime.

Upon graduation from Michigan, Kohn went to work for the *Detroit Free Press* and wasted no time diving into that city's darkest problem: heroin. Posing undercover, he mingled with junkies, and a series of articles resulted in arrests and more acclaim for Kohn. Gradually he fell out with the Detroit police, as his articles began to spell out the shameful indifference on the part of Detroit's Finest to the smack trade. His articles described their arrogance, their brutality. In a particularly damning series, he disclosed that a man in jail these past eighteen years for the murder of a grocer was apparently framed by policemen. The convict was granted a new trial and released. Word went out: the cops were lying low for Kohn, waiting for just one slip-up. Meanwhile, the police commissioner, a mayoral candidate as it happened, announced, "Kohn's dope war is pure fiction."

In 1971, Kohn began to accumulate evidence that Detroit policemen were themselves steeped in the drug mafia. It took nearly two years after that to sort out all the labyrinthine leads. The first corruption stories were published in April of 1973. Kohn and his family began to receive death threats. A $20,000 contract was levied on the farm boy's head. His stoolies were vanishing one by one. Howard Kohn did what most people in that situation would have done: he bought a gun. Unfortunately, a license-to-carry required a three-month waiting period. Kohn could not walk the streets defenseless for the next ninety days. He kept the Sterling six-shot in his glove compartment.

One evening a shady informant kidnapped Howard Kohn, seized his gun and threatened to execute the reporter and his family if he did not reveal his sources. Kohn stalled for hours, then found the moment and lunged for the gun. The kidnapper shot at Kohn, narrowly missing him, and ran off. The shaken reporter told his editors and the police about the kidnapping the following morning, but claimed that the gun was owned by the assailant. In their zeal to nail Howard Kohn, twenty policemen were assigned to the case. Details of his story failed to check out.

"The *Free Press* had gone to the wall for me, over and over," said Kohn. But this time the heat was unbearable. Howard Kohn, who would later that year win the Detroit Press Club Award for his investigation, was fired, charged with filing a false police report and sentenced to six months' probation. His marriage subsequently fell apart, and in the late summer of 1973 he arrived in San Francisco—a rural boy disgraced in the city streets, a quiet crusader with, as he put it, "a huge millstone of failure around my neck."

Kohn freelanced here and there, hoping for a new lease on life. He told his story to a journalist friend, who thought it might make a good feature. The article was pitched to Jann Wenner at *Rolling Stone*.

At the same time, Kohn met David Felton and later Joe Eszterhas. His background impressed them; they urged him to think up article topics. In November of 1973 Kohn remarried, and while honeymooning on the Russian River he picked up a newspaper and read about the strange death of Karen Silkwood, a Kerr-McGee employee who'd become convinced that the nuclear power plant was contaminating its employees.

Howard Kohn cut his honeymoon short and returned to San Francisco. He marched into the 625 Third Street headquarters and made a beeline toward Felton's office.

Felton was sitting there in his barber chair, contemplating who could say what, papers strewn about as if dropped through the ceiling. "I've got a great idea," said Kohn.

The associate editor looked up anxiously at the sound of Kohn's voice. "No," interrupted Felton. "Forget about it. We've got a perfect story for you. We're sending you to Oklahoma."

To investigate the Silkwood death. Howard Kohn took this as a promising omen.

For two months he labored, winning the trust of Silkwood's boyfriend (a *Rolling Stone* fan) and a handful of her fellow workers, though, as Kohn put it, "there was a wall of apprehension all around Kerr-McGee. Workers at the factory thought their jobs—and who knows, maybe even their lives—might be in jeopardy."

For Howard Kohn, however, danger was an old friend. The few reporters dispatched by their editors to Oklahoma dwindled further in number. Eventually, even the *New York Times* reporter whom Silkwood was on her way to meet the night her car ran off the road was taken off the case. ("There was no question in my mind," said Kohn, "that pressure from the industry had been applied, and as a result his work just sort of disappeared.")

As there were no obvious means of "getting at" *Rolling Stone*, Kohn's investigation continued unmolested, though without a moment's cooperation from Kerr-McGee. At the end of January in 1975, Kohn turned in his piece to David Felton. Felton did not change a single word.

Jann Wenner was thrilled by the Silkwood piece. He met Kohn for a drink at Jerry's Inn, accompanied by Felton and Eszterhas. The editor did not mince words. "I'd like to see your name on the masthead," he said.

Eszterhas butted in. "Let me just put this on the table," he said, "because it's bound to come up sooner or later." The senior editor brought up Kohn's controversial departure from the *Detroit Free Press*. Eszterhas, who only a couple of months before had been tarnished in the Supreme Court case, knew something about skeletons in closets.

Kohn's heart sank, but he said nothing.

Jann Wenner waved off Eszterhas's warning. The Silkwood article, he said, spoke for itself. Howard Kohn was made an associate editor of *Rolling Stone*. He cast off the millstone and combed the Bay for a story.

———

On April 9, 1975, a San Francisco attorney named Michael Kennedy approached Kohn and David Weir, a close friend of Kohn's since college and now mining the same territory as a Bay Area freelancer. Kennedy had a client he wanted the journalists to meet.

The client, Jack Scott, was a sports activist who was suspected by the FBI of having ties with the Symbionese Liberation Army: the ragtag leftist tribe which, on February 4, 1974, abducted nineteen-year-old newspaper chain heiress Patricia Campbell Hearst in her Berkeley apartment. Three months later, on April 15, Patty Hearst was seen participating in a bank robbery with other SLA members. She announced herself as Tania, so named after the Cuban revolutionary who died with Che Guevara in the jungles of Bolivia. Instantly she became a heroine to radicals who believed the heiress had renounced the Hearstian opulence for the Revolution. Not long after that, the SLA safe house in Los Angeles was incinerated in a police ambush, killing all but William and Emily Harris . . . and Patty Hearst.

She'd not been seen since. And now here was Jack Scott, in legal trouble, wanting favorable press and telling Howard Kohn and David Weir some rather incredible things—namely, that Scott had seen the Harrises and Hearst, had in fact helped to find them refuge and might well be able to trace their whereabouts today.

Kohn and Weir weren't prepared to swallow without a little chewing. "The tales he told," said Kohn, "so clearly skirted his involvement that certainly some doubts were raised. His explanations were so obtuse and roundabout—but still we had no doubt: he'd seen Patty. So we took what Scott gave us and proceeded to talk to three or four other sources. Laying the stories side by side, it all began to check out."

The reporters notified Jann, who orbited into seventh heaven. It was the best *Rolling Stone* story since the 1972 McGovern campaign: a tale of bungled investigations and tattered old vestiges of the New Left, a violent psychodrama the conventional media could only blink at. It was, for that matter, the hottest story of the year, one of the hottest of the decade. Everyone wanted to know where Patty Hearst was, and whether she had been brainwashed or freely radicalized. Jann Wenner could see it plainly: Patty Hearst was *Rolling Stone* territory. She was a rock & roll star.

The editor instructed them to follow the trail Scott had described and thus determine whether the details meshed with his account. Above all, said Jann Wenner, keep this one a secret.

The two reporters flew to Pennsylvania, rented a car and began to trace the SLA escape path. They located the abandoned farmhouse outside of Scranton, jimmied their way inside and took photographs. They found rifle shells in the fields, evidence of target practice. Jack Scott had claimed that he himself had driven Patty from the West Coast to this very spot, and interviews with neighbors confirmed the description of his vehicle. Scott was telling the truth. Patty Hearst had been here, and was now somewhere in northern California. They had a story.

Unfortunately, so did *New Times*, another general-interest magazine with offices in San Francisco, whose news coverage often overlapped that of *Rolling Stone*. Word reached Kohn and Weir that the *New Times* reporter didn't yet know about the Pennsylvania safe house, but he, like the FBI, was piecing together Jack Scott's role in the disappearance of the last SLA members. If *Rolling Stone* didn't react quickly, they'd lose one of the biggest scoops of the seventies.

The reporters huddled with Jann and Paul Scanlon. Publicist Anne Wexler was brought into the loop. "We've got to have a media strategy," she said, and began to outline a plan for containing the Hearst story until the very moment of release.

Howard Kohn and David Weir manned the typewriter, working around the clock for four straight days, sequestered from the rest of the staff. A radical fringe group discovered what the reporters were up to and added the names of Kohn and Weir to their death list. Pinkerton security guards were posted outside the office doors. Doggie Diner burgers were brought to them. Kohn's car was parked in front of the office, within plain view, where it received $500 worth of parking tickets that were later picked up by Jann.

One evening a staffer burst through the door. "They've got her!" he said, and Howard Kohn instinctively ripped the paper out of the typewriter. Patty Hearst had been captured by the FBI. Yet even the feds didn't know where she'd been before the arrest in San Francisco. The story was still untold. Kohn put the paper back in the carriage, and he and Weir resumed. The writers would not sleep. Kohn's fingers thudded against the typewriter keys at a torturously slow pace.

On Monday, September 22, 1975, traffic manager Dan Parker arrived at the magazine's printing press in St. Louis with the flats for "The Inside Story." Parker stayed at the printer's all week long, accompanied by guards who stood by all entrances and frisked employees as they left the building. That Friday, Kohn and Weir were taped for an interview on the *Today* show while Jann Wenner rounded up the entire staff minus Parker and transported them 152 miles south of San Francisco to Ventana, the elegant Big Sur country inn. By now "The Inside Story" was known to most staffers, and Jann didn't want word leaking out.

On Monday, September 29, publicist Bryn Bridenthal showed up for work at nine in the morning, only to find the entrance blocked by reporters. An ad hoc press conference was called in the Raoul Duke Room. Present were Bridenthal, Kohn, Weir and Scanlon. Conspicuously absent was Jann Wenner, who had been too nervous to handle the press—though later, said Anne Wexler, "he got mad at Howard for being so visible."

"You couldn't have gotten another TV camera or radio mike in the conference room with a shoehorn," said Bridenthal, who massaged the media for thirteen hours that day as they peppered the *Rolling Stone* reporters with questions about their sources, their methods and, inevitably, Howard Kohn's problems with the *Detroit Free Press*. A man posing as a reporter was found by security guards rummaging through files in Jann's office. Later that evening, David Weir attempted to elude reporters by checking into a hotel with his wife. Photographers took pictures of the couple, and the next day's papers alluded to a "mystery woman"—an SLA source?—accompanying Weir.

Issue No. 198 sold out instantly, with a clamor for reprints. Jann, his publicists, his editors and his new star reporters gathered in his office on the evening of September 29 and watched one major television network after another lead off with the incredible "Inside Story" of Patty Hearst's life on the lam. No publication had pulled off this kind of coup since the *New York Times* printed the Pentagon Papers five years ago. The fucking *New York Times*! *Rolling Stone* wasn't just *on* the map, it was *all over the map*, an American sensation, and the editor, Citizen Wenner, uncorked a bottle of champagne. His eyes watered as he raised his glass, and as the others did the same it might well have been another time and another place, eight years ago in that grubby little printing room on Brannan, when a chubby young man with long hair held high his champagne and let the tears fall from his sweet blue eyes and proclaimed that he just couldn't imagine his little magazine ever, *ever* getting any better than this ...

———

But Ralph Gleason no longer shared the triumph.

There were some at *Rolling Stone*—Paul Scanlon, Charlie Perry, Ben Fong-Torres, Alan Rinzler, Sarah Lazin and, above all, Jann Wenner—who truly believed that the magazine's co-founder was still an asset to the publication. Most of those who had joined the magazine after 1970, however, could not conceive of the *San Francisco Chronicle* critic as anything but a worn-out old joke. In fact, they resented him: his position on the masthead despite his never shedding fortnightly blood at 625 Third Street; his careless verbiage which he nonetheless would let no editor alter; and his tired championing of musicians no one else seemed interested in. While the children of the sixties had grown up and come to terms with the System, there was Old Man Gleason, his hair now grown out like LBJ's in his final days, murmuring "groovy," stranded in a depleted era.

The drumbeat he marched to was not *Rolling Stone*'s, or vice versa. While Hunter Thompson was leading the magazine into the bowels of presidential politics, Gleason was lobbying the editor to think about creating a music trade publication similar to *Billboard*. While Felton, Eszterhas, Lewis and Cahill were taking New Journalism to wilder altitudes, Gleason was scolding Jann and Scanlon for failing to scoop the *New York Times* on the *Godspell* production and on Paul McCartney's latest plans. A year later, the *Chronicle* columnist urged Jann to find a topic that could net *Rolling Stone* the coveted Pulitzer Prize. Gleason had just a subject in mind: the suppression of rebel students in California universities.

Often he sent notes to Jann and Scanlon, excoriating them for missing the point in stories or for overlooking stories altogether. Usually his missives were ignored. His sphere of influence was now limited to his "Perspectives" column, which he defended like a grizzly protecting its cub. Occasionally Jann would kill his submission altogether, explaining that it read like the stuff of newspapers, not a stylish biweekly like *Rolling Stone*.

This incensed Gleason. "Columns are not news stories and they are not feature articles," he wrote angrily in a letter to Jann. "They are personal columns. Poems, if you will. And if you want them and want me to write them, this is the only way I can write them, and if this isn't what you want, good luck."

It did not take much insight to detect Ralph Gleason's chagrin as *Rolling Stone*, and Jann Wenner, rolled past him. Yet Jann did little to soothe the sting. The editor was now a millionaire, a *celebrity*, who took no pains to remind interviewers that he could not have done all this alone, that he would not be standing on the mount today were it not for the patronage of Ralph J. Gleason. Gleason saw no great riches for his early financial and creative contributions. In fact, time and again the magazine skirted bankruptcy, its stockholders left wringing their handkerchiefs while the wunderkind boarded the next flight to London or Tangiers.

By the middle of 1973, Gleason decided he'd had it up to here with the ungrateful little brat. In June he had lunch with Max Palevsky, who had just resigned as chairman of Straight Arrow, and urged him to initiate a stock takeover of the corporation. Palevsky balked, citing his friendship with Jane Wenner.

A few months later, Bob Dylan returned to the West Coast on a national tour, and Jann was heard to brag that he'd scored an exclusive interview with the legendary singer/songwriter. At the concert, the editor sauntered up to the backstage entrance and showed them his pass, but was sent back to his seat. Gleason, in the meantime, skirted through without incident and was embraced warmly by Dylan.

When Gleason returned to his seat, Jann was beside himself. "How did you get backstage?" he demanded. "You don't have a backstage pass."

Gleason could not resist a jab. "Anybody can get backstage with a pass," he noted suavely. "The trick is to get backstage without one."

Jann assigned himself the task of editing Gleason's Dylan article. He savaged the piece, resulting in a three-page single-spaced protest from Gleason, to no avail. Ralph Gleason vowed to wash his hands of *Rolling Stone* once and for all. He announced that he wished to sell the rest of his Straight Arrow stock. Jann told Alan Rinzler to offer Gleason $16 per share, which to Rinzler seemed like a spitefully low offer. Gleason had to agree. "Next time you see him," he told Rinzler, "punch him in the mouth for me."

He began to call up Larry Durocher, who had never before spoken with Gleason and knew nothing of his quarrels with Jann Wenner. Jon Landau had told his fellow New Englander that Ralph was something of a father figure to Jann, that the two bickered occasionally. But none of this prepared Durocher for the bile Ralph Gleason unleashed in his conversations with him. "His feelings about Wenner were not best described as anger," he said.

"They were feelings of contempt and disgust. He thought that Wenner was a lowlife."

The dean of music critics had enjoyed tremendous moments of late: an ASCAP-Deems Taylor award in 1973 (his second) for an article published in *Rolling Stone* on Louis Armstrong, and even more ennobling, a spot on the Nixon White House's Enemies List. He had an office of his own at Fantasy Records, where he was at last an insider, closer to the industry's big red buttons than ever before. Yet he could not elude mortality's cold shadow. His health had been poor: diabetes, a hand operation, the mindless onslaught of old age. His very main man, Duke Ellington, had died in 1974, whispering "Kisses, kisses, kisses" in his final breaths. His music would live forever, but Ellington's life was itself a song, and God how Ralph Gleason would miss that grand old serenade.

"I wonder sometimes if you really trust anybody," wrote Ralph Gleason on April 25, 1975, in a long letter to the Berkeley dropout he'd taken in and even now, after the lowball stock offer, could not bring himself to abandon:

> Your instincts are great, but you get seduced by something else. I'm not sure exactly what; sometimes I think you are a perpetual groupie: first music, then writers, then politics. But it gets in the way of your mind and destroys your perspective. . . .
>
> If you would let me I could show you how to change the image fruitfully over a period of time, how to alter the approach to the record business usefully, how to expand the audience and how to handle the things you have not been successful handling. For Christ's sake hire me as a consultant or something. But do something!
>
> And if you don't know by now that I neither want to ruin you nor steal the paper from you, you will never learn anything; use the resources you have which you can trust, and by God and by Jesus I am the number one on your side.
>
> Think about this, old friend. . . . Write when you get work.
>
> Ralph Gleason

He died of a heart attack five weeks later, at the age of fifty-eight. Paul Scanlon gave Jann Wenner the news. He had never seen a grown man burst into sobs so quickly.

There was to be a wake at the Gleason household, in the fine Irish tradition. Ralph's personal secretary, Gretchen Horton, called her old boss Jann to notify him.

"Please go with me," he begged her. "I can't go in there by myself."

She met him at a corner, where they left his car, and in Horton's car they drove together to the Berkeley house on Spruce Street that Ralph had purchased after selling some Straight Arrow stock in 1971. Hordes of people were there—musicians, writers, lefties, professors, he had so many friends—and Jann Wenner cried throughout that evening and drank heavily and snorted cocaine, and Gretchen Horton would not let Jann drive back across the Bay Bridge and so ordered him to stay at her house, and to this he blearily acquiesced.

He returned to the office, to his family, but nothing could lift his despondency. Ralph had wanted to sell his stock; Jann would not let his father figure break the chain. And yet he had reached out to Jann in his letter, an offer that was as much a cry for help . . .

He called for Toby Gleason, Ralph's only true son, a young man who had grown up in the hyperactive shadow of an interloper named Jann Wenner. At times he had hated Jann like no other. Now they shared grief and Jann's cocaine as the editor handed Toby a manuscript, an epitaph he'd written. "I want you to edit it," he told Ralph's son. "You're the only one who can."

There was to be a Ralph Gleason issue, and in honor of the great man's departed soul, assistance came from distant quarters. Greil Marcus and John Burks returned to the fold, writing and assigning pieces, gathering memories from the many who'd been touched by Gleason. Jann petitioned Toby Gleason for a photograph the young man had taken of his father. He wanted to put it on the cover. Toby refused. Ralph Gleason, he insisted, would never allow a goddamned music critic to be on the cover of *Rolling Stone*. The editor grew heated. What other kind of gesture could he make, how else could he show his love and assuage his guilt without putting the man who'd done so much for him for so little in return on the cover of *Rolling Stone*? Toby *had* to let him do this, *he needed to do this* . . .

In his epitaph—pared down drastically by Toby, for the original draft rambled and trembled like a child roaming a house now deserted—he wrote:

Later on it became "Janno," and if I was on some trip or another, blithely avoiding common sense like an infantry kid ten steps into a minefield, Ralph's words would invariably be, "Janno, this is Ralph here." It was a code between us meaning, "back to reality, old pal"—and a lot of other things, but it aches to explain it any further, to remember the warmth of those words. And even though just a random memory from the ten years in which Ralph guided me toward adulthood, it hints at what none of us who were close to Ralph want to face—that to define any of it is to admit the finality. And he always used to say, "Don't define it, dig it." The stories are easier—they signify life, they are nearly all joyful times, even those that at the time were difficult. I think that there will always yet be a story we haven't heard before. And none of us will die having heard all that can be relived about Ralph, and in this way, he still lives, and we can "dig it."

Jann Wenner never spoke about being liberated by the death of his father figure. But now this rampaging, groping, pulsating ball of boundless energy and appetite was untethered. Never again would he hear a sharp but gentle voice coo into the phone receiver, "Janno, this is Ralph here." All those once present to tweak his conscience and remind him how much left he had to learn—Ralph, Rinzler, Palevsky, Durocher—no longer stood over him, mussing his hair.

And let there be a reason for this! He was Jan Wenner, then Jann Wenner, and now the masthead read Jann S. Wenner—a man of greater distinction; his own man. *Known fact! New Yorker* cartoons made mention of his magazine. Jackie Onassis was photographed reading an issue. He'd met Jackie, in fact. Escorted her daughter to the theater, grinned at the paparazzi while Caroline clung to his arm.

And those bastards at the *Examiner!* "Caroline Kennedy," the photo caption read, "with unidentified man." Vintage wise-ass San Francisco. They had never, ever given Jann Wenner his due. Every chance they got, they stuck it to him. People still slapped the barnacled old back of Warren Hinckle. And when Francis Ford Coppola started up his new magazine, *City*, you'd've thought he was the resurrection of Henry Luce, William Randolph Hearst and William Shakespeare all balled up into one bearded package.

Unidentified.

His good friend Jon Landau had struck it big, the jerk. "I have seen rock & roll future and its name is Springsteen," he wrote in Boston's *Real Paper*—why not in *Rolling Stone?*—and with that neobiblical rhetoric launched the career of the Asbury Park, New Jersey, musician. Landau had quit the magazine to become Springsteen's producer and manager. Their very first collaboration, *Born to Run*, put the Boss on the covers of *Time* and *Newsweek*. But not on the cover of *Rolling Stone*, despite Jann's love for the album. Some said it was jealousy. Many said that.

Unidentified.

A new rival appeared on the other coast: Clay Felker, editor of *New York*, the prototype for all city magazines to come. A genius, they said; and now he was taking over *The Village Voice*, and as a further encroachment, starting up *New West* in California. The two editors had been amicable, flattering each other in national publications. Then Felker offered the *Voice*'s top editorial post to *Rolling Stone* copy chief Marianne Partridge. She accepted.

"You fucking cunt!" Jann screamed, and threw a chair across the room. She had betrayed him. He had her former New York office repainted immediately after she vacated it, and openly grieved for days like a lover spurned.

When he saw his chance for revenge, he took it. At a restaurant in New York, he sat with a business associate and spied Clay Felker at another table. He followed Felker out the door, put his arm around him, chatted in his ear. Felker departed, and Jann returned to his associate, looking like a boy who'd just picked the lock on the candy store.

"I told him some things about Marianne," he bubbled. "He'll never trust her now!"

That was a great moment, one of many in the city that had become his home away from home. Or perhaps simply *home*. Jann was born here, after all, though he had scarcely a memory; and Jane was a New Yorker, and often mentioned her desire to return. They had a home here now, an apartment on posh East Sixty-sixth—walking distance from *Rolling Stone*'s New York office, which was looking more and more like headquarters whether anyone in the 625 Third Street office liked it or not.

———

The man responsible for this new phenomenon was not a New Yorker, but rather a Texan. Joe Armstrong was his name, a tall and lanky young man from the West Texas city of Abilene, the Buckle of the Bible Belt, as it were. In 1973 Jann hired Armstrong, a transplant with almost no magazine credentials, as *Rolling Stone*'s advertising director. This displaced Laurel Gonsalves, the equally uncredentialed woman who, in keeping with the ethos of the early seventies, operated more as a business "conscience" than as a saleswoman. A savvy, unruffled presence, she nonetheless, in Durocher's words, "tended not to hire anyone who might pose a threat to her job security."

In 1973, about 88 percent of the magazine's advertising revenue was derived from the music business, and as long as the industry was healthy,

Gonsalves and her subordinates could afford to sit placidly by the phone and take the orders. Yet was this dependence, with all its inherent risks, so very necessary? And especially in light of the magazine's foray into four-color art in 1973, the time seemed ripe to scratch around for new markets.

Before Armstrong, Porter Bibb's "hippie reps" roamed Manhattan like Woodstock poster children, and the ads *Rolling Stone* published in the trade magazines declared, "*Our* readers brush their teeth, too." A San Francisco business staffer once visited the city to meet loan officers with Dan Parker and, winking to Parker, said, "I believe I'll set the tone for this meeting," and proceeded to undo his ponytail and let his long white hair obscure his shoulders.

Madison Avenue was unpersuaded. Testimonials about the "sweet-steppin' folk who read *Rolling Stone*" rang like clattering hubcaps in these polished hallways. This was a magazine, after all, that never missed an opportunity to use the dreaded F-word, that printed its pages on newsprint as *Screw* (and no other major magazine) did. Worse still, Jann Wenner had established himself most unfavorably here. He'd lied about *Rolling Stone*'s ad rate base, showed up drunk at luncheons, peddling his apple-cheeked charm in a sector where charm got you into the janitor's closet, maybe, if you knew how to dust windowsills.

As a result, *Rolling Stone* found itself in a peculiar position. The magazine was adored by its media peers but reviled on Madison Avenue. How to improve the latter situation without tampering with the former would become Joe Armstrong's daunting task.

Without bothering to apologize for his lack of publishing experience, thirty-year-old Joe Armstrong proceeded to weave a miracle in a city that believed in few. He recruited his own sales force, initiated a slick promotional campaign with peanuts for a budget and started banging on doors. First he courted the stereo market, pointing out to Pioneer and Sony what his predecessors had not bothered to point out: that the *Rolling Stone* readers who bought all those records must play them on *something*. Then came liquor accounts—unheard of, surely, in 1967, yet now that Charlie Perry was pronouncing alcohol "the drug of the year" in his 1974 drinking column, the rank and file did not grumble.

Tobacco companies were a different story, and when Armstrong suggested pursuing them, veteran staffers cried that this was a bridge too far. Armstrong pointed out that "there sure were a lot of ads in the back of the book about smoking"—meaning rolling papers, pipes and other paraphernalia. ("I didn't know what the fuck a bong was," confessed Armstrong. "I thought maybe that was something like a miniature bongo.") Clearly there was a distinction to be drawn, but Jann chose not to do so, instead heartily encouraging Armstrong to go after the tobacco accounts.

And he could hardly complain about the results. In 1974, ad revenues jumped 50 percent. In 1975—a recession year that saw nearly every single periodical in America wither on the fiscal vine—*Rolling Stone* billings soared *another* 50 percent. Joe Armstrong had made New York safe for Jann Wenner. His reward was the title of publisher—"and in this case it means not just a super ad sales title," Jann wrote in a memo, "but the old-fashioned full scale person in charge of all publishing operations." To underscore this, the editor also conferred on his publisher the titles of president and chief operating officer of Straight Arrow Publishers, Inc.

Joe Armstrong returned the favor in early 1976. He procured Volkswagen—the account Jann had courted like a teenaged Casanova six years ago.

———

Staffers took notice when Jann celebrated his thirtieth birthday in Manhattan. His affection for the Big City was getting serious.

They could imagine what he was doing there. New York always knew how to treat a celebrity. There would be a table for him at Elaine's, Felkers and Rosenthals and other high-toned literary wags squeezing his shoulders and buying the next round, private clubs whose doormen did not even have to look on their sacred lists to know that his name was there, that suite at the Sherry Netherland for old times' sake . . .

Despite its economic doldrums, Jann openly expressed his faith that New York City was on the precipice of a renaissance. President Ford had told the city to drop dead, but New York dined on defiance. And now, in 1976, it appeared that Ford might be the main course. *Rolling Stone* would play its role, of course. Though Jann would openly declare his intent *not* to cover the '76 campaign—he prophesied that it would be "the most over-covered campaign in history"—he had a mojo wire delivered by truck to the Owl Farm in Woody Creek, Colorado. Hunter Thompson elected to "lecture" his way through Australia rather than return to the campaign trail, so Jann then turned to Gore Vidal, who demurred as well.

Nonetheless, Thompson responded when notified that the magazine wanted his comments on the Democratic candidates. He'd been impressed with Jimmy Carter, a man he once lumped in his 1972 coverage with the "bums and hacks" comprising the new Democratic party leadership. Several times since then he'd met the candidate, was startled to hear that the former Georgia governor loved Dylan and the Allman Brothers and began to think that there was more to this peanut farmer than met the eye.

On May 4, 1974, Thompson attended Governor Carter's address to the University of Georgia, somewhat by accident. What he heard sent Thompson's post-Elko heart to fluttering. It was "a king hell bastard of a speech," he wrote, adding, "I have never heard a sustained piece of political oratory that impressed me any more than the speech Jimmy Carter made on that Saturday afternoon in May 1974."

These words were printed in the magazine's June 3, 1976, issue, under the cover headline "Jimmy Carter & the Great Leap of Faith: An Endorsement, with Fear & Loathing, by Dr. Hunter S. Thompson." The headline was David Felton's, not Thompson's, and the Gonzo journalist protested to some that he'd been misrepresented. Yet as Felton would say: "It *was* an endorsement, whether Hunter wants to call it that or not."

Thompson was not the only writer to object to *Rolling Stone*'s unapologetic support of Jimmy Carter. Marianne Partridge thought the endorsement cheapened the magazine. Joe Klein didn't think it was kosher for publicist Anne Wexler to be putting "Carter for President" bumper stickers on the office doors. But then, Wexler was doing advance work for the candidate, and Thompson himself was developing a closeness to the Carter children that betrayed any suggestion of Fear & Loathing. All lines were blurring, the contours of the dancers dissolving in the swirl of the dance.

On July 12, 1976, Jann Wenner, Anne Wexler and *Rolling Stone* threw a party in honor of the Jimmy Carter staff. It was an event Jann took very seriously—a coming-out affair, set of course in New York, and the staff women would have to wear nice dresses and the drugs would have to stay hidden. When new reviews editor Dave Marsh flatly refused to hand over his Rolodex of musician addresses to Wexler, Jann advised him to comply if he wanted to hang on to his job. Marsh passed on the addresses to his boss.

The invitation list read like a Jann Wenner fantasy scroll: David Brinkley, Robert De Niro, Bob Dylan, Jackie Onassis, Norman Lear, Dan Rather, Robert Redford, George McGovern, Abe Rosenthal, the Carters, the Kennedys, the Lennons, the Allmans . . . All told, there were five hundred on the spangled list. "I think we're in!" Jann confided to a friend as the date approached.

He was in, as it turned out, beyond his wildest speculation. On the appointed night, seemingly thousands pressed up against the doors of the

Automation House on East Sixty-eighth, until the whole block was crummy with celebrities of every stripe. Inside, the scene was somewhat subdued, with Jann embracing his guests and Anne Wexler cursing the grossly violated guest list and Hunter Thompson inhaling amyls in the closet.

But outside, the masses swelled into a near-rumble of frantic New York journalists and actors and politicians—many of whom would have agreed with Madison Avenue's earlier uncharitable assessment of this "little music paper from San Francisco" not so very long ago. But there was a craziness now to *Rolling Stone*'s momentum. Richard Avedon was taking celebrity photographs for an issue. Watergate felon John Dean was covering the Republican convention for Jann, and his quotation of Agriculture Secretary Earl Butz's assessment of what American Negroes crave would fry Butz like a flounder. Jack Ford would be on a cover, David Eisenhower would be assigned a piece, the staff of the next President of the United States was eating the caviar out of Jann Wenner's uncallused hand . . .

———

Unidentified.

The February 26, 1976, issue of *Rolling Stone* was devoted to San Francisco, ten years after the unnatural childbirth of the psychedelic era. It was a tender, bittersweet collection of memories—unavoidably sad, for nowhere did the issue indicate that the beautiful Bay City had anything left to offer American youth culture.

Not long after the issue was published, Jann met with publisher Armstrong, senior editor Scanlon, publicist Wexler and a few others. The site this time was not Big Sur, but rather Hilton Head, North Carolina, a trendy corporate conference center.

There the unspeakable was spoken for the first time: it was time, said Jann Wenner, for *Rolling Stone* to move to New York. Nothing was keeping the magazine in San Francisco. It was only gathering moss there.

His lieutenants were hardly surprised, but the speech Jann gave to the rest of the staff on October 1, 1976, jolted the listeners. "We're all going to New York!" he began enthusiastically, standing on top of a chair. Then he added, "Or at least some of us are."

Anxious stares were traded as their leader ticked off the ever so obvious advantages: a greater talent base, easier access to national news, massive savings on long-distance phone calls, overdue recognition from the rest of the press, a cultural renaissance in the making. . . . The editor in his smart vested suit dismounted his chair and paced as he talked, gathering steam, while staffers nodded and sat stupefied, hardly knowing what to say.

Charlie Perry knew what to say: "Not me." He'd been briefed in advance by Jann, who offered his old copy chief a variety of options—but not, in his view, a single good reason for moving the magazine. The news shattered him. In a day and age that seemed so complicated back then but seemed so painfully simple now, he had regarded himself as Jann's first fan. And now Charlie Perry bitterly took to describing himself as "Jann's first sucker."

"I had given them my goddamn life's blood," he said. "And now it seemed to me a betrayal of everything that I did. I'd been suckered into seeing *Rolling Stone* as this new voice, and now it was obvious that he just wanted to publish the same people that were being published everywhere else."

Ben Fong-Torres elected to stay and run a San Francisco bureau. The Bay was his home; his family was here, and six years after his brother's brutal gangland murder, there was still healing to be done.

The season changed, then the year, and on Third Street emotions spiraled and crisscrossed and sailed off the graph in all directions. There were goodbyes, too many of them: Cindy Ehrlich, Dan Parker, Tim Cahill, dozens of minor employees whose imminent departures would leave gaping holes in this motley family quilt. But soon there would be hellos: Joe Klein, Dave Marsh and Chet Flippo were in New York. And an adoring world awaited them, for Jann, God damn him, was right: *Rolling Stone* was hot, had been hot for some time, and its star journalists and artists were due for a ride on the town.

———

At the close of work, around midnight, art director Roger Black and picture editor Karen Mullarkey slouched against the brick wall adjacent to the office parking lot and the coffee company's loading docks, the way they always did. Even in the darkness they could look up and see the chimney stack Jann always feared would topple down onto the office and crush him. Beyond that hung streetlights, and farther west stretched that deep sparkling infinity of water, seals weaving around in her, barking at the hotel where Hunter Thompson once wrote about McGovern and Nixon and how those god-damned seals were driving him crazy.

It was a San Francisco night, as quiet as a dream. Neither Black nor Mullarkey hailed from the Bay, but both could see an argument for this being Nirvana. *Rolling Stone*, madness and all, was part of Nirvana. They'd both joined the magazine rather recently, in 1975. But it seemed much, much longer than that. Roger Black had been reading *Rolling Stone* since its early days. As a kid in Houston he once stood in line with twenty other people at the neighborhood newsstand, waiting for the second installment of "Fear & Loathing in Las Vegas" to arrive.

Now he and Karen Mullarkey had arrived. They were crucial elements in a magazine they both regarded as utterly without peer, without rules, without limits of any kind. Perhaps they were spoiled, and so what if they were. The world, they were convinced, needed them. In return, they at *Rolling Stone*, anytime they wanted, could tell the rest of the world to take a flying leap.

They sat in this paralyzed night, depleted of idle talk since they'd worn their asses out putting another issue to bed. A joint was rolled, and as Mullarkey pulled at it, her gaze fell to the nearby railroad tracks girdling the loading dock, and the little shards of glass on the tracks that caught the streetlight and winked at her and at Black and at the old coffee building now dark and soon to be emptied of their strange and wonderful melodrama for all time.

Karen Mullarkey blew out smoke and said, more to the Bay breeze than to Roger Black, "I wonder if it's going to be like this in New York?"

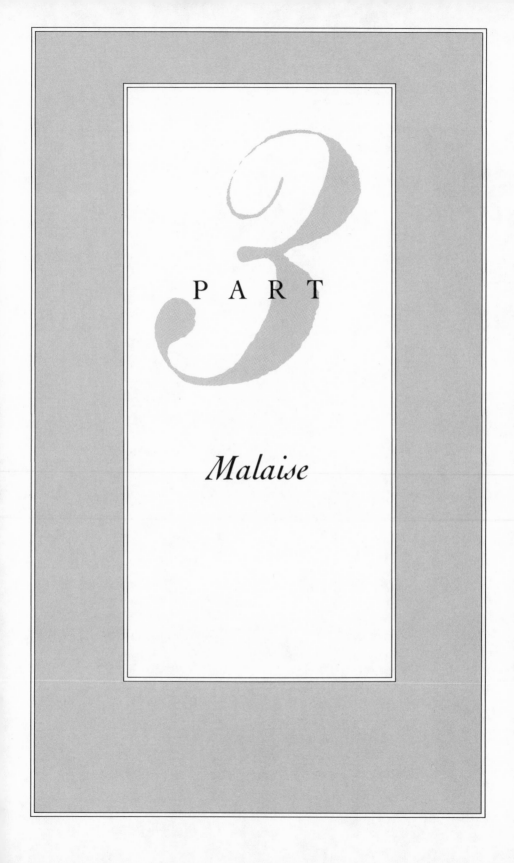

PART 3

Malaise

Chapter Fourteen

BIG CITY OF DREAMS

"So, uh, Truman. Know any good writers in New York?"
— *Jann Wenner to Truman Capote*

*G*ranted, it was a slow news day. But the television camera crews bunched up around 745 Fifth Avenue could just as easily have been dispatched to Ed Koch or Bella Abzug or one of the other mayoral candidates—or perhaps to Yankee headquarters to catch George Steinbrenner in one of his periodic fulminations. The New York media could always find something better to do than to cover the official opening of a magazine's new headquarters.

But *Rolling Stone*—the unwashed glitterati from the Bay, the new kids on the block—would get the royal treatment.

Parties, parties everywhere—endless affairs, the booze gushing long past those ridiculous West Coast liquor curfews and oh, check your denim at the door, no objections to semi-nudity as long as you don't dance like a hippie. Welcome to the Mudd Club, to Studio 54, to CBGB, your names are of course on our doorman's list, file past the more hiply dressed but alas uninvited throng, we do not encourage open display of drug taking but we should warn you that if you're discreet you'll be considered a bore and bores aren't on our doorman's list, just thought you should know. We see you've already met Andy and Truman, and before long we'll have you arm in arm with our other hot new friends, the Saturday Night Live *gang. This NBC pass will get you backstage to every show. Who knows what else it'll get you.* Ciao, baby . . .

. . . and hello, darling. Welcome to Elaine's, to our new opening, to this-that-and-the-other exclusive soirée. Diana Vreeland of Vogue *notices you're not wearing your shoes and she thinks that's simply di-vine, you're just what she imagined you'd be. Standing over there in a glass-swishing inner circle are some of our city's finest writers, and their circle will part for you—in fact, they not only want to meet you, they want to write for you, yes you you gorgeous bumpkin! Now walk over here, I want you to meet the Honorable Gerald Ford, and the Honorable Abe Beame, the Honorable—oops, I almost introduced you to your own editor, all primed for another night on the town with Art Garfunkel or John Belushi or . . . good God, is that Jackie's perfume I smell on him . . .*

All of this happened during the otherwise turgid New York summer of 1977.

——

The architect had flown to San Francisco, had carefully taken notes as the various big guns of *Rolling Stone* described the structural requirements of the new office. What he came up with won him glowing notices in the *New York Times* and *Architectural Record*. Neither publication, however, bothered to consider the views of *Rolling Stone* staffers. Nor had the architect, apparently.

Veteran receptionist Judy Lawrence, the Mouth of the South, Director of Rumor Control, would be placed behind a plastic security wall, like an imperious bank teller. Sarah Lazin's research department, once the center of editorial activity, was now shunted off to the fringes of the art department. The darkroom was painted white; its doors would not close. The ceiling in the color-separation room was too low for the camera to be raised, thus rendering tens of thousands of dollars' worth of fine German equipment absolutely useless. There was not a single supply closet in the office. The architect could hardly have done a better job of subverting the office flow of *Rolling Stone* had he burned the facility to the ground.

The evolution—from the old Brannan wooden beams to the cubicles and exposed brick on Third Street to these four floors of antiseptic white walls, upon which no posters would be hung—was unsettling. "The editors had these big corporate offices and their assistants had cubicles outside their offices, which was a big change," said Sarah Lazin. "It really imposed a hierarchy that had not existed. When we got there, Harriet [Fier] and Christine [Doudna] and I just looked around and there were all these assistants who were not really editorial assistants at all, but secretaries, with their Bloomingdale outfits and their high heels and their makeup, sitting outside the offices of the editors, who were inside being important.

"And we said, 'This isn't the dynamic of the magazine. Where's the place where we all sit around and talk about cover heads? Where's the place where we go over the galleys together?' Instead of all the open space, there were offices. Offices with doors. People walked into the offices and closed their doors and stayed in there all day—or they brought in their friends and just stayed there. It got very clubby, and very elitist, and very isolating.

"And that architect won an *award* for this."

Yet the blueprint, they all knew, was not the architect's. It was Jann Wenner's. The only surviving founder of *Rolling Stone* had plopped his brainchild down on Fifth Avenue, abandoning the $6,000 annual lease on Third Street for space that would cost him over fifty times that sum. Staffers noted, somewhat bitterly, that their boss could have bought property in SoHo outright with that first year's $330,000, and spent that amount in succeeding years promoting editorial excellence.

Yet new digs in lower Manhattan would suggest only that *Rolling Stone* had moved, not that it had arrived. No, Jann S. Wenner belonged right here on Fifth Avenue and Fifty-eighth, overlooking not that hateful chimney stack but rather Central Park and the Sherry Netherland. It was a vantage point he prized. "How can you leave this?" he asked an employee who was resigning, sweeping his arm across the twenty-third-floor window like a game-show model. Having now arrived, how could anyone *consider* returning? Why should an angel clip his wings so as to walk with mere mortals?

The oversized corner office now featured a telescope. "Look across there," said Jann to one of his writers, pointing to the Sherry Netherland even as he squinted through the lens. "Diana Ross lives in a suite right . . . over . . . there."

He lingered for some time, hunched over the telescope, this Berkeley stargazer now delivered to a constellation more spectacular than any dream. Then he looked up and sighed. "Too bad she keeps her blinds shut," he said.

No one would begrudge the man his bite from the Apple. Yet *Rolling Stone*, the window into Jann Wenner's mind, was now foggier than ever. The feature inventory now included profiles on Princess Caroline of Monaco and Diana Vreeland, articles by David Eisenhower and Caroline Kennedy—and an entire issue about New York, with restaurateur Elaine Kaufman on the inside and Andy Warhol's portrait of losing mayoral candidate Bella Abzug on the cover. Articles were now subjected to what was referred to as "tight editing," meaning the days of the 20,000-word Eszterhas opus were twirling westward. When writer Chris Hodenfield complained about the shrinking of editorial space, Jann Wenner spelled out his priorities with yet another loving gesture toward Central Park.

"Well," the editor explained, "we traded twelve pages for a view of this."

It was the kind of talk they dreaded. "Whatever problems people on the staff had with Jann," said Harriet Fier, "*Rolling Stone* was Jann's magazine. And he was, in his time, a brilliant editor, with great ideas. And we respected that." Yet if one of his blue eyes was focused brilliantly on his creation, the other wandered here and there, searching, they feared, for something *Rolling Stone* could not provide him, something in fact at odds with the magazine's vitality.

Charlie Fracchia had taught Jann how to throw his money around. Porter Bibb showed the young editor that *Rolling Stone* could be a merchandising center. Larry Durocher ushered in a more conventional format. His replacement, a southern California Republican named Richard Irvine, had revived in Jann the yearning for a media empire. Irvine's successor as publisher, Joe Armstrong, had ignored the old taboo and brought tobacco and automotive ads into the magazine. To the staff, some of these fellows seemed quite nice and others less so. But as Tim Cahill put it: "I considered the people on the business side my adversaries. I didn't know 'em, and I didn't want to know 'em. From afar they seemed to be greaseballs one and all, without exception."

Said Fier, "We were always glad to see them go."

And now, inexplicably, Joe Armstrong was gone.

One minute he and Jann Wenner were chumming it up at Hilton Head, wearing T-shirts that sported a photo of the two, and the editor was warmly complimenting his publisher in memos and telling Armstrong to his face, "We're like Lennon and McCartney." Then, on May 1, 1977, Armstrong was frantically packing his belongings and moving out of his office before tendering resignation, not knowing how irrationally Jann would react. And on the following day, Jann was ordering a symbolic emasculation: the cutting in half of Joe Armstrong's office.

Armstrong's departure stunned everyone. His star had risen higher even than Jann's in New York—and maybe, some suggested, that was the point: perhaps, as some reports put it, the town was not big enough for both of them. Yet no one could recall ever hearing the editor grumble about all the press his publisher was amassing. Nor had Armstrong seemed any less gung ho about Jann and the magazine heading east than he'd been at Hilton Head.

Many on the San Francisco staff had been uneasy about Armstrong. They didn't like the "Meet the New Team" trade ads that showed Armstrong flanked by his staff of advertising whiz kids. To them, there was only one "team," and that was the 625 Third Street crew. To them, Rolling Stone's recent financial success had less to do with any fancy-talking Texan and more to do with Thompson, Kohn, Eszterhas, Crouse et al.

Yet for the most part their objections to the publisher derived from the usual creative-vs.-corporate paranoia inherent in the business. And this was hardly fair, as Armstrong was a classic "church/state" publisher: supportive of the magazine's editorial stance while not meddling in its affairs. Jann Wenner himself could hardly have done a better job of walking this razor line.

Armstrong was a handy man on the lecture stump, coining phrases like "impact journalism" to describe Rolling Stone's mission ... and protecting that mission, as well as defending the magazine's editorial integrity, even when an electronics company jerked its $75,000 ad account because the magazine did not rank the company in its stereo review. At the same time, said Paul Scanlon, "he was the only publisher—and I knew them all—to invite me to advertising functions. Most of the sales reps had never talked to an editor before. So I'd speak to them, tell them what editorial does, and it was very useful, a very smart thing for Joe to do. He was always my favorite publisher."

And he'd been Jann Wenner's favorite publisher as well. Armstrong had, in fact, been the first individual ever to make money for Rolling Stone hand over fist. Yet the issue was personal, not financial. Armstrong groused to others about the editor's business ethics, worrying aloud that Jann's erratic behavior would undo much of the publisher's accomplishments. Gradually the message became clear: Jann had willingly given up much of Rolling Stone, and now he was snatching it all back again. He would not arrive in New York City as anybody's right-hand man.

Joe Armstrong battled. Then he withdrew. The thrill was gone in a flash, it seemed; but it was gone for good. Armstrong was himself a star now, and other ventures beckoned. He gave Jann Wenner back the title of publisher, saddled up and was out of Dodge before dawn.

———

Thanks largely to Armstrong's efforts on Madison Avenue, Straight Arrow Publishers, Inc., found itself with an unheard-of $2 million war chest by 1976. And even more revenues were available, the publisher suggested in a memo to Jann, if *Rolling Stone* could find a way to capitalize on the swelling advertising budgets of wilderness equipment companies. The Armstrong memo suggested a special "outdoor supplement" as a surefire advertising magnet.

Associate editor Harriet Fier caught wind of the scheme and was not amused. She slapped the memo down on Jann's desk and said to her boss, "This is advertising dictating editorial. This is *not* classy."

The editor's blue eyes seized her attention. "You be in charge of it, then," he directed her. "You *make* it classy."

Before the Fier supplement—even before Armstrong's memo—the old fire in Jann's Hearstian loins had been rekindled. He now had a syndicated "*Rolling Stone* Radio Hour," a *Rolling Stone* Lecture Service (featuring Jon Landau ruminating on "The Place of Rock in American Pop Culture," Hunter Thompson on "whatever your pleasure" and David Felton on "Interviewing and Creative Ignorance") and scattered book projects. Now he had money to back his lust for empire.

Two magazine projects tossed around in his head. One he called "the poster magazine," patterned after the photo-laden publications so popular in Great Britain. The other dealt with the growing interest among Americans in outdoor recreation—a trend Jann could not help but notice as he dodged fellow tourists on Aspen ski slopes.

Neither idea was strikingly novel. In fact, Bob Guccione, Jr.—the son of *Penthouse*'s editor and publisher—was already marketing a poster magazine in the States. Proposals for outdoor magazines were also kicking around, but none had yet found financial backing.

Jann paid a call on Michael Rogers, the Grover Lewis protégé who had since become one of *Rolling Stone*'s finest contributors, particularly in the area of science writing. The editor asked Rogers to put together a magazine prospectus. Jann also asked Rogers if he'd like to be the publication's editor.

Rogers, a frequent backpacker, passed on the job offer—"I could see that in being a full-time editor, the great irony would be I'd never get to go outdoors again," he said. Nonetheless, Rogers set to work on the prospectus.

The next recruit was William Randolph Hearst III. The grandson of the famed newspaper magnate had been a useful pipeline of family information for Howard Kohn and David Weir during their investigation of Hearst's cousin's kidnapping. Inevitably, at a dinner party thrown by Ralph Gleason's widow, Jean, the heir and the editor met.

"It was a natural friendship," said Hearst. Both were young and wealthy San Franciscans with quick, impatient minds. ("Will, like Jann, had the attention span of a flea," said art director Hans Teensma, who worked with them both.) Unlike Jann, Will Hearst was born into social standing and was enormously self-conscious about money, spurning opulence in favor of a secondhand mattress during his college years. If Jann Wenner was impressed with the Hearst aura, Hearst in turn had to admire the *Rolling Stone* editor's entrepreneurial spunk, his power beyond birthright.

The two began to see more of each other, and one day Hearst took his gaping friend to the legendary family castle at San Simeon—an event satirized in Garry Trudeau's "Doonesbury" strip a few days later. If others snickered at the mention of Jann's new social acquisition, the twenty-five-year-old Hearst didn't feel especially cheapened. "There are people who drop names to make themselves important because of who they know," said Hearst. "But I always felt Jann had a real fan's mentality. He wanted to hang out with Mick Jagger because Mick was cool, not because he wanted to tell people that *he* was cool as a result of knowing Mick."

Hearst was a committed outdoorsman, and told Jann one day he'd like to help out with this magazine idea he and Michael Rogers were conceptualizing. Jann later rejoindered, "Here's the deal. You're either the editor or there's no other offer. That's the way I want to do it."

Hearst, taking stock of his negligible experience as a magazine editor, agreed anyway.

Months later, Jann recruited another big name for the masthead: twenty-four-year-old Jack Ford, the President's son. Ford had been a natural cover subject for *Rolling Stone*, as he'd openly admitted smoking pot and had brought George Harrison and Bianca Jagger over to the White House. His duties at the new magazine were less clear. Jann signed young Ford to a contract the night before his family left the White House, awarded him the nebulous title of "assistant to the publisher" and sent him off on a variety of publicity functions. "I liked Jack, and I thought he was a decent guy," said managing editor Will Hearst. "But he always struck me as a celebrity guest."

Now Jann had two celebrities with fancy titles and not a dime's worth of experience between them. The search began for a veteran senior editor. One of the finalists was Jon Carroll, late of the 1970 John Burks rabble and now the editor of *New West*. Carroll, after some deliberation, demurred, explaining that he was married now, and just starting to raise a family, and he hoped that Jann would—

"See you around the day-care center, asshole," Jann Wenner interjected, and hung up the phone.

The man Jann settled on was Terry McDonell, who'd logged several years with Max Palevsky's *L.A. Magazine*, Francis Ford Coppola's *City* and Warren Hinckle's *San Francisco*. A man, that is to say, who had withstood every flavor of ego and temperament. McDonell was hardly ruffled when the only question Jann Wenner asked him during their interview was "Do you know how to cross-country ski?"

"No," said McDonell. "But I'd love to get the chance."

In preparation for the *Rolling Stone* outdoor supplement, the staff trio of Fier, Cahill and Rogers thumbed through existing outdoor magazines, trying to get a sense of the possibilities. "We were looking through magazines with names like *Canoeing*," said Cahill. "You know, here's a magazine that tells you eight times a year how to paddle a canoe. And then there's the fishing and hunting ones, the splash and bang magazines. And we figured: The guys we want to address probably are not that interested in killing animals. Maybe they're more interested in going to India, and running the rapids in the Himalayas, and reading truly literate outdoor articles."

McDonell was especially keen on the latter subject. "I had this idea," he said, "that the way to do the magazine was to use fiction writers in a very old-fashioned way, in the sense that we could send them out into the wilderness to have an experience. And then we'd get interesting personal journalism that would hark back to a more traditional kind of travel writing, as opposed to just dead fish and stuff."

Hearst, who "didn't see people going out in the woods with manuscripts in their hands and reading while fishing," wasn't sure the *Rolling Stone*-type reader would go for this approach. His mind's eye conjured up not Hemingway but a mountain climber: "They represented in the outdoor movement what the rockers represented in popular music. They had taste and style, but they also had an irreverence, a kind of hang-the-Establishment outlook."

Jann's own vision for the magazine, said Hearst, "was the hardest one

for me to get ahold of. But it was maybe something along the lines of
Surfing—a magazine with a very pop quality to it."

Michael Rogers's prospectus incorporated these disparate themes, the
sum of which recalled nothing so much as *Rolling Stone*: broadly defined but
with a distinctly literate and individualistic tone. And now it was time for a
title. The most obvious choice, *Outdoors*, was owned by Weyerhaeuser, and
the company would not part with the name unless dearly. Jann went with a
simple alternative: *Outside*.

———

In the summer of 1977, just after Joe Armstrong's departure, the minds met
at a weeklong conference in Montauk, Long Island: the New York business
staff, the creative heads of *Rolling Stone* and the new editors of *Outside*. As
could have been predicted, sobriety was seldom in force, unlikely sexual
partnerships developed and a limousine driver was routed back and forth
between Manhattan and Montauk, unwittingly transporting envelopes filled
with cocaine so as to fortify the troops.

Just as predictably, the meetings were dreary, with staffers oversleeping
and staggering in half drunk, observing bitterly that the humidity had turned
the cocaine to mush. John Belushi, along for the ride, lent the conference
some levity by delivering the art department's presentation and launching
into a "Samurai Editor" routine that sent the audience into hysterics. Yet
the Montauk conference was marked by more than boredom, comedy and
debauchery. Tension hung in the blanketlike air. The three factions represented here all vied for the attention of Jann Wenner, and it was widely
suspected that he could not heed all three at once.

Though the *Outside* presentation impressed the veterans, the notion that
Rolling Stone had suddenly become "a heavily freighted ship" was bandied
about. Additionally, the new financial officers at Straight Arrow weren't like
Joe Armstrong. They didn't use phrases like "impact journalism." To them,
it seemed, *Rolling Stone* was no more than just a magazine, and in fact wasn't
even a magazine: it was a mere commodity, a ware to peddle.

One late morning, one of the new ad salesmen rose to give a presentation.
He was a young man, short-haired, and he wore the collar on his peach
polo shirt straight up. As this was, after all, morning, his words were barely
attended to, until after a few minutes the message was inescapable: *Rolling
Stone* was going to accept an advertising account with the ROTC.

Gasps and murmurs were general throughout the room. Obscenities
followed. Pencils and wadded-up paper were thrown at the befuddled young

rep. Jann rose to put in his two bits, but so did another individual. His name was Dave Marsh, a former Detroit street kid and editor at *Creem*, an erratic publication made credible in part due to Marsh's intelligent writings. Now Marsh was *Rolling Stone*'s reviews editor and following in the footsteps of Greil Marcus and Jon Landau as a brilliant theorist who nonetheless conveyed rock & roll's passion as only Ed Ward and Lester Bangs could.

Marsh was choked up even before he spoke. "Look," he managed. "What *Rolling Stone* sells is not just an editorial product. It sells its credibility. It *stands* for something. If you take these ads, you will not stand for that any longer; you will stand for the opposite. The ROTC may seem a neutral, harmless thing. But I'm here to tell you, from everybody I know who got killed in that war or who went there and got their lives ruined by it—this is wrong. You don't do this. *You don't do this. Rolling Stone* will not be the same *Rolling Stone*."

Even as Jann Wenner nodded his assent, others from the business staff rallied to the rep's defense. Broken sentences flew back and forth. Whereupon Virginia Team, the art director of *Outside*, stood up and declared, "I've had about all this shit I can stand," disrobed on the spot, marched outside and jumped into the nearby swimming pool.

Others on the art staff followed her. Then the cry went up: "Everybody into the pool!" And Jann Wenner laughed and collared Dave Marsh and they fell into the pool together, and the account with the ROTC was thereby tabled.

Editorial had whipped business. It would not happen again.

———

On Friday, August 26, 1977, *Outside* assistant to the publisher Jack Ford sat in the wicker gondola of a hot-air balloon parked on a Fisherman's Wharf pier. The balloon, intended to be launched over the Sierras as a promotional stunt for the magazine's first issue, would not float. Shifting winds rocked the vessel until finally, after repeated effort, Ford removed his crash helmet, climbed out of the gondola, lit a cigarette and called it a day.

The magazine itself got off the ground, but faced gusty winds from the very beginning. Jann had never seen fit to draw up a formal business plan for *Outside*, figuring that situating the magazine next to *Rolling Stone* on the newsstands would magically turn the trick. Therein lay the folly. Balloon stunts and celebrity editors notwithstanding, people didn't know what *Outside* was. They would not seek it out on the newsstands. The publication would have to find its reader, rather than the other way around, and the only way to do that was an all-out subscription drive.

Yet Jann knew only the *Rolling Stone* newsstand approach. *Outside* hit the racks in late August with stories by Tim Cahill, Michael Rogers and National Book Award winner Tom McGuane; with an astonishing fifty-nine pages of ads (none of which came from tobacco companies); and with striking, elaborate artwork. Sales, however, were disappointing. All talk became financial. The *Outside* staff, still situated in the old 625 Third Street office, was bombarded by missives from the New York business staff. Color separations were becoming exorbitant. The photo subjects were hippies—wrong image. The boss was in a rage. "You're hemorrhaging us!" they told Will Hearst and Terry McDonell.

True, *Outside* was pushing its budget to the wall, and here and there exceeding anticipated costs. But, said Terry McDonell, "you can't sink a ship with that. Our problems were more along the lines of promotion and strategy errors that we made about whether or not it was a subscription magazine or a newsstand magazine. We dumped a whole bunch of 'em on the newsstands and they sat there."

Said Will Hearst, "The charge never was 'You are spending more money than you are budgeted.' It was 'We have to restrict the budget. The cost of doing this magazine is not being offset by the revenue that's coming in.'

"I would agree, though, that nobody at the high end of *Outside*—by that I mean above me—had ever really sat down and said, 'What do we want to accomplish with this magazine? How does this fit into *Rolling Stone* Incorporated?' Those were the kinds of things that an Armstrong might have done. But Armstrong wasn't there."

Hearst had been told that *Outside* would be allotted $1.5 million of Straight Arrow's $2 million war chest. Yet the move to New York had by itself cost over $1 million, with nearly half that spent on office renovation alone. Now *that* was over budget.

Panicking, Jann ordered that *Outside* put a rock & roll star, Jimmy Buffett, on the cover. Louder colors were used. Tobacco ads were accepted after vigorous debate, which ended with a resigned Will Hearst observing, "Look. We can either do this magazine with cigarette ads, or we can *not* do it with*out* cigarette ads." Finally, while Hearst was vacationing, Jann decided to convert the monthly magazine into a bimonthly to shore up costs. The managing editor blew a fuse when the news eventually reached him.

Jann was frank. *Outside* was out of money. "Why don't you buy it?" he asked Hearst. Instead, Hearst—who, in Tim Cahill's words, "was not a good editor when he started, but a year later was *damn* good"—took a hike from *Outside*.

For the first time since 1973, when Joe Armstrong became *Rolling Stone*'s advertising director, the company was in debt. The well seemed to be leaking from all sides. The biggest holes came from *Outside* and office renovations, but there were others. Writers couldn't ply their sources with two-dollar Doggie Diner burgers in New York. Drinks cost three times what they had at Jerry's Inn.

More ominously, *Rolling Stone* was being sued for $100 million for a story written by Howard Kohn linking Richard Nixon, Howard Hughes, the CIA and the Mafia. The article brazenly accused Resorts International, a casino operator in the Bahamas, of being run by the mob. Jann stood courageously behind the story and his writer, but Resorts had enormous legal firepower, and the suit, said one *Rolling Stone* business staffer, "nearly brought us to our knees" before a six-figure settlement was eventually agreed upon.

Though Jann later claimed that "it wasn't a financial crisis," he openly fretted at board meetings about whether Straight Arrow would have to dip into its final $500,000 in CDs and totter on bankruptcy's precipice. At one of these meetings, it was judged that the *Outside* venture would mean *Rolling Stone*'s ruin if it wasn't folded. A $1 million line of credit was obtained from Chemical Bank, whose officers then examined Straight Arrow's books and recalled the loan, requiring a second bailout by the Continental Bank of Illinois.

In the fall of 1978, Jann Wenner officially declared defeat. *Outside* was sold to a competing magazine, *Mariah*, after which the two magazines consolidated into *Outside* and became a financially successful, award-winning magazine. The Straight Arrow empire was decimated once again, and its chairman was $500,000 less Hearstian than two years before.

———

Yet the financial disquiet of 1977 bore no resemblance to earlier crises. Long past those bootstrapping days, *Rolling Stone* now dealt with these matters calmly and quietly. No one on the *Rolling Stone* staff was laid off; no wages were cut back. No brakes were applied to the fast-lane lifestyle the San Franciscans now led.

In the old Third Street office, the resident drug dealers stocked only marijuana. Here in New York, pot's somnambulent charms were not con-

ducive to the city's frenzied, out-all-night pace. Before long, the in-house
merchants were selling cocaine, and the office room in which they did so
came to be known as the Capri Lounge, after the gathering spot on the TV
show *Mary Hartman, Mary Hartman.*

Uppers had been a common feature of Third Street's deadline nights.
With few exceptions, however, they took the form of pharmaceutical speed,
an essentially nonrecreational means of pulling the necessary all-nighter.
Staffers continued to work late hours on Fifth Avenue, but the benefits they
derived from coke were not strictly functional. The drug's high was more
pleasurable, less wicked; it connoted both style and rebellion, a seventies
version of radical chic. Cocaine's high price tag only bolstered its exclusive
status.

It was the ultimate drug for the urban social climber, clean and compact,
leaving no odor, causing no hallucinations or red eyes or nausea or primal
urge for junk food. Studies indicated that coke, far from deadening intelligence, actually stimulated the brain cortex. A thinking man's drug. A
hipster's drug. Certainly New York's drug. When interviewing a local ap-
plicant, a top staffer pulled out a joint, took a hit and held it out. The local
fellow withdrew in surprise, refusing the reefer. The staffer got the message.
Back-to-nature drugs didn't make it here. There was no nature in the city;
only cold concrete.

Musicians snorted coke. Reportedly, White House Chief of Staff Ham-
ilton Jordan snorted coke. Jann Wenner snorted coke. And now so did his
employees: editors, writers, production artists, secretaries and even business
staffers, visiting the Capri Lounge just after cashing their checks (or anytime
they pleased, if they had a line of credit). If discretion was advised, it was
not practiced rigorously. The Lounge's walls were covered with Polaroid
photos of its clients happily snorting away their wages.

One new editor thought he'd impress the boss. While conversing with
Jann in the latter's office, the editor made mention of this exceptional coke
he'd scored.

"Really?" asked Jann, adding eagerly, "Do you have any with you?"

"Sure," the editor said, and withdrew a little paper wrapper.

Jann promptly dove in, nostrils flaring, and snorted nearly all of the
contents. The editor learned the same hard lesson others had before and
would later: "Don't do any coke around Jann. He'll snort it all himself."

The lessons Annie Leibovitz learned were far more concussive. For all
her magnificent talent, Leibovitz was still susceptible to self-doubt, to ac-
cusations that she was second-rate, or worthless without drugs. Her insecurity

was many-tentacled, and it lay at the very heart of her complex relationship with Jann and Jane Wenner. Said one of her closest friends at the time, "She was so naïve, so grateful to Jann for having given her this break. And he was very much a Svengali. He was able to keep that song playing in her head. And she wanted to hear it—she liked the sense that Jann made her and that she owed it to Jann, because it all played into her feelings of insecurity."

Leibovitz and the editor's wife had been close for years, but their friendship was strange and manipulative, and fellow staffers did what they could to avoid its manifestations. One editor received an office call from Jane, who was furious because Annie had walked into the Wenner house in the middle of the night, helped herself to a beer and left the empty can on the drainboard. Another staffer answered her home phone well past midnight. It was Jane, wanting to know if Annie was over there. To those standing on the sidelines, it all seemed childish but vaguely wicked, and certainly messy. It was intense enough simply working for Jann.

Annie Leibovitz had bitten off more than she could chew. She'd gone on tour with the Stones as their official photographer, developing a mean crush on Mick Jagger, stubbornly believing that he had written "Memory Motel" about her. Her career had taken off like a bottle rocket, but its toll was impossible to overlook. People began to call Annie Leibovitz a prima donna. She arrived late at photo shoots, sometimes did not arrive at all. She agreed to photograph Dave Marsh's wedding. The best man, Jon Landau, made the mistake of catching a ride with her. Both missed the ceremonies.

She continued to report lost cameras on her expense sheet, though insiders knew the equipment was being traded in for drugs. She formed a side business with a friend, who discovered that the photographer was taking checks from the back of the checkbook. Annie Leibovitz walked with the dark princes—John Belushi, Keith Richards, Hunter Thompson—but she could not stand the pace. Twice she overdosed and nearly died.

A friend and fellow *Rolling Stone* staffer let herself into Leibovitz's Dakota apartment one afternoon. The photographer had just completed a shoot of Keith Richards—an infamous session, capturing the Stones guitarist in a slack-kneed, gaping, wall-eyed heroin stupor; there were light fixtures and lenses all about the room. And there was something else. Blood on the walls, thin red spurts. Blood on the bathroom walls as well. She'd been shooting up again.

The friend hesitated by the bedroom door, then walked in. She feared she'd see Annie Leibovitz's cold body tangled up in the sheets. But no, there was no body, only more blood. The friend retreated. She needed a thousand drinks. Outside, a St. Patrick's Day parade rolled gaily through the streets, and the friend wove her way to a nearby pub, where she tossed back innumerable bourbons. Whereupon she lurched outside and joined the march, and had not gone a great distance before she marched into a lamppost—much as Annie Leibovitz had herself done a year or so back, at a London airport, wearing only her pajamas and colliding with a pillar after a long day with Mick Jagger—and saw stars.

———

Jann Wenner was gathering no moss. This was a town for big plans, and he was full of them. Buying a Rolls-Royce. Opening a nightclub of his own. Being seen—oh, and was he being seen! *With Jackie*. They were friends. She had taken it upon herself to help Jann establish contacts in Manhattan. Ms. Onassis even recruited him for a Save Central Park campaign that opened with much fanfare and then fizzled into obscurity. Jann escorted her around the new offices, the former First Lady displaying hardly a flicker of disapproval when Jann opened a door behind which stood two staffers puffing on a joint. In return, Ms. Onassis had the Wenners over for Christmas. Jann took pictures of this hallowed moment and carried them around with him. Now, if he could only meet Telly Savalas of *Kojak* . . .

In April of 1977 he accepted *Rolling Stone*'s second National Magazine Award, this time for the 1976 Richard Avedon special photographic issue. That issue—featuring photographs of Establishment leaders like Ronald Reagan, Barbara Jordan and George Bush (none of them under the age of thirty)—was as emblematic of the tony and refined New York *Rolling Stone* as the award-winning Altamont and Charlie Manson issues typified the rough, painfully earnest San Francisco antecedent. More than ever before, Jann began to speak of that magic circulation number, 1 million; only few doubted him now.

He could have it all. A magazine declared Jann and Jane Wenner likely candidates for "New York's celebrated couple of 1977." Surely this was all Jane Schindelheim Wenner had hoped for: a return to her roots, escape from her daily fear that the city she lived in would be ruptured by a terrible earthquake.

But utopia wasn't supposed to move this fast. She spoke with Charlie Perry that year, and confided to Jann's old copy chief that all she'd wanted was for Jann to have a nice business and a nice house in the country. She hadn't counted on all this urban royalty. Jann, on the other hand, had taken to it all too well. On the all-night circuit he'd acquired a new interest, vodka, and now freely slugged away on a chilled bottle of Wodka Wyborowa during office hours. Friends from San Francisco couldn't help but notice how much weight he'd put on.

A staffer from the old days, Chris Hodenfield's older brother Jan, had dinner with the Wenners one evening in Manhattan. The reporter who covered Woodstock for *Rolling Stone* listened quietly as Jann and Jane talked about the new office, their East Side apartment, their new friends.

Then Hodenfield put down his fork and asked, "Yes, but how has living in New York *changed* you?"

There followed silence. Both Wenners shifted nervously in their seats. Then one of them changed the subject. Jan Hodenfield knew he'd touched a throbbing nerve.

Jane wanted a baby, and spent much of the summer of 1977 on the beaches of Long Island with a basal thermometer in her mouth. Their efforts failed. Jane Wenner despaired. She separated from Jann. Jann was seen publicly with Caroline Kennedy. ("He asked Jackie's permission," Paul Scanlon smirked.) He moved in with actor Richard Gere in the West Village. In time they got back together, then separated again.

In place of the Great Earthquake, there was the nuclear spill at Three Mile Island. The disaster threw Jane into hysterics. She phoned the office and demanded that receptionist Judy Lawrence charter a jet that would seat twenty-five and deliver Jane, Jann and the magazine's most crucial staffers to the Tennessee Valley—the area in the vicinity least susceptible to nuclear contamination.

The nuclear threat passed, but the malaise did not. In this big city of dreams, the Wenners discovered Fear & Loathing.

———

The year 1977 was surely intended for celebration. *Rolling Stone* had helped put a Bob Dylan fan in the White House, had moved to New York, had launched a sister publication . . . and was now ten years old.

Jann Wenner decided to do it up right. The magazine would congratulate itself on nationwide television with a two-hour special on CBS. In one of his last acts as publisher, Joe Armstrong lured producer Steve Binder—known best for Elvis Presley's televised comeback in 1968—to the project. The show would be simulcast on fifteen major-market FM stations. Possibly a sound-track record of the event would be released.

With a $1 million budget and two months to prepare for the November 25 broadcast, writers David Felton and Ben Fong-Torres began drumming up skits. Jann pushed his own ideas; Felton and Fong-Torres pushed back, urging the editor to devote himself to attracting a roster of talented guests. Jann began to call on his multitude of famous friends: Mick Jagger, John Belushi, Rod Stewart, Lily Tomlin, Richard Pryor, Jack Nicholson, Dan Aykroyd.

To his chagrin, almost everyone declined. Others, like Belushi (who was to play Hunter Thompson in a skit) and Aykroyd (who was offended by the request that he take Belushi's place), begged off at the last minute. One tailor-made sketch after another was subsequently trashed, and others still never made it past the CBS censor.

The patchwork lineup for "*Rolling Stone*: The 10th Anniversary" seemed to miss every conceivable boat. The show, with Bette Midler as emcee and Donny Osmond playing Jann in a skit, did not exactly embrace the raucous spirit of rock & roll. Nor, however, did it reflect Jann Wenner's latest conquests. There they were, Jimmy Messina and Art Garfunkel and song-writer Jimmy Webb, those tattered remnants of the early seventies ... and only comedian Steve Martin to suggest that the *Rolling Stone* editor had established remote contact with late-seventies hip.

Even before the show had aired, David Felton had renounced the special. "I think it's a horrible show," he told reporters, and later wrote an article in *Rolling Stone* publicly apologizing for his role in the disaster.

Picture editor Karen Mullarkey walked into Jann's office a month before the special was aired. A screen was set up in the office, and the editor motioned for Mullarkey to pull up a chair and watch a particular skit that had recently been completed.

Mullarkey could hardly believe her eyes. To the tune of the Beatles' wonderfully psychedelic "Strawberry Fields Forever," a chorus line of girls danced around, costumed as strawberries.

The editor was gleeful. "It's great!" he said. "It's just great! What do you think? Isn't it great?"

Mullarkey, though in mild shock, did not have trouble finding the proper words. "I think it's shit," she said. "This is like Las Vegas! What do you mean, having all these strawberries dancing—"

"What the fuck do *you* know?" bellowed Jann. "Get out of my office!"

Karen Mullarkey got out and promptly booked a ticket to Jamaica. She returned to New York a month later, on November 25. At the magazine's expense, she chartered a limousine and dispatched the driver to art director Roger Black's house, where she picked up her severance check.

On the way back from Black's house, she flipped on the television set in the limousine. There it was, the anniversary special, and those damned dancing strawberries again. She shook her head. Had it really been only months ago that she and Black sat on that deserted loading dock, smoking weed, trying to imagine what kind of life they'd lead in New York? Those swaggering, arrogant, innocent old days had vanished in a puff of marijuana smoke. And now here they were: the Big City of Dreams, the Capri Lounge, limousines, celebrities, dancing strawberries ...

Mullarkey gave the driver new instructions. She decided she'd better cash her check right away.

Chapter Fifteen

A FINAL ROAR

Yet the magic had not altogether dissipated. On August 16, 1977, the *Rolling Stone* editorial and art staff went through the last motions of putting the magazine's 248th issue to bed. The special issue on New York, with its Warhol cover and its articles celebrating all things Manhattan, was fittingly the first *Rolling Stone* issue to be produced from the offices of 745 Fifth Avenue.

Putting together No. 248 had been a particularly trying experience. Much of the office furnishings had yet to be delivered from San Francisco. Staffers sat on folding chairs in front of rickety tables and manual typewriters or spread their work out on the floor. Exposed wooden beams jutted out of the unrefurbished ceiling.

Smart and classy as the New York issue was, not all hearts were bent toward the project. Only a few short weeks ago, they'd said goodbye to San Francisco, to Jerry's Inn and old lovers and the soft, bountiful Pacific sky. And now they were in Manhattan during a summer of soaring temperatures and blackouts, playing the role of City Booster while a young man named David Berkowitz who heard the voices of dogs in his head roamed the parks and killed women he never knew and told the world to call him Son of Sam.

It was a foul and sticky Manhattan August, and the office air-conditioning system did not work. The *Rolling Stone* sweat brigade rolled up their sleeves, pushed up their windows and got on the floors and worked. There was a saxophone player outside the building, not an altogether good one. He played and played. He would not shut up. To this sick, long-winded dirge they put the finishing touches on No. 248, laboring to celebrate their new home.

Then word came in that Elvis Presley had died.

It reached Peter Herbst, the magazine's new music editor, who promptly walked into Jann Wenner's office. He was surprised to find the editor/publisher crying.

"It's ... it's a cover," blubbered Jann, his face red and wet.

Herbst said he didn't understand.

"It's a cover!" said Jann Wenner, and then the music editor understood all too well. The New York issue, already in the can, would be postponed. Issue No. 248 would revolve around the King.

Staffers protested feebly, knowing they had four days to muster an entire issue from scratch—knowing their boss would not budge, knowing he was right about this. And so the magic was woven. From the cradle to the grave, they would embrace Elvis. Joe Klein was dispatched to Tupelo, Mississippi; Chet Flippo, to Memphis's Forest Hill Midtown Cemetery; Ben Fong-Torres, to Los Angeles to interview Presley's former bodyguards. (Ingloriously but with a cunning eye to public relations, Jann brought in a piece written by Caroline Kennedy, who had been the only "reporter" to gain entrance into Graceland after Presley's death. Caroline was interning for the *New York Daily News* at the time, but that paper rejected her article. Jann obtained a copy, passed it on to Harriet Fier and told her to "do something with it." It was rewritten from top to bottom.)

Calling from Maui and with Jack Daniel's in hand, Greil Marcus read his brilliant tribute over the wire. Dave Marsh, Chris Hodenfield and Robert Palmer turned in fine copy with no time to spare. A 1971 concert review by Jon Landau and an excerpt from Jerry Hopkins's biography of Presley were located and tossed into the feature well. The dead man about whom they wrote was not the corpulent, pill-popping, karate-practicing recluse of the seventies, but rather the tough and gorgeous Southern boy who became the American Dream for all the world to see.

Meanwhile, at 745 Fifth Avenue, staffers worked for four days straight, catnapping on cots when a spare hour could be scrounged, doing their best to ignore the fatigue and that merciless saxophone noise screeching in their ears and the humidity that dragged across their faces like a cat's tongue. Fier, Herbst and Barbara Downey coordinated the flow of copy, but the mastermind, the man with the whip and the pillow, was once again Jann Wenner, the Wenner of old. "He absolutely *did* that issue," said Fier.

And when it was done and the presses rolled, Peter Herbst held an early copy of No. 248, the Elvis issue, in his hands, and looked out his window at Central Park, and cried. They had served the King well. "It was definitely the most emotional moment I had in journalism," he said. "And for the magazine, it was one of the last great moments."

One item assigned by Herbst didn't make it into the issue. Thinking it might be a good idea to cover the reaction overseas to Elvis's demise, he telephoned London. Eventually Herbst located a particular New York *Rolling Stone* writer, relatively new to the ranks but already showing signs of being its most sensational voice since Hunter Thompson lumbered off to the lecture circuit. The writer, in London on assignment, reluctantly agreed to find a suitable quote from a British rock luminary on how the United Kingdom was taking the horrible news of Elvis's death.

The writer's research yielded this tender tribute:

"Fuckin' good riddance to bad rubbish."

———

The young man quoted was John Lydon, a.k.a. Johnny Rotten, the cruel-voiced and mutilated lead vocalist of the Sex Pistols. The young man quoting him was Chuck Young, a.k.a. the Reverend Charles M. Young, *Rolling Stone*'s newest star.

Since the early seventies, *Rolling Stone* had become so adventurous, so rich with maturing homegrown talent, that the creeping mediocrity of its music pages nearly escaped attention. The magazine, like the music industry, was now older, more prosperous and increasingly mass-conscious; both *Rolling Stone* and the rock & roll business had become key spokesmen for the New Establishment.

Barely conscious of their own widening distance from youth culture, *Rolling Stone* record reviewers regularly bemoaned rock's sallow new phase. They lauded their old titans, or kicked them, and regarded the field with wrinkled noses. New York's scabrous underground—the Velvet Underground, the New York Dolls—warranted only the barest acknowledgment.

David Bowie and the other perpetrators of Glitter Rock amused the magazine's critics, somewhat. Bands like the Allman Brothers and Led Zeppelin inspired scores of imitators but relatively scant coverage. *Crawdaddy!*, not *Rolling Stone*, broke Bruce Springsteen. And black music—despite Landau's presence, despite 1974–75 music editor Abe Peck's varied tastes and despite the occasional brilliant profile (especially Ben Fong-Torres's searing glimpse into the private lives of Ike and Tina Turner)—was usually discussed only with great discomfort.

In these matters *Rolling Stone* mirrored its readership. At no time was this more disquietingly apparent than during the disco craze. "There's no question," said Greil Marcus, "that *Rolling Stone* didn't have a clue about disco. It was just something everybody hoped would go away."

Peter Herbst agreed. "We all hated disco. It was something that existed outside of the rock & roll population that we belonged to personally and that we thought we were catering to. It was a different audience, blacks and gays and women. And in retrospect some of the stuff was terrific. It was a music like any other music, and some of it was good and some was bad. But we resisted all of it."

Bowing to advertising pressures, *Rolling Stone* published halfhearted "special disco issues" in 1975 and 1979. Both sold poorly and drew decidedly racist missives from its readers—the same individuals, presumably, who proudly sported "Disco Sucks" T-shirts and demolished records by the ton at a Comiskey Park anti-disco event in 1979. Episodes like these told staffers more about their readers than they wished to know.

Had it not been for the discovery of a teenaged southern Californian named Cameron Crowe, *Rolling Stone* might have trundled through the seventies like a blind man in a wheelchair. Crowe was all of fifteen years old and writing record reviews for the *San Diego Door* when music editor Ben Fong-Torres, during one of his periodic visits to Los Angeles, noticed the kid hanging out at a well-known PR agency in 1973. By the end of the year, Crowe was writing cover stories for *Rolling Stone*.

Crowe, despite his limited writing experience, was an invaluable acquisition. "With the exception of Marsh, Landau and Ben," said Abe Peck, "the senior writers of the magazine were probably growing more distant from the music. And then here's Cameron, reacting the same way that everyone from Jann on did in 1967. This is his first flush of rock & roll. He's the guy that's still getting a kick out of the dressing room experience, a kick out of dangling groupies out the window and a kick out of the music in a way that thirty-year-olds weren't. He was the guy who could bring in a cover story on all the big white bands. He was our man with the Eagles."

Rolling Stone's veteran writers took a dim view of the decade's mainstream acts like the Eagles, Poco, Yes, Kris Kristofferson, Led Zeppelin, Deep Purple, David Bowie, the Allman Brothers, Joni Mitchell, Neil Young, Linda Ronstadt, Peter Frampton and Crosby, Stills and Nash. Crowe, a genuine fan, filed stories on each artist. Such a task might have proved impossible for any other writer, as most of the above-mentioned musicians (particularly Joni Mitchell and Led Zeppelin's Jimmy Page) had been stung by past encounters with *Rolling Stone* reporters. But Cameron Crowe, a gangly and long-haired West Hollywood rendition of Beaver Cleaver, could melt any frost with the first flash of his gee-whiz smile. Said Ben Fong-Torres, "He used a combination of spunk, humor and charm to score some pieces and befriend some people that *Rolling Stone* had been dissociated from."

It eventually came to pass that many Los Angeles artists granted interviews to *Rolling Stone* only under the condition that Crowe would be the reporter. By the mid-seventies, the teenager had a virtual lock on America's most popular acts. Under other circumstances, this might have infuriated some of the magazine's more sensitive egos. In truth, however, none of the other writers wished to follow the Eagles around, and besides, they themselves were not immune to Crowe's exuberant charm. "Cameron possessed the ability to make people root for him," said Abe Peck. "He was a very engaging kid. I remember driving up California Avenue with Cameron in my car and Jann passing us in his car and Cameron mooning Jann. He was probably the only person besides Hunter who could do that and provoke hysterical laughter rather than a more dire response."

An unaccomplished stylist in his early articles, Crowe's work reflected maturity and insight by 1977. At root, however, he remained a fan, speaking no ill of his favorites. Some *Rolling Stone* writers expressed unease about Crowe's "lack of critical edge," as Peck put it; others suggested, somewhat lamely, that there was perhaps no other way to approach a Peter Frampton or a Fleetwood Mac. It did seem, in any event, that Cameron Crowe embodied all the traits of mid-seventies American rock—amiable, unoffensive and enormously successful; and if the Crowe Approach was the only means by which to win the trust of these artists and thus land their stories on the cover of *Rolling Stone*, so be it.

In the meantime, the magazine's veteran music writers took refuge wherever they could find solace from the seventies: Jim Miller in the Beach

Boys, Chet Flippo and John Morthland in country & western and Jonathon Cott in nonrock artists like pianist Glenn Gould and violinist Stéphane Grappelli. Cott, a friend of Jann's since 1966, won privileged showcasing for his zealous, sometimes intellectually overwrought profiles. Nonmainstream artists covered by other writers, however, typically found themselves in the back of the *Rolling Stone* bus. The magazine that once put Captain Beefheart, the MC5 and Sun Ra on its cover was no longer in the business of breaking obscure acts.

Instead, *Rolling Stone* used mainstream cover stories to expose music-oriented readers to the magazine's brilliant young corps of nonmusic writers. Even without Grover Lewis and Joe Eszterhas, *Rolling Stone* by 1976 was the most dazzling publication in America. Howard Kohn, David Weir and Joe Klein filed powerful and high-risk investigatives in the finest tradition of Joe Armstrong's "impact journalism." Michael Rogers's coverage of a total eclipse in the Sahara Desert won the American Association for the Advancement of Science Award for Distinguished Science Writing, yet he eclipsed himself with his report on a genetic scientists' conference in 1975. Tim Cahill's piece on the death of a retarded marine at boot camp was among the year's most resonant. Donald R. Katz, a twenty-three-year-old American studying at the London School of Economics, decided to try his hand at writing and instantly became *Rolling Stone*'s best international politics journalist.

The magazine's virtually highbrow reputation began to attract writers of a stripe most alien to *Rolling Stone* circa 1970. British travel writer Jan Morris, introduced to Jann by Richard Goodwin, began to contribute essays regularly. Famed correspondent Daniel Schorr wrote on the CIA and on the movie *Network*; Lillian Hellman interviewed Rosalynn Carter. *Village Voice* columnist Ellen Willis, referred to Jann by Max Palevsky, shared a column with Michael Rogers. Greil Marcus returned as a book critic, applying his energetic intellect to a regular column that covered considerable turf, and with considerably more adroitness than almost any other book column published at the time.

Absent any heroes to glorify, the magazine's music writers roamed harder edges. Chet Flippo (with Austin writer Joe Nick Patoski) examined the Rubin "Hurricane" Carter Benefit that became a financial disaster, while Jerry Hopkins reported on the plundering of the Jimi Hendrix estate. "American Grandstand" columnist and record reviews editor Dave Marsh was himself a hard edge. A moralist like Ralph Gleason and an unapologetic fan of pop music like Cameron Crowe, Marsh nonetheless considered market-engineered stars like Peter Frampton pap and said so.

Beyond that, Marsh's transition from his Motor City days at *Creem* to the more cautious mannerisms of *Rolling Stone*'s music coverage was not a smooth one. At *Creem*, Marsh used to rumble with Lester Bangs over the subject of rock & roll, and literally had the scars to prove it. Here, the magazine seemed to be reserving all its passion for general-interest articles. Marsh, who jumped ship to *Rolling Stone* as a logical career move, wasn't a dunce when it came to market realities. Still, despite his reverence for Marianne Partridge—"a person who knew nothing about music," he said, "and who had utter respect for the people who wrote about it well"—Marsh believed *Rolling Stone* mined its musical turf with "a fundamental contempt for the subject matter."

Jann was delighted to have Marsh on board, but was clueless as to how to deal with him. He reflexively awarded Marsh a choice assignment, an interview with Mick Jagger, only to learn that Marsh didn't particularly like the Stones and would rather not have anything to do with Mr. Jagger. Jann made Marsh do the interview anyway, and the results pleased no one. Marsh's tastes tended to run "blacker and weirder" than Jann's, and he was permitted to reflect this in the appropriate ghettos of the magazine. But no fringe artists would find a home in *Rolling Stone*'s feature well. The magazine, after all, was going places. Those who came along would have to behave.

———

Chuck Young did not behave.

He had abandoned the practice at the end of junior high school, when he discovered that repressing his hostility toward authority figures had given him an ulcer. Young had been raised in Madison, Wisconsin, by libertarian parents who nonetheless believed in respectable conduct. His father was a Presbyterian minister, and his mother never told a lie.

He grew up in the tumult of the sixties, but Chuck Young was fitted at birth for the straitjacket of the preacher's kid. Young did not wear the role well. His father lectured him when he showed up at church with Democrat buttons on his coat lapel. The boy felt rotten for not measuring up, resentful that he should have to and inadequate to the very core. He sulked at home while *The Beverly Hillbillies* and *Petticoat Junction* played on the television set in front of him, and he could dream up no doom more glorious than to attend a naval academy.

He began his rebellion in nearby college bookstores, reading William Burroughs and the Marquis de Sade. "My mother's idea of teaching me about sex," he said, "was to check a book out of the library about sperms and eggs and leave it on my bed, like the tooth fairy. She said, 'If you have any question, just ask.' And she was obviously terrified when she said that. And I read this book and it talked about sperms and eggs, and what I wanted to know was, How do you fuck?"

School, church and life made him want to scream. Guitars screamed for him. He distrusted the Beatles—"they sounded too happy and too many girls liked them"—but found sanity in the rhythmic menace of the Stones, the Yardbirds and the Animals. Hearing the Fugs was a particular revelation. Obscenity on vinyl! For public consumption! Someone was lying to Chuck Young. There was no joy in respectability.

His parents took him to a therapist, who "convinced me that I wasn't ugly and stupid, which I was convinced that I was." Yet his misery dragged on through the bleak conformity of high school—until eleventh grade, when his English teacher told him a short story he'd written was the funniest she'd ever read, and that her husband had read it as well and had pronounced him "a budding Jonathan Swift." Whereupon Charles M. Young checked out every Jonathan Swift book he could find, began writing satire and found his talent as a class cynic.

The editor of the high school paper—a cheerleader, one of the prettiest girls in school and thus terrifying to Chuck Young—asked him to write a regular column. His hostility exploded in his writings. He'd read and reread Joseph Heller's *Catch-22*, and came to believe that "this book isn't about World War II—this book is about my high school." School regulations— the dress code, the hair code, daily recitations of the Pledge of Allegiance —became Young's punching bag. He wrote, he marched, he petitioned the school board.

And he won these battles, but at the cost of any lasting friendship with his high school principal. Dr. Gorton kept two portraits on the wall just behind his desk: one of John F. Kennedy, who urged youngsters to "ask what you can do for your country," and the other of Teddy Roosevelt, wielder of the big stick. That stick came down hard during Chuck Young's senior year, when Dr. Gorton—in an effort to prevent smoking in the bathrooms—ordered all doors removed from the school's toilet stalls.

Young thought this was degrading, but the school board ignored his sermon. The boy then dug through city ordinances at the Madison Public Library and emerged with a citation that mandated doors on toilet stalls.

His next column was an open letter to Dr. Gorton and the school board, placing them under citizen's arrest. The principal censored the column and subjected his young enemy to an abusive discourse, but Chuck Young's father took the matter up with the school board. Christmas came, and then 1969, and students returned for the spring semester to find doors on their toilet stalls.

Chuck Young, implausible campus hero, wrote the senior class play and everyone laughed and suddenly all the torment and the vomiting before class was worth it. At graduation, Dr. Gorton handed Young his diploma, shook his hand and said, "You see there? I'm still shaking your hand even after all those things you said about me." Twenty years later, Chuck Young returned for his reunion and provided the music for the dance. His band was called the Dr. Gorton Experience. The principal was not there to hear him play, but the noise was loud enough to rattle every door on every toilet stall in every high school in Madison, Wisconsin.

———

"I went to Macalester College," said Young, "and I spent two years there looking for other toilet stall doors to write about. I was like the protagonist in *Rabbit, Run*, replaying the last free throw."

In a desperate attempt to fire his imagination, he tried out as a defensive back for the football team and wrote a behind-the-scenes column in the campus paper. Macalester immediately descended into a vicious losing streak (fifty straight, an NCAA Division III record). "I was the worst player on the worst team," he said. "You could make a case for me being the worst player in the history of college football. They didn't play me very much. They'd wait until the game was something like 46–0, and then they'd put me in for two minutes and the other team would throw a couple of touchdowns over my head just so I could be ashamed along with the rest of the team."

Young was not a model player, but the coaches needed every warm body they could suit up. Besides, his column was immensely popular, especially among the players, who twice awarded him the trophy given to the player who contributed most to team morale. Again Chuck Young graduated at the peak of popularity, and again he found himself starting over. He returned home and took a job in a sheet-metal factory. After a year of trying to figure out the proper career path to literary greatness, he enrolled at Columbia University's Graduate School of Journalism.

In 1975, *Rolling Stone* advertised its first annual student writing contest. One of Chuck Young's professors suggested that he submit one of his pieces.

Young did so, having fantasized about writing for the magazine ever since its fourth-anniversary issue with Hunter Thompson's "Fear and Loathing in Las Vegas" on the cover.

He won. The $500 check arrived at a time when Young had forty-six cents to his name. More importantly, *Rolling Stone* advised the young writer to contact New York bureau chief Chet Flippo about possible assignments. Flippo was himself a preacher's kid, and before long Charles M. Young was a *Rolling Stone* reporter.

His beat was Manhattan's Lower East side and the bands that had been gigging in the gloomy Bowery area for the past two years. In the summer of 1975, at a Bowery cavern known as CBGB, Young saw the Ramones for the first time. The band wore black leather, was loud and mangy and played a twelve-to-fifteen-minute set consisting of twelve to fifteen songs about sniffing glue and banging heads. They could just barely play their instruments.

Young thought the Ramones were the funniest thing he'd ever seen. But the joke, he knew, was not on them. As much as Young liked *Rolling Stone*, the acts featured on the magazine's covers bored him stiff. He'd waited for someone like the Ramones to come along and mock the prissy harmonies and self-indulgent guitar solos that characterized these bloated golden calves of the seventies. He'd been longing for someone to rear back and spit on what he would refer to as "the Frampton flotilla."

Chuck Young fell in love with the boys of the Bowery—progenitors of what New York music critics were labeling "punk rock." Months after the release of their debut album, Young's article on the Ramones appeared in the middle of the magazine's music section. The piece was funny, and the new kid received a number of compliments from the staff. After his second article, on the notably nonpunk Jefferson Starship, Flippo called Young into his office. "We want you to apply for the job of 'Random Notes' editor," he said.

The interview was conducted by Jann Wenner, who seemed to Young to be nursing an awful hangover. The writer braced himself for a lengthy interrogation. But the editor, who did not seem familiar with Young's work, instead asked, "What's your favorite Rolling Stones record?"

Young, thoroughly rattled, could not recall a single album by his favorite band. Finally he blurted out, *"Beggar's Banquet,"* adding hastily, "though of course *Exile on Main Street* is probably the masterpiece."

The answer seemed to please Jann. "How about your favorite Bob Dylan record?" he asked.

Young replied that he wasn't a Dylan fan—discovering too late, by the sour look on the editor's face, that he had committed first-rank heresy. He sputtered out an ingratiating footnote, but the editor looked distracted.

"I don't have time for this now," said Jann, looking here and there. "Come back tomorrow."

Certain that he'd blown his big chance, Young bought a six-pack and retreated to his apartment and drank it. He woke up the next morning depressed and hung over, and shuffled his way to the bureau office. He sat outside Jann Wenner's office, unshaven and shoddily dressed, primed for rejection.

Jann poked his head outside his office. "Let's cut the suspense," he told Chuck Young. "You're hired."

As "Random Notes" editor, Young did what neither his predecessors nor his successors did: he made the column funny. The idea was strangely novel. Though "Random Notes" occasionally infuriated musicians with tales of backstage debauchery, it usually gave them the velvet-gloved star treatment. Publicists, well aware of the column's popularity ("Random Notes" always topped readership polls), eagerly supplied innocuous tidbits.

The job, however, was not an easy one. Said Fred Schruers, who replaced Young as "Random Notes" editor in the middle of 1978, "You had to not only run around to a lot of parties, of which New York had a surfeit in those days, but you also had to research stuff that happened on the West Coast. You were responsible for the whole world, in a way. And 'Random Notes' was like the semi-permeable membrane through which all the rock groups entered the magazine."

"Random Notes" editors burned out every year or so, in large part due to the hawk-eyed presence of Jann Wenner, who read every word of the column long after he'd stopped reading most of *Rolling Stone*'s editorial content. "Random Notes," after all, was the magazine's society column; it rewarded Jann's friends, took digs at his foes and kept him abreast of celebrity's ongoing gang bang.

Young's "Random Notes" sought to smear the cult of celebrity that so infatuated his boss. Rock & Roll, in his view, didn't mix with royalty. The messy, breathtaking performances of the Ramones said it all: *Don't you dare worship us.* Rock & roll was for nerds, for socially malnourished middle-class kids like Chuck Young. "It was a response to decadance," he said. "It was barbarians at the gates, saying, 'We're gonna come in and ravish your daughter and burn down the palace, but in the process enrich the race with our strength and our wildness.'

"Jann completely identified with the celebrity aspect of rock & roll, the new royalty. It's like the difference between Mick Jagger and Keith Richards. Mick Jagger is a celebrity. Keith Richards is a rock & roller. And Jann I don't think was in any way conscious of the distinction."

The editor stormed into Young's office one day and demanded to know why the last "Random Notes" column had not mentioned that Art Garfunkel was at work on a new album. Young was surprised by his boss's vehemence. "Jann," he said, "Art Garfunkel has never sold many records. No one cares about Art Garfunkel. He's not interesting."

"Yes he is!" said Jann. "He's a major star!"

Only when he reported the incident to Flippo did Young find out that Garfunkel was, if not a major star, certainly a major friend of Jann's. The incident infuriated Young, as did Jann's insistence that he phone the sixty or so names on the "Random Notes" "beat list" every week to dredge up celebrity gossip. Sometimes Young made the calls. Whenever he could, however, he relied instead on weird morsels, such as the report that an obscure British musician had contracted a peculiar disease from giving one of his sheep mouth-to-mouth resuscitation.

One day, on his own defiant initiative, Chuck Young undertook to produce a "Random Notes" column composed entirely of items pertaining to Mick Jagger. He also polled musicians ranging from Linda Ronstadt to the Damned's Rat Scabies, asking, "Which would you rather do: read another 'Random Note' about Mick Jagger or pull your own teeth?" (Keith Moon replied, "I'd rather pull Jann Wenner's teeth.")

To his surprise, each editor approved the column, including Jann, who later mentioned at an editorial meeting, "Mick thought it was funny, too." Young and a number of other people laughed. Jagger may have gotten the joke, but did Jann?

He did not, in any event, censure Young. The writer possessed a fine comic touch which, when combined with his reportorial skills, produced compelling feature pieces on otherwise dreadful topics. By inserting his own character into the story—owing less to Hunter Thompson than to David Felton's subtle moralism—Young forced his subjects to be honest. This worked to dramatic effect when he interviewed Gene Simmons, the leader of the teen metal band Kiss:

I ask who he voted for in the 1972 presidential election. He says McGovern and admits there may be something wrong, on occasion, with mass taste. "But nothing is right or wrong in music. There are just certain tastes. People in New York hate Lawrence Welk, but he sells half a million records every time out and he's got about 30 releases."

"Will you admit it's still shit?" I ask.

"Somebody out there likes it."

"Jacqueline Susann sells more books than Shakespeare, but she's still shit and Shakespeare is still Shakespeare."

"Wait a minute!" Simmons exclaims. "I think Shakespeare is shit! Absolute shit! He may have been a genius for his time, but I can't relate to that stuff. 'Thee' and 'thou'; the guy sounds like a faggot. Captain America is classic because he's more entertaining. If you counted the number of people who read Shakespeare, you'd be very disappointed."

"No aesthetics exist aside from what people buy?" I ask.

"You bet."

In similar participatory fashion, Young argued with avowed master of the jungle Ted Nugent about gun-control laws and played the gong in the orchestra touring with Emerson, Lake and Palmer. His style, alternating straight reportorial prose with slang, often put him at odds with *Rolling Stone*'s somewhat stuffy copy editors. Eventually, however, his copy was untouchable. Young was Jann Wenner's golden boy. He was a star.

———

The November 6, 1975, issue of *Rolling Stone* featured glamorous rock icon Rod Stewart and his sexy new girlfriend, Britt Ekland, on the cover. On that same day, a nasty and thoroughly incompetent four-piece band calling itself the Sex Pistols performed for the first time, at the St. Martin's School of Art in London, for ten minutes.

Midwifed by a shrewd clothing store entrepreneur named Malcolm McLaren, the Pistols lunged out into the world like a rabid alley dog, spraying saliva everywhere, ravaging the Rod Stewarts of the rock aristocracy. The band's lead singer, Johnny Rotten, wore a T-shirt that said "I Hate Pink Floyd" and denounced Mick Jagger as a twisted, pompous old crock.

It was not in the cards for Jann Wenner to embrace punk rock. When Chet Flippo returned from London with the Sex Pistols' first singles in his briefcase and popped "God Save the Queen" on Jann's turntable, the editor was appalled. "It's just fucking noise," he declared.

Flippo and Young didn't think so. For months now, Young had been going to the mat with Jann over "Random Notes" items pertaining to the

Ramones, the Dead Boys, the Dictators and especially the Sex Pistols. Sometimes the editor relented, as the punk stories were usually funnier than the average Jagger factoids. But Young was more accustomed to the grating refrain: "Quit writing about punk rock!"

Despair was always tempting. Jann's tastes were either social (Jackson Browne, Boz Scaggs and other recent cover subjects) or sentimental (Dylan, the Beatles and the Stones), and in both cases antiquated. While the staff were arguing among themselves about the merits of punk, the *Rolling Stone* editor was still captivated by every apocryphal rumor that the Beatles would reunite. At an editorial meeting, Jann announced that he'd gotten a reliable tip that a reunion was in the works. Young groaned, and aired his belief that such an event would be anticlimactic. Jann seemed hurt and bewildered that anyone would think such thoughts.

Years later, after the memorial ceremony for John Lennon in Central Park, Young ran into a teary-eyed Jann Wenner back at the office. "God, Chuck," said the editor. "Didn't you think the music was great down there?"

"No," said Young. "I thought it was terrible."

The editor gaped.

"They played his most insipid shit," Young continued, "and they didn't play a single rock & roll song."

Jann shook his head emphatically. "That would've been completely inappropriate," he said.

Young wanted to say that the ceremony had characterized Lennon as a sorry-ass celebrity crooner rather than a rock & roller, but he could see the argument was going nowhere. Both Jann Wenner and Chuck Young had spent their adolescent years as creative but socially insecure middle-class rebels, pelting authority figures with their literary slingshots even as they yearned for acceptance among their peers. Yet subtle quirks in each's value system erased all similarities. The yearnings diverged violently—the debutante photograph in one direction, the toilet stall door in the other. And now the two young men spoke different languages.

Nevertheless, Young—with the assistance of Flippo and music editor Peter Herbst—finally convinced Jann to fly the writer to London to interview the Sex Pistols in August of 1977. And so it was that while America mourned the loss of its most spectacular music hero, Charles M. Young fell into the loutish company of Sid Vicious, Johnny Rotten and the rest of the Pistols, rapt as they spewed out their denunciations of Elvis, Jagger, hippies, sex and food. While America laid to rest the man who'd had it all, Young listened to Rotten lay out a cynical filmmaker who, after remarking casually that all movie directors were whores, then asked the vocalist, "John, wouldn't you make yourself look like a cunt for a million dollars?"

Sneered Johnny Rotten, "How could you make me look like a bigger cunt than I am? The joke's on you."

Young returned to the States and entered 745 Fifth Avenue with spiked hair, a masticated T-shirt and makeup that gave Young's face the appearance of having been smashed repeatedly against a fire hydrant. An old lady in the elevator swooned when she saw him. Judy Lawrence did not recognize Young and would not unlock the security door.

Chuck Young reported what he'd seen to Flippo and Herbst. The Sex Pistols weren't just some warped publicity stunt. They represented sheer anarchy in a country choked by its economic strictures; they preached the destruction of rock's Trojan horses. But the weapon they chose was humor. The Pistols didn't believe for a second that they were heroes of any kind. "Have a laugh on us," they told Chuck Young, who later wrote about a brief smile Johnny Rotten flashed from a nightclub stage:

> Did that mean, "Look at how great I am!" or "Look at them have a good time!" Those have always been divergent roads in rock & roll. The Sex Pistols took the latter, the one less traveled by, and that has made all the difference.

Young pled with Flippo and Herbst to put the Sex Pistols on the cover. Herbst, a James Taylor fan, shared Jann's distaste for punk. But the star writer was vociferous. In the end, said Herbst, "Chuck convinced me that what they were doing was what every kid in England was talking about and that we would be feeling reverberations shortly." Young went so far as to bet his music editor twenty bucks that the Sex Pistols would crack America's top twenty.

Jann, who had not put the Pistols back on his turntable since Flippo subjected him to "God Save the Queen," was not warm to the idea. The piece was hilarious, Young's best yet, but he couldn't imagine the Sex Pistols gracing the cover of *Rolling Stone*. Even when he relented, Jann issued the dire prediction that the issue would die on the newsstands.

He was right. The Sex Pistols issue sold an anemic 178,000 copies. The Pistols themselves never made it past number 108 on the American charts. Chuck Young lost his bet.

But that was all he lost. The reader response, though severely polarized, was tremendous. Young's brazen advocacy of punk marked the first defiant stance *Rolling Stone* had taken since putting Hunter Thompson's 1972 campaign coverage in the front of the book. From Berkeley, Greil Marcus called Young and congratulated him. The veteran critic's sentiments were sincere, but they jostled the chip on Young's shoulder. "It was like the Pope calling up some novice priest and saying, 'Nice job at the altar today,' " said Young. "He was like the number one authority figure deigning to give me a pat on the back. So even as he was complimenting me, I was resenting Greil."

One staffer who didn't massage Young's ego was Dave Marsh. Marsh couldn't stand the Sex Pistols piece, and for reasons broader than musical taste. Where Young searched for nihilism and laughs, Marsh preoccupied himself with, as he put it, "the possibilities of the backbeat." The "American Grandstand" columnist—who did not attend college, and wore that fact alternately as a badge on his heart and a chip on *his* shoulder—probably did not intend to refer to himself when he wrote, "Little rock criticism is concerned with music, because most rock critics are less concerned with sound than sociology." Yet on the subject of punk, Marsh waxed positively sociological: "Punk to me was never just music or style," he wrote, "but a set of standards, a code of behavior, founded on friendship, acting on principle." Marsh believed, as did Young, that "God Save the Queen" was the most important song of 1977. But while Young found joy in the smartassed humor of punk rock, Marsh openly fretted about the movement's repercussions. "I don't trust movements in music, or in culture generally," he said. "And so my thing was, 'Well, wait a minute, what's comin' in the back door?' And what was comin' in the back door was the smart guys crowdin' out the street guys. That made me feel threatened."

Young didn't exactly know what to make of Marsh, and was somewhat afraid of him. Marsh was given to violent outbursts; once, for reasons no one could remember, he kicked a hole in his office door. The critic often lambasted musicians for showing no sense of humor, yet Marsh apparently chose not to display his around the office.

Marsh, in turn, thought Young's emotional development had been arrested at the seventh-grade level. One Friday evening, Marsh walked into his office and discovered that someone had overturned a carton of yogurt in his typewriter. He immediately suspected Young and David Felton, who had been in the office recently. Marsh left the office, returned with two cartons of yogurt and placed them, unopened, next to Felton's and Young's typewriters.

A few minutes later, the two writers appeared in Marsh's doorway, wanting to know if Marsh was responsible for the yogurt. "Yeah," he replied. "I could've done what you did, but I'm a little too grown-up."

(Young and Felton were not the only perpetrators of jokes at Dave Marsh's expense. The critic was severely acrophobic, so much so that he refused any office with an exterior window. Knowing this, staff writer Fred Schruers enjoyed climbing outside the window by the reception room whenever Marsh was likely to walk past. Marsh would look up, see Schruers dangling from a twenty-third-story ledge by his fingers and "would just go bananas," he admitted. "Everybody else thought it was immensely funny. All I could think of was: Man, if this guy makes one mistake, he's gonna die!")

———

After the Sex Pistols piece, Chuck Young the preacher's kid became the Reverend Charles M. Young, his prose now sage with references to the Old Testament. A photograph was run in the table of contents showing the writer in full ministerial regalia. More than his share of fan mail, hate mail and solemn memos from the UFO Committee packed the 745 Fifth Avenue mail room. He was, Lord spare him, "king of the dunghill." He took shit from no copy editor.

He became the office mascot, the resident punk. This did not translate into unanimous adoration. Said Joe Klein, "Seeing Chuck Young was the first sense I had that the sixties really were over. This was the next generation, and they were shmucks."

A fellow staffer called Young up and tipped him off to a party taking place at an editor's house that night. Young hopped on the subway and, while en route, took the liberty of inviting everyone in his subway car to join him at the affair. Some twenty individuals of every known disposition followed him and stood behind him as he knocked and was let in. As they flooded through the editor's door, hollering and fingering the editor's tasteful bric-a-brac, the guests already present sat in a frozen cluster by a table, their hands hidden from view. Young realized then that he'd barged in on an intimate cocaine party. The editor guided Young's friends back out the door. He let Young stay, but if the editor ever hosted another party, Young did not find out about it.

In the spring of 1978, Young got word that the Eagles had been trounced in a softball game against a team led by concert promoter Bill Graham. He ran the item in "Random Notes," and another just like it a few issues later—throwing into question, it seemed, the very manhood of the mellow rockers. Drummer Don Henley rejoindered immediately, challenging Young and the rest of the *Rolling Stone* staff to a softball match.

Bad blood ran between the magazine and the Eagles. The band, perhaps more than any other, typified the music of the seventies and the state of the industry itself. They were America's most commercially successful band, veterans of the L.A. studio underground, former Linda Ronstadt backups, tuneful and laid back and clever, faceless stars, spokesmen for no cause save the guilty pleasures of the fast lane. The Eagles exhaled one flawless, ephemeral single after another: Jackson Browne's "Take It Easy," "Witchy Woman," "Peaceful Easy Feeling," "Desperado," "One of These Nights," "Lyin' Eyes," "Hotel California" and, of course, "Life in the Fast Lane." Guitarist/vocalist Glenn Frey and his cohorts fancied themselves outlaws— desperadoes under the eaves, as fellow L.A. rocker Warren Zevon would put it—but in fact they were consummate insiders. No one understood the big business of rock better than the market-conscious Eagles, and long before 1978 they had the bank accounts to prove it.

The *Rolling Stone* critics loathed the Eagles. Where Dylan had been rock & roll's mind, the Beatles its heart and the Stones its loins, the Eagles represented a new and almost parasitic entity—spongelike, it seemed to the critics, sopping up the genre's very blood. Greil Marcus, Dave Marsh, Peter Herbst and of course Young had each taken swipes at the band. Predictably, Cameron Crowe had penned a quote-driven, easygoing Eagles cover story in the fall of 1975. Since that time, however, the magazine's incessant barbs won the band's animosity, and no further interviews were forthcoming.

An additional edge could be found at the corporate level. As a short, brash, brilliant upstart in the record business, Eagles manager and MCA Records president Irving Azoff served as a natural rival to Jann Wenner. Each seldom missed an opportunity to take the other to task. When Jann attended a party for the Eagles in Hawaii, he telephoned the office, demanding that the next "Random Notes" include the fact that the Eagles served cheap vodka. A later entry discussed Azoff's role in depriving his client Boz Scaggs of the opportunity of being on the twenty-two-million-selling *Saturday Night Fever* sound track. (The "Random Note" punned that the five-foot-three Azoff "was rather short with RSO Records . . . when RSO asked to use Boz' hit 'Lowdown' in a movie sound track.")

The latter "Random Note," penned by Fred Schruers, resulted in an obscenity-laced phone polemic from Azoff, ending with Azoff telling Schruers, "You fucked me, asshole! Now make it right!"

Schruers was scared neither of twenty-third-story ledge-dangling nor of short, livid record company executives. "Irving," he said, "I don't have to listen to that, even from you." He hung up the phone. Then he went down the hall to Jann's office, figuring he'd better report the incident.

Jann's eyes became very large. "You put it down in the cradle so that he heard it click?" he asked his writer.

Schruers nervously affirmed this.

The editor's face fell into a devilish grin. For ten full seconds he smiled at his audacious reporter. Suddenly his eyes became almost wild. "He manages the five most important acts in America!" yelled Jann, scrambling from behind his desk toward a startled Schruers. "Call him!"

Azoff did not take Schruers's call. Not much later, however, Azoff wrote to correct a Dave Marsh story on Bruce Springsteen that claimed, incorrectly, that Springsteen had sold out two shows at the L.A. Forum. The Asbury Park, New Jersey, rocker might be the critics' darling but, as Azoff pointed out in his letter, the number one band in America was the Eagles—who had, in fact, sold out at the Forum.

For the softball game, Young suggested modest stakes. If *Rolling Stone* won, the Eagles would grant an interview; if the magazine lost, the staff would treat the band to Manhattan hot dogs at Nathan's. Jann insisted that the ante be upped. Peter Herbst proposed that the game be made a charity event, with ticket proceeds and a $5,000 donation from the losing team being earmarked for the UNICEF World Nutrition Program. The stakes were agreed to, while on the side Jann and Azoff established a sizable bet of their own.

"Jann," said a worried Herbst, noting that the Eagles took their softball very seriously, "we're not very good."

The editor dismissed the remark. "We can beat those guys," he said.

A team of fifteen or so *Rolling Stone* personnel was assembled, flown to the West Coast and booked into the University of Southern California Hilton Hotel for a week of team meetings, batting practices and late-night acts of petty vandalism at the Eagles' households. The sudden departure of key staffers like Young, Herbst, Marsh, Crowe, Howard Kohn and Joe Klein did not amuse associate editor Harriet Fier, who was left to produce an issue with a decimated staff while the boys played their grudge match.

On Saturday, May 6, 1978, at USC's monstrous Dedeaux Field, the *Rolling Stone* Gonzos took batting practice while the Eagles slouched in the bleachers, hurling vile epithets. The Gonzos, though generally slipshod, were blessed with the addition of advertising director Claeys Bahrenburg, a brawny former hockey player, and chief financial officer Jim Dunning, who had once been recruited by the Baltimore Orioles. When the Eagles' turn came, Dunning and Bahrenburg joined Jann in scouting the opposition. To their horror, one of the Eagles' players—a former minor leaguer—repeatedly bashed pitches over the wall. They also noticed that the Eagles were wearing shoes with metal spikes.

"Somebody might get hurt," Jann protested to Azoff.

The Eagles manager leered. "How exciting," he replied. "Do your writers ever think about that?"

Faces were glum at that night's team dinner. Team captain Jim Dunning, disturbed by the Eagles' auspicious batting practice, proposed a new lineup in which several once integral Gonzos who'd been flown in from New York would now be replaced by more talented athletes from the West Coast ad staff. Jann ratified his chief financial officer's suggestion. He then informed the team of his exchange with Azoff, and argued that the Gonzos should pull out of the benefit if the Eagles showed up in spikes.

Young, the team captain, the old Macalester College morale booster, rose to give a pep talk. "Where's your manhood?" he demanded. "This is as close as we're ever gonna get to the World Series. We have the rest of our lives to get over any injuries we might incur. Let's go out there and do the absolute best we can, and we'll have great stories to tell afterwards. But for God's sake, let's not wimp out now!"

Despite Young's exhortations, the Gonzos voted to withdraw if the Eagles used spikes. The following morning, Jann and Dunning bought the entire team shoes with soccer cleats. The cleats did not sink into the hard turf and did more harm than good. The Eagles, clad in tennis shoes, battered the Gonzos, 15–8. Irving Azoff—whose jersey wondered rhetorically, "Is Jann Wenner Tragically Hip?"—had gotten the last laugh.

And though goodwill between the teams was traded at the Eagles' victory bash that night, Chuck Young was demoralized by the experience. It had been a game, just a game. He knew that; the Eagles knew that. Why did Jann Wenner have to turn it into a negotiations battle? Did fun have to have teeth?

A year later, a nearly identical situation emerged. In August of 1979, Jann convened an editorial conference at New York's Shelter Island. The meeting was uneventful but for the ad hoc formation of a *Rolling Stone* house band, consisting of new associate editor Tim White on drums, Herbst and assistant editor Kurt Loder on guitars, David Felton and assistant editor Jon Pareles on keyboards, editorial assistant Debbie Hurst on vocals and Young on bass guitar. With few exceptions, the writers played music about as well as they played softball. They called themselves the Dry Heaves, and if a more aurally offensive band was hatched that year, it did not inflict itself upon an audience.

After the conference, the Dry Heaves hoisted their secondhand instruments up to the twenty-eighth floor of 745 Fifth Avenue. They rehearsed on that floor's conference room after the business staff departed for the day, determined to play for the magazine's 1979 Christmas party even if no one asked them to, even if asked not to. *Rolling Stone*'s annual event had by now become a posh, see-and-be-seen affair, with scores of uninvited celebrity guests. It seemed like a perfect setting for the Heaves to provide, in Timothy White's words, "absolute proof that writers should never play rock & roll."

One evening, someone else brought a guitar, a red Gibson, up to the twenty-eighth floor. Everyone looked at each other. They had no idea Jann could play a musical instrument.

Instantly the editor took over the Dry Heaves. "I knew that if we were going to do a Christmas party in front of the Rolling Stones and everybody, we had to have a tight set," said Jann. "You can't get up and just endlessly jam. I mean, that bores the shit out of people. And not that we were professional, but we had to be organized. . . . So we had to rehearse. And somebody had to run the rehearsals. And it was me, as usual."

Organized they became, but at a price. Jann began to schedule rehearsals for the Dry Heaves during office hours, four or five hours a day, three days a week. Harriet Fier was beside herself. Eleven kids had just been crushed to death at a Who concert in Cincinnati, and her best reporters were five floors above her, giving each other earaches.

Jann paid Fier no mind. He had a band to run. With Straight Arrow money, he bought the Heaves thousands of dollars' worth of new equipment. He brought in a professional equipment manager to oversee the sound. A formal song list was mandated; sheets with lyrics and chord changes were drawn up. Jann's good friend Peter Wolf of the J. Geils Band suggested a uniform look, so the editor rented tuxedos. When rehearsals carried on through dinnertime, he ordered Chinese food to be delivered. Keyboardist Jon Pareles saw that the tab for one of the deliveries was $200. We could have gotten a real band for that amount of money, he thought.

"Jann got to the point where he was holding our jobs over us," said Timothy White. "He'd say, 'You guys have gotta rehearse. I'm very pissed off at you and I'm not gonna take it, and I think it's an indication of your attitude toward everything here.' It got blown out of unbelievable proportion in his mind, because he wanted to show Jagger and some of his friends that we had a little skill in this area. But the whole point of the gag was that we had no fucking credentials! And anytime that cracks were made along those lines, he didn't laugh—quite the opposite. He'd say, 'You aren't taking this seriously!' "

"There I was," said Jann, "cracking heads again, making it not so fun for everybody—but getting it done." But Chuck Young, like White, thought that missed the point. Sure, the editor's presence had lent the band some much needed focus. But why would he not let up? This wasn't a magazine they were putting out. This wasn't even a goddamned softball game. It was a one-set, one-shot, deliberately incompetent music gig. How could it possibly matter what Mick Jagger thought of them? How could a band calling itself the Dry Heaves, and featuring a guitarist named Jann Wenner who could not for the life of him keep his Gibson in tune, even entertain the *notion* of impressing the Rolling Stones?

The Christmas party, as it turned out, was a raging success. The Heaves were predictably awful, but they brought the house down. Jann, without a trace of irony, sang "Don't Let Me Be Misunderstood" while a bearded Mick Jagger stood at the edge of the stage, hollering gleefully, "Jann Wenner! Fuckin' Jann Wenner!" Young, during his performance of the Sex Pistols' "17," unveiled every cheap punk trick in the book: hanging a microphone out of his fly, sticking his head in a bass drum, flopping around on the stage and smashing his guitar à la Pete Townshend. As an act of defiance, a couple of songs were spontaneously (and thus without Jann's approval) inserted into the set list, and Young altered the lyrics to "Eve of Destruction" to reflect his raging disdain for Jann and the business staff.

Young was drunk as a monkey and, by his own admission, "made a complete jerk of myself on the stage. But I went out into the audience afterwards, and several women made it abundantly clear that they were available for the evening."

Now the Reverend Charles M. Young had groupies. He had peaked. From this great height, he could only fall.

———

He was burning out, taking on more assignments than his creativity could bear. The magazine had no other true stars, and Chuck Young had nowhere else he wanted to go. He dated women at the office, did drugs there, hung out in bars with Felton and Flippo and White and Fier after hours. . . . He'd become friends with John Belushi, and one night Young took the raucous star of *Saturday Night Live* to CBGB to see the Dead Boys, and on another they went to the Palladium, a hip Manhattan disco, and on the club roof Belushi began to cry, sobbing to Chuck Young about the pressures of the TV show, how hard it was to be a star. Young could imagine, he truly could, but in these climes there were no more toilet stall doors. One had to find exaltation in fame's misery.

Yet his disaffection was becoming positively cancerous. He spent an inordinate amount of time—at work, in bars, lying awake in bed—thinking about Jann Wenner: What kind of mood he would be in, how he would react to Young's next piece, whom he would holler at during the next editorial meeting? The editor was driving Young insane with fury. One minute Jann would be hunched over the writer's copy, swigging out of his bottle of vodka, snarling "This is shit" and demanding to know information that was provided in the very next sentence. Or he'd put in a rare 9 A.M. appearance and fly into a fit because his entire staff weren't cranking out copy at their typewriters. Then the editor would disappear for a day or two, usually emerging just at deadline to tear the scheduled issue completely to ribbons.

He did what he could to mollify Jann. For a time they were almost friends. But it was hard to be buddies with a fellow Chet Flippo described as "a shark swimming through water, nothing going on inside him except appetite." Once, Young brought Sex Pistols manager Malcolm McLaren, suitably bedecked in bondage pants, up to the office to meet the editor. Jann would not give McLaren the time of day, and Young felt humiliated and pissed off. Not too long ago, he had told a writers' group in Madison, Wisconsin, that his ambition was to write for *Rolling Stone*. Now he was doing just that, and the experience was turning him into an anarchist and a drunk.

Young began to think of Jann Wenner as the New York Yankees regarded their owner, George Steinbrenner. The difference was that no one at *Rolling Stone*, save Jann, was a millionaire. No writer was at the magazine to get rich, and that certainly included Young, who did not even file expenses on his first feature articles. But he began to consider financial inequities when the Sex Pistols issue featured an article on journalists working for the CIA, written by Watergate reporter Carl Bernstein. For that article—a "really terrible" piece, according to Harriet Fier, who devoted an unusual amount of time to editing it—Bernstein was reportedly paid $27,000, more than Young and his fellow associate editors were making that entire year.

True, the Bernstein piece attracted considerable publicity. Young could see this. But now he saw, for the first time, just how much cash *Rolling Stone* had to throw around. So why was it that Jann would promise a Tim Cahill

$3,000 for an article and then pay him only $2,700? Why was it suddenly decreed that foreign subsidiary rights were the exclusive property of the magazine, thus depriving writers of the occasional $200 checks that floated in from overseas sales of articles?

One day, chief financial officer Jim Dunning came down to the twenty-third floor to pay Chuck Young a visit. "I've got some really good news," Dunning told Young. "*Rolling Stone* is going to start doing a radio show. And we'll pay you an extra fifty dollars for the taped interview of whoever you're going to write an article about."

Young balked. "Jim, I don't really have a tape recorder that's suitable for that," he said.

Dunning waved that off as a nuisance easily surmounted. "We'll let you use a professional tape recorder that you can carry along with you," he said.

The writer shook his head. "Jim, if I carry a big tape recorder around like that, along with microphone booms and stuff, it's really gonna interfere with my reporting style. And besides," he added, "fifty dollars isn't very much money."

Dunning upped the fee to $75. Young turned him down. Later, he spoke with the disc jockey in charge of the radio show. *Rolling Stone*, Young found out, was charging a $40,000 syndication fee per show. "And that was Dunning and Jann's idea of a fair deal," he said. "Fifty bucks for the guy who does the work; $39,950 for Jann. It was unfathomable to me."

———

In 1978, Jann's rival Irving Azoff produced *FM*, a dull movie about a hip radio station that despite its intense mediocrity made good money and gave Azoff an entrée into the movie business. Two years before, promoter Bill Graham made his screen debut in *Apocalypse Now*, playing a sleazy press agent. Now Jann wanted to go to Hollywood. Paramount signed him to a lucrative production deal, empowering the editor to create and executive-produce three major movies.

Before long, stationery reading "Jann S. Wenner Motion Pictures" began to pile up at 745 Fifth Avenue. Hunter Thompson was recruited to write a screenplay about gunrunning in the Everglades; Ben Fong-Torres, for a movie about San Francisco during the sixties; and Cameron Crowe was asked to produce a treatment for a high school flick.

Crowe, in fact, was writing a book based on his own high school experiences: *Fast Times at Ridgemont High*. The former teenaged *Rolling Stone* mascot was now twenty-one. His days of hanging out in recording studios with L.A. superstars were receding. That beat was no longer exclusively his. Since the Eagles softball game, Chuck Young had struck up a friendly correspondence with drummer Don Henley—culminating, improbably, in the punk journalist getting the choice assignment of covering the Eagles' tour in the fall of 1978. Crowe had learned a thing or two about trends in Los Angeles, and this one suggested he'd better not put all his eggs in Jann Wenner's basket.

The future of Cameron Crowe as Hollywood's keenest ear for adolescent angst glimmered in the near distance. He decided to write the *Fast Times* screenplay not for Jann but rather for Irving Azoff. This sudden severing of the umbilical cord constituted in the editor's mind an act of betrayal every bit as egregious as Marianne Partridge's decision to bolt *Rolling Stone* in favor of Clay Felker's *Village Voice*. Later, when Crowe produced the first interview Joni Mitchell had given *Rolling Stone* in ten years, Jann ran the story on the cover but would not award his prodigal son a cover byline. Four years after, *Fast Times at Ridgemont High* star Sean Penn was the subject of a *Rolling Stone* cover story. Yet the feature scarcely mentioned the movie that had made Penn an overnight sensation.

Jann called Chuck Young into his office. He wanted Young to write the treatment for the high school screenplay. Young was flattered, but a little bit confused. Only a few days before, he'd shown the editor a first chapter of a novel he'd been contemplating. Jann had helped to secure Young a contract, had given the writer a leave of absence.... Now this.

"I'd like to," apologized Young. "But I'm really psyched up to write the novel."

"I'll pay you $50,000 to write the script," said Jann.

The offer staggered Chuck Young. Still, he refused.

A few days later, Jann raised the offer to $75,000. "It's not the money," Young protested. But a few days after that, when the offer became $100,000, Young froze in his tracks. After mulling it over, he accepted.

Only $1,500 of the advance was provided up front. Young, now off the *Rolling Stone* payroll, was running up research expenses but having trouble paying his bills. He asked Jann to press Paramount for more funds, but if the editor petitioned the studio, it had no effect. Young could not afford groceries. He snuck into staff deadline dinners and was thrown out.

After several belt-tightening months, the writer produced his treatment. What he came up with was nothing at all like Crowe's good-natured adolescent romp, but rather a dark, vicious drama—Young's Sex Pistols, in essence, to Crowe's Eagles.

"At the time," said Young, "I had a very inflated idea of my own capabilities. I really felt I was Superman. Everything I tried at *Rolling Stone* at that stage had turned to gold—not necessarily in terms of selling the magazine, but in terms of work I was proud of, work everybody else seemed to think was funny and good."

So the Reverend Charles M. Young had every reason to feel cocky the night Jann Wenner invited him over to discuss what the editor had just read. Within moments, he was cut down at the knees.

"These characters you've got in here—they're just caricatures," said Jann. The treatment was nowhere near what he had in mind. Paramount would be appalled if they saw what Young had come up with after months of work. ("Too oppressively dark and desperate" was their eventual verdict.) The editor had recently read an article about a high school student who'd had an affair with his teacher. Now *that* was hot stuff.

But this . . . The editor put down the screenplay treatment. "If this is the truth about American teenagers," he declared, "I don't want to know it."

Young returned home, utterly humiliated. He had expected the screenplay to make him a ton of money, to deliver him to some astounding new plateau. Instead, he was broke, emotionally at rock bottom and somehow made to feel as if his flawed vision of American adolescence had betrayed Jann. Momentarily he felt guilt, then indignation. The final, lasting emotional stage was unalloyed hatred for Jann Wenner.

He did not complete a successful rewrite of the treatment. He did not complete his novel. He did return to the magazine, a malcontent ghosting the hallways, of little use to the magazine or to himself. He wrote articles that were not printed. Finally, he did not write at all.

"As soon as you went to work at *Rolling Stone*," he would later say, "it enveloped you completely. It took care of your professional, artistic, social, sexual, drug needs. Everything you needed to get by in New York City, *Rolling Stone* sort of furnished for you. It was a complete womb. And I didn't want to leave that womb when the time came. I left kicking and screaming like a traumatized baby."

At a small staff Christmas party in 1980, held on the twenty-eighth floor, Chuck Young lurched drunkenly around the desks of the business staff, trying to amuse himself. He found, on top of one desk, a bullwhip. He took it from the desk and caressed its handle. Then he lashed it against the ground. The whip made an agreeable noise. Young grinned. He began to lash objects off tables and desks. He was making a mess of things up here on the twenty-eighth floor. It felt right.

From a hallway emerged Jann Wenner and Hunter Thompson. Young and Thompson had met only once, though Young suspected Thompson had been so out of it he probably wouldn't remember. Before and since, he'd seen the immortal master of Gonzo visit the office, and Young had been too awed to approach his old hero. The old Woody Creek renegade represented everything wild and splendid about the *Rolling Stone* Young had once dreamed of writing for.

Chuck Young had come too late. Those days spilled out like gold dust through the floorboards. And now here walked Hunter Thompson with the object of Young's seething contempt. In crooked, inebriated motions, Young lunged toward Jann Wenner and wrapped the bullwhip around the editor's neck.

Thompson watched this, and others did as well. Jann looked up at his writer with an expression that suggested real terror. Young grinned back, too drunk to know what his own intentions were. Words from somewhere in the room pleaded with him not to strangle the editor.

Chuck Young loosened the bullwhip from Jann's neck and stepped back. He looked up at Hunter Thompson, who stood there with his normal incalculable expression intact. Young advanced toward Thompson, bullwhip raised, and Thompson neatly kicked the Reverend Charles M. Young in the balls.

He went down like a sack of potatoes. Thompson looked at the groaning writer on the floor, then walked away with Jann Wenner at his side.

The editor looked back at his fallen star, then at Thompson. "He has an authority problem," Jann explained.

Chapter Sixteen

CAMELOT
ABANDONED

Art director Roger Black delivered the news to Jann that he was quitting *Rolling Stone* over a late lunch at the Sherry Netherland café in August of 1978. In fact, Black felt awful about the decision. He'd been the magazine's art director for longer than anyone save Robert Kingsbury. By designing *Rolling Stone*'s own typeface, Black's imprint was literal and lasting. He would go on to become the art director of the *New York Times*; but even from that pinnacle of prestige, Roger Black would wax nostalgic about those enchanted seasons: 1975, 1976, 1977; Patty Hearst to Jimmy Carter to the Sex Pistols; the days when *Rolling Stone*'s voice was the clarion blast of a triumphant generation.

Only now it was 1978. The ship of state, both for America and for *Rolling Stone*, was a vessel of driftwood. No moral consensus had emerged from the generation that delivered Carter to the Oval Office. This was the

Me Decade, a time not for communal benevolence but rather for narcissism, ethical relativism and ultimately despair.

And as Jon Landau wrote in the magazine's tenth-anniversary issue: "Today's music documents a world in which people are out for themselves instead of for each other, in which people are growing apart instead of coming together." How to portray this phenomenon without being sucked into the dismal vortex was a creative challenge *Rolling Stone* simply could not meet. The barnacled anchors of the past were plopped down again in 1978: two Bob Dylan covers, two Mick Jagger covers, plus two Who covers and three Linda Ronstadts in the span of a year. Jane Fonda, heroine of the sixties, now appeared on the cover of *Rolling Stone* looking for all the world like Fleetwood Mac's Stevie Nicks. Did the new, "civilized" Fonda capture the very image *Rolling Stone* sought in the waning years of the amoral seventies? Other covers reflected other postures: Brooke Shields, the decade's would-be Lolita; punk poet Patti Smith; giddy, manic *Saturday Night Live* comedienne Gilda Radner; or Linda Ronstadt, herself shuffling styles, discarding one look after the next like cheap lingerie.

If music was no longer "the rock & roll of the seventies," then what was? Surely not politics, not after Carter. Movies? Comedy? (One issue led with a profile of Bill Murray in its music section.) From each dubious hook *Rolling Stone* dangled limply in 1978. "This was a time," said Roger Black, "when *Rolling Stone* especially needed leadership, because the times were changing, the music had gotten bad and the old formula just didn't work any longer."

The magazine needed a leader, but Jann Wenner wasn't available. He was hitting Manhattan's late-night haunts, poking his nose around in Hollywood, enjoying the celebrity accorded him at last. In 1978, Jann had in fact entertained a serious offer to sell *Rolling Stone* to Ziff-Davis. An elaborate proposal was drawn up and considered; then the editor raised his demands, and the deal was off. Some would suggest later that Jann only wished to reckon the market value of his magazine. But the fact remained that *Rolling Stone* was now viewed by its founder as a commodity, an object to which a price could be assigned. The man was disconnected from the magazine.

Jann, who was immensely fond of Black and his work, did not want to see his art director leave the fold. He wanted to know what it would take for Black to stay.

"One of two things," said Black. "Either raise me"—and here the art director named a figure to which Jann Wenner could not possibly agree— "or come back and be the editor."

Jann immediately knew what Black was saying, and his answer was just as immediate. "I'm not going to do that," he said. And with that Roger Black gave notice. By the end of the month he was gone. A month later Black paid an angry call to 745 Fifth Avenue, demanding that Jann remove his name from the masthead.

———

The choice of Harriet Fier as *Rolling Stone*'s managing editor seemed gloriously inspired. Fier personified the magazine's history, its cultural sincerity and its brash ambitiousness. In 1972, the former Smith College Phi Beta Kappa member, rock & roll musician and hitchhiker showed up at 625 Third Street, hoping for a job as an office grunt. The application asked for her sun sign, her rising sign and her moon sign. Stumped, Fier wrote "Gemini" in all three blanks.

The woman who took her application drew back. "Triple Gemini!" she exclaimed. "How do you cope?"

Harriet Fier became the night switchboard operator, an attractive, well-educated "office chick." Like everyone else in the office, she eagerly volunteered for whatever needed to be done: proofreading, writing promotional blurbs, conjuring up the occasional headline—there was always work for idle hands. In 1973, when publisher Larry Durocher converted *Rolling Stone* into a flatfold, four-color publication, Fier was shifted over to circulation to assist with the burgeoning subscriber list.

Her break came in 1974, when copy chief Marianne Partridge rescued Fier, Sarah Lazin, Christine Doudna and Barbara Downey from their drudgery and announced that the women were now editors. The titles came first, respect later. Fending off the chauvinistic wisecracks became second nature for Fier. When "Random Notes" editor Jim Kuntsler eased up to her and cooed, "I can see my unborn children in your big brown eyes," she did not blush. "Fuck off," she advised Kuntsler, and returned to her work.

She attended the women's meetings held outside of work, but as a feminist stopped short of stridency. Unlike the other women, Harriet Fier enjoyed belting back a few at Jerry's Inn, matching wits with the boys. When one of the first issues of *Ms.* arrived at the office, Fier flipped a few pages, noted its somewhat shrill tones and returned the copy to receptionist Judy Lawrence. "Not for me," Fier said.

The relationship between Jann and Marianne Partridge had always been laced with nervy melodrama. Fier was brassy but not given to Partridge's histrionics. Jann liked her style, her looks; Fier was a rock & roller and a feminist who comported herself like a classy New York editor. Her mentor, Partridge, had schooled her well in getting the best out of writers. Jann assigned Fier the task of putting together the *Outside* supplement, and was much impressed by the results. And it did not escape his attention that while others bemoaned the magazine's impending move to New York, Fier was buoyant. She was a native New Yorker; she would hit the ground strutting.

After Marianne Partridge bolted for *The Village Voice*, her lieutenants —Fier, Sarah Lazin, Christine Doudna and Barbara Downey—spoke often of feminist solidarity, pledging to edit *Rolling Stone* by committee. But Jann wasn't about to turn his magazine over to a cabal.

Harriet Fier knew this. There was only one desk available. Jann wasn't going to give it back to Paul Scanlon, whose contributions had dwindled. And of the women, she as features editor seemed next in line for the post. Said Jann, "She was the strongest one of the girls, the most assertive and savvy. She was the only one who really could step up to the next level. The rest of them couldn't handle it."

The job, it seemed, was Fier's to refuse. And she did not refuse it. In fact, Harriet Fier openly assumed authority over her peers even before she was awarded the title. Everything about her—the way she spoke to them, her sense of humor, even how she carried herself when she walked—seemed haughty. Her friends were shocked. "We all thought Harriet had a personality transplant," said Doudna.

When the other women confronted Jann, one after the other, and learned that Fier was pushing her new weight around with his blessings, they realized it was the sudden end of the miracle they'd lived together. For some time after that, said Downey, "there was a lot of fighting, the way women fight: a lot of not recognizing the other person exists, leaving the bathroom without a conversation and letting certain comments get back. It wasn't direct confrontation. It wasn't blatant. But it was very intense."

By the end of 1978, both Doudna and Paul Scanlon left *Rolling Stone*, and Lazin took the reins of the newly formed Rolling Stone Press. Only Barbara Downey stayed behind to work for Harriet Fier.

———

"At *Rolling Stone*," said Harriet Fier, "we had our moment, our Camelot." But Camelot had already been deserted by the time Fier became managing editor in 1978, and by the time she left, those days were barely even a memory.

The seventies, the vastness of the music industry, Jimmy Carter and New York had changed *Rolling Stone*. Then again, all magazines had changed. In 1974, Time Inc.'s *People* magazine was launched. "Our focus is on people, not issues," proclaimed *People* managing editor Richard Stolley, adding dubiously, "We will not pander to baser instincts." Yet pander it did, delivering spicy nuggets to people who did not read, casting images on paper much like the flickering of faces on the television screen. By the end of the seventies, the message behind *People*'s ghastly success was like a high-pitched whistle blowing through the darkness, and the entire publishing business, like neighborhood dogs, stood up and barked. Overnight, it seemed, articles in nearly every American magazine shrank to a size that could be digested while perched upon a toilet. Political pieces no longer took. People were tired of reading about how horrible their leaders were. The time had come for a sweeter diet.

Once a writer-driven magazine, *Rolling Stone*'s middle management now consisted of editors who rarely sat behind a typewriter. More than ever before, there was talk about the editorial "mix," the contrived ratio of hard news to music pieces to personality features. And there became, said Joe Klein, "the cult of the editor. You would hear editors in the hallways at the new offices saying, 'That was a good piece by Klein,' and the other editor would say, 'Well, you should have seen it before I rewrote it.'"

Rolling Stone was fast becoming another New York magazine, and this cut several ways. Star writers like Michael Rogers, Tim Cahill, Howard Kohn and Chris Hodenfield saw the magazine as unworthy of their loyalty, and one by one moved on to more lucrative arrangements. Conversely, writers whose work regularly appeared in other New York publications began to submit pieces to *Rolling Stone*. But the effect of using talented but ubiquitous writers like Roy Blount, George Plimpton and David Halberstam was hardly to distinguish *Rolling Stone* from the pack. Being different was no longer the game.

The business side saw to this. Jann Wenner spent more and more of his time up on the twenty-seventh floor, in Joe Armstrong's old office, mulling over the advice of his new financial triumvirate: associate publishers Kent Brownridge, Jim Dunning and Claeys Bahrenburg. The words they whispered in Jann's ear were disquieting. They spoke of "market forces," of *Rolling Stone* being out of step with the publishing trends begun by *People*. If Jann wanted mainstream profits, they told him, the magazine's look and content would have to become more "market-responsive."

Kent Brownridge had been an advance man for Jimmy Carter and other politicians, and his role at *Rolling Stone* was rather nebulous. But he soon developed a fascination with circulation, with what made a magazine move off the racks. Brownridge took it upon himself to master this obscure but remunerative science. He especially focused on a matter near and dear to Jann: the magazine's cover. For this preoccupation with numbers, the editorial staffers labeled Brownridge Mr. Charts & Graphs; for his eagerness to please Jann, they called him simply Brownnose.

On the twenty-seventh floor, Jim Dunning had emerged as something of a hero for obtaining the bank loan that saved *Rolling Stone* from bankruptcy in 1977. But Dunning was a breed apart from the Joe Armstrongs and Larry Durochers and Porter Bibbs of yesteryear. Brought in from Publishers Clearinghouse, he had never read so much as a word of *Rolling Stone* and was completely ignorant of the culture from which the magazine had sprung. His interest was strictly financial. Dunning was there to keep the company viable. But that didn't just mean commiserating with bankers. In Dunning's view, the editorial staff was "holding on to the old security blanket of journalism—long stories, trying to find investigative stories—and the stuff *stunk*. The reality was that there wasn't a constituency for that old agenda anymore. Clearly there was a path for a new agenda, and if you responded to it, you had a chance—there was no guarantee, but at least you had a chance. But the magazine had to change, or it wasn't going to be around anymore."

Claeys Bahrenburg's mission was to crack the big ad accounts *Rolling Stone* hadn't yet won: American automobile companies, and farther down the road, the Army. The problem, as one business memo put it, was that many mega-advertisers believed that *Rolling Stone*'s "editorial environment did not always seem appropriate or supportive." When Bahrenburg first penetrated the inner sanctum of Detroit, a Ford rep greeted him by saying, "Young man, I just want to let you know that over my dead body will you ever get an account with us." Ford and other conservative would-be advertisers still perceived *Rolling Stone* as a journal of the drug-addled left. The magazine's frequent use of "shit" and "fuck" ended many business conversations before the matter of politics even came up.

The traditional "church/state" arrangement between business and editorial began to deteriorate even before Harriet Fier got her new business cards. Dunning, Brownridge and Bahrenburg often descended from the twenty-seventh floor—"turkey heaven," David Felton called it—to the twenty-third; their presence was impossible to ignore. There were Bahrenburg and his ad reps, jawboning, suggesting more and more supplements so as to attract new accounts, new "ad scams" as they came to be known on the twenty-third floor. There was Dunning, slapping a few backs—"this little blond munchkin in his dapper blazer," said music editor Peter Herbst, "telling me that he really loved the magazine, when it was antithetical to everything he'd ever done in his life." And there was Kent Brownridge, who spent Saturday mornings riding horses and would show up at the office on weekend afternoons in knee-high leather boots, tapping his riding crop against his palm, a taskmaster lording over his sweating minions.

"These guys were shoe salesmen," said Fier. "They could be selling *anything*. They didn't have the kind of attachment that we had to *Rolling Stone*. We resented them for the fact that they didn't love this magazine, that they were mere moneymakers. They were the enemy."

Often Fier met with Jann and his business trio. The managing editor usually emerged from these meetings of what Jann called "the Joint Chiefs" cursing under her breath. During one encounter, Fier was informed by Jann that *Rolling Stone* was instituting a zero-based budgeting scheme, wherein every single item in the magazine's budget would have to be justified quantitatively. The Carter administration was employing zero-based budgeting, and the concept was all the rage in the private sector as well. But how was Fier to justify, for example, photographs? *Rolling Stone* had photos on nearly every page, and the reasons for this were aesthetic, not quantifiable.

The photos stayed, but staff writers went. The printouts indicated that writers like Chet Flippo and David Felton weren't justifying their salaries in terms of sheer word count. Whether the numbers lied or not was not the point, in Harriet Fier's view; the point was that writer productivity was a matter for her to decide, not a man like Dunning, whom she regarded as a fascist.

The business lieutenants, in turn, thought Fier was in way over her head. This was a woman, after all, who didn't see any need for *Rolling Stone* to grow—a woman who once thought it would be politically and cosmically correct for the magazine to fold when Nixon resigned. Fier seemed to believe that financial instability was an integral part of the *Rolling Stone* experience. She routinely approved advances to writers without regard for the budgetary consequences. She had no patience for Brownridge's statistics indicating that certain colors and photographic poses performed better on covers than others.

And when Bahrenburg finally got Ford to buy a full page, what did Fier do? She placed the ad opposite a story which contained, by Bahrenburg's count, over twenty instances of "fuck" on that page.

(Bahrenburg eventually took matters into his own hands. When the ad director went to Washington to court the Army, he neatly removed each page from the sample issues that contained the word "fuck." Bahrenburg suspected the folks at Army headquarters wouldn't notice the disjointedness in the text. He was right.)

Ironically, Jim Dunning greatly appreciated the only two writers Harriet Fier truly developed at *Rolling Stone*: Chuck Young and Timothy White. "They saved the magazine," said Dunning. "Like when Chuck Young interviewed Carly Simon. We *had* to have it. White and Young went out there and got us the stories of the only music personalities we could put on the cover and expect to sell."

This was especially true of Timothy White, who entered *Rolling Stone* in the late fall of 1978 like an electrical current in a copper bathtub. White was passionate and enormously energetic at a time when *Rolling Stone* was neither. In his adolescent days, White often gazed longingly at the *Rolling Stone* masthead. Yet he scarcely imagined that the magazine would depend on him to remind it of its vitality.

Though it was White's brilliant music reporting in *Crawdaddy* that caught Fier's eye, he'd done his real learning as a reporter for the Associated Press. That experience, said White, taught him that "everybody has a story, and failure to get it is always the writer's fault." When no one else wished to write about immensely popular but critically snubbed acts like the Bee Gees, Stevie Nicks, the Doobie Brothers and Billy Joel, White eagerly signed on (to the delight of both Dunning and Fier). In this manner he recalled Cameron Crowe, the writer whose record for *Rolling Stone* cover stories White would smash. White was a far more thorough reporter than Crowe, approaching the subject not as a fan but as an inquisitive stranger; but he admired "the kind of proximity that Cameron provided," and sought the same intimacy in his profiles.

Timothy White wasted little time infuriating individuals who already felt alienated from Harriet Fier. At his second editorial meeting, he attacked Dave Marsh's columns and articles for their incessant references to *Rolling Stone* veterans Greil Marcus and Jon Landau—a "claustrophobic and lame" practice of backscratching that no other magazine saw fit to engage in.

But it wasn't just White's irreverence that irked veteran staffers. To Donald Katz, the magazine's talented international rover, White's rising star was emblematic of *Rolling Stone*'s new mass-market, personality-oriented posture. Katz, the last nonmusic staff writer *Rolling Stone* would hire in the seventies, correctly perceived this trend as a threat to his livelihood. He saw himself as a link in the chain that clasped together Joe Eszterhas, Tim Crouse, Howard Kohn and Joe Klein. Katz wrote nonrock pieces in a rock magazine, scrambling from Spain to Northern Ireland to Monaco to Italy, consorting with revolutionaries and princesses. Back in the States he covered Republicans, police brutality, autism and, at Jann's request, Jane Fonda. His early work attracted the attention of *New Republic* editor Marty Peretz, who tried to hire Katz away from Jann's magazine. While Katz agonized over the choice, Peretz told him, "Look. If you want to be a star, stay with *Rolling Stone*. It makes its writers stars." Donald Katz stayed. Surely Jann Wenner had big plans for his young reporter.

Alas, Katz was tailored for the past, not the future. His patron, Paul Scanlon, was gone. So were the others he cavorted with: Klein, Kohn, Christine Doudna. *Rolling Stone*'s new heavies, like Chuck Young and Timothy White, wrote about the Sex Pistols and John Belushi. Editors sat at their desks thumbing through back issues of *Time* and *Newsweek*, looking to the Establishment weeklies for inspiration. Editorial meetings were listless, except when David Felton would use them as an opportunity to humiliate Katz, who began to wear a neck collar around the office because the place gave him muscle spasms.

After writing a piece on the bloody revolution in Ethiopia (which later won the Overseas Press Club Award of 1978), Katz received a letter from a reader:

> Dear Mr. Katz,
> Young people risked their lives to talk to a *Rolling Stone* reporter so that stoned-out young teenagers can read about it between gossip and music reviews. What's the point, Mr. Katz?

Katz made copies and circulated them, with his comment at the bottom: "Having trouble answering this letter. Any input would be appreciated."

Morose though he was, Katz understood the situation. "The business question facing Jann," he said, "was whether to grow up with the baby-boom audience, which would entail becoming the *New Yorker* of its generation, or to go after the teenagers in the grocery stores. He chose the latter, which obviated the need for people like me." When Katz returned from an assignment and found that his office overlooking the park was now occupied by someone else, he knew he'd be having a conversation with Jann shortly.

It happened. "You haven't worked out like I expected," the editor told his writer. Jann gazed out the window toward Central Park. "You know," he said, "you really should be writing serious political work in journals or something. You're too serious for *Rolling Stone*."

Instead, Donald Katz became a business writer, specializing in, among other subjects, office politics.

———

If alienated writers like Donald Katz and Dave Marsh believed *Rolling Stone* was descending into trivia and anti-intellectualism, the new managing editor professed the contrary. "I really thought we were doing God's work," said Harriet Fier. "I believed in it, I was committed to it and I thought we were writing and doing things nobody else was doing."

When Fier wasn't fighting with the business staff over obscenity and the ad/editorial ratio, she was grooming her pet writers, maternally soothing them, buffering their fragile egos from Jann Wenner's blistering whims. When Chuck Young experienced stomach pains while writing a John Belushi cover story under extreme deadline pressure, Fier hastened to a grocery store and returned with Pepto-Bismol and apricot juice for her writer. "She was the all-giving, all-knowing earth mother at *Rolling Stone*," said Young. "The writers who didn't hate her loved her, and some of them had mad crushes on her. Besides being your editor, she was sort of your Muse as well. She had such big, sympathetic brown eyes. . . ."

She sought to salvage the shipwrecked journalistic careers of *Rolling Stone*'s two greatest writers, Hunter Thompson and David Felton. Since the Jimmy Carter article of 1976, not a rustle had been heard of the Gonzo journalist, but Fier reopened communications. Soon she was staying up late by the 745 Fifth Avenue mojo machine, spreading out Thompson's disjointed "inserts" on the floor, reestablishing that venerable tradition of Thompson-induced office angst. Fier did not extract from Hunter Thompson his most inspired work; indeed, his coverage of the Ali-Spinks title match in 1978 was the dullest Thompson piece *Rolling Stone* had ever published. But getting the Woody Creek recluse to write at all was a triumph, and the mail pouring in from *Rolling Stone* readers reflected an abiding appetite for Gonzo no matter how stale.

The matter of David Felton was more troubling. Felton had never eclipsed his brilliant Charlie Manson and Mel Lyman epics of 1970 and 1971—had never even come close. His attention now focused on his chief love, comedy, and in fact his profiles of Richard Pryor, Lily Tomlin, Steve Martin and Bill Murray read more like nightclub shticks than the amused but subtly righteous insights that once characterized Felton's greatness.

He could be, and usually was, clever. Jann Wenner continually found uses for Felton's wit when other editors would long before have cast him out to sea. But the withering of David Felton's astonishing talent was no laughing matter. In the magazine's tenth-anniversary issue, Felton wrote a piece entitled "Lifer," in which the veteran associate editor described the incestuous and narcotic powers of *Rolling Stone*—a magazine from which he'd been fired three times, but to which he always returned. To some of his fellow staffers, the portrait amounted to gallows humor at best, and at worst, Felton's admission of incapacitation. "It was an abject expression of David's pathetic state," said a staffer who greatly admired Felton's earlier work. "It essentially said, 'Thank you for letting me ruin my life in shelter.' "

Though Jann Wenner missed few chances to jab Felton during editorial meetings—"I can be mean, David! You know I can, you sack of shit!"— the editor truly liked his longtime employee. Out of fondness, but against his better judgment, Jann commissioned Felton to write a long profile of *Hustler* publisher Larry Flynt. The writer spent a year on the project. He recorded hundreds of hours' worth of interviews. Annie Leibovitz shot rolls and rolls of film. Chuck Young read Felton's lead and pronounced it fabulous, Felton at his absolute finest.

But David Felton did not write another word after that. "I tried everything I could to get that piece," said Jann. "I would advance him money. I would deprive him of money. I actually held the money in front of his face—I'd say, 'Just finish the piece, David, all this money is sitting here, just turn in the piece.' He was desperate for money, I knew, and I told him he'd be living on a steam grate somewhere unless he turned in that piece. I tried everything I knew how to do.... And it agonized me personally that I couldn't do anything—it was beyond my power to help him."

Disgusted, the editor restricted Felton's presence at 745 Fifth Avenue to "wandering privileges": he could visit, but there would be no desk for him. And so Felton wandered, his principal way station being Harriet Fier's office. Fier thought Felton was wonderful. She wanted to help him any way she could. She gave him little assignments so that he could meet his child-support payments, kept him on the company insurance plan, befriended him.

She was—to use the terminology of Alcoholics Anonymous, which Felton later joined—his enabler.

———

Felton, Chuck Young, Tim White and Chet Flippo looked upon Harriet Fier as a noble matriarch, battling back Jann's idiotic schemes and the greedheads on the twenty-seventh floor. Their gratitude went out to her when the managing editor emerged from Jann's office shaking her head, rolling her eyes heavenward, sighing, "I had another fight."

Yet others weren't so sure Fier was fighting all that hard. "It got to be kind of a joke," said one of her subordinates. "All the time she'd say, 'I had a real fight with Jann about this.' It wasn't always that believable. I thought she was blowing her own horn."

Joe Klein, at first firmly in Fier's corner, began to wonder if the new managing editor was up to the formidable task of dealing with Jann. "Scanlon's most valuable function," said Klein, "was that he'd go into Jann's office, and Jann would have six story ideas, four of which were completely insane and ridiculous, one of which was pretty good and one of which might be genius. And Scanlon was a pillow. You'd throw all of this energy into Scanlon and he knew enough to hold back. But one of Harriet's real problems was that she took all six ideas seriously. And they weren't only story ideas. They were ideas about people. You know, 'Let's fire him, he's no good,' or 'Why don't we hire this hot new so-and-so,' or 'Why don't we get Sissy Vanderbilt to write a story about shoe imports?'

"My dream was that *Rolling Stone* was going to become the *New Yorker* of our generation. But Jann was becoming very conservative with the magazine, moving it away from politics and back to rock & roll and shorter stories, a market-packaged type of thing. And Harriet was the willing agent of this. I think that power corrupted her terribly."

Fier's copy chief, Barbara Downey, remained loyal to the managing editor, but the chemistry of their friendship was never the same. "It was a multiple blow when she became managing editor," said Downey. "She was much more in Jann's corner than in the editorial corner where she'd once been. Who would have guessed that she would change loyalties so completely, and so nonsensically in many cases?"

To some, she seemed bedazzled by her exclusive access to Jann Wenner. Fier would herself recall, with obvious affection: "Every Friday night, we'd have dinner catered—deadline dinner. I'd go in Jann's office and close the door, and we'd eat on these plastic plates. We'd sit there, and he would tell me stories, and talk to me about things. The meetings were great. I learned a lot about the history of the magazine, and he got through to me on a lot of stuff."

If Downey, Klein and others were disturbed by Fier's companionship with Jann, the editor's wife was downright incensed. Jane Wenner despised Harriet Fier ever since the tenth-anniversary issue, when—in a section devoted to photos of various *Rolling Stone* alumni—a picture of Jane was run with the caption "Jane S. Wenner as sex symbol." The photo, showing Jane's naked back and her face peering drowsily over her shoulder, was quite glamorous. But she thought the caption was catty and demanded that Jann scratch it off the printing rotogravure, which he did—though too late to eradicate the caption from all copies of the issue.

Quite regularly, Jane Wenner phoned Jann's secretary, Mary McDonald. "Who's he with?" she would demand. "Is he with Harriet? Are they at lunch together? Check with her secretary!"

———

In the summer of 1979, a born-again Bob Dylan released *Slow Train Coming*. The album was almost universally panned, but not in *Rolling Stone*. Jann Wenner wrote the review himself, hailing *Slow Train Coming* as "one of the finest records Dylan has ever made. In time, it is possible that it might even be considered his greatest."

Beneath Jann's affection for that album lurked a tale. The year 1979 had been one of hopes burned to cinder. Jane had finally gotten pregnant, only to miscarry. Cameron Crowe had taken *Fast Times at Ridgemont High* away from Jann.

On May 7, Jann Wenner was hired by French publishing magnate Daniel Filipacchi to be the editor in chief of *Look*. Instantly Jann phoned Harriet Fier, vacationing with a boyfriend on St. Maarten, and begged her to fly back to New York for the weekend. Fier reluctantly did so. Jann picked her up at the airport. That night, at Frankie and Johnny's Restaurant on Forty-fifth Street, the two sat over dinner and mapped out *Look*'s editorial content. The editor was nearly breathless with excitement.

Later that evening, en route to Elaine's in Jann's chauffeur-driven limo, he warned Fier, "Whatever you do, don't say a word to 'em. If anyone comes over to our table and asks about *Look*, you don't know anything. We've got to keep this under wraps."

As soon as they sat at a table and ordered a drink, Watergate reporter Carl Bernstein sauntered up and said, "Hi, Jann, what's new?"

The editor flew up out of his seat. "We just took over *Look!*" he blurted out.

The new editor of *Look* seized Fier's entire *Rolling Stone* feature inventory and transferred it to the new magazine. He decided immediately to ease editorial and financial pressure by converting *Look* into a monthly. His first day on the job saw wholesale dismissals, ending with Jann firing the secretary whose job it had been to call in the victims one by one.

Among the few who stayed was former *Rolling Stone* associate editor Christine Doudna, *Look*'s senior editor at the time of Jann's entry. "I'd definitely had the entire range of feelings about Jann," she said. "But my main thought at that point was that I'd escaped him. When Jann reappeared in my life, I certainly had mixed feelings.

"Amazingly," Doudna said, "it turned into a fabulous time for all of us. It was the best I'd ever seen of Jann." Those who saw him during the months of May and June saw the Jann Wenner of old: showing up for work before noon, staying all night, editing articles, bouncing from desk to desk, hurling thousands of ideas into the void. He was having a blast—in Jim Dunning's words, "coming alive again."

The *Look* that Jann Wenner inherited was losing half a million dollars per issue. Two issues into the enterprise, the Wenner-operated *Look* was economically profitable—and a vast improvement editorially. He brought Paul Scanlon into the fold. Dave Marsh and Chris Hodenfield were assigned pieces. It was Jann Wenner's renaissance, *Rolling Stone* all over again— except that it wasn't his.

Daniel Filipacchi pulled the plug on *Look*, choosing to fold it even when Jann offered to buy the magazine. Jann was devastated. He'd never been fired before. How could that arrogant French bastard end his dream? The sudden removal of *Look* from Jann Wenner's life was a personal miscarriage.

Slow Train Coming came out the week *Look* folded. Jann listened to the record some fifty times that month. He coaxed people into his car, played them his cassette. Tears formed in his eyes when he heard the legend's familiar rasp, singing through the darkness about faith and hope. The last time *Rolling Stone* reviewed Dylan's work, both Greil Marcus and Dave Marsh savaged the legend, calling him a rank comic. Jann had been moved to issue a rebuttal. This time, there would be no rebuttal. The first and last word would be Jann's:

Faith is the message. Faith is the point. Faith is the key to under-standing this record. Faith is finally all we have. . . .

I don't go to church or to a synagogue. I don't kneel beside my bed at night. I don't think I will. I have yet to face the terror I read about in all the great literature. But, since politics, economics and war have failed to make us feel any better—as individuals or as a nation—and we look back at long years of disrepair, then maybe the time for religion has come again, and rather too suddenly—"like a thief in the night."

"Don't change a word!" Chuck Young pleaded with Harriet Fier after reading the rambling, hypersentimental draft in Jann's shaky scrawl. "Let the bastard hang himself!"

Fier wouldn't do it. The magazine reflected upon her as well as upon Jann. "I tried to talk him out of writing it, I tried to talk him out of running it and then I tried to fix it up," she later said. "That was my job."

That she allowed the piece to run, polished up or not, dismayed several on the staff. After reading the Dylan review, Dave Marsh decided that *Rolling Stone*'s sick slide into mediocrity was irreversible. Mick Jagger told Chet Flippo that the review had exposed Jann as a fool, making Flippo feel foolish by association. Shortly after the *Slow Train Coming* essay ran, assistant editor Jon Pareles left *Rolling Stone*, frustrated by its timid musical tastes and Jann's corrupting influence on the record reviews section. Pareles went on to become the pop-music critic of the *New York Times*, where he won acclaim for the kinds of insights he never could publish at *Rolling Stone*.

Here and there, the magazine found its mark: a rare and penetrating interview with Johnny Carson by Timothy White; Chet Flippo's dissection of the tragic Who concert in which several fans were trampled to death; guest appearances by Gabriel García Márquez, Frederick Exley and Tom Wicker; a pseudonymous piece on the cocaine trade by Michael Thomas. But not since the back-to-back Elvis Presley, New York and Sex Pistols issues in 1977 had the Harriet Fier regime produced any edition of sustained power.

"The issues were much less interesting," admitted Barbara Downey. "It's like we'd sit around and say, 'What are we *doing*?' I didn't have the answers, and neither did anyone else. And then the issues wouldn't sell, and we'd feel really bad."

They felt even worse when *Look* took its plunge and Jann Wenner returned. Shortly after the magazine folded, music editor Peter Herbst was summoned to Jann Wenner's office. Jann was, in Herbst's words, "drunk as a skunk."

The editor looked up at Herbst, who gulped at the sight of Jann's clenched face. Said the editor, "You're looking at a man who just lost a magazine."

Before Herbst could inject his sympathies, Jann growled, "I'm gonna make everybody's life here hell."

Thereafter, said associate editor Alan Weitz, "people came to work in the morning with their stomachs in a knot, praying throughout the day that Jann wouldn't call them into his office—praying that somehow they would get through this day without having to see Jann.

"He ran the office in a terrible way. Jann would come bustling in, with all this contained energy, sort of bursting at the seams, and you'd have this vision of papers flying in his wake and people running after him. He'd speak in short staccato bursts, and someone would be called into his office and he'd lay into them for a while, and then it'd be someone else. Everyone got their turn."

Jann began to call regular editorial meetings again—vodka bottle in one hand, gavel in another, curled up in his chair like a serpent contemplating a mouse. He marshaled his troops before him and told them where to sit. Chuck Young came to these meetings shaking. Barbara Downey left them in tears. Jann lit into Felton for trying to inject levity, Dave Marsh for being too serious, Timothy White for showing too much enthusiasm. Throughout, Harriet Fier seldom, if ever, said a word.

"Jann would pick a goat at the meeting," said Peter Herbst, whose slightly prim demeanor led Jann to present his music editor with an ironing board for a birthday gift at one meeting. "He'd just make fun of our ideas, or what we were wearing—whatever he could find. It was a little bit like a gong show, and so it took some courage to either voice your ideas or disagree with Jann."

Yet the editor's bullying was somewhat justified. A spark was missing from *Rolling Stone*. Headlines lacked wit. Beyond Young and White, Fier's attempts to cultivate new writers met with failure. (Some prospects simply didn't pan out. Others might have, had they received even marginal encouragement. When Jon Pareles resigned, a somewhat surprised Harriet Fier quipped, "Jonny, we hardly knew ye." The future *New York Times* critic had to wonder whose fault that was.) With its heavy reliance on hip comedy stories, the magazine was beginning to look like a *TV Guide* for *Saturday Night Live*. Cover stories were not conceived until the very last minute—

sometimes with disastrous consequences. (Fier and her associates could not come up with an acceptable cover image for a special disco issue, and so settled on a photo of the Village People—a colorful band that nonetheless represented the most aggravating, least substantial aspects of that genre. The issue bombed. Months later, at an editorial conference in which the magazine's creative lethargy was discussed, Chet Flippo was still growling, "It was that goddamned Village People cover that poisoned the well!")

"Every three issues or so," said associate art director Hans Teensma, "he'd get everybody together in his office, and he'd give a little page-by-page critique of the issues. And he would not miss a trick. I mean, no matter what this guy was coming off of, he'd catch every mistake, down to the last typo. He was very, very sharp."

Except when he wasn't. The editor's music opinions were seldom appreciated. "Punk," Jann would grunt at the very mention of the Talking Heads—a band no closer to punk than the Rolling Stones. His bubbly predictions of an imminent Beatles reunion sent eyes to rolling. When new writer Kurt Loder made plans to interview the Pretenders, an upstart British band fronted by American journalist Chrissie Hynde, Jann showed little interest. Then, when he learned that Pete Townshend was a big fan of the band, the editor told Peter Herbst to find a celebrity writer to replace Loder. Herbst ignored Jann, and the resulting cover story helped establish both the Pretenders and Loder.

At Jann's orders, a cover story was written on the benefit concerts staged by Musicians United for Safe Energy (MUSE), spearheaded by Jann's friend Jackson Browne and *Rolling Stone* reporter Howard Kohn. The shows were in fact not well attended, except for the two sellout performances by Bruce Springsteen—the one musician who would not sign the MUSE political statement released to the press. Yet writer Daisann McLane was told to play up the event anyway, and Jann added his own editorial, complimenting the MUSE concerts for being "smoothly run" and the audience for being "friendly."

His haphazard conceptualizing the staff could deal with, more or less. But his hands-on attempts at editing, at one time greatly admired, were now openly derided. Jann's skills as a line editor had degenerated badly, and writers came to dread what they called "the coke edit." This meant, said one staffer, that "the first two paragraphs would be rewritten sixteen times, with little notes in the margins you couldn't read. Then on the second page he'd change one word. The rest of it would be intact."

MAX AQUILERA-HELLWEG

PHOTOGRAPH © 1989 BY JILL KREMENTZ

DEACON CHAPIN

Until the mid-seventies, female staffers at *Rolling Stone* shared the workload but not the glory. That began to change in 1974 when copy chief Marianne Partridge (third from left, top) made editors out of former secretaries Harriet Fier, Christine Doudna and Sarah Lazin. Center: The brilliant Annie Leibovitz – with Wenner at the 1976 party for the Jimmy Carter staff – and shooting Wenner's friend Boz Scaggs for a *Rolling Stone* cover (right).

Final days in San Francisco. Wenner, associate editor Barbara Downey and art director Roger Black toast the future in 1977.

Harriet Fier (far right) whose ascension to managing editor sharply divided the New York staff. Among those who did not get along with Fier was Kate Wenner (left), Jann Wenner's sister, who was briefly in charge of the editor's ill-fated *College Papers*.

The two men responsible for bringing *Rolling
Stone* to New York were publisher Joe
Armstrong (left) and Wenner. But the former
quit three months before the move took place.

Reviews editor Dave Marsh (right) thought Wenner treated music critics "with contempt." Teenage rock journalist Cameron Crowe (below) left the fold to write *Fast Times at Ridgmont High,* and later married Heart guitarist Nancy Wilson.

The Reverend Charles M. Young.

The *Rolling Stone* softball team of 1978 was stomped by the Eagles after a longtime feud between magazine and band.

The Dry Heaves, living proof that rock journalists have no business onstage. (Clockwise from left) guitarist Jann Wenner (note broken string), vocalist Deborah Vare, keyboardist Jon Pareles, bassist Charles M. Young, drummer Timothy White and guitarist Kurt Loder.

Rolling Stone entered its third decade in a spiritual daze. Its chief sponsor, the music industry, was taking a brutal beating. Punk was dead; New Wave was a commercial failure. For the first time since 1973, when Joe Armstrong became *Rolling Stone*'s advertising director, the magazine's ad revenues began to plummet.

The *Rolling Stone* masthead included the names of Charles Perry, Jon Landau, Hunter Thompson, Ralph Steadman, Tim Cahill, Joe Eszterhas, Paul Scanlon, Joe Klein, Timothy Crouse, Cindy Ehrlich, Tim Ferris, Cameron Crowe and Michael Rogers. Not a one of them had the vaguest connection to the *Rolling Stone* staff of 1980. It was a list of the past, tattered by ambition and alienation. By the end of 1980, Ben Fong-Torres, Dave Marsh, Chuck Young, David Felton, Chet Flippo and Peter Herbst would join the ranks of the bygone. So would Harriet Fier.

The traditions were now bloodless and stripped of meaning. Stories were still late, but seldom were they worth the last-minute agony. Staffers put in long hours, staying up all night on Friday issue closings, visiting the Capri Lounge to obtain their fuel and spreading the white powder in shaky lines across the smooth teakwood tabletops of the twenty-third floor.

The office morale boosters, David Felton and Chuck Young, were now part of the morale problem. Even Timothy White was starting to burn out. More and more supplements were filling the magazine's pages, and on at least one occasion, supplement editor Alan Weitz was told by one of the boys on the twenty-seventh floor that if a particular audio manufacturer wasn't included in the issue's Ten Best Car Stereos list, the magazine stood to lose a full-page ad. Weitz heard this tune sung by the ad reps every time a supplement came up. This time, he did as he was advised and added the name to the car stereo list. What the hell difference did it make anymore?

Jann Wenner's missions were new and yet not. He'd started another doozy, *College Papers*, a magazine proposed by Jim Dunning as a youth marketing vehicle even as Dunning was getting seasick aboard a tuna boat off the coast of Florida. Jann hired his sister, Kate Wenner, to edit *College Papers*. Despite her lack of prepublication magazine experience, Kate was a sharp and focused editor, a natural. *College Papers* was not. Caught between Kate's desire to gear the magazine toward Ivy League tastes and Jann's yearning for a mass-market, *Animal House* approach, *College Papers* withered away after a few issues before anyone could figure out what it was.

The fast lane still preoccupied the editor, only now the road veered westward. Mr. Wenner had gone to Hollywood. His first three-picture, $150,000 movie development deal with Paramount bore no fruit, as the scripts of Chuck Young, Hunter Thompson and Ben Fong-Torres were never satisfactorily completed.

This deterred neither Jann nor Paramount, who signed Jann up to a similar deal. The studio had every reason to keep the faith. Irving Azoff had delivered gold with *Urban Cowboy*; editor Clay Felker, in whose *New York* the article that inspired *Saturday Night Fever* had appeared, was developing scripts as well. Record executive David Geffen was being courted by studios. Rock & roll had crossed over to the screen, and who would better capture this intersection than rock publishing's wunderkind?

Jann recruited Paul Scanlon to read scripts. A treatment was developed to showcase Bette Midler. Joe Eszterhas was paid $120,000 to write a screenplay set in Pittsburgh. Others came. All of them went. None of the projects undertaken by Jann S. Wenner Motion Pictures ever saw the light of day.

Of his disappointment in Hollywood, Jann Wenner would later shrug his shoulders and say, "I made a lot of friends." But the experience stung him. People limped away from show business every day of the week with hard-luck tales. But those people didn't have boxes and boxes of unused stationery to remind them of just how loudly they'd failed.

He did not say goodbye to Paramount, however, without inflicting his predicament upon *Rolling Stone*. So as to ingratiate himself with the studio, Jann ordered several cover stories, in the presence of Fier's subordinates, on performers featured in recently released Paramount movies. Harriet Fier fumed but did as she was told. Staffers were stunned to find the voice of the counterculture putting Mary Tyler Moore (*Ordinary People*) on its cover. Their astonishment became unvarnished disgust when they beheld the next cover: Michael Douglas and Jill Clayburgh (*It's My Turn*) embracing, accompanied by the headline "Sooooo Sexy."

Sooooo Sexy. Rolling Stone had hit rock bottom. Even Harriet Fier's closest allies wondered how she could sleep with herself after that one.

———

Jann Wenner's love affair with President Jimmy Carter ended just after it began. Annoyed that Jann's chaotic New York party for the Carter staff in 1976 had become such a celebrity-studded mess, the Democratic nominee's aides responded by giving the editor and his wife bad seats at the Democratic convention. Whatever access to the White House Jann had expected was not forthcoming. He met Carter once, in a receiving line, and was never invited for a personal visit at the Carters' new home on Pennsylvania Avenue.

By midway in the Carter term, items in "Random Notes" began to quote rock stars who'd met the President and come away unimpressed. Jann, of course, hardly stood alone in his disdain for Carter. The man who had run on a platform of sincerity and respect for the common man had appointed a Cabinet full of Georgia cronies and unimaginative Washington bureaucrats. Carter seemed to embody the worst traits of American liberalism: pious arrogance, indecisiveness and a fundamental ignorance of his own constituents. The peanut farmer from Plains, Georgia, was making a laughingstock of the counterculture that helped elect him.

Jann threw his support behind Ted Kennedy, who was challenging Carter for the Democratic nomination. A cover story on Kennedy hit the stands several weeks prior to the convention. The *Rolling Stone* office sponsored a party for Kennedy and his staff. Elaborate plans were made; Secret Service agents combed the floors. Jann Wenner made the rounds, toasting and flattering the various celebrities who cluttered the affair, but he looked in vain for Kennedy, who did not attend his own party.

Harriet Fier brought in *Village Voice* political columnists Alexander Cockburn and James Ridgway to cover the election. The editor gave his blessings, though in the past the columnists had slighted *Rolling Stone,* compelling Jann to refer to Cockburn as "Cockroach." The columnists' first installment, on George Bush, was brilliant; the succeeding ones, less so. No more or no less than any other political writers in America in 1980, Cockburn and Ridgway wrote as if they were themselves prisoners of the Carter malaise. Readers began to send letters begging for the return of Hunter Thompson. *Rolling Stone* issued this clearly frustrated reply:

Attention all you readers who are constantly on our backs about where the hell Dr. Hunter S. Thompson is. Please write to him yourself and tell him to get off his ass and start writing again: c/o Woody Creek, Colorado 81656.

—Ed.

As Kennedy's hopes faded, as the capture of the American hostages by Iranian terrorists underscored Carter's impotence, Jann Wenner began to do what most other Americans did: he considered Ronald Reagan, the Republican candidate. The former California governor didn't seem so bad to Jann, but he conveyed this to his business staffers, not to anyone on the twenty-third floor.

"He didn't run around saying 'I'm for Reagan,' " said one of his business lieutenants. "But he was thoroughly and totally disillusioned with Carter. I think his attitude was, 'Well, let's give Reagan a chance.' "

In the spring of 1970, when the voice of *Rolling Stone* was both smaller and prouder, Ralph J. Gleason explained to a reporter from the *Chicago Daily News* why he, and the generation in which he placed such unshakable faith, believed that the magic of rock & roll would set a nation free:

> I don't think it is possible for a generation that has listened to Bob Dylan and listened to "Maggie's Farm" and listened to "Desolation Row" and the rest of it even to look at the idea of working for IBM and retiring with a pension when they're 65 the way their fathers did. The message of rock has fundamentally altered their values in the way they look at the world, and that is going to affect society inevitably. There's no way to avoid it. It's going to be better as a result, if we haven't blown up the world in the meantime or choked to death through ecological overload. Eventually, Nixon dies. He will not live to be 150. When he and his kind die, the young people who take their places will be different, they can't help but be, and rock, the music, [will have] much to do with it. They can't help but be better.

October became November; the fall advanced. And one afternoon, Timothy White walked into managing editor Harriet Fier's office to find her staring out the window, crying. Jann had fired her. Because Jim Dunning had urged him to? Because a Straight Arrow board member had told Jann his magazine had gone flat? Because Jane Wenner was jealous? Because of the expenses on the Cockburn and Ridgway articles? Because she wouldn't fire one of her assistants at Jann's request? Because she was too stubborn at times, too compliant at others? Because it was a new decade, and Jann Wenner was entering it bruised and hostile and betrayed by the Jimmy Carters and the Harriet Fiers of his last ten years?

Because of all of these. Ring in the new. That month, Ronald Wilson Reagan became the oldest President of the United States in the nation's history. The victory was a landslide. Perhaps, when all the votes were counted, Ralph Gleason died a second time.

A Gathering

of Moss

Chapter Seventeen

WHEN THE MUSIC DIDN'T MATTER

*I*t seemed only fitting that John Lennon, the man featured on the cover of *Rolling Stone*'s first issue, should again grace the cover for the magazine's 1981 rebirth as a periodical printed on slick paper. But the issue Jann Wenner and his staff had in mind wasn't going to glorify the former Beatle, not by any means.

Double Fantasy, Lennon's first album in nearly six years, featured his wife, Yoko Ono, and a host of generally cheery, frivolous songs. Eager to promote the record, Lennon and Ono made themselves accessible to various reporters. Among these was *Rolling Stone* veteran contributor Jonathon Cott. The material Cott obtained wasn't much different from the quotes Lennon furnished other reporters. In fact, Harriet Fier's replacement as managing editor, Terry McDonell (the former senior editor of *Outside*), grumbled to staffers that the interview wasn't very newsworthy, adding that John Lennon hadn't done anything recently to merit prominent coverage in *Rolling Stone*. About the only notable features of the Cott interview transcript were the passages *Rolling Stone* wasn't about to print: the forty-year-old musician's vicious denunciations of editor Jann Wenner.

Lennon had never really forgiven Jann for publishing the famous December 1970 *Rolling Stone* interview in book form. Jann's repeated insistence that Straight Arrow Books chief Alan Rinzler was to blame did not quell Lennon's suspicion that the editor could not be trusted.

Not once since that interview had Lennon or Ono appeared on the magazine's cover—though Paul McCartney had on three different occasions, twice with his wife, Linda. Jann, of course, could hardly be blamed for John Lennon's virtual disappearance from the rock & roll landscape. Indeed, *Rolling Stone*—led by Jann and Ralph Gleason—sounded the loudest and most passionate blasts among the American media in opposing Lennon's deportation from the United States in the early seventies. But the man who once compared his band favorably with Jesus Christ perhaps felt a sense of entitlement with regard to *Rolling Stone*. Lennon's nude photograph with Ono in 1968, and the interviews he granted Cott in 1969 and Jann in 1970, helped sustain the magazine's credibility. *Rolling Stone*, those instances suggested, enjoyed a direct pipeline to Lennon's inner sanctum. Apparently, however, the pipeline worked in only one direction. John Lennon wasn't going to get any unearned strokes from a magazine that no longer needed his sponsorship.

It did not help matters that Jann Wenner's magazine no longer kissed Lennon's sandals every time the ex-Beatle put his mouth up to a microphone. His three albums of the seventies—*Imagine, Mind Games* and *Walls and Bridges*—drew irreverent analysis in *Rolling Stone*. *Double Fantasy* would be no different in this respect. Reviewer Stephen Holden's dispassionate remarks, balanced but hardly worshipful, were already set in type on the evening of December 8, 1980, the day a Beatles fan named Mark David Chapman paid a visit to the Dakota Apartments with a copy of *A Catcher in the Rye* and a Charter Arms .38 revolver in his jacket pockets.

Terry McDonell was drinking with his old *Outside* compadre Will Hearst at Runyon's on Second Avenue when news of the five bullets that killed John Lennon reached the managing editor. McDonell took a taxi to 745 Fifth Avenue and began making phone calls. There would still be a Lennon issue, but now of an entirely different nature. Among the first McDonell called was Jann, who was himself burning up the phone lines from his home on

East Sixty-sixth, across the park from where the legendary Beatle's blood stained the sidewalk.

Unlike McDonell, Jann was not phoning reporters. He was revisiting his past, tearfully seeking kind words from deserted friends. He called Jean Gleason, Ralph's widow, to reminisce about gentler times. He called Harriet Fier. He stayed on the phone for hours until there was no one left to call, and then Jann Wenner dispatched his driver to 2 West Seventy-second, where the editor stood across from the Dakota, one of hundreds of sobbing souls that bitter December night.

The next morning, a red-eyed Jann Wenner confiscated all office copies of the Cott transcript with Lennon's scathing remarks about the editor. The interview was excerpted; Stephen Holden's record review was rewritten. A moving photograph of a naked John Lennon clinging to a fully clothed Yoko Ono—taken by Annie Leibovitz on the afternoon of Lennon's death—was placed on the cover without any headlines or captions. Chet Flippo, Dave Marsh, Greil Marcus and Jan Morris contributed their memories and reportage. Chuck Young's description of the bizarre, Felliniesque weeklong crowd vigil outside the Dakota didn't run. Deemed equally inappropriate by Jann were the eyewitness accounts of the shooting—which caused the editor to burst into tears when McDonell described them to him—and a profile of Mark David Chapman. This was not a time for objectivity. This was a time for remembering, for praising, for grieving and for begging forgiveness of the dead.

Without telling his editors, Jann wrote in tiny, scratchy letters within the fold of the issue:

John, I love you I miss you you're with God I'll do what I said "Yoko hold on"—I'll make sure, I promise XXX Jann

The Lennon memorial issue sold a record 1.45 million copies. As with the Elvis issue (which sold just over a million copies), and the Jimi Hendrix and Janis Joplin issues years before, the tribute to the fallen Beatle displayed *Rolling Stone*'s continued effectiveness as the focal point of a generation's celebration and mourning.

———

At the time, however, the *Rolling Stone* business staff was mourning a different matter. In 1977, the year Joe Armstrong quit as publisher, *Rolling Stone* had reached a peak of 1,241 advertising pages. That figure plateaued in 1978, though a sizable ad rate increase allowed revenues to jump 25 percent. After 1978, however, the slide began. Only 1,162 pages were sold in 1979, and only 985 in 1980.

The business staff blamed music—both the economically depressed state of the industry and the undesirable image rock & roll triggered in the minds of advertisers. Major clients were no longer enraptured by magazines catering to the 18–24 age bracket. The baby-boomers were growing up, having children, rocking out less and less.

Rolling Stone conducted one readership study after the next, hoping to come up with data to convince Madison Avenue that its readership was older and more upscale than otherwise perceived. And one study after the next defined the average *Rolling Stone* readers: eighteen-year-old boys. Jim Dunning, Kent Brownridge and Claeys Bahrenburg knew the numbers would have to improve if the magazine wanted to enter a comfortable profit picture.

No longer a cultural phenomenon, rock & roll was now a fact of everyday existence—a steady sound track rather than a rousing anthem. In 1981, rock & roll still stood, but the industry behind the sound was infirm and slouching in a wheelchair. In the early eighties, *Rolling Stone* rolled away from its crippled old friend. The music didn't matter anymore.

"We were trying to make the magazine for older people," said Terry McDonell. "We were trying to deemphasize music and do more intensive movie coverage, start TV coverage and run fiction now and again. Instead of rock & roll stars, we put a lot of people who were not in the music business on the cover. Partially that was a reflection of the interests of those of us who were working there, which in turn was a reflection of what was going on in the culture. Music wasn't that interesting."

Not that McDonell had ever been in the business of following music trends. The former *Outside* senior editor had the newsroom acumen of John Burks, with a fondness for the kind of literary adventurousness that made *Esquire* famous in the sixties—and *Rolling Stone* famous in the early seventies. After quitting *Outside*, McDonell had gone on to start *Rocky Mountain* magazine, an often brilliant, if short-lived Denver-based publication that featured essays by Western literary eminences like Thomas McGuane, Peter Matthiessen, James Salter and William Kittredge, along with the work of *Rolling Stone* stars like Tim Cahill, Michael Rogers and Howard Kohn.

What caught Jann's eye, however, was the exclusive cover story McDonell had scored on Robert Redford for *Rocky Mountain* in its June 1979 issue. That McDonell appreciated the drawing power of a Redford and could deliver an extensive interview (conducted by Michael Rogers) said something about the man's professionalism. Jann asked him to be the editor of *Look*. McDonell declined, and after *Rocky Mountain* folded he wrote a novel, sold it and bought a ranch in Montana.

When the call came in November of 1980, McDonell told Jann he'd have to think about it. Later he phoned the office and asked longtime receptionist Judy Lawrence, "What's Jann like these days? Has he gone completely New York?" Still, the gig of managing a magazine that at one time "had run without question the best journalism I'd ever read" was too good to pass up. Besides, Jann knew what he was getting with Terry McDonell, and it wasn't a rock groupie. As writer P. J. O'Rourke would tell Jann, "Terry wouldn't know the difference between the Motels and the Ashtrays."

The *Rolling Stone* staffers didn't know quite what to make of the new managing editor. McDonell showed up for work that first day in his boots and jeans, a big and rugged rancher, utterly antithetical to Harriet Fier. He put out a beefy hand to the switchboard operator, Chris Connelly. "My name is McDonell," he said.

End of conversation. McDonell stalked past the reception room, walked into Harriet Fier's old office, picked up the telephone and did not emerge for the rest of the morning. Connelly said later, "It was like the beginning of a television series."

Indeed, Chuck Young called McDonell Lou Grant. His gruff exterior took some getting used to, and Harriet Fier's pet writers never did manage to adapt to McDonell. Timothy White continued to write through the middle of 1981, but with dwindling spiritedness. His friends Young, Flippo, Felton and Fier were gone. Jann's tantrums, in the wake of his failed foray into Hollywood, were jangling White's nerves. And McDonell, for all his talents, seemed altogether alien to the *Rolling Stone* experience as White knew and lived it. There McDonell was, in Harriet's old office, making one call after the next so as to obtain the serial rights to *The Hotel New Hampshire*, by John Irving. Hey, Irving was great and all, but excerpting novels was the kind of thing *Esquire* did, not *Rolling Stone*. In the meantime, McDonell had discontinued the practice of running authors' bylines on the cover—a tradition White had long advocated, arguing that it benefited both the magazine and its writers. McDonell retorted that cover bylines should be an honor, not a routine.

White didn't feel like arguing. His main quarrel was with Jann anyway. Their relationship had never been a comfortable one. Even when the two spent Sundays together at a movie theater, Jann would pepper his writer with very personal questions, adding, "I gotta figure you out, Timbo, I gotta figure you out." White got the distinct impression his boss was probing for weaknesses.

Jann did not have to look hard. Timothy White harbored an Old World work ethic matched only by the fiercely protective Irish pride he placed in his work. When he was at *Crawdaddy!*, White fired off an angry letter to *Rolling Stone* reviews editor Dave Marsh after one of Marsh's reviewers quoted heavily from a White article on Beach Boy Brian Wilson without attributing the quotes. (White and Marsh never got along after that.) Later, *Rolling Stone*'s most prolific writer saw red when Jann waved one of Jim Dunning's productivity studies in his face, suggesting that Timothy White wasn't working hard enough to earn his keep.

After the Lennon memorial issue was put to bed, Jann informed White that the writer's upcoming exclusive profiles on Walter Cronkite and his replacement at CBS News, Dan Rather, would simply run in question-and-answer format, without any embellishment. White protested, but the editor snapped, "You work for me. You'll do what I tell you to do."

White would have quit right then, but he was hot on the trail of a Frank Sinatra interview—a coup of virtually historic proportions, as the wall of bodyguards and managers surrounding Ol' Blue Eyes had not been penetrated by the press in many a year. But White had impressed Sinatra's agent, Lee Solters, who finally, after a year's wooing, relented.

"Jann," White said, the excitement surging out of every pore as he stood over the editor seated at his desk, "I just talked to Lee Solters, and the Sinatra thing is settled. He's gonna do it, and Annie's gonna take the photos, and it's a happening thing."

Jann looked up. His eyes were as flat as a butcher blade. He had only one thing to say to Timothy White: "Why you?"

A couple of weeks later, White returned from an interview with Goldie Hawn on the West Coast to see a news blurb by Howard Kohn on Sinatra's alleged ties to the mob, laid out and ready to roll. White stormed into McDonell's office and demanded to know what in the hell was going on. The managing editor shrugged. "Jann called Howard," he began.

"Are you insane?" yelled White. "I had an interview with Sinatra all set up! This is gonna completely queer the deal!"

McDonell gaped. "I had no idea you were so close to getting the interview," he apologized.

White shook his head. "I'm gone," he said, and so he was.

McDonell deeply regretted the Sinatra episode, and later wrote Lee Solters, exonerating White from the whole mess. Apart from this blemish, Terry McDonell spent his first few months undoing the damage wrought during Harriet Fier's tenure. Deadlines were enforced, thus shortening office hours; Jann's abusive editorial meetings were abandoned. Headlines became meaningful, less pun-stricken. And the same people who thought Fier easy prey for Jann knew McDonell was a different story.

After the managing editor bolted out of Jann's office one afternoon, his face wrinkled with wrath, a staffer asked, "Are you and Jann through meeting?"

"Jann and I don't meet," growled McDonell. "We collide."

That collision began during their first week together. When Jann refused to formulate the Lennon issue as a comprehensive news package, complete with eyewitness scenes and a profile of the killer, McDonell threatened to quit. The managing editor stayed only after promises of autonomy were issued. The solemnity of these oaths was debatable, as McDonell learned when Wenner buddies Peter Wolf of the J. Geils Band and Art Garfunkel landed on back-to-back covers in 1982.

But Terry McDonell's biggest brawls were with Jim Dunning, who in McDonell's view "had no business in journalism. I never blew a budget, but I would continually get these preposterous memos about financial planning. I was allotted about $1,000 per page in the budget, which was fine—I would spend $1,500 on this page, $500 on the next. Dunning would not go for that. We would have endless arguments, with him saying things like 'If you can do this page for $500, why do you have to spend $1,500 on this one?' I once slammed the door so hard in his office that the doorknob went through the wall."

McDonell didn't win all the battles, but editorial staffers appreciated the vitality he instilled in the magazine's pages. As expected, McDonell brought his Western literary cadre to *Rolling Stone*. But he also enticed some of the magazine's finest writers from the past to quit their disaffection and return to the fold. Howard Kohn was assigned the Washington bureau and produced "Newsfront," the section that now appeared at the front of each issue. Tim Cahill was told he could write on whatever he pleased, and so chose Jack Nicholson and other movie personalities. Greil Marcus, who had stopped doing his book column—"It wouldn't have made any sense to continue in the midst of all that glitz," he said—was given the same sort of offer, and ended up interviewing Elvis Costello and author John Irving.

"I wanted the magazine to be informed by a sense of a larger world," said McDonell. "I wanted to bring back writers who had a political orientation to whatever they wrote about. Thus did I immediately go and drag Joe Klein screaming back into *Rolling Stone*. Joe Klein is not the kind of guy you fire, after all. You just don't. He's too good."

Then McDonell found the biggest, sharpest treble hook in his tackle box and cast it out to Woody Creek, Colorado. He wanted Hunter Thompson back.

Thompson and Jann continued to stay in touch, but the latter had essentially given up on the former's ability to contribute to *Rolling Stone* in a continuing, meaningful manner. In 1977, the Gonzo journalist penned an uncharacteristically sentimental tribute to Oscar Zeta Acosta, his Chicano attorney sidekick, long presumed dead. Six months later, however, Thompson produced for Harriet Fier the two-part Ali article that amounted to lame self-parody. Fier got nothing more from him after that.

Thompson's wealth and celebrity somehow rose in inverse proportion to his output. He'd sold his life story to Universal Artists for $100,000, resulting in *Where the Buffalo Roam*, a surprisingly dull and predictable movie starring Bill Murray as Thompson. Around the time of the film's release in 1980, Thompson moved to Hawaii for a year, during which time he wrote *The Curse of Lono*, a book spinning off an assignment *Running* magazine gave him to cover a marathon in Honolulu. His editor at Bantam Books, one Alan Rinzler, was compelled to raid Thompson's office after the writer flouted his deadline and make off with every grocery bag and napkin that had been scrawled upon, which motley collection became the manuscript for *The Curse of Lono*, for which Hunter Thompson netted another six figures.

At the time McDonell wrote Thompson from a hotel in Baja California, proposing a $50,000 fee for twenty-five columns a year, the writer had just sold the film rights to a book in progress for $250,000. Money was the last thing he needed; twenty-five deadlines a year, the next-to-last. Also, knew Hunter Thompson, the world had changed since his days of comparing Nixon to Hitler and Humphrey to a rodent in heat. Replying to McDonell, he wrote:

We are no longer operating on the ground rules of the *New York Times vs. Sullivan*, which I was fortunate to have on my side for ten very volatile years. The rules are a bit different now. *Time vs. Firestone, Goertz vs. Chicago*, etc. And it may be that the new legal definition(s) of libel could make my kind of journalism too risky to have any fun with. . . . I am a recognized expert on libel in its most extreme forms, & if I decide to write a regular "column" it will almost certainly raise questions in that area. I will naturally have to make my peace with the new rules, whatever they are. . . .

The *real* question is whether or not writing a regular high-profile "column" on the back page of every issue of *Rolling Stone* would be *a good thing for me to do.* Because it would obviously—if it works —be a good and demonstrably profitable thing for *RS.*

Thompson agreed to give the column a whirl, but failed to follow through. He did, however, suggest an acceptable replacement: William Greider, the *Washington Post's* fine national affairs reporter who had indicated to Thompson his restlessness at the *Post.* Greider's column was launched in the summer of 1982, and relentlessly hammered away at the Reagan administration while the rest of the news media genuflected. Readership surveys during this intensely conservative period showed that *Rolling Stone's* readers by and large ignored Greider's well-researched harangues, but McDonell and Jann stuck with the columnist nonetheless.

Meanwhile, McDonell baited the hook with another proposition: a long feature on the celebrated divorce trial between Peter and Roxanne Pulitzer in Palm Beach, Florida. Though other editors eventually worked on the piece, it was Terry McDonell's brilliant conception, with all the obvious Gonzo elements: sexual perversity (rumors had Roxanne Pulitzer sleeping with women, animals and, finally, a trumpet), a campaignlike media circus and the decadence of the bourgeoisie.

"And I was in that mood," wrote Thompson. "I needed a carnival in my life: whoop it up with the rich for a while, drink gin, drive convertibles, snort cocaine and frolic with beautiful lesbians. Never mind the story. It would take care of itself."

The Gonzo journalist entered Florida with a splash, ripped to the tits on cocaine and terrorizing car rental agencies while the media gaped in awe. Thompson declared that he'd uncovered a missing link in the messy divorce—meaning drugs, though he could prove nothing and finally settled for declaring West Palm Beach the bestiality capital of the world. Whereupon Hunter Thompson lashed out his article, insert by insert, and then departed to the Ramrod Key to begin a novel on "the Cuban flotilla trade," leaving West Palm Beach to ponder what it had seen.

The 10,500-word "A Dog Took My Place" (a title *Rolling Stone's* attorneys tried to veto, fearing libel suits) was Hunter Thompson's finest piece since his 1972 campaign writings: ferocious but coherent, with an attention to detail and character development he'd lacked since consigning Nixon to the rubble of Watergate.

> Roxanne Pulitzer is not a beautiful woman. There is nothing especially striking about her body or facial bone structure, and at age thirty-one, she looks more like a jaded senior stewardess from Pan Am than an international sex symbol. Ten years on the Palm Beach Express have taken their toll, and she would have to do more than just sweat off ten pounds to compete for naked space in the men's magazines. Her legs are too thin, her hips are too wide, and her skin is a bit too loose for modeling work. But she has a definite physical presence. There is no mistaking the aura of good-humored out-front sexuality. This is clearly a woman who likes to sleep late in the morning.

The New Journalism saw its return under Terry McDonell. The music section, in the meantime, was moved to the back of the magazine, like a senile uncle in the basement. It was a grim concession to commercial reality: the most interesting music in the early eighties wasn't selling, and the most popular stuff was simply disposable. "We were in hand-to-hand combat with that fact every week," said Chris Connelly. "The bands that were selling records were bands like REO Speedwagon and Foreigner—bands that you just knew, in your gut, weren't going to sell on the cover."

Under Terry McDonell, outstanding profiles were written of Fleetwood Mac's spacey Stevie Nicks (by Timothy White), of the terminally underappreciated Ringo Starr (by eventual senior editor Brant Mewborn) and of reformed alcoholic Warren Zevon (by Paul Nelson). Just as often, however, the music writing in McDonell's *Rolling Stone* reflected frustration. Staffers wrote about the facelessness of eighties rock, about the commercial failure of New Wave. A particularly wistful issue saw *Rolling Stone* "Look Back with Longing" at the sixties, when music fueled ideas and action. One evening, McDonell, Jann and Hunter Thompson went so far as to discuss writing an essay proclaiming "the death of rock & roll."

The essay was canned, but its sentiment poisoned the pages of *Rolling Stone* throughout the early eighties. The September 17, 1981, issue featured Jim Morrison on the cover with a headline that would become one of the magazine's most memorable: "Jim Morrison: He's hot, he's sexy and he's dead." (Though Jann Wenner today insists that the headline was his, current and former staffers dispute this. Assistant managing editor David Rosenthal, they say, came up with the line. In fact, Rosenthal insists that Jann at first considered the headline too risqué, and gave in only when no alternative could be conceived.) Though the story's premise was a revived infatuation with the Doors' vocalist, the cynical tone of the article was set in the lead, in which a young girl being interviewed said she loved Jim Morrison, but admitted she couldn't name any of the Doors' songs. The suggestion was plain: today's fans don't care about music; they want a superstar. But was this really their yearning, or *Rolling Stone*'s?

Three issues later, *Rolling Stone* published excerpts from a controversial Elvis Presley biography by Albert Goldman. McDonell had obtained an advance copy of the book and passed it on to Dave Marsh, who thought the unflattering portrait was trashy, and thus commercially very viable. That was enough for McDonell, who said, "I believed in big audiences and I wanted to expand the magazine's circulation, and rock & roll wasn't sacred to me—or Elvis Presley wasn't."

Jann had to be convinced. His mentor, Ralph Gleason, once labeled Goldman a charlatan in the pages of *Rolling Stone* for the author's ugly depiction of Lenny Bruce. Only four years ago, *Rolling Stone* had virtually deified Presley: "the first King we ever had," "How Great Thou Art . . ." But enough. Goldman's stuff was controversial, he wrote Jean Gleason by way of apology, and controversy was cold cash. Besides, McDonell had bought the serial rights for a meager $8,000. That was a small price to pay for a bareback ride on rock & roll's most sacred cow.

(Almost exactly eight years later, *Rolling Stone* would denounce Albert Goldman for his biography of John Lennon, a figure nearer and dearer to Jann than Elvis. The October 20, 1988, issue mounted its rebuttal with an article attacking Goldman's research methods—and more tellingly, with an excerpt from the Ono-sponsored book *Imagine* along with photographs of Lennon hugging anyone within reach and beaming wholesomely. As Jann told *Newsweek* reporter David Gates: "There is nothing mean or nasty in John's life.")

Terry McDonell was having his way with things. The Presley excerpts sold well (though hate mail arrived by the ream), newsstand figures were way up over those of 1980, he was revitalizing the magazine's literary spirit and did not have to make rock & roll his major concern. That was now the responsibility of *Record*, a new sister publication established to attract music advertisers while *Rolling Stone* levitated to more "adult" climes. Yet McDonell had his own writing and publishing interests, and at times was given to sigh, "Here I am, almost forty years old, and I'm having to check with Fleetwood

Mac about a 'Random Note.' " His contract with Jann had expired, was renewed and expired again, and by the end of 1982 McDonell was ready to move on. He did so, the only *Rolling Stone* managing editor ever to leave under amicable circumstances.

Assistant managing editor David Rosenthal was McDonell's replacement. Rosenthal, formerly the executive editor of *New York*, wiped *Rolling Stone*'s journalistic slate clean. Replacing the magazine's hallowed old voices were names from Rosenthal's Rolodex: Mark Jacobson, Gerri Hirshey, Rosemary Breslin, Lewis Grossberger, Lynn Hirschberg, Steven Levy, Aaron Latham, Nancy Collins. Some of them were very good, and what most of them did best was what *Rolling Stone* now emphasized: movies and television. Certainly Rosenthal, who himself penned profiles of Meryl Streep and Jessica Lange, was happy with this. So were the business lieutenants, who saw the magazine's median age climb dramatically from 1982 to 1983.

And Jann Wenner was happy too. *Rolling Stone* was making money without him having to lord over Rosenthal. He could attend to his own affairs, which by 1982 had almost nothing to do with music.

———

"In December 1980," said Jann during a speech he gave at a luncheon in 1982, "a friend of mine was shot, murdered in New York City. It was one of those senseless, meaningless killings; and might never have occurred— or at least not have ended in death—were it not for the availability of handguns. . . . I am referring to John Lennon. The days and weeks following his death were among the most unhappy and hopeless of my entire life. My despair was widely felt."

After despairing, Jann reacted as he always did: he sought to use *Rolling Stone* to attain his goals—in this case, to push for gun-control legislation.

"He adopted gun control as a personal cause," said Howard Kohn, whom Jann assigned to write an article on the National Rifle Association. "I had no disagreement, but it wasn't my cause or my passion. But he was passionate about me doing it."

Jann wanted Kohn to use his acclaimed investigative powers to take down the gun lobby—"to break new ground and arouse public anger about the NRA," said Kohn. But the writer's research pointed to a glum conclusion: "The reason the NRA is so damn successful is that people like their idea. I didn't put this in the story, but I talked to various congressional leaders, and regardless of what they said in public, the fact was that even liberal congressmen owned guns, and so did their aides and their constituents.

"I don't think Jann knew what he wanted. But what he certainly didn't want to hear, what no one wants to hear, is that the heart of the enemy is yourself and your friends."

Jann placed Kohn's investigation on the cover of the May 14, 1981, issue, the last purely political cover *Rolling Stone* would run. But the article's fatalistic message disappointed him, as did the indifference accorded its publication. The editor then tried a new approach. He formed the Foundation on Violence in America, and with $75,000 that he raised, commissioned a poll by Peter D. Hart Associates to determine public attitudes on handgun control. The results confirmed Kohn's thesis, but suggested that the public could be swayed to support gun control if policemen were used to educate their communities about the dangers of handguns.

Jann contacted Betsy Gotbaum, director of the New York City Police Foundation, and asked her to spearhead his organization. "He said that he not only had a lot of money in his foundation," said Gotbaum, "but that he could raise an enormous amount of money because of his connection to rock stars."

Though Gotbaum was happy where she was, the offer flattered her, and the apparent depth of Jann's financial well added further appeal. While she deliberated, Gotbaum and her husband received several calls from associates who were well aware of Jann's reputation as a businessman. "You'd be making a big mistake," they told her. Among these was an editor of a major New York daily, who wrote a long letter outlining Jann's past transgressions. Another was one of Jann's past editors, a woman Gotbaum didn't even know.

Gotbaum took the job anyway, changed the organization's name to the National Alliance Against Violence and moved her headquarters onto the twenty-seventh floor of 745 Fifth Avenue. Instantly she encountered problems. The foundation had only $38,000. Her new boss was impatient for results but refused to deliver his or his rock friends' money. It occurred to Gotbaum that Jann was interested in using her and her husband, Victor— the city's well-known union leader—for social cachet. But after a dinner party meant to introduce Jann to various social notables, Victor Gotbaum commented to his wife that Jann Wenner's drunken behavior had thoroughly embarrassed him and his friends and that he would have no part of her boorish new employer.

Gotbaum could hardly blame her husband, or foundations who didn't want to award grants on account of *Rolling Stone*'s "drug aura." After all, there was Jann in his office, openly snorting cocaine and chugging vodka, or showing up for meetings red-faced and belching. (This despite the cocaine-related death of his friend John Belushi and himself suffering a blocked gallbladder that almost necessitated an operation. The doctors advised Jann to lead a less adventurous lifestyle, but as Jann could remorselessly subvert any diet, so too could he flout physician's orders.) Gotbaum once insisted that Jann cut his virtually shoulder-length hair before meeting with city officials. She was awarded a telephone call by Jane Wenner, who heatedly advised a startled Gotbaum to keep her nose out of Jann's personal affairs.

Betsy Gotbaum began to believe she'd bitten off more than she could chew by coming to work for Jann Wenner. He wrote her long, incredibly fond letters for a time, saying he felt closer to her than to anyone but his wife. Then the letters stopped. Jann accused Gotbaum of incompetence, and at a board meeting proposed giving half of the National Alliance Against Violence's funds to another organization. The board voted him down. Jann did it anyway. Betsy Gotbaum quit, the Alliance was disbanded and in 1988 the American public elected a lifetime member of the National Rifle Association as its forty-first President.

––––

Though Jann would tell *Mother Jones* in 1986 that "Ronald Reagan has done a decent job in some ways," the editor was offended by Reagan's hawkish sensibilities. "Jann thought Reagan's total militancy towards the Russians was just crazy," said a business staffer.

This predisposed Jann in favor of Senator Alan Cranston, who in 1983 announced that he was running for the presidency. Cranston, a veteran liberal politician from southern California, rested his candidacy on the issue of nuclear disarmament, and was regarded by the press as the darkest of Democratic dark horses.

But Jann was thoroughly taken by Cranston's performance at one of *Rolling Stone*'s editorial "meet the candidate" roundtables in 1983. (Such meetings were generally sluggish, as they were held in the morning, when *Rolling Stone* staffers were not at their most inquisitive. Bill Greider, however, culled useful information for his columns, and Jann seemed entranced that the 1984 Democratic candidates were coming to *him*, one by one. The only ungracious visitor was Walter Mondale, who was not overly fond of a *Rolling Stone* article depicting him as "monochromatic." He huffily informed his audience, "I have more than one suit!") Jann's predictable first impulse was to support Cranston editorially, and assigned Bill Greider to write a profile of the candidate.

The profile was not completely flattering. Though Greider cited Cranston's fine legislative achievements, he also noted that the senator was given to pork-barreling and shirking the Liberal Conscience role for that of Consummate Politician. "I thought it was a very fair piece," said David Rosenthal. "I would say it was more favorable than not favorable, but there were some digs in there. And Jann wanted all the digs out. He marked up the galleys and crossed out every negative reference in the piece."

Rosenthal went to the mat with his boss on Greider's behalf, and Jann eventually let the piece stand. But this did not mitigate his enthusiasm for Cranston. When it became clear that the best way to help the candidate at this point was financial, Jann volunteered to host a fundraiser. Attending the thousand-dollar-a-plate luncheon were Yoko Ono, Peter Wolf, David Cassidy and other rock cronies. The benefit netted over $25,000, more than Cranston had received from any group thus far.

"Alan instantly thought he had hit the jackpot," said one of the liaisons between the editor and the candidate. "He figured Jann was going to organize rock stars to put on concerts for him and make all this money." Cranston awarded Jann the title of finance director, and there ensued dizzy talk of a million-dollar concert, of the youth vote being delivered, of Cranston staging an astonishing upset.

Yet none of this was to be. When Cranston's aides point-blank asked Jann about making the rock benefit a reality, the editor balked. "I can't make a rock star do anything," Jann told them. "It's flattering that you think I have this power, but I don't. The magazine frequently criticizes these people, they're beholden to no one and I can't order them to put on a rock concert. You can do it just as easily as I could."

This was not exactly what Cranston's operatives wanted to hear. They hadn't made Jann Wenner their finance director to give the editor something to brag about at parties. Money talked, and Jann wasn't delivering. Alan Cranston's funds withered away before the primaries officially began, and the man *Rolling Stone* dubbed "monochromatic" took the 1984 Democratic nomination before losing to Reagan in a landslide.

———

Throughout 1983, Jann Wenner spent his days on planes, in board meetings and at his house in East Hampton. He seldom showed up at 745 Fifth Avenue more often than twice a week. The magazine he entrusted to his two *Rolling Stone* chiefs, associate publisher Kent Brownridge and managing editor David Rosenthal.

"Ours was a varying relationship, to say the least," said Rosenthal of his dealings with Brownridge. At *New York,* working with both Clay Felker and Joe Armstrong, Rosenthal was accustomed to the classic church/state division between editorial and business. At *Rolling Stone,* he found the sales staff reviewing copy before it went to press and Brownridge regularly vetoing photographs or cartoons that showed bare buttocks, dildos and the like.

Yet Brownridge had educated himself well in the matter of magazine publishing, and Rosenthal himself understood their joint mission: to "age" *Rolling Stone*'s readership from a median age of twenty-three to twenty-five by shifting coverage away from music, in the process attracting greater ad revenues. To aid the cause, Jann recruited Henry Marks, the man credited with scrubbing up *Playboy*'s lascivious image and increasing that magazine's ad pages from 776 in 1976 to 1,433 in 1980.

Perhaps Rosenthal pursued this mission too zealously. He came to be known, in writer Lynn Hirschberg's words, as an editor who "hated rock & roll and actively said so." Under Rosenthal, said another of the managing editor's writers, "there was an attitude that music wasn't worthy of respect, that music should be treated with a certain snottiness."

As Rosenthal would admit, "I had expressed to Jann my *complete* disinterest in running a rock & roll magazine. And he knew that one of the only reasons I went to work there was the sense, both from Terry and Jann, that this was not going to be a rock & roll magazine anymore—it would be a general-interest magazine, with a special coverage of music."

Rosenthal had never read an issue of *Rolling Stone* before coming to work for Jann, nor did he care much about what the magazine once stood for. All the same, music coverage did not entirely suffer under his reign. The May 26, 1983, issue described a strange but vital South Bronx music/dance phenomenon known as hip-hop—thus predating the general press's discovery of rap music by several years. For the first time since the infamous Village People cover of April 19, 1979, Rosenthal put a black musician on the cover of *Rolling Stone.* That musician was Michael Jackson, on the eve of his chart-busting album *Thriller.* Though the issue did not sell particularly well, the article on Jackson by Gerri Hirshey garnered much attention later, as it was the last interview the timid young star would ever grant.

Rosenthal didn't know much about rock, so he relied on the tastes of his writers: former switchboard operator Chris Connelly, Kurt Loder, Parke Puterbaugh and music editor Jim Henke. In many ways, his dispassion freed him to approach music from a more journalistic standpoint. Visually or artistically off-the-beam artists like Annie Lennox of the Eurythmics, Boy

George of Culture Club, Prince and the Talking Heads intrigued him, as did the Blitz/New Romantic fashion movement emanating from England. Each became cover stories (except for the Talking Heads—not mainstream enough, Jann decreed); and so it happened that Rosenthal, the Man Who Hated Rock & Roll, brought *Rolling Stone* closer to the musical cutting edge than it had been in years.

But David Rosenthal also brought a certain venom to which the magazine was not accustomed. Because he was a writer's editor, his allegiance was to the story, not the subject. At times, the results were tough but effective. Too often, however, Rosenthal's *Rolling Stone* was malignant with cynicism. The magazine sponsored contests on "the year's worst rock video" and "the last funny thing said on *Saturday Night Live*." A special issue was devoted to "the Age of Junk," with articles on junk food, junk sex, junk government and the junk generation of the eighties. "The Most Overrated People in America" were listed; among those included were Albert Goldman and John Irving, both published in *Rolling Stone* less than two years ago. Jann Wenner would later declare of his former managing editor, "It wasn't just that he hated rock & roll. He truly hated everything."

The magazine's pages took on a gray pallor. Articles dwelled on trans-sexual murders, a son killing a father, a feminist implicated in two murders; the back page was now devoted to obituaries; and Rosenthal himself was quoted in newspapers about the commercial viability of dead musicians. Brilliant and meaningful articles on AIDS (one of the very first ever published) and rich kids addicted to heroin seemed lost amid the tangle of this necrophilic orgy.

Though Rosenthal's disinterest in music sometimes resulted in rock pieces with interesting angles, the effect was often cheap and degrading. The punnish cover headline on a David Bowie story—"David Bowie Straight"—said it all: *Rolling Stone* wasn't interested in Bowie's new music, but rather in his new heterosexual wardrobe. The Duran Duran cover story, written by music editor Jim Henke, began with the revelation that vocalist Simon LeBon wore blue underwear.

Perhaps David Rosenthal figured that readers wouldn't notice the condescension, or wouldn't care. Like John Walsh and Terry McDonell before him, Rosenthal was a deft editor, popular among most staffers and highly respected in the publishing business. His dispassionate sensibilities would have been a boon to most any other magazine. At 745 Fifth Avenue, however, he seemed to mock *Rolling Stone*'s very premise. And if the music didn't matter, its ennobling institutions mattered even less. Certainly "The *Rolling Stone* Interview" under David Rosenthal ended all pretense of integrity. Kurt Loder, the magazine's best music writer, pumped Joan Baez for details about her sex life and Bob Dylan's religious conversion. Nancy Collins's formidable interviewing skills were unleashed to quiz John Travolta on his sexual obsessions. The *Rolling Stone* motto of "All the News That Fits" seemed damningly quaint by 1983; "Inquiring Minds Want to Know" was, sadly, already taken.

————

Two funny things happened in the fall of 1983 that David Rosenthal did not find amusing.

The managing editor was sitting behind his desk one Monday morning when Jann popped in and announced cheerily, "I'm back, and I'm really gonna be running things now."

Rosenthal didn't take this seriously. Then he had to. True to his word, the editor resumed his old practice of tearing up issues at the last minute, ordering cover changes, firing off a barrage of memos through the newly installed office computer system and cracking the managerial whip. (When Jann discovered that an issue's table of contents didn't track to the correct page, he ordered an investigation to determine who was at fault. The blame fell to copy chief Parke Puterbaugh. Jann gave in to Rosenthal's plea not to fire Puterbaugh—one of the staff's best music writers—but insisted that the copy chief be docked for his transgression.)

"It's Jann's candy store," Rosenthal would remind himself. If the editor shot down the managing editor's movie covers in favor of a Mick Jagger or a Beatles photograph—"evergreen covers," Kent Brownridge called these, instant cash—then that was his prerogative.

But something more ominous was in the wind. Henry Marks, the man brought in to engineer *Rolling Stone*'s demographic shift to a more adult readership, was up in arms. They'd *over*succeeded, Marks was moaning. The readership was now *too* old. All those covers of Jessica Lange, Dudley Moore, Sean Connery and bodybuilders had attracted a sizable number of readers in the thirty-five-plus age category—above and beyond the coveted twenty-five-to-thirty-four bracket, and thus utterly worthless as a marketing tool. In the meantime, clients were now scrambling about like rats in a silo, trying to sink their teeth into a burgeoning youth market that had all of a sudden taken up a most bizarre battle cry: *I want my MTV.*

When twenty-seven-year-old MTV masterplanner Bob Pittman took Jann Wenner out to lunch in 1981 to discuss his scheme, the editor informed Pittman, "It'll never work. People don't want to hear the same thing again and again, day in and day out."

By the fall of 1983, however, the music video station had raided millions of homes, revolutionized the pop-music charts and accomplished what the music industry, radio programmers and *Rolling Stone* could not accomplish: it attached faces to sounds. Now a transfixed fifteen-year-old boy in Des Moines could *see* Boy George, Billy Idol, Cyndi Lauper and Men at Work —artists whose music the boy might have ignored on radio, whose worldviews he might have deemed unworthy of scrutiny in the pages of *Rolling Stone*. Visual personas could be attached to the otherwise mundane: Phil Collins would now be cast as an impish blue-eyed soul man, Huey Lewis as pop music's Regular Guy, ZZ Top as hirsute pranksters with inexplicable sex appeal. *Everyone* would have sex appeal. Every over-the-hill rocker would appear on the television screen with a brace of miniskirted vixens at his boots. No fantasy would go unconsummated. *I want my MTV!*

Its impact on the industry was manifold and simply impossible to ignore or discount. "MTV essentially re-created Top 40 radio," said senior editor Chris Connelly, who would one day join the station's ranks as an entertainment newscaster. "In particular, it got women and dance music back into the mainstream." New bands broke into the marketplace with unprecedented speed. Veteran artists left for dead now got new hairdressers and enjoyed spectacular resurrections. (None more than Tina Turner, onto whose bandwagon *Rolling Stone* climbed only after MTV made her suitably commercial. Senior editor Brant Mewborn, the magazine's resident champion of sixties music, pushed hard for a major Turner feature, but Jann and the other editors waved him off. Said Mewborn, "The attitude was, 'Tina Turner? Who cares? She's not even with Ike anymore.'")

If there existed a new wave of music marketing, this was it. Slumping record companies took notice, and so did Jann Wenner, who was well aware that advertising budgets were limited and MTV would likely command a hefty percentage. Jann personally considered MTV boring and ridiculous, and his estimation of Bob Pittman wasn't much higher. When David Rosenthal suggested a major cover story on MTV, Jann rejoindered with a flat no. He didn't want to give Pittman's creation publicity of any kind.

Rosenthal persisted. He knew Jann had an itch to put Michael Jackson, pop's crossover sensation, on the magazine's cover again. Jackson and Paul McCartney's new $300,000 video of "Say Say Say" could provide the rationale. Jann relented, then changed his mind again after seeing freelancer Steven Levy's manuscript. "He hated it violently," said Rosenthal. Levy's essentially negative piece nonetheless conceded MTV's extraordinary influence on eighties rock, and painted Bob Pittman as a wunderkind for our times, a Jann Wenner of the eighties. The flattering portrayal of Pittman particularly galled the editor, who ordered a complete rewrite from top to bottom.

A month later, Rosenthal delivered the galleys of the MTV piece for Jann to approve. The editor was amazed. "What did you do?" he asked. "It's brilliant now. It's terrific."

Rosenthal had not changed a word.

Levy's well-researched polemic gave *Rolling Stone* the opportunity to take the righteous road and accuse MTV of the very sins for which *Rolling Stone* had long been condemned. Now it was MTV who was getting fat off the music industry, who ignored black musicians, who plugged docile nitwits while shunning those acts deemed offensive to suburbia's palate. Now it was MTV, not *Rolling Stone*, who "sells out rock & roll," according to the headline.

"Ironically," said David Rosenthal, "in retrospect MTV is what saved the magazine." What Jann Wenner initially perceived as a potential threat became free advertising for *Rolling Stone*'s cover subjects, and in fact a useful tool for determining future viable covers. (For example, Brant Mewborn's heroine Tina Turner graced the cover of *Rolling Stone*'s October 11, 1984, issue—three years after Mewborn pled her case at an editorial meeting and, for that matter, thirteen years almost to the day since Turner had last appeared on the magazine's cover.) Above all, MTV had revitalized rock & roll, giving *Rolling Stone*'s business staff impetus to scramble back to reclaim its younger readership, which, for editorial staffers who'd been fretting over the magazine's lost identity, was very, very good news indeed.

———

But it was very bad news for David Rosenthal, whose days were numbered the moment it became clear that *Rolling Stone* should return to its rock roots. Jann fired Rosenthal in March of 1984.

Doomed too was *Record*, the magazine created by Jann to keep music advertisers in the Straight Arrow Publishers, Inc., stable. *Record* had in fact never quite achieved its objective—partly due to a low editorial budget and unoriginal ideas ("If you want to know what's in this month's *Record*," went the joke on the twenty-third floor, "read last month's *Rolling Stone*"), partly due to a disastrous packaging shift from quarterfold to slick and partly due to its "Hit Man" column, which regularly attacked its music advertisers for sponsoring mediocrity. (Later, the column was replaced by Dave Marsh's "American Grandstand," but that too was canned by Jann after Marsh wrote a column attacking Michael Jackson for not spreading his wealth among underprivileged blacks.)

Record limped onward until 1985, at which time *Rolling Stone* was competing with its sister publication on virtually every page. There was nothing left to salvage except Jann Wenner's pride. But by now the editor of six failed publications could take his losses with a dose of humor. When Jann decided to fold *Record* at the end of 1985, he called the magazine's publisher into his office and sat him down. Without explanation, Jann withdrew a music box and put it on top of his desk. He lifted the music box's lid. A song played.

It was the theme from *The Godfather*. The *Record* publisher blanched. Jann Wenner's blue eyes laughed. A final head rolled as *Rolling Stone* rolled tunefully through the eighties.

Chapter Eighteen

PERCEPTION/
REALITY

*J*ann Wenner, an actor? Jane Wenner didn't see it.

"All the other editors in town are already jealous of Jann," Jane told *Rolling Stone* writer Aaron Latham, whose article on health clubs as the singles bars of the eighties was about to become a Columbia Pictures movie. The 1985 film would be *Perfect*, but Jann wasn't. The editor hadn't acted since boarding school, and besides, he was severely overweight. The critics would be lying low for her husband, Jane Wenner feared. If he embarrassed himself on the screen, they'd never let him forget it.

Although resistant at first, Jann warmed to producer/director James Bridges's idea that he play Mark Roth, *Perfect*'s barely fictionalized *Rolling Stone* editor. "Getting to star in a movie about yourself—it was like a dream come true," he said. Besides, Bridges and Latham had rejected Jann's suggestion that the Mark Roth character be played by Michael Keaton, or Peter Riegert, or Richard Dreyfuss, or Jeff Bridges, or Jann's buddy Michael Douglas. They had in mind the brilliant but short and decidedly unsexy Wallace Shawn. Merely mentioning Shawn's name was enough to send the editor into groaning paroxysms.

But Jane remained unconvinced until Jann had Bridges, Latham and John Travolta (who would play *Rolling Stone* reporter Adam Lawrence) over for dinner one evening. "They just turned their charm on Jane," said Jann. "John just walked into our apartment, looked at Jane and said, 'You are *so beautiful!* You are *so good-looking!*' And when it was over, I was off to Hollywood."

The night before Jann's first screen test, he hit the Hollywood party circuit. Along the way, he ran into Michael Douglas and Warren Beatty, each of whom gave the editor acting tips. Prominent among their suggestions was that Jann should be his natural energetic, histrionic, bullying self. Jann practiced a few lines with his actor friends. He called it a night at 3 A.M.

Six hours later, in the old office of legendary producer David O. Selznick, Jann Wenner gave it all he had. He rolled his eyes; he mugged; he sprayed out his lines; he flapped his arms about like a demented seabird. Bridges and Latham traded worried looks. They called for a recess. Latham took Jann upstairs and tried to relax him by talking about politics.

Travolta joined them and, in Latham's words, "helped peel off another layer of Douglas, another layer of Beatty." Jamie Lee Curtis, the female lead in *Perfect*, lent moral support. Jann gave his best rehearsal, and Jim Bridges signaled for the cameras to roll.

After breaking for lunch, Latham, Bridges, Travolta and Curtis studied Jann's screen test. Though Travolta allowed as to how it was one of the best tests he'd ever seen, the others thought it was horrible. Jamie Lee Curtis in particular expressed serious doubts about Jann Wenner's ability to pull off the Mark Roth role. Producer Bridges decided to go with the editor anyway.

Staffers couldn't help but be excited. The movie was about their magazine; it would be shot in their offices; they would all be extras, immortalized in celluloid. Enthusiasm dimmed somewhat when word spread that Columbia had elected to use a different location for the office scenes. Still, there was much to arouse curiosity. For days thereafter, photographers nosed around the twenty-third floor of 745 Fifth Avenue, taking detail shots of the *Rolling Stone* office for set design purposes. Travolta himself showed up, notepad in hand, and asked the magazine's writers a few rather simplistic questions about reporting. (Later, the actor played real-life reporter by conducting a question-and-answer session with Jann in Andy Warhol's magazine *Interview*.)

Jann's first scene as Mark Roth was shot in Manhattan's Le Relais Restaurant on the corner of Sixty-third and Madison Avenue, sealed off from rush-hour traffic. The scene was to feature Carly Simon, in the presence of Jann, throwing wine in Travolta's face for trashing her in an article. Jann was nervous but excited. Hollywood had come to him in a rush, its unblinking eyes surrounding him. This was his moment.

Then life imitated art.

Onto the set marched actress Debra Winger. Winger was a friend of Latham, Bridges and Travolta, who'd respectively written, directed and starred in *Urban Cowboy*, the movie that established the actress as a star. But Winger was no friend of Jann Wenner. Twice she'd been bumped from the cover of *Rolling Stone*: first, when *Cannery Row* turned out to be a box-office dog; then a year later in 1982, when the lead actress in *An Officer and a Gentleman* was told she'd have the cover, only to discover that Jann instead awarded the honor to his friend Richard Gere, Winger's co-star but by no means her buddy.

Debra Winger sat down at the table where Jann, Latham, Bridges and Travolta were sitting. Wasting hardly a second, she lit into the editor. "You're a sexual dilettante, Jann," she spat. "You're always fucking people in your magazine. You don't really fuck them—you just fuck them over. But you don't know the difference, do you?"

Jann turned a ghastly white. His apologies only seemed to incite the temperamental actress further. After a few more abusive moments, Jann Wenner retreated from the table and scurried outside. Bridges rushed after him. The actress had reduced the editor to psychic rubble. All Bridges and Latham could do was render the classic Hollywood advice: "Use your emotions. Channel them into your lines."

It worked. The show went on, despite Debra Winger, despite the fears of a few *Perfect* associates that the editor would drink and drug himself into blithering incompetence. As it turned out, Jann Wenner was the least of their worries.

Despite Jann's laudable performance as himself, and despite his shameless promotion of the movie in *Rolling Stone* (which sported Travolta and Curtis on its cover just at the time of the movie's release), *Perfect* stiffed. For the editorial staff, the movie—which portrayed a *Rolling Stone* reporter as someone who asks stupid questions, sleeps with his article subjects, deceives his interviewees and somehow emerges as a heroic individual—was a thorough embarrassment. They came out of the private screening cursing and shaking their heads. "What a depressing moment that was for everybody who worked on the editorial side," said a staff writer, "to sit in that theater, see that scummy, stupid, soft-porn misrepresentation of everything *Rolling Stone* was about. I think a lot of people felt sold out by that movie."

After the screening, a party was held at the posh Parker Meridien Hotel, out by the pool. Several staffers drank to excess that night. *Perfect* was a smear that would not soon wash off. Though they had to admit their boss had done a decent job on the screen, "we were concerned that, by his being a part of it, Jann sort of lent a credibility to this picture of *Rolling Stone* which just wasn't credible at all," said senior editor Brant Mewborn. Yet the concern was unfounded, for in the end no one took *Perfect* seriously except its associates, including Jann Wenner.

For his acting and consulting roles in *Perfect*, Jann was paid $200,000. The money was nice; the stardom was nicer still. Jann began to talk to Aaron Latham about other acting roles he'd like. A few directors made inquiries. He was the center of attention, and loving it. When former *Rolling Stone* associate editor David Weir ran into his old boss and commented, "It must be difficult making the transition from editor to actor," Jann shrugged.

"Not really," he said, his blue eyes beaming. "Not when you have so much natural talent."

———

While filming a few scenes in Hollywood, Jann and Jane went out to dinner with *Rolling Stone*'s first copy editor, Charles Perry. Perry was now a restaurant critic for the *Los Angeles Times* and doing fairly well, having survived personal bankruptcy and *Rolling Stone*'s departure from his life—the one connected to the other, as Perry had been contracted to write for the magazine after its move to New York, after which, according to Perry, "Jann totally reneged on the contract. Out of sight, out of mind, out of pocket."

But that was years ago. Perry was always an amiable and sentimental sort, not one to harbor grudges, and so he picked up the Wenners at Michael Douglas's house in Beverly Hills and treated them to dinner. The evening was a pleasant one. Jane gave her old confidant a book about pizzas, and Jann entertained with wry gossip about David Felton and other wayward *Rolling Stone* alumni.

While Perry's former boss wolfed down his food—his appetite as boundless as ever—he talked incessantly about *Perfect* and about his exciting new life. Jann dropped a lungful of movie star names, only now he was among that unreachable constellation, twinkling haughtily above the mortals he'd once smoked pot with. The Mark Roth role was only the beginning, Jann told Perry. He'd actually heard, in fact, that Hollywood directors were casting about in their film projects for "Jann Wenner types."

Perry laughed, thinking, God, is Jann full of himself. It surprised him, and pleased him, that the Wenners seemed to be getting along well. He'd always had a soft spot for Jane, and, he supposed, for Jann as well. They'd had some savage times together. Perhaps, after all that booze and coke and celebrity chasing in big bad beautiful New York, the editor had forgotten some of those moments and what they meant. Not Charlie Perry. The devastation he experienced after the love of his life rolled eastward was exceeded only by the humility one feels for having been privileged to touch, embrace and be swallowed up by greatness.

Well, yes. The memories could still take his breath away. He was the better for those bygone days. Rolling Stone Press had published his book on the Haight-Ashbury, with the help of his agent, former research editor Sarah Lazin. These days he took friends, including fellow war horses like Grover Lewis, out for posh dinners on the tab of the *L.A. Times*. He had his own house, his own home computer, and on a regular but by no means frenetic basis, he pounded out his reviews—signing them Charles Perry, though just by his computer sat a dusty old nameplate with the moniker he'd given himself when he was less bald, less soft in the belly and less doubtful of one scruffy magazine's ability to change the world: Smokestack El Ropo.

Perry and the Wenners laughed and ate and drank. There wasn't much to discuss, as he and they had so little in common now. But it was fun to hear about the New York Wenners and the New York *Rolling Stone*—fun and distantly resonant, rather like a high school reunion, or the chance meeting of old lovers a decade after the sparks had fallen to ash. Perry even enjoyed hearing Jann's boasting again. He dropped them back off at the house of Michael Douglas, and they all agreed it had been a nice evening.

Charlie Perry watched them walk toward the movie star's mansion. He never saw them again after that night.

———

Ah, change. The man whose birth certificate read Jan Simon Wenner swore by shifting sands and new winds blowing. Since at least 1976, when he'd considered starting up a pop art magazine before electing instead to publish *Outside*, the glimmer of a European-style color-photo-oriented publication had never fully receded from his mind's eye. In May of 1985, Jann Wenner and Straight Arrow Publishers, Inc., put up a paltry $2.5 million and purchased 25 percent of *Us* magazine, the snappy, if sappy biweekly competitor to Time Inc.'s weekly money machine, *People*. Since its inception in 1977, *Us* had been something of a monkey's paw, passed with grimaces from its parent, the *New York Times*, to MacFadden Publishing and then to Jann, losing money like a boy with holes in every pocket. As he had with *Look*, the editor thundered through his new property, dismissing all but one editorial staffer and discarding the entire feature inventory.

(In at least one instance, Jann also raided *Rolling Stone*'s feature inventory, converting reporter Guy Martin's 12,000-word profile of Julio Iglesias into an *Us* snippet barely one tenth its original length. Martin was in Africa at the time. Those privy to the incident couldn't help but recall the scene in *Perfect* where editor Mark Roth took Adam Lawrence's health club story and had it completely rewritten while the reporter was in Morocco. Though Jann later assured reporters that he would never treat his writers as Roth treated Lawrence, it appeared that life had imitated art once again.)

In 1986, Jann's first full year with *Us*, the magazine lost $12 million; in 1987, several million more. Most of the money wasn't his to lose (Lorimar/Telepictures, Straight Arrow's partner, had put up the lion's share in the buyout), but the editor decided he'd better devote his energies to business all the same. He thus recruited Anthea Disney, the *New York Daily News* assistant managing editor whose work on that paper's sassy entertainment section earned her high regard, and awarded her his title of editor. He also gave her his office—at Disney's insistence, as this would ensure that Jann wouldn't be hanging around.

Disney's notion was to move *Us* away from *People*'s quasi-sensationalistic bailiwick and try for a more high-profile approach. "I thought we should go through the front door," said Disney, "and meet the celebrity—always have the interview and always do a photo shoot. Jann loves change, so he got terribly excited by all this."

Between Anthea Disney's editorial repositioning and Jann's business efforts, *Us* by 1988 began to see daylight. Throughout, however, Disney wondered if her boss understood just what she was trying to do with *Us*. Much as Jann took a special liking to *Rolling Stone*'s gossipy "Random Notes," he also tittered over "Faces & Places," the *Us* celebrity section Jann brought over from his days at *Look*.

"The only arguments we ever had," said Disney, "were that he basically loved tacky, which is odd because *Rolling Stone* isn't tacky at all. He really loved supermarket tabloids and tried to inject that stuff in there."

Disney didn't share the fixation, and by the summer of 1988 was sick of her all-celebrity diet. When she departed for Condé Nast's *Self* magazine, Jann was furious and sued her new employers. Change, after all, was for him to decide; change was *his* department. And this, of course, would never change.

———

In November of 1984, Ronald Reagan ran for reelection and annihilated his Democratic challenger, Walter Mondale. Surveys later showed that the majority of *Rolling Stone*'s readership—those who were eighteen or over, that is—had cast their ballots for the wealthy former movie star.

This did not surprise Jann Wenner, who always understood *Rolling Stone*'s readership better than his employees or his critics. By 1985, the magazine had reached the coveted circulation figure of one million. *Rolling Stone* was officially mass market. There was nothing fringe, Jann knew, about his magazine's readers. If America voted for Reagan, then so did they. And now it was time to drive home this point to Madison Avenue.

Despite a promotional budget of virtually zero, *Rolling Stone*'s ad revenues had grown steadily since 1981 until its Henry Marks-inspired demographic contortions caused a 7.4 percent drop in 1984. Yet even in the best of times, *Rolling Stone* continued to receive mere morsels from the big media buyers, and virtually nothing from the food and personal grooming industries. Convinced by his business staff that this wall could not be surmounted without a significant promotional effort, Jann Wenner in April of 1985 paid the upstart Minneapolis firm of Fallon McElligot Rice $500,000 to design a trade advertising campaign for *Rolling Stone*.

What FMR copywriter Bill Miller conceived came to be known as the Perception/Reality ad campaign. Playing off Madison Avenue's apparent view that *Rolling Stone* and its readers still lived in the muddy, incense-choked atmosphere of the sixties, Miller took every hippie stereotype he could think of and countered each with a stereotype of Madison Avenue's beloved yuppie consumers—that is to say, *Rolling Stone*'s true readers. Page one of the two-page ad would feature, for example, a marijuana roach clip and, above that, the word *Perception*. The facing page would show a dollar-bill clip with the word *Reality*.

Miller found that the formula could be used endlessly, that "it really had legs," in his words. *Perception*: a psychedelic van. *Reality*: a smart-looking sports car. *Perception*: George McGovern. *Reality*: Ronald Reagan. *Perception*: a blank page. *Reality*: a bar of soap. What the photos and the headings didn't spell out, Miller's ad copy drove home. Under the bar of soap, for example, the ad declared, "If you think *Rolling Stone* readers are the great unwashed, this should send that sort of thinking down the drain. In the last 7 days alone, *Rolling Stone* readers worked up a lather with soap and shampoo 40 million times. If you've got health and beauty aids to sell, you can clean up in the pages of *Rolling Stone*."

(In at least one instance, Miller's images were judged unsuitable for publication. For the *Perception* page, Miller used a peace sign; for *Reality*, the hood ornament of a Mercedes-Benz. Kent Brownridge liked the images, but wistfully observed that *Rolling Stone*'s readers weren't Mercedes owners. Jann thought the pairing mocked the peace sign and vetoed it altogether.)

The concept was simple and flawless. Fallon McElligot Rice launched the Perception/Reality campaign in July of 1985, with ads showing a frizzy-haired sixties specimen on the *Perception* page (a "real-life hippie," not a model, FMR gleefully revealed later) and a jacketed, presumably affluent preppie on the *Reality* page. The results exceeded even the most breathless of expectations. By the end of the year, ad pages jumped 10 percent over 1985; by 1986, 23.1 percent; by 1987, another 20.4 percent over the previous year. Revenues poured in, flooding *Rolling Stone* and Jann Wenner with unforeseen wealth, while in the meantime Bill Miller sat at his desk in Minneapolis, busily spewing out images that were guaranteed to penetrate the stony skulls of Madison Avenue.

Skulls were penetrated, contracts were signed. It was all good fun and shrewd marketing, said Miller. "We weren't intending to deride the magazine's roots." But when one woman who'd once been a staff writer for *Rolling Stone* saw that first trade ad, she put down the issue and began to cry.

Chet Flippo, who had written for the magazine from 1971 into the next decade, was purely disgusted by the stark images peering back at him. A cancer on a perfect body, he thought. Flippo had heard about the Perception/Reality campaign from Harriet Fier, who called him in a state of shock and horror. She'd just seen the trade ad that consisted of two song titles: "All You Need Is Love," countered by "What's Love Got to Do with It?"

Rolling Stone's former managing editor knew a clever ad campaign when she saw it. She also knew that those long days and nights in San Francisco meant more than the glib, sniveling revision of *Rolling Stone* that Jann Wenner was now advertising. "I was detached, I had my own life," she said. "But I was also nostalgic, emotional and idealistic enough to say, 'No more soul. They've sold the soul.' It was a denial of what happened in the sixties—a denial that the sixties ever happened. *It broke my heart.* Not for *Rolling Stone*, but for the time; for the notion that all that stuff is now grist for the mill, that we can now make fun of all that."

The present occupants of 745 Fifth Avenue's twenty-third floor did not share the former staffers' sense of personal violation; nor, however, were they thrilled to see the business staff's yuppified depiction of their magazine. "We were all mortified and appalled, of course," said senior editor Lisa Henricksson. "We grumbled about it a great deal. But there was nothing you could do about it. In the end, it wasn't worth going to the mat over. You were almost always going to lose."

David Rosenthal's replacement as managing editor was Bob Wallace, a former fact checker in the early seventies who became Harriet Fier's assistant managing editor in 1979 before quitting at the end of that year and moving on to *Newsweek*. As managing editor, Wallace restored the music section's front-of-the-book status, brought order to the magazine's chaotic editorial flow and ended for all time the eleventh-hour production of *Rolling Stone*. A low-key, almost folksy Westerner, Bob Wallace encouraged the sort of levity staffers hadn't dared show in many a year.

Good humor was essential, for the magazine's editorial integrity was suffering body blows constantly, and the Perception/Reality campaign was only the most obvious example. By July of 1985, the *Rolling Stone* cover was glossy, and its cover subjects even glossier. Obsessed with newsstand sales, Kent Brownridge began to submit potential covers to focus-group tests. Individuals who fit the magazine's standard demographic profile were literally taken off the street, brought upstairs to a conference room and seated. Placards of potential cover subjects were mounted on easels. Questions were asked of those seated: How often do you listen to music? How many records do you buy? Who on these placards do you recognize? Which of those are you interested in reading about?

When Brant Mewborn learned that his story on Annie Lennox of the Eurythmics—thought by many on the staff to be hot cover material—would be subjected to a focus group, he decided to peek through the conference room's one-way glass and see what was going on. What he saw were college-age kids squinting at a barely recognizable placard of Lennox. Mewborn wondered where the business staff had come up with the photograph. When he saw the kids react most favorably to a placard of Bill Cosby, the senior editor retreated in disgust. Cosby didn't make the cover, but neither did Annie Lennox.

Nearly everyone on the editorial staff thought the use of focus groups was ludicrous and, on a creative level, profane. Didn't the cover of *Rolling Stone mean* anything anymore? Particularly offended were writers and editors who had worked for other publications whose reputations were stodgier than that of *Rolling Stone* but who would not have dreamed of letting a panel of consumers determine what went on their covers. Said one such staffer, "Whoever tested best in the focus groups would likely end up on the cover whether they'd done anything interesting lately or not. Eddie Murphy tested great. So did Jack Nicholson. But what was there left to do on those guys?"

Former *Vanity Fair* staffer Lisa Henricksson observed one such test and, she said, "was sufficiently appalled that I never wanted to go again." The main subject being tested was Van Halen's David Lee Roth. One of the participants identified Roth as actress Dyan Cannon.

The in-house tests were later abandoned in favor of mall surveys by Peter D. Hart Associates. These were more accurate, but the fallacies inherent in focus-group testing seemed rather obvious to Bob Wallace, who opposed it from the start. "I think they represent a trend in this business toward a need to create a science out of something that is fundamentally not a science," he said. "If you could predict accurately, based on a focus group, what a magazine should be and how it could be successful, then I'd be all for it and there'd be a lot of millionaires around. But that's not the way it works. Putting out a magazine is a function of the editors, and a good editor with good instincts is going to be right not all the time, but will probably have just as high a percentage as the information that is going into the focus groups.

"Also, by emphasizing focus groups, in a way you are letting the readers lead you, and most people want to be *led by* a magazine; they want the magazine to introduce them to something new. If you only put out what readers *think* they want, you are only giving them what they already know. That has always been my position, and Jann knows it."

But Jann was not always interested in Wallace's position. By 1987, advertisers—through general manager Kent Brownridge—were controlling enough of the magazine's content to compel staffers to ask themselves, in one's words, "Who's wearing the pants?" Fights over obscenity were being lost; reporters were being asked to "clean up" quotes, even when the use of "fuck" was illustrative and not gratuitous. Staff writer David Handleman was told by Jann to "tone down" his article on the Beastie Boys, a band whose stock-in-trade was four-letter words. The editor told his writer that ad reps had complained about the piece. Ad reps? What the hell were they doing reading the proofs? And since when did they have a say in how a piece on the Beastie Boys should be written? Who was wearing the pants?

In the summer of 1984, during an "executive agenda meeting," the goal of luring fashion advertisers into *Rolling Stone* was established. When results proved disappointing, Jann approved the business staff's suggestion that the magazine begin running fashion spreads. Though the editorial staff made clear its opposition—"I felt like a Martian there," said Laurie Schechter, *Rolling Stone*'s first full-time fashion editor—the decision proved to be a financial bonanza. When Schechter was hired in 1986, the magazine was running only 20 pages of fashion ads annually. Two years later, the figure increased to nearly 500.

Among *Rolling Stone*'s first major fashion advertisers was Benetton, well-known designers of attire catering to what could be called preppies. In his somber essay on the decline of liberal arts, "Down and Out at Bennington College," *Less Than Zero* author Bret Easton Ellis lamented the growing conservatism on college campuses. In one passage, Ellis described the average preppie female student, decked out in her Benettons—not only an innocuous reference but arguably the kind of identification Benetton paid thousands for in advertisements. But the business staff didn't want to take a chance. The reference was ordered to be deleted.

When Brownridge's lieutenants took note of the fashion section's magnetic powers, they began kicking around other ideas. Food advertisers were mentioned. This time Bob Wallace and Lisa Henricksson reacted quickly and vehemently. The food column proposal was strangled in its crib.

But the victory was notable for its rarity. When the side of *Rolling Stone* that viewed the magazine as a creative organism clashed with the side that saw *Rolling Stone* as a product, the outcome was foretold. Advertisers wanted their ads facing editorial pages; hence, "feature wells" were diluted. Advertisers wanted more special issues, so Bob Wallace was told to come up with ideas. The "Hot Issue" was born. A "Comedy Issue" followed. By 1989, fifteen of the magazine's twenty-four issues had some sort of theme, a hook on which clients could hang their advertisements. "All the News That Fits" now had an entirely new meaning.

Of course, *Rolling Stone*'s editorial staff enjoyed good company. All over New York, editors were losing battles to what publishing's financial wizards were terming "marketing realities." It took no fighter pilot's eyesight to behold the general shriveling of feature space, the predominance of "special issues" where once magazines touted actual editorial concepts, the replacement of words with pictures and the preference for personality profiles over what were now sneeringly referred to as "think pieces" and "voice pieces." *Rolling Stone* could actually endure these impositions better than most magazines. After all, its existence was not dedicated to lyricism or muckraking, but rather to rock & roll, "the magic that can set you free." So long as *Rolling Stone* stood behind the magic, *Rolling Stone* made a difference.

Then *Rolling Stone* rolled over.

In 1986, associate publisher Les Zeifman inaugurated a *Rolling Stone* advertising newsletter entitled *Marketing Through Music*. Its purpose was simple but striking: to encourage corporations to discover the power of rock & roll as a marketing tool.

Corporate sponsorship of rock was hardly new. Elvis Presley lent his name to Southern Maid doughnuts in the fifties; the Jefferson Airplane and the Who to Levi's and the U.S. Navy, respectively, in the sixties. The Rolling Stones' tour of 1981 was underwritten by Jovan perfume, and thereafter beer and soft drink manufacturers began to get in on the act. Zeifman read the graffiti on the wall: if corporations began to understand the marketing power of rock & roll, the magazine he liked to call "the *Wall Street Journal* of rock & roll" would surely derive enormous advertising benefits.

And so *Marketing Through Music* entered the world cheering odd partnerships: tobacco companies who sponsored concerts, beer companies who cajoled rockers into peddling their products on television, detergent companies who altered classic rock lyrics for gung ho radio commercials and perfume companies who signed up "celebrity spokespersons." The newsletter, said Zeifman, did "anything that it could to perpetuate the use of music marketing"—even going so far as to suggest marketing strategies. "Isn't it time that some hot sauce marketer, say Tabasco, used the Red Hot Chili Peppers in an ad campaign?" read one item. Another championed teenaged pop star Tiffany for, of all things, Tiffany's jewelry.

Zeifman and *Marketing Through Music*'s editor, David Rheins, didn't bother asking these artists whether they had any interest in plumping for corporations. Nor did they solicit the opinions of the *Rolling Stone* editorial staff, who did not enjoy reading in *The Village Voice* that "*Rolling Stone*'s current cutting edge is corporate sponsorship of rock & roll."

Eventual managing editor Jim Henke would remark, "There's certainly no relationship between the guy who puts that out and anyone on this floor." Certainly Henke wished that this was so. For if ever a topic met *Rolling Stone*'s "All the News That Fits" criterion, the Faustian ethics of corporate sponsorship did. Private funding of culture had always been a thorny subject, and the corporate backing of an art form with anti-Establishment roots even more so. When was sponsorship desirable, when was it safe and when did it exceed tasteful limits? The matter was debated by the press, at music seminars and in all levels of the record industry.

On national television, pop singer Phil Collins sang his haunting description of a marriage in tatters, "In the Air Tonight," as a jingle to a beer commercial. Was the song now about the pleasures of tossing back a cold one? Or was Collins still singing about divorce, this time a divorce from the fans who cared enough about him to seek out his music in record stores and plumb its contents for meaning?

Surely, as other publications had, the magazine that lectured politicians for censoring rock lyrics and MTV for "selling out" rock & roll would take a stand! But *Rolling Stone* did not. It could not. After all, the magazine's parent company, Straight Arrow, was corporate sponsorship's official sponsor.

After watching Neil Young's scathing video parody of rock jingles, "This Note's for You," music editor David Wild walked into Bob Wallace's office and said, "You know, I feel like we're on the wrong side. It's like being on the wrong side of abortion or the death penalty."

"Yeah," was the managing editor's soft reply. "I agree." But there was nothing to be said after that.

For projects like *Marketing Through Music* did not materialize without Jann Wenner's blessings. If Jann wanted editorial's input, he would have asked. But he didn't—not on *Marketing Through Music*, not on the Perception/Reality ad campaign, not on the rash of special issues or the regular full-page ads *Rolling Stone* now took from the military. These were orders from on high, and never at *Rolling Stone* was the distance between editor and editorial staff so formidable.

The old mantra, "It's Jann's magazine," was invoked as never before. The editor's fingerprints were all over *Rolling Stone*, of course—only now the effect was, with few exceptions, to smudge the magazine's editorial integrity. Actor friends Michael Douglas and Richard Gere seemed to make the magazine's cover no matter how undistinguished their latest film happened to be. Other friends, like Judy Belushi and Tom Cruise, were permitted to alter quotes in stories that involved them. A review of Mick Jagger's album *Primitive Cool* was assigned, rejected for its mild criticisms, then reassigned to a different critic and heavily edited by Jann. Yoko Ono's trip to Europe and subsequent peek behind the Iron Curtain drew inflated coverage in *Rolling Stone*—perhaps, though the articles did not mention this, because Jann and Jane Wenner accompanied Lennon's widow.

In 1987, *Rolling Stone* devoted a special issue to the "100 Best Albums" of the past twenty years. Critics were polled; results were tabulated. At the top of the list was *Sgt. Pepper's Lonely Hearts Club Band.* Second was *Never Mind the Bollocks, Here's the Sex Pistols,* an album which sold less than one tenth as many copies as *Sgt. Pepper.*

The results angered Jann. Though he had never actually listened to more than a few minutes of the Sex Pistols' record, he could not fathom its lofty rank in the poll. Besides, he demanded, "where's Loggins and Messina on this poll? Where's *Hotel California?*"

When the magazine ran its "100 Best Singles" special issue a year later, the editor took matters into his own hands. He ordered music editor David Wild to put singles by his friends Billy Joel and Foreigner's Mick Jones on the list. Then Jann personally manipulated the tabulations, a puppetmaster jerking his subjects up and down the list. Thus did the deathless classics "Uptown Girl" (by Joel) and "I Want to Know What Love Is" (by Foreigner) receive the respective designations of 99 and 54, while Stevie Wonder's "Superstition"—originally given the 6 rank—languished at 73.

It was demoralizing enough that the editor no longer awarded cover bylines to staff writers while at the same time displaying Tom Wolfe's name on twenty-one of twenty-seven covers over the course of 1984 and 1985. (For $150,000, Jann commissioned Wolfe to publish *The Bonfire of the Vanities,* one chapter per issue, in *Rolling Stone.* Despite the enormous success of *Bonfire* when published in novel form, the *Rolling Stone* entries—inferior in both form and content to the novel version—received little attention, commercially or otherwise.) Jann Wenner favoring celebrity journalists over his own—well, he'd been doing that for some time now. But here was Jann Wenner telling his staff, in effect, "When I must choose between loyalty to my friends and loyalty to my employees—well, hey, guys, it's only a job."

Or as the editor told senior editor Brant Mewborn after his Annie Lennox story failed the focus-group test: "Look at it this way. It's all going to be paper in the gutter in a week anyway."

In 1987, *Rolling Stone* magazine celebrated its twentieth year of publication. Four special issues—on style, live performances, records and the sixties—commemorated that tumultuous passage of time. A two-hour ABC television special celebrated the music that in many ways defined those two decades. Jann Wenner was rightfully proud of the productions. They were insightful, faithful to the times and thoroughly professional. Taken together, the specials epitomized *Rolling Stone* at the absolute height of its power, confidence and wisdom.

Absent from the issues or the television show was any mention of the magazine's own past—its sons and daughters, celebrated and unknown, who helped Jann Wenner whirl a $7,500 San Francisco tabloid through America like a jagged diamond. The media nodded thoughtfully at *Rolling Stone*'s phenomenal success and the price of that success; there was much discussion about Jann Wenner, now forty-one and fabulously wealthy, and occasionally of Hunter Thompson, an eminence no longer in view. But the ghosts of the sixties and seventies trembled darkly in the walls. This triumph was not theirs.

It was a triumph for Jann Wenner, and for the *Rolling Stone* staff that congregated in black ties and evening dresses at the South Street Seaport under the Brooklyn Bridge, toasting a history of which they had little comprehension, except perhaps that in this history rewards came in strange and disparate forms, and that this was no less strange or less appropriate a reward than those previous. In a grandly appointed restaurant at the banks of the shimmering East River, the staff listened not to the Dry Heaves but to Marshall Crenshaw, a brilliant pop musician who nonetheless shared with the Dry Heaves an inability to break through his cult status and thus make the cover of *Rolling Stone*.

Crenshaw's music was wonderful if somewhat overamplified, and the spread of food and beverages was like no other staff party before or since. The view, of course, was immaculate. Out here by the river, the breeze was crisp and the sky aflame with the headlights of a thousand taxicabs flying across the bridge. Ah, New York; none other. Who could imagine Jann Wenner elsewhere? They had to hand it to their boss, this man they barely knew: Jann Wenner could do it up right. This brilliant, boyish bastard, this somehow father of theirs—whatever else people said about him, Jann Wenner could seize a moment. And tonight this moment was his. Tonight, in fact, there would be no seizing. All things would come to him at last, at last.

———

Perhaps, as he often said, a generation gap no longer existed. But Jann Wenner was doubtful enough of his own words to commission Peter D. Hart Associates in 1986 to survey the attitudes of Americans born after World War II.

The results were, as Pete Townshend would say, "bleedin' quadrophrenic." The new generation held views that seemed to elude any unifying value system. They embraced Martin Luther King, Jr., as their hero while shunning nearly all forms of civil activism. They voted for a Red-baiting hawk in 1980 and 1984, but themselves espoused no willingness to fight for their country. They rated negatively George Bush, the man they would vote for in overwhelming numbers two years hence. The most economically privileged generation in the history of mankind was preoccupied with the pursuit of success. Free sex now scared them; they were homophobic, and saw merit in mandatory AIDS testing. Children of Woodstock they were, yet almost half of them cited rock & roll as a bad influence on their children. Disciples of the revolution they were, yet they now viewed themselves as less involved in community and civic affairs than their parents had been.

Jann Wenner understood. Like the vast majority of his generation, he neither went to Woodstock nor marched in political rallies. He'd always claimed that his peers weren't monolithic, and *Rolling Stone*, he believed, reflected this. Out there in that many-shaded field of *Rolling Stone* readers, there were Joe Eszterhas fans and "Random Notes" followers, Hunter Thompson freaks and Dave Marsh disciples. He would have them all, the readers and the writers who reflected their interests and his. Inside *Rolling Stone*, the world could rejoice in, or be appalled or amused by, his naked interests.

Beliefs could be interesting, for a time. They could also get very dull; and if you were Jann Wenner, you moved past your dull beliefs like a feature article that rambled on for too long. You turned the page, but your beliefs were still back there somewhere, easily returned to in moments of emptiness or despair, or of sheer restlessness.

In the spring of 1988, Jann Wenner turned back the pages. He received his old friend and former employee Howard Kohn in his office on the twenty-third floor of 745 Fifth Avenue.

Kohn had written virtually nothing for the magazine since 1981, when he and Jann traded sharp words over the approach of his National Rifle Association piece. Their close relationship had seen Kohn through the press furor over the Patty Hearst pieces, the chilly atmosphere of the Karen Silkwood investigation and the Resorts International lawsuit. He'd come to depend on that relationship, and now it wasn't there. Now *Rolling Stone* was an office full of strangers churning out material without much moral spine as far as he could tell.

Given no compelling reason to stay, Howard Kohn went on with David Weir, the co-author of the Patty Hearst articles, to found the Center for Investigative Reporting, with offices in San Francisco and Washington. At the Center, Kohn and Weir established a resource station for young reporters who yearned to take on heavies as the former *Rolling Stone* journalists had done throughout the seventies.

Fully two years passed before Howard Kohn spoke with his former boss again. During the Christmas season of 1983, Jann called Kohn to congratulate him on *Silkwood*, the Meryl Streep movie based on Kohn's reporting of the case. The editor told the writer he'd like to interview him for *Rolling Stone*. That didn't pan out, but Jann later called again, this time with politics on his mind. The two discussed the looming 1984 presidential campaign. The Alan Cranston effort was for naught, Jann said, adding that he'd voted for Reagan in 1980 and probably would again in 1984. Kohn couldn't believe Jann would make the same mistake twice.

The writer agreed to send Jann a piece on presidential candidate John Glenn's campaign finances. But Kohn had no desire to reinitiate their employer-employee bond. "Jann and I had an unspoken understanding that we weren't going to force a professional relationship," he said. Instead, the two relied on a new commonality: fatherhood. They began to send each other pictures—Kohn of his daughter, Jann of his two newborn sons—and speak of their children the way they once spoke of their work. Gradually, the frayed strands connecting them strengthened.

By 1987, Howard Kohn had completed *The Last Farmer*, a memoir exploring the ties and tensions between Kohn, the citybound man of letters, and his father, a proud sentinel of the soil. The book emerged from an essay Kohn wrote in *Rolling Stone* in 1977, so he made sure that Jann received an advance copy. Jann, who had become close to his own father only within the last few years, was deeply moved by *The Last Farmer*. He told Kohn this when the two met in his office that spring afternoon in 1988.

But there were other things on the editor's mind as well. A few months back, the CBS news magazine *West 57th* profiled *Rolling Stone* for its twentieth anniversary. Former staffers like Hunter Thompson, Roger Black, Chet Flippo, Ben Fong-Torres and Harriet Fier were interviewed, and their views about the magazine's direction were not altogether charitable. Jann tried to shrug off the show as one long exercise in shoddy journalism, but clearly he was stung by their remarks. He'd gone so far as to contact Thompson, telling him, "Well, Hunter, if that's the way you feel about the magazine, why don't you come back and do something about it?"

Sure, the editor now conceded to Kohn, things were different. Whole weeks passed without *Rolling Stone*'s co-founder having any hand in the running of the magazine's affairs. Jann Wenner did not for a moment regret the time he spent with his new family, but yes, his detachment from *Rolling Stone* felt a little strange.

"The magazine's gotten better and better," Jann assured Kohn. Even the writing had improved, he claimed. But he missed the old writers, the partnerships he enjoyed with daredevil journalists like Howard Kohn. He and Kohn, they'd taken on some pretty ferocious subjects: kidnapped news-paper heiresses and dead nuclear power plant employees; yachtjackers, plu-tonium merchants and mob affiliates; town bullies, anti-environmentalists, crooked politicians . . .

"I want you to write for us again," the editor said. As always, he had a million story ideas: the Defense Department, the Justice Department, George Bush's past, a host of other Washington-based stories. His words were a seductive blur. It was the Jann Wenner of old, the unvanquished Jann Wenner, and if Howard Kohn was somewhat amused and more than slightly apprehensive, the editor's guileless sales pitch still aroused dormant appetites in the writer. Kohn was no circus rube, but this was a ride that was tough to resist.

But for Jann Wenner, the former *Detroit Free Press* reporter might never have gained readmission. The editor of *Rolling Stone* gave the controversial journalist a second chance, and stood by Kohn when others might have cut their losses. They might have kept him on a short leash; Jann Wenner encouraged Howard Kohn to run wild. As Kohn would say: "He's always been willing to let me raise hell in the pages of *Rolling Stone*."

In return, one simply took Jann Wenner's rantings and bouts of knav-ishness with as much humor as one could conjure up. That was the devil's bargain in journalism, a deal the Lutheran farm boy agreed to back in Michigan's Saginaw Valley at about the same time Jann Wenner was shuffling through London in his porkpie hat, hoping for a glimpse of Mick Jagger.

Sure, said Howard Kohn. He'd return to *Rolling Stone*, from time to time.

———

Bob Wallace, now *Rolling Stone*'s first-ever executive editor, was delighted to have Kohn's work in his magazine. The old blended nicely with the new: David Breskin's teen suicide and adolescent Nazi investigations; Mike Sager's detective-style narratives of dead porn prince John Holmes and Rob Lowe's sex tapes; Lewis Cole's alarming piece on crack, which laid much of the blame for the epidemic at the feet of the Reagan-Bush administration; Larry Wright's damning portrayal of the fallen Reverend Jimmy Swaggart; and the lively profiles of staff writer David Handleman, a winner of the 1982 *Rolling Stone* College Journalism Award as Chuck Young had been six years prior. Critics sneered at the Michael Douglas plugs and sabotaged critics' polls, but between the slick covers and the fashion ads resided evidence that the *Rolling Stone* tradition of good reporting had never gone away.

"I look at it like this," Wallace would say. "My idea of what's important in a magazine really centers around the quality of the journalistic standards within any given piece. Now, magazines are owned by individuals, and if Jann wants to have John Travolta keep a notebook [as Travolta did for the infamous *Perfect* issue], that's his business. I'm not gonna go to confession or feel bad because we ran it. I *would* feel bad if we ran a piece on teen suicide and tried to paint a picture that kids aren't in trouble out there, that it's just an aberration, when you know it's not true. I mean, those are the important things."

Quick to point out the magazine's often disastrous editorial forays in the sixties and seventies, the *Rolling Stone* staff could now take pride in the mistakes it did *not* make. "Consistency counts for something," one of the business chiefs would say, noting the well-rounded editorial mix comprising each issue: a front-of-the-book music section, followed by coverage of movies, television and national affairs; a feature well usually consisting of three rock-related articles, one actor profile, one "serious" piece (drugs, international affairs, murder stories) and one less so (profiles of brain surgeons, race-car drivers and entrepreneurs); a fashion spread or special section; record reviews; a column devoted to audio, video or other technology; and, of course, a carefully chosen cover. The system was a sensible one, covering all turf, pleasing rock fans, older readers and advertisers alike.

Yet Bob Wallace was an editor, distrustful of business formulas. By 1988, he'd restricted the use of focus groups. The following year, he noted with some satisfaction that *Marketing Through Music* suspended publication. Wallace had his editorial mix—every good editor did—but to cross it now and then, he turned to the magazine's resident loose cannon, P. J. O'Rourke, a *National Lampoon* alumnus now charged with covering "Irrational Affairs" for *Rolling Stone*. Unlike any other staff writer beyond the inactive Hunter Thompson, O'Rourke was a familiar name to readers, infusing his unapologetically wise-assed persona into his unorthodox travelogues. If O'Rourke, a Republican "innocent abroad," was no Thompson, he nonetheless generated controversy and helped retain a semblance of the outlaw spirit for which *Rolling Stone* was once known.

Few could deny that the magazine looked more professional than ever.

Though Annie Leibovitz left *Rolling Stone* in 1983 and rebuffed Jann's attempt
to lure her away from *Vanity Fair* in 1988, the magazine regularly featured
stunning visuals, resulting in back-to-back National Magazine Awards for
design in 1987 and 1988. *Rolling Stone* assumed the hip and upwardly mobile
look of the consumers its advertisers sought.

Despite *Rolling Stone*'s inglorious silence on the matter of corporate
sponsorship, the magazine tackled every other major music story of the
eighties in the manner expected of it. An editorial sternly contradicted the
record industry's claims that home taping was costing it billions annually.
(Some record companies immediately pulled their advertisements from the
magazine as a result.) Reporter Michael Goldberg covered the industry's
payola hearings with far greater vigilance than had his *Rolling Stone* ante-
cedents. The historic Live Aid concerts of 1985 were discussed as musical,
sociological and media phenomena, leaving to others the foolish claim that
the concerts amounted to a "Woodstock of the eighties." And *Rolling Stone*
wasted little time before lambasting the rock censorship aims of Tipper
Gore's Parents' Music Resource Committee—though perhaps the most
revealing piece on the subject was a dialogue published in *Musician* between
Mrs. Gore and *Musician* contributing editor Charles M. Young.

Rock & roll, Wallace knew, still buttered *Rolling Stone*'s bread. That
the magazine still churned out credible music journalism was a triumph unto
its own. The days of Ben Fong-Torres hanging out at David Crosby's house,
Robert Greenfield observing the Rolling Stones juggle groupies and Chuck
Young spending a year snorting cocaine with the Eagles were a decade gone
and unlikely ever to return. Publicists now called the shots, and the shots
did not always favor the magazine that pioneered professional music journalism. Seemingly every publication in the land, from *Penthouse* to *People* to
Vogue to *USA TODAY*, had a music reporter on its staff. Some offered
glamorous photo spreads; others guaranteed covers. And the stories, as often
as not, featured familiar bylines: Fong-Torres, Young, Chet Flippo, Ed Ward,
John Morthland, Timothy White, Jon Pareles . . .

Dave Marsh's aggressive newsletter, *Rock 'n' Roll Confidential*, seemed
to spend half its time beating *Rolling Stone* to the punch on industry news
and the other half attacking Marsh's former employer for the usual reasons.
A new magazine, *Spin*, launched by the *Penthouse* founder's son, Bob Guccione, Jr., in 1985, announced plans to "kick *Rolling Stone*'s ass." Guccione,
a brash and energetic young American with a British accent, was heard to
declare at one *Spin* editorial meeting, "*Rolling Stone* is Johnny Carson; we're
David Letterman." *Rolling Stone* editors regarded this as mere wind in sails,

yet *Spin*'s devastating story on David Crosby's drug problems proved that the more established magazine could be scooped.

Rolling Stone had never been particularly hard-hitting in its coverage of dope-addled rockers. Ironically, it now fell to the magazine in the late eighties to grapple with the polished flip side: clean & sober musicians. The rehabilitation of alcoholic Warren Zevon at the beginning of the decade proved to be a harbinger. Out of this ignoble closet shuffled Eric Clapton, Pete Townshend, Ringo Starr and others, one by one, led by their publicists. *Rolling Stone*'s music writers now found themselves wading through story lines epitomized by that of former Go-Go's vocalist Belinda Carlisle: rising pop star stuffs her swollen head with drugs; disappears from the charts, hits rock bottom; gets help, marries a Republican public relations man, swears off drugs for aerobics; returns as a beautiful rising pop star with a well-packaged story to tell.

MTV had rejuvenated rock & roll, it was said. But the cable television station had also created a pantheon of artists with a distinctly, and often exclusively, visual appeal. The stories young MTV stars like Tone Loc, Taylor Dayne, Tiffany, Rick Astley and Debbie Gibson had to tell lacked any sense of history or creative anguish. *Rolling Stone*, having made its bed as a mainstream rock magazine, was obliged to cover popular acts. Beyond acknowledging their popularity, however, there was often nothing left to say.

What *Rolling Stone* music writers longed to do was break obscure artists, coronate princes and defrock pretenders. A number of factors conspired to make this mission a difficult one. Chief among them was their boss. "Jann still thinks he's an expert," one staffer would sigh. "He thinks that because he hangs out with a few record company executives and rock stars, he knows what's going on today. And you know, Jann's knowledge of music pretty much stopped in the mid-seventies."

As a result, U2 and the Talking Heads were awarded covers in 1985 and 1987, respectively—in each case after *Time* or *Newsweek* had run a cover story on one of the bands. ("I personally found that embarrassing," admitted Jim Henke, the magazine's music editor at the time.) In 1989, Jann confessed to a staffer that he'd never heard a record by the most critically acclaimed songwriter of the past decade, Elvis Costello—explaining, perhaps, the magazine's meager coverage of Costello. And *Rolling Stone*'s proclamation at the end of 1987 that REM was "America's best band" seemed to arrive at least a year after any argument on that subject had been settled.

"*Rolling Stone* had power and influence and authority," said contributing editor Mikal Gilmore. "They were tastemakers. At this point, they're taste trackers." Yet this was where the magazine found itself at the close of the eighties: respected but no longer relied upon, a force among other forces —an institution, surely, and like many such institutions, disregarded.

After listening to the debut album of American singer/songwriter Peter Case, music editor David Wild knew he'd heard genius and sought to spread the word. "I went and wrote a review," he said, "that I thought was along the lines of 'I've seen the future of rock & roll'—assuming then, logically, that Case would become the next Bruce Springsteen.

"And then, of course, nothing happened."

———

Oh, but the fans were still out there, watching and dreaming and anticipating, ready to believe, to cheer once more and then again, suckers as always for dazzling new heroes. The world in 1990 still had a few things in common with the world Ralph J. Gleason beheld a quarter century ago from the balcony of the Longshoreman's Hall in San Francisco. There remained a thousand reasons to despair, a few strands of hope worth holding on to— worth living for—and still occasions for joyous misconduct. And each such occasion was good enough for a flicker in Gleason's vigilant glare, good enough for another pipeload, for another round at the typewriter. These puzzling, puzzling times—and still throughout, Lord knows how, they danced beautifully.

In a drab and poorly tended motel on L.A.'s Sunset Boulevard, a young man named Rodney and a girl named Lisa Marie went at it. She had her hands down his underwear, he had his between her legs. It was definitely getting steamy, especially with all the camera lights baking their semi-dressed arching bodies and the curtains pulled back to flood the dismal room with sunlight.

Across the motel hallway, a man peered through his binoculars at the couple pawing at each other and, for reasons of his own, called the police. Two squad cars arrived just as Rodney and Lisa Marie were leaving the room, heading toward their van. The policemen climbed out of their cars. Rodney tried to walk past them, and was pushed by one, and pushed back, and the sticks came down on him. When the young man tried to fight back, his head was slammed through the plate-glass window of a motel room. Rodney's face was dazed and blood-slick. Lisa Marie screamed.

"This is a shoot!" protested Laurie Schechter as the police handcuffed her, the photographer and the two models and stuffed them into the back of the two police cars. "It's a *fashion story*! For *Rolling Stone* magazine!"

They went downtown anyway, where finally a detective could be found who would sit still long enough to listen to Schechter's tale of how she, as fashion editor of *Rolling Stone*, had recruited the two young actors to pose for a fashion spread on blue jeans. And yes, Rodney and Lisa Marie, being boyfriend and girlfriend and all, were not timid with each other, and yes, things got a little hot in the room, but no, this was *not* pornography—this was *Rolling Stone*. This, as anyone not named Mr. Jones and sweating all over his binoculars could see, was rock & roll.

The story made the papers the day Laurie Schechter flew back to New York City. The man waiting for her as she stepped out of the plane and into the landing gate was alight with glee, his blue eyes like soft little fires. "Laurie?"

"Yes?"

Said Jann Wenner, the original fan, "You're a hero."

EPILOGUE

I t's just beautiful out here, isn't it?" Jann Wenner says as he plops down into a poolside chair. "It's so nice getting away from the city for the summer. The beaches here are the most beautiful in the world, better than the Riviera, and all my friends are here, and"—he adds without pausing to laugh or blush or bluster or in any way qualify his sentiment—"I deserve it."

The editor/publisher of *Rolling Stone* magazine spends some four months out of the year in Long Island's East Hampton, at his three-story, 1912-erected Georgian manor just down the road from Mr. and Mrs. Billy Joel. Out here on this magnificent estate there is little suggestion of even so much as momentary discomfort or fleeting regret. Or, for that matter, isolation. The phones ring constantly here, and visitors show up at all hours, bearing tennis racquets or unreleased studio recordings. For a man of Jann Wenner's restlessness, there is no perfect getaway, but this is as close to retreat as he will ever experience. The long, strange trip ends here.

An Asian couple busy themselves in the elongated kitchen, preparing for tomorrow's dinner party featuring Yoko and Sean Ono and whoever else drops by. A rather formal-looking butler fixes afternoon cocktails in the living room. Between the house and the immense back lawn—where a young man tends the French-style landscaped garden—sprawls a patio littered with toys of every sort. Four-year-old Alex and his three-year-old younger brother, Theo, jump in and out of a space tepee while a young nanny sits nearby, reading a Beatles biography.

Jane Wenner emerges with a cup of coffee for her guest. Even in a pullover and faded blue jeans, the editor's wife is no less the sleek Mediterranean beauty than she was when Jann first set eyes on her twenty-three years ago, in the mail room of Warren Hinckle's *Ramparts* magazine. She has always appeared doelike and translucent, a little too frail for the *Rolling Stone* lifestyle; but through innumerable winters of discontent her dreams of wealth, motherhood and a country life have endured, and at long last, prevailed. Today she catches bugs in the garden for her two sons and takes tennis lessons on the backyard court. All good things have come.

Her smile is almost jovial. "We're celebrating our twenty-first anniversary next month," she says. "I don't know anyone our age who's been married as long as we have." Her Long Island accent betrays detached wonderment. She has not forgotten the burnt rubber on the road.

But she has learned her lessons; she need not look back. "I've gotten all the craziness out of my system," she says, then smiles flirtatiously and adds, "Well, not *all* of it," and then Theo interrupts to ask for a new bug, as the captive in his little wicker box needs a companion.

Jann Wenner wears a sleeveless *Rolling Stone* T-shirt that is amply but solidly filled. He is tanned and as youthful in appearance as ever but for the psoriasis on his forearm and lower leg. Several times this year he has checked into the Canyon Ranch, a posh health retreat in Tucson, where Jann sweats alongside Mary Tyler Moore and climbs mountains with Billy Joel's wife, Christie Brinkley. Today's papers carry the announcement that the *Rolling Stone* editor/publisher now wants to conceive a men's travel/fitness/fashion magazine. The void his magazine will fill is not immediately apparent, but it will likely be required reading at the Canyon Ranch.

It does not seem possible that he could own all this: the country manor with its brace of servants, the five-story Manhattan town house he bought from the Perry Ellis estate, the Gulfstream II twelve-passenger private jet he plunked down a million in cash for yesterday, plus the Mercedes limo that the family driver, Jeff Spiller, is commandeering toward East Hampton while this gathering takes place. In his T-shirt and shorts and well-padded smile, Jann Wenner does not dress or look or behave like anyone's idea of a multimillionaire. He does not appear tough enough or worldly enough to have earned anything. More plausibly one could imagine him as an heir, a playboy offspring entrusted (against everyone's better judgment) with the family estate.

No mere magazine editor lives like this. But magazine publishers do— a few of them, anyway; and owners of successful magazines live as they please. In 1985—the year Jann starred in *Perfect*, launched the Perception/ Reality ad campaign, purchased *Us* and bought his country manor—the Wenner couple bought back thousands of shares of Straight Arrow stock at $100 a share. The company is theirs exclusively. And so today, Jann Wenner, all other titles notwithstanding, is *Rolling Stone*'s owner, nothing more and nothing less. He approves cover photos, writes cover heads when he feels so inclined, talks daily with general manager Kent Brownridge, delivers scattered editorial ideas (some which come as orders) to executive editor Bob Wallace and leaves it to others to mind the shop.

At a party in 1988 for Michael Douglas (who stayed with the Wenners in East Hampton during the filming of *Wall Street*, for which Douglas won an Oscar), Jann introduced Wallace to several of his friends. "He's the executive editor of *Rolling Stone*," Jann explained. Then he added with a grin, "He's really the editor, but I like to keep the title."

It was a remarkable admission for a man who has guarded his brainchild like a hungry pit bull. But Jann Wenner's lieutenants know him well enough by now to act in their employer's interest. Yesterday he convened his top staffers at the nearby Montauk Yacht Club for a daylong conference. "I asked everybody sitting around the table how long they've worked at the magazine," he says. "And with only two exceptions, it was something like twelve years. Incredible! It's probably as stable a company as there is on the face of the planet."

He is perhaps aware that members of the *Rolling Stone* shadow government wish they, rather than their inactive boss, received more credit for the magazine's successes. On the other hand, Jann Wenner believes the magazine's vitality owes much to his participation. "I have a role in it and still contribute good ideas," he says. "If somebody comes along with better ideas and is a better editor and publisher, I'll probably say, 'Well, go start your *own* fucking magazine!'

"I hope that by the time I'm sixty or so, there'll be somebody who can run it so I can nicely step away from it without a lot of reluctance. But right now I can be on vacation and be with my family five months a year, and seven months a year work as intensely as I've always liked to work. And at the same time, turn out what is still regarded as one of the two or three or whatever best magazines in the United States, and have a lot of fun doing it."

There is a vague complacency to this statement, a suggestion perhaps that the journey has come to a close, that it is time to rest and gather moss. But charges that *Rolling Stone* has gone flabby bring him out of his chair. He paces out by the long, deep pool surrounded by Corinthian pillars dressed in ivy; he stares into the water and his words spill out of him. It was never his aim to establish a training camp for New Journalism, and it no longer serves his interests for writers to dominate *Rolling Stone*. Banned from the magazine are the 20,000-word epics of old. "There's less need and opportunity for it," he claims, "and less writers available to do it as well as it has been done." Cover bylines don't promote sales (he admits they don't hurt sales either) or anything else other than the writer, says the editor; and so that practice has ended as well. Celebrity journalists are another matter, of course. "Putting Tom Wolfe's name on the cover *does* serve my purposes," he acknowledges.

But all this talk about *Rolling Stone* discouraging fine journalism, favoring advertisers over writers, sacrificing integrity for the sake of high newsstand sales—it's bullshit, says Jann Wenner, the kind of grousing one would expect to hear from disgruntled former editors, egotistical writers or jealous competitors.

"I get a little defensive and angry and hostile about it," he says as he paces, "because I hear it so much, and it's so boring, and it really is so begrudging. Because it doesn't deal with the essential facts. Yes, *Rolling Stone* is a success; and what has *Rolling Stone* done with that success? Has it remained true to its basic aesthetic and moral principles and what it set out to be? Is it good on its own terms as a journalistic thing?

"The real point is that it's a great magazine and *deservedly successful*. And those two things are not irreconcilable. You can be highly commercially successful and put out a very high-quality magazine that's full of integrity. That's what we do. And I wouldn't do anything less."

He says that some of *Rolling Stone*'s obvious advertising magnets—the "Hot Issue," for example—have also been among the magazine's strongest efforts editorially. If he was so preoccupied with pleasing advertisers, he'd ban the use of "fuck" in the magazine; if newsstand sales were the only thing on his mind, he'd eliminate *Rolling Stone*'s left-leaning national affairs column.

He freely disclaims any responsibility to promote the high-quality contents of his magazine unless that content will earn him more money. In the past, *Rolling Stone*'s award-winning features—Altamont, Charles Manson and Richard Avedon's photo essay—were placed on the cover. In 1985, however, David Black's award-winning two-part AIDS investigation took a backseat to cover photos of Richard Gere and Don Johnson. "To put it on the cover," he says, "would be to take a hit of 100,000 newsstand sales. I *know* so. It would go down as one of our worst-selling issues. So what would be the point of doing that? After all, why did we do the article in the first place? Why did we spend two years and all that money?

"It was *my* idea to do the piece. I saw that as a story and gave somebody over a year to do the piece. We were ahead of all the other publications in the country. That was vintage *Rolling Stone*. And we'll do it again. We'll do it again."

But when they do, there will be another highly commercial personality on *Rolling Stone*'s cover. And Jann Wenner admits that this kind of packaging helps fuel the perception that his magazine panders and stoops in a way that the *Rolling Stone* of years past never did. "If we put AIDS on the cover and did more heavy-duty stuff like that instead of putting personalities on the cover, then yes, absolutely, we would alter that perception," he says. "But among who? Among people I don't really care about. Among people who are not germane to the success of the magazine or the happiness of my life."

Happiness is the day every two weeks when Jann Wenner receives advance copies of his two magazines, *Us* and *Rolling Stone*. He says that he always reads his entertainment magazine first. "Many people are fascinated by that stuff," he says, adding, "*I'm* fascinated by it." But *Us* claims no emotional hold over him; nor, likely, will the one-hour television specials he plans to broadcast twice a year or the men's magazine due to launch in 1990. These are not propositions of the heart, as *Rolling Stone* was. What he calls "my first love" will in all likelihood be his last.

There may yet be other purchases, though his interest in the whole business of magazines is overstated. His publishing passions, what is left of them, still reside on 745 Fifth Avenue's twenty-third floor. He still refers to his business staff as "the people upstairs." As for the people downstairs, Jann Wenner would be doing well to recite the names of half of them. "You're, uh, 'Random Notes,'" he will say. Or "You did, uh, didn't you do the Ringo piece? Yeah. Good piece." To him they are still family, somehow. To them he is an eminence, somehow.

They meet, really, in the pages of the magazine, for that is where his whims and their talents are each made known to the other. Tenuous though the bond may be, Jann Wenner depends on it. *Rolling Stone* has given him much more than money; the loss of his magazine would be a primal blow.

"It would be too dangerous to contemplate," he says, now seated, sipping at his wine, talking rapidly as always but in lower, more somber tones. "I don't know what I would do. I mean, there is only so much you can spend money on. And I love being with my children—they're satisfying to an enormous extent . . . but not night and day. And I don't know that I'd ever stumble upon an idea that would be as satisfying to me. It's a once-in-a-lifetime thing.

"Half of what I do is connected to that magazine," he says, the earnestness in his voice suggesting a far greater percentage. "The access, the power, the ability to influence—it's all connected. You know, it's a *big voice*. I want a big voice. I've always wanted it. And to take it away from me—I would miss it terribly. It would take me out of being in the center of the things I like, and that so many of my friends are connected with, which makes me more a part of their lives and in the swing of things. Like any journalist wants, desperately: to be in the middle of the action."

Jann Wenner squints as he looks across his immaculately tapered acreage. "I mean, you know, I love it out here. But after a few months . . ."

———

Busily he seeks out pleasures in the summertime, puttering down the silken Long Island roadways on his Harley, visiting the Jon Landaus and the Billy Joels and the Mick Joneses. Often the Wenners entertain at home, as they did this past Fourth of July. Former *Outside* and *Rolling Stone* managing editor Terry McDonell would later recall this affair, a warm gathering of somewhat sedentary rockers, Mick Jones strumming the guitar and Billy Joel playing the piano, and Jann Wenner leading the throng through a few verses of patriotic standbys. Boy, McDonell thought as he watched the editor among his friends, he's really *happy*.

On the patio he wrestles with his two boys, teasing them, urging them to say clever things to the guest. Jann Wenner the father thinks about the world his children will inherit. Wealth will shield Alex and Theo for a time. They will not, in all likelihood, see crack invade their classrooms or knife fights clot the hallways of their school. "They'll have the best education money can buy," says their father, almost apologetically. "It's tragic about everyone else."

He believes Gorbachev (whose hand he shook in 1987) wants to slam the door on the Cold War, if only America will let him. Like many Americans, he has begun to take the environment seriously and personally. Tears welled up in his eyes when he saw the gruesome images of the Alaskan oil spill on his television screen. Immediately he ordered Bob Wallace to dispatch a writer to Alaska, without regard for the cost.

When Jann Wenner holes up at the Canyon Ranch, his music staffers send him CDs of current artists in hopes of indoctrinating him. Because of his affection for sixties music, they send him 10,000 Maniacs; because he loves the Stones, they include INXS. Some of these hit home. But when Jann Wenner is asked to talk about music, he talks first and foremost about heroes and fellow travelers: Mick Jagger, Robbie Robertson, Jackson Browne, Billy Joel, Mick Jones. Just a month ago, he relistened to the entire Bob Dylan catalogue. He still has not listened to any record released by Elvis Costello or the Sex Pistols. Likely he never will.

He became a board member of the Rock & Roll Hall of Fame partly out of reverence for the past—but really, he freely acknowledges, for the fun of it. Laughing quietly, he says, "Yeah, you know, that's what Ralph would preach to me all the time. 'You young people, you just don't pay enough attention to history!' Ralph was always saying that."

Ralph Gleason, a permanent fixture on the *Rolling Stone* masthead, is part of a history to which its present staff feels little if any connection. Today's *Rolling Stone* writers, weary of hearing that they don't measure up to their predecessors, are inclined to repudiate their own heritage. They've read the old issues, they say, and much of the old stuff stinks. Record reviews were comically overwrought, as if the writers had some deep emotional investment in each song. Feature articles were long, repetitious and showy. Didn't they have editors back then? The past, says today's *Rolling Stone*— a chorus of writers and editors and financial officers and advertising representatives—was not so goddamned great. Let it be buried, they say, and let us go on.

———

On rolls their fearless leader. On August 18, 1989, Jann and Jane Wenner board a Concorde with Elizabeth Taylor, Walter Cronkite and hundreds of other celebrities, bound for Tangier. There they celebrate the seventieth birthday of the man Jann calls Forbesy: Malcolm Forbes. The press labels the bash garish and insensitive. To Jann Wenner, it's fun and great company.

From there the Wenners and the Calvin Kleins board Calvin's private jet and wend their way toward Europe. Maybe Spain, maybe Italy; there are many, many friends to see. But before all of this, before doing the Old World up right with fashion czars and attending Forbesy's bash, he directs his own jet westward, where Jann Wenner's boys will for the first time behold the place of their father's youth.

He has not been back to San Francisco since 1977, the year *Rolling Stone* moved to New York. He has just been so busy. But he knocks on old doors while Jane trolleys the kids around, and among those he sees is Jean Gleason. They talk about their children, Jann's new jet, his father, who died nine months ago, her husband and his mentor dead these fourteen years. She mentions that she's trying to gather Ralph's old radio productions from the sixties, but that she's encountering legal difficulties. Jann offers to have his own attorneys untangle the mess. Jean Gleason declines, but his unprompted generosity makes her smile. She will forever regard him as Peter Pan, a child with a universe of toys, willing to share if not challenged to do so. Why he behaves with such ruthlessness, with so little regard for how others will suffer for his actions, she will never know. But she knows that the child has a heart.

The journey through his youth thrills him, but one San Francisco night he and Jane are awakened by an earthquake, jarring loose the old phobias. They rise easily to the surface, these reasons to belittle his past and short-shrift the people who deserted him or who were expelled from his life. Yet when he reaches for the memories, rather than they for him, his words are fond and even proud.

Leaning forward, his face red with recollection's mirth, Jann Wenner says:

"We used to have these editorial meetings. And oh!—they were just one of the best experiences you could have. There'd be Felton, and Paul Scanlon, who is a great wit, real dry. And Charlie, who is brilliantly funny.

And Charlie and David didn't like each other. And Eszterhas was there—he was grouchy all the time, this and that, you know. And who else was there? Annie was usually at the meetings, and whoever was floating in and out—Cahill, he'd be there.

"And boy. These things would sparkle, and they would just ripple—the story ideas, and then we'd get to writing the headlines. God, we'd all spend two and a half hours on headlines! And not really for the purpose of writing headlines, although we'd get headlines out of it. But for one-liners, you know.

"And it was just, and Felton, he would just go at it, it would be so *hysterical!*" Jann Wenner is not in East Hampton, at the end of his road, when he says this. He is absolutely backpedaling, roaring through the San Francisco seventies—childless, a boy himself, reveling in his brilliant mess with a small band of misfits and lunatics who simply could not be convinced that they did not have the world by its balls on a downhill tug. He and they did not know half what they know today. They were such fools for the possibilities. They were all such wicked little believers.

All scattered now. Perry, a restaurant critic. Felton, a writer for MTV. Scanlon, an assistant managing editor at *GQ*. Eszterhas, a wealthy screenplay writer. Cahill, jumping out of planes and stumbling through caves for *Outside* and other magazines. Annie, shooting for *Vanity Fair* and a host of commercial clients. John Burks and Abe Peck, teaching journalism to the next generation. Hunter Thompson, flouting deadlines at Will Hearst's *San Francisco Examiner*. (When hired as a columnist, Thompson pledged to Hearst, "We will chase them like rats across the tundra.") Greil Marcus, Ben Fong-Torres, Jim Miller, John Lombardi, Jon Carroll, Chet Flippo, Ed Ward, John Morthland, Grover Lewis, Timothy Ferris, Tim Crouse, Cindy Ehrlich, Chris Hodenfield, Richard Goodwin, Howard Kohn, David Weir, Joe Klein, Jim Kuntsler, Don Katz, Michael Rogers, Dave Marsh, Chuck Young, Tim White, Jon Pareles, Kurt Loder, Chris Connelly, Aaron Latham—Jann Wenner sees their names every time he picks up a newspaper or magazine or every time he visits a bookstore. He'd flung them, or they'd flung themselves, like wild seeds into a hurricane. Dizzy they'd stay from that mad ride, no matter where or when they landed.

"Those were a lot of fun times," says Jann Wenner. Slowly he returns. His voice, still young and anxious, is informed by yesteryear's pain. "But there's other things in life, you know. And there's other ways of running a magazine that are just as satisfying as that adrenaline-addicted deadline mania we finally brought to an end. Because that was not producing a good magazine anymore. All it was doing was exhausting everybody for no good purpose. It was damaging people.

"Damaged people don't do good work," he says. "So we brought it to an end."

The butler brings gin and tonic. Storm clouds blow eastward and darken the fragrant lawn. Jann Wenner accepts his drink, chews on a stubby fingernail. "I used to spend twenty-four hours a day at *Rolling Stone*," he says. Quietly he adds, as a vow, "I'm not about to do that again."

ACKNOWLEDGMENTS

I first decided to write a history of *Rolling Stone* magazine in 1987, when Jann Wenner's publication celebrated its twentieth anniversary. Like many of my generation, I grew up reading *Rolling Stone*—relying on it, perhaps, as my parents relied on *Time* and the evening news. As a journalist, I often crossed paths with those who'd put in time at *Rolling Stone*. Their stories enchanted me, especially upon discovering that most were true. And it occurred to me that these anecdotes, hitched together reasonably well, might tell a tale far more meaningful than that of a magazine's mindless journey through time.

Three *Rolling Stone* affiliates—my good friends Bob Simmons, John Morthland and Ed Ward—helped me lay the groundwork for research. They attached personalities to names, explanations to events. Without their crucial early assistance, I might well have leaped from the starting blocks and broken both legs.

My greatest debt is to the two hundred or so individuals who donated their time, memories and insights to this book. Only midway in my research did the full extent of my outrageous good fortune become apparent to me. I simply could not have written a credible history, for example, without the help of Ralph Gleason's widow, Jean, who gave me full access to the *Rolling Stone* co-founder's files. I missed out on the privilege of meeting Gleason, but in these writings and videotapes he came alive, and I hope that my rendering of him does the man justice.

A number of former *Rolling Stone* associates had long made it a practice not to discuss with the media their association with Jann Wenner or his magazine. I want to extend particular thanks to those individuals who broke their silence and put their trust in me: former reviews editors Greil Marcus and Jon Landau; former publishers Larry Durocher and Joe Armstrong; ex-senior editor Marianne Partridge; and former receptionist and Director of Rumor Control, Judy Lawrence.

In understanding the pre-*Rolling Stone* life of Jann Wenner, I'm particularly indebted to Susan Weigel Pasternak, Susan Read Adam and Denise Kaufman. In helping me reconstruct the magazine's San Francisco era, the following deserve particular thanks: Gretchen Horton, Jann's first secretary; Michael Lydon, Baron Wolman, Bob Kingsbury and John Burks, crucial staffers in the earliest days; Ben Fong-Torres, Grover Lewis, Paul Scanlon and Tim Cahill, the brilliant editorial nucleus; Max Palevsky, Porter Bibb, Tom Baker and Alan Rinzler, for insights into the magazine's business affairs; former traffic manager Dan Parker, for his unique perspective; and especially former copy chief Charles Perry, whose thoughts and recollections I found indispensable. I owe additional thanks to two of the magazine's most famous writers, Hunter Thompson and Howard Kohn, who extended particular hospitality and support.

In my depiction of the magazine's more complicated New York years, I came to be especially grateful for the insights provided by the following: Sarah Lazin, Joe Klein, Dave Marsh, David Felton, Peter Herbst, Terry McDonell, David Rosenthal, Harriet Fier, Donald Katz, Brant Mewborn, Patty Fitzgeorge Dunning, Karen Mullarkey and Roger Black. For the enormous time and honest evaluation they devoted to this project, I owe particular thanks to Timothy White and Chuck Young. For offering perhaps the most reliable perspective of the San Francisco–New York transition period, I am indebted to Barbara Downey Landau.

Numerous current *Rolling Stone* staffers appraised their magazine with surprising candor. Many would not wish to be named, but I should in any event acknowledge the useful observations of Bob Wallace, executive editor; Jim Henke, managing editor; David Wild, senior writer; Kent Brownridge, general manager; David Obey, circulation director; and Les Zeifman, associate publisher.

I reserve particular gratitude for Jann Wenner. The editor, publisher and co-founder of *Rolling Stone* was understandably leery of my aims at the outset. Yet even as he deliberated over the extent to which he would personally involve himself in this project, Jann graciously allowed his staffers to speak with me—and on several occasions, encouraged reluctant sources to submit to interviews.

In the end, he decided to air his views, expansively and colorfully, for the record. If it were Jann Wenner's pleasure to write a book on this subject, his account would doubtless differ from mine. I nonetheless hope he agrees with me that this book is the better for his contribution.

My agent, Madeleine Morel, my editor, Paul Bresnick, and Paul's assistant, Mark Garofalo, were essential co-conspirators. For their suggestions, but most of all for their faith, I will be forever grateful. Friends who helped see me through my travels include my brother and sister-in-law, John and Laura Draper; Nadine Eckhardt, Julie Moline, Colin and Hazel Willis, Raye and Noble Robinson, Alan Cheuse, Mike and Tracy Dileo and Jerome Simon; and especially Kate Herrmann. My transcriber, Michele Michael, deserves special mention for her devotion to this project.

My deepest thanks are to my wife, without whose love and support this book would have been scrapped and filed with earlier unfinished works. Through the last four months of our engagement and the first sixteen months of our marriage, Judy Frels patiently endured my monomaniacal interest in *Rolling Stone* magazine.

When I mentioned this to Jann Wenner, the editor did not miss a beat: "Yeah, well, *my* wife certainly wouldn't know what that must feel like."

INDEX

NOTE: The abbreviation *RS* refers to *Rolling Stone*.

BOOKMARK

The text of this book was set in the typefaces
Cloister and Cochin by Crane Typesetting Service Inc.,
Barnstable, Massachusetts.

It was printed on 50 lb. Glatfelter, an acid-free paper
and bound by R. R. Donnelley, Harrisonburg, Virginia.

Designed by Viola Adams